Analysing Networked L
in Higher Education and
Professional Developmei

CW00450056

TECHNOLOGY ENHANCED LEARNING
Volume 4

Scope

The rapid co-evolution of technology and learning is offering new ways to represent knowledge, new educational practices, and new global communities of learners. Yet the contribution of these changes to formal education is largely unexplored, along with possibilities for deepening our understanding of what and how to learn. Similarly, the convergence of personal technologies offers new opportunities for informal, conversational and situated learning. But this is widening the gulf between everyday learning and formal education, which is struggling to adapt pedagogies and curricula that were established in a pre-digital age.

This series, *Technology Enhanced Learning*, will explore learning futures that incorporate digital technologies in innovative and transformative ways. It will elaborate issues including the design of learning experiences that connect formal and informal contexts; the evolution of learning and technology; new social and cultural contexts for learning with technology; novel questions of design, computational expression, collaboration and intelligence; social exclusion and inclusion in an age of personal and mobile technology; and attempts to broaden practical and theoretical perspectives on cognition, community and epistemology.

The series will be of interest to researchers and students in education and computing, to educational policy makers, and to the general public with an interest in the future of learning with technology.

Analysing Networked Learning Practices in Higher Education and Continuing Professional Development

Edited by

Lone Dirckinck-Holmfeld
Aalborg University, Denmark

Chris Jones
The Open University, Milton Keynes, United Kingdom

Berner Lindström
University of Göteborg, Sweden

SENSE PUBLISHERS
ROTTERDAM/BOSTON/TAIPEI

A C.I.P. record for this book is available from the Library of Congress.

ISBN 978-94-6091-005-0 (paperback)
ISBN 978-94-6091-006-7 (hardback)
ISBN 978-94-6091-007-4 (e-book)

Published by: Sense Publishers,
P.O. Box 21858, 3001 AW
Rotterdam, The Netherlands
http://www.sensepublishers.com

Printed on acid-free paper

CONTENTS

PETER GOODYEAR

FOREWORD

"...whereas for farmers and herdsman, the tool is an instrument of control, for hunters and gatherers it would better be regarded as an instrument of revelation."

Ingold, 1993, p. 441

"...you should not confuse the network that is drawn by the description and the network that is used to make the description."

Latour, 2005, p. 142

INTRODUCTION

First up, I want to try to describe how this book succeeds in avoiding three of the endemic failings of the educational technology literature. This will help position it in the intellectual landscape where technology and learning meet and, I hope, will help explain why it is worth reading.

The literature is suffused with material produced by innovative practitioners, whose enthusiasm is catching, but whose shareable insights are limited by the constraints of everyday language. Reflection without theory is trapped in the idea scape of folk psychology. Of course, there is also a small and impressive literature which is deeply coloured by theory – especially the theory of high modernity which can paint any practical activity into a corner. Foucault and co have been terrific at helping us see the invisible: the insidious intrusions of power, the power of language, the incoherent flux of the self. But critical theory can be seen as a luxury enjoyed by the intellectual aristocracy who live on the rents of cultural capital. It is not of obvious use to those who must work for a living. Then we have the books on self-improvement – the 'how to' manuals that explain the best way to catch the latest wave. These draw on theory, but so simplify the world that one wonders about their possible relations with action.

This book is rich in theory – it cuts below the surface and upsets everyday assumptions about people, tools and learning. It is by people who work for a living. For good and ill they are enmeshed in the imperatives of action. They teach and design and want to get better at doing what they do. Their action, experience, reflection, teaching, learning and writing are disciplined by a sense that what matters is not always obvious.

Secondly, I want to consider some key terms.

Networked learning is a diffuse idea. It's hard to believe that it would work analytically – that one would be able to distinguish between 'networked' and 'non-networked' learning situations, other than in trivial cases. In all of the studies presented in this book, everyone has access to the Internet and significant parts of what they do, and what they learn from their activity, involve connections that depend upon the net. Everything is networked learning. Perhaps it is better understood as an organisational fiction, of a pedagogical kind. People involved in networked learning agree to make sense of what they are doing by acknowledging the salience of technology-mediated connections. *Then* we can study what this *means* to them, and how it differs from other mutually defined pedagogical arrangements. Or perhaps what one needs to do, rather than patrol definitional boundaries, is look at characteristic practices. Some of these chapters do exactly that. For instance, engaging in online textual discourse, attenuated over time and space, or packed densely into a realtime chat, is a central practice of much networked learning and teaching. Richer conceptions of text and language; persistence and evanescence; genre, voice, writer, speaker, reader and listener, can help us all towards a better understanding of how to act in helpful and comprehensible ways.

Neither is *learning* straightforward, as an idea. It can be implicit or intentional. It can happen in formally arranged circumstances, but often doesn't. There's some fudging about whether it denotes a change in a person – in what they understand or what they can do – or a set of cultural practices. I'm probably odd in preferring the former, and wanting the freedom to be able to talk about what people think, believe and take with them as they move from place to place. Of course, what one thinks, and can do (and believing involves both) is bound up with place in subtle but powerful ways. These things are situated. But they *are*.

I think there is real merit in distinguishing between learning – seen as change in an individual's capabilities – and the complex mix of activities that are intended to provoke one's learning. Reading, writing, listening, explaining, searching, browsing, puzzling; flicking through notes, highlighting quotes, drafting, polishing; tidying one's books, sharpening pencils, finding peace and quiet...all these things are necessary, from time to time. All of them count, when we are thinking about how activity is structured and how technology and activity shape each other.

If nothing else, my writing about educational design has insisted upon the centrality of activity – what people do when they are trying to learn is what should matter to teachers and/as educational designers. Tasks, tools, resources, infrastructure succeed or fail in relation to such activity.

Understanding the character and limits of *design* is important in networked learning. I originally used analogies with ergonomics and especially with architecture to rethink educational design and I still find them useful sources of insight. Architecture involves the crafting of affordances, rather than deterministic logics of human control. Architecture has methods for managing complexity – not just complexities of construction but also complexities of representation and design. Architecture draws on multiple sources of knowledge and combines ways of knowing. It understands people from – at least – the perspectives of biology, psychology and culture.

It understands – at least – the physics, geometry, economics, aesthetics and history of buildings. Its practices are imbued with epistemic fluency, to a degree that makes many educationalists look, unexpectedly, like members of the Spanish Inquisition.

It is not much of a stretch to think architecturally about relations between activity and infrastructure (a strong sub-theme in this book). Educational design *has* to do this. In the case of networked learning, design attention has to be paid to the pros and cons at multiple choice points where tools and artefacts can be offered in material or digital form. The accelerating substitutability of material and digital versions of elements of infrastructure adds to the complexity of design. We no longer have a simple choice between local and distance learning, or between online and face-to-face courses. It becomes easier to construct a blend of many different components – but this *adds* complexity to *design*. So does the growing availability of tools and artefacts, and other elements of infrastructure, that combine material and digital components. These design considerations can be located on an axis linking space; place and activity (see Figure 2 in chapter 1, below). On this axis, teachers and other educational designers co-configure learnplaces with students. Moreover, this co-construction has both consciously planful and organically evolving moments. Vernacular design, like gardening and *bricolage*, is not easily separated from everyday action. Buildings, gardens and cities are shaped by repeated actions, as well as shaping those actions. They bear the traces, and in some ways *are* the traces, of repeated action. As Stewart Brand would put it, good buildings learn from their inhabitants. In the same way, the shifting mix of digital and material tools, artefacts, etc that come to constitute the infrastructures for networked learning are shaped and reshaped by their 'users'. Learnplaces are places that learn, as well as places for learning. Understanding the force of *indirection* in design requires at least this sense of the multiple agencies at work.

Moreover, the notions of indirection and architecture do not just apply to infrastructure. There are also architectures for the division of labour – for the multitude of ways that people, as students, might usefully be invited to work together and identify with one another. From dyads to global communities of inquiry, thinking about the design of architectures of collaboration invokes the axis I have (awkwardly) labelled 'organisational forms – community – activity'. To catch it simply, the place – space axis is concerned with the physically situated aspects of activity; the organisational forms – community axis is concerned with the socially situated aspects of activity. The first is about things; the second about people – how they work together, what they feel about each other, etc. This 'people' axis identifies an important design component. It says nothing about the value of one division of labour, or set of social arrangements, over another.

Looking beyond things and people, there are also architectures of outcomes, of tasks and activities, of cognition, beliefs, practices, etc. My point is not to use architecture as some way of smuggling back in some kind of structuralist supremacy. Rather, it is to help say that teachers can:

– work within the tight confines of classical instructional design, with its determinism and logics of control, or

- abandon all hope of taking useful action – leaving it to students to sort themselves out, or
- accept the challenge of discharging their professional responsibilities in a design environment which is complex and challenging, but not unlike the design environments in which other professionals (such as architects) have learned to survive, and sometimes succeed.

If this third way is accepted, and I see no other route forward for networked learning practitioners, then at least three significant implications follow. First comes an acceptance of the need for epistemic fluency: that no *one* way of knowing or source of knowledge is enough. We need psychology, anthropology, philosophy, ergonomics, computer science and more. We need to see how each of these can inform different kinds or levels of design decision. (For example, screen-based communication cannot ignore what we know from studies of perception in Human Computer Interaction. Reading this literature does not make us traitors to the cause of social practice theory.) Secondly, we need to be much more energetic and noisy in explaining to all those who shape curricula, learning infrastructures, educational quality assurance policies, etc, that macro and micro are not independent and both are important. Universities, in particular, are singularly inept at linking infrastructure planning and pedagogical planning, and at seeing how decisions at the macro level can thwart the best of intentions at the micro level. Several chapters in this book are particularly good at examining the meso level, which turns out to be key in understanding the interactions up and down the scale levels in educational organizations. Finally, we need to locate design in the context of self-organising systems. Networked learning systems – let's pretend they exist – evolve through the actions of teachers and students (and others, like IT developers). It's not clear that evolution as the consequence of a multitude of *independent* actions, rather than socially-organised actions, is necessarily the best way to advance. So part of the design challenge is to strengthen self-awareness. That is, a networked learning system might be seen as evolving most successfully when the people involved in it spend at least some of their time thinking and talking about, and acting on, the system level. In an important sense, *pace* Bruno, a healthy networked learning community needs tools to describe itself.

This is where the book in front of you plays an essential role. I cannot recommend a better toolkit for networked learning communities in search of self-understanding.

REFERENCES

Ingold, T. (1993). Tool-use, sociality and intelligence. In K. Gibson & T. Ingold (Eds.), *Tools, language and cognition in human evolution* (pp. 429–445). Cambridge, UK: Cambridge University Press.
Latour, B. (2005). *Reassembling the social*. Oxford, UK: Oxford University Press.

Peter Goodyear
CoCo Research Centre
University of Sydney, Australia

CHRIS JONES AND LONE DIRCKINCK-HOLMFELD

ANALYSING NETWORKED LEARNING PRACTICES

An Introduction

O! this learning, what a thing it is.

> *William Shakespeare, The Taming of the Shrew*

We live in an age of rapid technological and social change. Education is fundamentally implicated in these changes. It is affected by changes arising in other sectors of society, such as the growth in new networked digital technologies and the rapid integration of economies on a world scale. Conversely education and training are themselves motors of social change. Governments and large business organisations see themselves as operating in a climate of economic competition in which knowledge and knowledge workers are key resources enabling them to gain competitive advantage over others. As a consequence education and training are central to contemporary social and economic change and they are key sectors actively engaged in the conception of the future bringing about the new social forms emerging alongside digital and networked technologies.

For the education sector in general digital networks seem to offer novel ways to make learning universal, while also offering us the potential to share human knowledge in a manner that would previously have seemed utopian. When Ivan Illich wrote about de-schooling society, in the very early days of computing, he imagined being able to network expertise and interests in ways that then seemed technically difficult, using a mix of computer databases, mail and telephone (Illich, 1970). It is still shocking to read Illich writing using the terminology of learning webs, educational objects, skill exchanges and peer matching. These ideas still find their echoes amongst the most technologically forward looking research activities today. The technological elements of Illich's learning webs are now available on any networked computer, both commonplace and relatively simple to use, yet educational practice has remained, in some significant ways, largely unchanged. How is it that digital technologies can infuse social life so fully and seem to offer such radical and simple solutions to educational problems but regularly turn out to be difficult to embed in day-to-day educational practice (Cuban, 2001)? This book sets out to examine what we know about productive learning in networked environments and to draw out some conceptual developments that may help us to bridge the gap between the potential of digital networks and current educational practice.

L. Dirckinck-Holmfeld, C. Jones and B. Lindström (eds.), Analysing Networked Learning Practices in Higher Education and Continuing Professional Development, 1–27.

To give readers a flavour of the changes taking place and how they affect student experiences of higher education we begin with three brief vignettes of life as it is already being lived in tertiary education in a networked society.

VIGNETTE 1 – THE 'NET GENERATION' UNDERGRADUATE

Anna is an undergraduate student at a large urban university. She lives in student accommodation that has a broadband connection available in every room. She has her own basic laptop computer and a good mobile phone both of which she uses for social life and pleasure as well as work.

When Anna gets up in the morning one of the first things she does is to turn on her computer. As she makes a hot drink she logs on to the network and launches her preferred social networking site and an instant messaging (IM) service launches automatically in the background. As she eats a quick breakfast she reads messages posted to her Facebook 'wall'. She reads that Nina has had her mobile (cell) phone stolen while she was out last night and is asking everyone to send her their mobile numbers so she can reconstruct her address book. Her boyfriend Tom, who is at another university has left a short message in which he complains about being up late writing his dissertation, "Dissertations suck!" is his main comment. He has been joined on her wall by her cousin who is a post grad in another city, she agrees with him that "dissertations suck" and she goes on to complain about the quality of supervision on her masters course.

As she begins to wake up Anna checks her schedule and re-reads the briefing for her next assessment. She isn't clear what the question means and sends an IM to Vicki, another student on her course to ask what she thinks the question means. She then leaves the computer to take a shower and get herself ready for classes.

The classes Anna attends are lectures and seminars that entail small group activities. The university buildings she works in are spread over a large area of the town. All rooms in the university buildings are equipped with computers, fast Internet access and projection equipment. Some of her classes are in dedicated computer labs but increasingly the university is replacing older class rooms with new areas that have wireless networks and are intended to enable an integration of mobile devices with the physical environment. These areas are more flexible spaces and look nothing like the old classrooms. Some have glass walls and can be easily reconfigured. Corridors are wide and comfortable interspersed with lounge areas and workstations where individuals and groups can stand around and discuss their work. There is wireless access and there are power points everywhere in the new areas. Anna takes her laptop with her and always has here mobile phone switched on, though she has it on silent during classes.

During the day's work Anna moves between online and offline status depending on her location. In the afternoon she works in the library, which has good wireless access but restricts the way she can work face to face with others because most areas are intended for quiet personal use. She arranges to meet her group after the library in the coffee shop because they can talk more freely and the wireless connection is good. She is always in touch with others, contacting her local friends and arranging meetings or discussing work. Often she is keeping up with her extended network of friends around the country and beyond.

In the evening she arranges to watch DVDs with some friends in one of their rooms. Before they meet she works online in her room, moving seamlessly between a number of applications on her computer, some involving work and others just for pleasure. She downloads music, sends email and has IM conversations and posts messages on social networking sites. She is rarely completely alone in the virtual world, even when she sits alone in her study bedroom. After watching DVDs for a few hours she returns to her room, checks her messages and puts the computer on standby. Sometimes when she cannot sleep she turns the computer back on and checks or sends messages. Her mobile phone is by the side of her bed, primarily as an alarm clock but it is also a source of further interruptions because messages come in even late into the night.

VIGNETTE 2 – THE DISTANCE STUDENT

Shah lives abroad and has recently signed on to a Distance University course because the university has a good international reputation and it is part of a national system that he thought would be well regarded by prospective employers. As an ex-patriot he could have signed up with a University back home but he thought this would work out better if he continued to work abroad or for other multinational companies – even if he eventually went back home. When he gets the chance he does some of his work in the office on the company Intranet, but this is not always reliable because of the local firewall, which blocks some content. It is easier for him than working from home because the place they rent is open plan and the kids are always playing when he wants to work. His computer is also the family computer and it is tucked away in a corner of the main room. His wife tries to distract the kids or take them out when he needs to work, but it isn't fair on her to do this all the time. The kids also want to use his computer, which is the best for games and the Internet. This means that he often works late into the night after they have all gone to bed, even though it makes him tired the next day.

Shah's job is very demanding and his studies have to fit in around his work schedule which isn't easy. For example, he had a piece of work due for completion this week but there was a project report for work due at the same time, so he found himself balancing two heavy demands on his time. Worse than that they were both tasks that needed 'thinking space' – it wasn't just the time he lacked – it was the physical and mental space needed to let his thinking develop and mature. He has begun to talk to some of the other students about this. As the course progresses he has found others on the course in a similar position to his own and one in particular in a similar job and time zone. They use IM to keep in touch day-to-day, but his other contacts with the course are less regular. His study is largely solitary and he works at times when most other students aren't online because of their different time zones and working patterns.

He has tried to use smart phone to read some documents but he finds it difficult to read anything very long on the small screen. He likes to listen to some things that are podcast and he can listen to them whilst driving to work. Shah tries to imagine the other students. Some have their own blogs and they have personal spaces on some social networking sites that gave a little insight into their lives. He finds it important to look at photographs of the people he is working with, even though he gets some sense of the person from what they write. In fact he has been shocked on some occasions when he saw a photograph and the person was not at all how he had imagined them to be. Shah wonders if that is because he does not know the places they come from so he has filled out the details of what he doesn't know with images from work or the TV. Perhaps they do the same when thinking about him. That is the reason he has started his own blog 'Ex-pat Tales', which isn't for study but helps him work out his ideas and present himself as more than just a student.

VIGNETTE 3 – THE BUSY PROFESSIONAL POST-GRADUATE

Laura starts her work in the Virtual U, the online university system on Sunday at lunch time. At the moment she is part of a group with four other students, all male and all with different professional backgrounds. One is a university manager employed as a student counsellor; another is an educational designer in an international company, while the others are teachers in higher education. Yesterday Laura arrived back from a seminar at one of the participating universities where the group was formed. The seminar ran from Thursday to Saturday and they were together for two full days. There will be four seminars held during the year. All Laura's other study activities take place in the online environment. On the first evening of the seminar the course groups for the full semester had been established. Laura is part of a group that totals fifty students this year and they are split into ten sub-groups. Laura was pleased that the process went surprisingly smoothly. The tutors had used a special technique to help them form the sub-groups. Laura had an idea of who everyone was before she met them because they had already presented themselves online, providing an initial introduction to each other before the seminar.

Laura thought that the seminar program was very comprehensive with a lot of activities. At the seminar, there was a hands on demonstration and an introduction to the online system. Laura was happy that they had included a session on communication and collaboration in networked learning environments because this was a new way of working for her. This session was run by older more experienced students so that each course group met a group of older students. Laura had enjoyed meeting with the more experienced students and thought this was a very effective way of introducing her to this new way of working and to a problem based style of teaching. On the Friday evening at dinner, the coordinator gave a speech about the history of the programme. Laura had enjoyed the informal part, singing some funny songs about the program and poking fun at the outdated technology they were still using. It seemed that despite its weaknesses everybody starts to love the programme when they become familiar with it. For Laura the seminar had been important because it became much clearer how the five universities worked together. She thought this was fascinating, bringing things together in a new way and providing insights into the different traditions at the participating universities.

Looking back at the experiences of the seminar Laura was a bit nervous that it would be difficult to build up an identity as a student at masters level. She wondered if she could set aside enough time for study because of her work. The strong feelings aroused by the seminar made her think that this masters programme had a very strong identity, and the problem based approach to group work would help. The approach would help her to work with problems from her own working life. Sometimes the theories seemed a little academic and out of touch, as if the authors have never been outside a university, but nevertheless Laura found the prospect of applying the theories very interesting and challenging. Her hope was that through the masters' network she might find new friends and colleagues with whom she could share experiences.

When she looked back to the start of the seminar she had been a bit nervous about the project and the group work. However it had been good fun and the technology seemed to work well. She hoped that the group would soon find a good way of communicating using the various tools in the online system. They were using a virtual learning environment, but Laura thought it felt like her old email system, although there were some synchronous tools as well. She wondered if the students would stay inside the system or if she could use something like Skype to talk to the other students via the Internet and her blog to keep a record of the course as it developed. Laura also wondered about the group work. She thought of herself as quite responsible in a group but some of the others seemed to work very quickly and to add comments all the time. Laura was concerned about whether she could keep up with them, especially if one of her children became ill.

NETWORKED LEARNING

The core subject for this book is the notion of networked learning. There are a variety of competing terms used to describe related approaches: e-learning, online learning, virtual learning, and web-based learning. We have chosen the term networked learning partly in order to link the processes of education and learning to more general societal changes. The idea of networked learning has developed some force especially within European research. It has been expressed in a number of publications and a series of international conferences. The definition of network learning arising out of this tradition is that networked learning is:

> learning in which information and communication technology ... is used to promote connections: between one learner and other learners, between learners and tutors; between a learning community and its learning resources (Goodyear et al., 2004, p. 1).

The central term in this definition is *connections* and the interactions this points towards include human interactions with materials and resources, but interactions with materials alone are not sufficient and networked learning requires aspects of human-human interaction mediated through digital technologies. This definition takes a relational stance in which learning takes place both in relation to others and in relation to learning resources.

Perhaps the most well known author to place networks at the centre of modern societies is Manuel Castells (1996, 2000, 2001). Castells has written about the architecture of relationships within and between networks, and the ways that they are enacted by information technologies, which configure the dominant processes and functions in our societies. Castells building on work by Barry Wellman (Wellman et al., 2003), has used the evocative term 'networked individualism' to describe the form of sociality in such societies (Castells, 2001, p. 129 ff). Networked individualism relates firstly to the way social relations are realised in interaction between on-line and off-line social networks (Castells, 2001, p. 126–127) and to a move from physical communities to personalised or privatised virtual networks. Secondly it is related to the way the new economy is socially organized around global networks of capital, management, and information, whose access to technological know-how is at the roots of productivity and competitiveness:

> Business firms and, increasingly, organizations and institutions are organized in networks of variable geometry whose intertwining supersedes the traditional distinction between corporations and small business, cutting across sectors, and spreading along different geographical clusters of economic units (Castells, 1996, 2000, p. 502).

On the other hand Castells claims that the work process itself is increasingly individualized:

> Labour is disaggregated in its performance, and reintegrated in its outcome through a multiplicity of interconnected tasks in different sites, ushering in a new division of labour based on the attributes/capacities of each worker rather than the organization of the task (ibid. 502).

The concept of networked individualism points to a contradictory process in which overall social organisation through networks is accompanied by a tendency towards individualisation.

This social trend raises fundamental questions about the relationships between the emerging networked society and the organization of learning environments in both formal education and training. Networked individualism might suggest that we need to take a more critical approach to the theories of education and learning that are based on community and collaboration. The term also suggests that we can do this without ruling out the central place of communication and dialogue in education and learning. Networked individualism suggests that community is re-configured within networks so that different aspects of community are supplemented whilst others are decreased. We argue that a key question for research is whether the Internet will help foster more densely knit communities or alternatively whether it will encourage more sparse, loose knit formations. Educational researchers may not see these as oppositions and may wish to design for both the individualising and communal aspects of such changes. Furthermore we argue that a significant question is whether designs for networked learning environments should reflect the trend towards networked individualism or serve as a counter balance to this trend, offering opportunities for the development of collaborative dependencies.

CONCEPTUAL FRAMEWORK

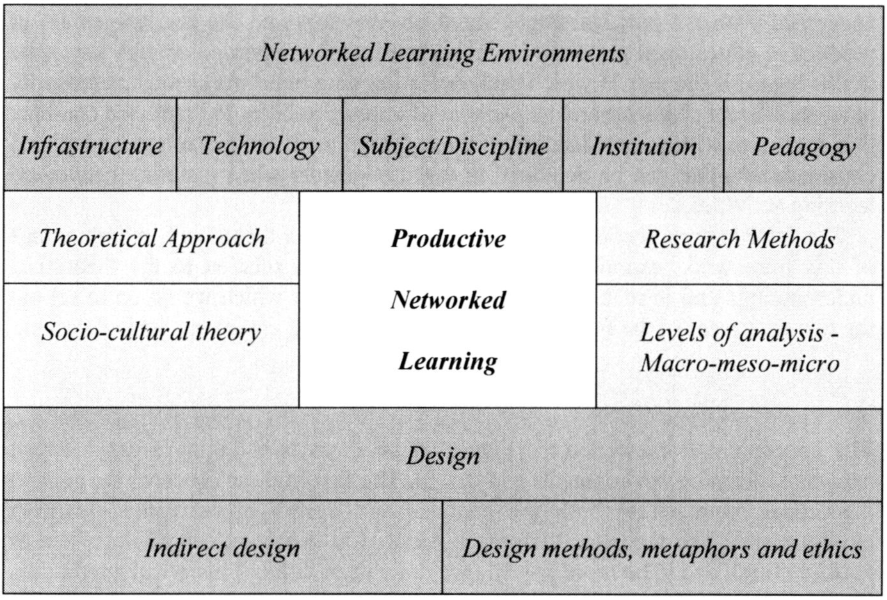

Networked Learning Environments				
Infrastructure	Technology	Subject/Discipline	Institution	Pedagogy
Theoretical Approach		Productive	Research Methods	
Socio-cultural theory		Networked	Levels of analysis -	
		Learning	Macro-meso-micro	
Design				
Indirect design		Design methods, metaphors and ethics		

Figure 1. Conceptual framework

The focus of our work is summed up in the term *productive networked learning*. We identify two central layers of concern in the promotion of productive networked learning, *networked learning environments* and *design*. By networked learning environments we mean the sets of technological and organisational arrangements in which educators and students work and study which are often given and over which they often have limited control. By design we identify those aspects of a setting in which educators can organise for future activities and developments. Between these two core layers we identify linking elements in the form of *theoretical approaches* that educators and students apply and engage with and in the *research methods* used. The research methods are included because they influence the kinds of information and outlooks that educators have at their disposal to understand the complex interplay of issues that arise in networked learning.

The book presents a framework for understanding and designing networked learning building on a socio-cultural theoretical foundation. An essential part of this framework is the interrelated set of conceptual tools that help us rethink some of the basic issues and concerns in the domain of networked learning environments, starting with the very definition of networked learning. These conceptual tools, infrastructure, technology, subject/discipline institution, and pedagogy are interlocking building blocks for the development of a theoretically sound and coherent under-standing of networked learning environments. Some of the elements are dealt with more fully than others and our focus being more directly on technology, institution and infrastructure than it is on pedagogy or subject and discipline. The book is not simply pursuing an abstract understanding of networked learning; rather it is concerned with the practical engagement of educators and the encouragement of productive educational practices in networked learning environments. A key issue in this regard is the way in which designs for learning in networks must necessarily have an indirect character and an element of unpredictability to them. We combine this constraint with a consideration of those design methods, metaphors and ethical considerations that can be deployed to assist educators when planning networked learning activities.

The introductory section of the book elaborates the theoretical underpinnings of this framework, examining the issues that arise in relation to the theoretical underpinnings and in relation to research methods after which we go on to set out the two core areas of the framework, networked learning environments and design.

THEORETICAL APPROACH

The conceptual framework (see Figure 1) suggests two linking areas between networked learning environments and design. The first of these concerns the general theoretical approach to both the analysis and design of networked learning environments. The theoretical approach adopted in this book can be described as socio-cultural, and to be more specific we draw upon cultural-historical approaches to learning, for example Vygotsky (1978) and Engeström (1987, 1999, 2001). We also draw on other social theories of learning, for example Wenger (1998), Brown et al. (1989), Lave and Wenger (1991) and Bakhtin (1986). The key elements of socio-cultural theories in terms of pedagogy are that:

– Learning is mediated by tools, both symbolic tools such as language and physical artefacts
– Learning is social and language and artefacts are both cultural and social products rather than learning being the products of individual minds.
– Learning is historic because we 'inherit' cultural tools we need to understand the history of their development.

A socio-cultural approach stands in contrast to cognitive and psychological theories of learning that take the individual mind as their starting point. This difference in approach affects both the unit of analysis, which for socio-cultural theory is always a social/activity system, and the idea of learning itself. Learning in the socio-cultural tradition is achieved socially using mediating tools and artefacts to support the socially and physically embodied individual's internalisation and co-construction of knowledge (Säljö, 1999).

In some part these discussions relate to the central focus on meaning making that several authors propose as fundamental to the field of Computer Supported Collaborative Learning (CSCL). Koschmann for example states that CSCL is a field of study centrally concerned with meaning and the practices of meaning making in the context of joint activity, and the ways in which these practices are mediated through designed artefacts. (Koschmann, 2002, p. 20), and Stahl states that meaning making can be treated as an essentially social activity that is conducted collaboratively by a community, rather than by individuals who happen to be co-located (Stahl, 2003, p. 523). The strong case that Stahl makes is that meaning making takes place not just in the context of social practices and mediation through artefacts. However, meaning making is composed of those practices and mediations (see also Wenger, 1998).

RESEARCH METHODS

The second linking area identified by the framework concerns some of the methodological issues pertaining to the conditions for productive networked learning. We claim that studies within the humanities and the social sciences must take into account the *intentional* nature of human action and the centrality of the concept of 'meaning' to such intentional action. We contended that each situation is unique both because of the exceptional nature of the elements involved and because of the unique way they interrelate in any given case. This uniqueness does not preclude the possibility of situations, actions, and contexts being prototypical in respect of their overall pattern or gestalt. It does, however, preclude the possibility of a positivist approach to the replication of situations and of postulating law-like generalizations on the basis of the investigation of representative cases. As a consequence the explanations sought for within areas of human activity will be of a different nature than explanations in the natural sciences. Likewise, the form of generality pertaining to case studies will differ from natural laws, and the validity of the analyses will relate to the complex, interwoven meaningfulness of the phenomena that they put in view, not to their corroboration by impartial observation and experiment.

In this stance we follow Winch and others (*e.g.* Winch, 1990; Taylor, 1985; Flyvbjerg, 2001) by drawing a distinction between causal and interpretive explanations. In studies of human activity, the latter kind of explanations must be dominant, *i.e.* actions must be explained by the meaning they have in the situation – for the agents themselves, for others, and for the organisational setting of which the situation is a part. These explanations must relate to possible differences in meaning for such agents and settings and to the consequences such differences have for further actions. In this book this approach is related to our emphasis on case studies that are situated within particular settings as both a source and background to our more generalised statements. In contrast to the causal explanations of the natural sciences, the interpretive explanations point only backwards in time, seeking to understand *reasons* for actions and *relations* in terms of meaning between such actions. Winch makes the important point that although it is possible to understand after an action *why* it was undertaken, it is not possible to predict an action before it takes place. Denying this asymmetry is denying the uniqueness of meaning of each situation and action. Therefore, instead of complaining about the lack of predictive theory leading to cumulative research results one should start further back with basic investigations regarding the kind of rationality that is essential to the conduct of research involving human learning activities in their contexts. Such an approach enables us to specify a more robust definition of validity that is suitable for applied science regarding context and learning.

This book in line with a broadly socio-cultural understanding of the social sciences does not seek a scientistic or positivist form of explanation. Rather we adopt what has been termed, following Aristotle, phronesis (Flyvbjerg, 2001). Phronesis concerns values and as such it relates closely to notions of practice and praxis. Phronesis steps beyond traditional analytic, scientific knowledge (episteme) and technical knowledge or know how (techne). Phronesis involves judgements and decisions made in the moment, on the fly, by what Flyvbjerg calls virtuoso social actors. Flyvbjerg summarises the point of departure for phronetic research in four questions:

– Where are we going?
– Is this development desirable?
– What, if anything, should we do about it?
– Who gains and who loses, and by which mechanisms of power? (Flyvbjerg, 2006, p. 374)

Flyvberg has written in defence of case study research and against what he calls five misunderstandings from the perspective of phronesis:

> By and large, the conventional wisdom is wrong or misleading... the case study is a necessary and sufficient method for certain important research tasks in the social sciences, and it is a method that holds up well when compared to other methods in the gamut of social science research methodology (Flyvbjerg, 2003, p. 432).

Flyvbjerg contends that phronetic research can yield pragmatic, context dependent and actionable knowledge based on experience and informed by value rationality. We wonder whether a phronetic research approach is a viable way of letting the holistic gestalt of the situation present itself and thereby showing generality through uniqueness. It is from this perspective that we both present our conceptual developments and our case study work in the separate sections of the book. Neither section could exist separately but the rich detail of each case is only able to be expressed in terms of the context dependant but necessary abstraction of the conceptual work.

LEVEL OF ANALYSIS – MACRO, MESO, MICRO

Often research in the CSCL tradition has naturally focused on the collaborative learning that takes place in single, small groups (Stahl, 2006). This is not a universal pattern and approaches to CSCL have also included attempts to link different level of analysis:

> The understanding of collaborative learning requires both a microanalysis of group interactions and a macro analysis with regard to the socio-cultural context in which learning occurs. (Dillenbourg in Strijbos et al., 2004, p. xvii)

The school of research derived from the early Soviet tradition of Vygotsky has retained an ability to deal with issues at different levels of granularity. In the hands of Engeström and others cultural historical activity theory is able to locate activity systems at various levels in any given social system, including whole institutions. Activity systems are not restricted to the level of single small groups and activity theory can be applied at various levels of analysis (Engeström, 1987, 1999, 2001). CSCL research while often confined to a micro level of analysis has clear connections to larger social networks and the macro level has been clearly acknowledged in work in this field.

We argue that it is necessary to supplement these approaches and to focus on what we have called the meso level of collaborative learning. Such an approach would focus on:
– How to design for collaborative learning at the institutional level, in organizations, university settings, and in networked learning environments
– Identifying the basic conditions that allow for collaborative learning in these settings
– Understanding how technologies and infrastructures afford and mediate the learning taking place

The meso level at its simplest can be thought of as the level of interaction that was intermediate between small scale, local interaction and large-scale policy and institutional processes. The idea of a tripartite division into macro, meso and micro levels is not new and has been developed most recently in the field of complex systems (Liljenström and Svedin, 2005). CSCL is in our opinion a classic example of a complex system with non-linear interrelationships between variables, including thresholds, lags and discontinuities. Most importantly CSCL systems include human agents and such systems are prone to both feedback and feed-forward loops and radical indeterminacy. The meso level can be characterised from this point of view as "the level in between the micro and the macro, as that is the domain where bottom-up meets top-down." (Liljenström and Svedin, 2005, p. 5). We would argue that differentiating between levels in this way can help us to identify the detail of what otherwise might appear as a simple or monolithic social system.

We would also suggest that it is possible to use levels and the distinctions between macro, meso and micro levels in a more analytic way. Used in this way the meso level points to the place of social practice as the locus in which broader social processes are located in small, local group activity (Schatzki, 1996; Schatzki, Knorr Cetina, and von Savigny, 2001). This suggested link with social practice also helps to connect the idea of a meso level of analysis with previous work in cognate research areas such as Computer Supported Cooperative Work (CSCW). In CSCW organizational concerns have been more generally addressed than in CSCL (e.g. Harper, Randall, and Rouncefield, 2000). The link to social practice also provides a bridge to broader concerns with organizations (e.g. Orlikowski, 2000, Wenger, McDermott, and Snyder, 2002). In this analytic form meso is an element of a *relational* perspective in which the levels are not abstract universal properties but descriptive of the relationships between separable elements of a social setting. In this view meso is not a characteristic that adheres to a particular set of arrangements it arises in the processes of relating these arrangements upward towards macro processes and downward into micro processes.

These elements in the relationships can be separated over both space and time. The term micro then identifies small group interaction with a highly local (not necessarily spatially local) setting occurring over short time periods. Meso would identify interactions in and with the settings beyond the small group, but still with a local focus that was open to routine control and intervention over moderate time spans. Macro would identify the level of interaction beyond meso that was general in character (even if represented locally) and not open to routine control within moderate or short time spans, such that it could on many, if not most occasions, be treated as a given.

NETWORKED LEARNING ENVIRONMENTS

We argue that networked learning *environments* are critical for networked learning. The term learning environment points to the physical or virtual aspects of a setting and the characteristics or arrangements of elements of that setting within which learning can take place. Of course learning can take place anywhere and the idea of a learning environment implies that these settings are intentionally designed and arranged to allow learning to take place. The term learning environment has at least two recent usages within educational research literature. One recent use of the term in the context of the use of computers and computer programmes in education suggests something small scale and self-contained such as a simulation or micro-world. This sense of learning environment although it is closely connected with computers and computer programmes, could also be applied to resources that are not computer based but which offer the student a contained experience where they might learn through the exploration and manipulation of objects. Modern museum exhibits often have this general approach to the design of a learning experience. A second use of the term learning environment is more encompassing and would include the totality of resources on which the learner can draw. This view is found more widely in educational literature and is particularly strongly associated with the relational or phenomenographic approach to learning (see for example Laurillard, 2002). More recently the idea of a learning environment has been strongly identified with commercial products marketed as virtual and/or managed learning environments. These computer-based environments could be thought of as being at the meso level, neither small-scale self-contained environments, nor encompassing a totality of resources. It is this level of learning environment that most concerns the authors of this book, environments that involve wider social processes and that offer significant control to practitioners who wish to actively design course environments.

The concept of a learning environment points towards the physical environment alongside the social organisation of the setting and as a consequence the idea of a networked learning environment points towards the socially and physically net-worked nature of learning environments distributed over space and time. From this we argue that the relationship between the design of a technology and the use of that technology is a central concern for networked learning. In this we follow

Vygotsky's socio-cultural approach in suggesting that tools fundamentally mediate both higher mental functioning and human action. In education we argue in favour of a focus on how digital and networked technologies function in the appropriation and understanding of conceptual knowledge (Säljö, 1999). Tools and technologies have a clear material form and persist as material objects even when they are not incorporated into the flow of action (Wertsch, 1998). Both the material and symbolic properties of tools are seen as having important implications for understanding how internal processes come into existence and operate. The technology of computer networks has generated a number of debates around issues that may impact on a networked learning environment. These include:

- Time shifts – Computer networks used in education affect the usual time patterns of education. Many courses delivered across networks are asynchronous.
- Place – The introduction of mobile and ubiquitous computing devices have begun to make the idea of education occurring at anytime, anyplace, and anywhere seem more feasible.
- Digital preservation – The outputs of synchronous and asynchronous activity are easily preserved in transcripts, logs and a variety of other forms including the archiving of web casts and audio interviews/podcasts.
- Public/Private boundaries – The preservation of what would otherwise be ephemeral materials alters the boundaries between what is public and what is private. Tutors can now view and preserve the details of student's interactions during group activities, making these available as tools for assessment.
- Forms of literacy – The still largely text based world of networked learning has generated new forms of writing that are neither simple text replications of informal conversation nor are they formal written texts. The integration of images and audio into digital environments has suggested new forms of multimedia literacy.
- Content – The boundary between content and process is shifting. Blogs and wikis can provide elements of content and cut and paste re-use is common practice. The idea that there is a clear distinction between activity/process and artefact/content is becoming strained.

Overall a claim can be made that computer networks disrupt and disturb traditional boundaries in education. If this is so then it is important to consider how this might affect the parameters of design.

We have argued that networked learning is necessarily learning mediated by technologies. Orlikowski has suggested that it may be helpful to make an analytical distinction between the *use* of technology and the *artefacts,* that is the bundle of material and symbolic properties such as hardware, software, techniques, etc. (Orlikowski, 2000, p. 408). This distinction is important for networked learning as it directs our attention to the way in which technologies are deployed and the complex nature of their use in education with both teachers and students having different claims to be considered as the primary users of any system, both of which need to be considered. She demonstrates that the same artefact used in different institutional contexts and by different social actors can evoke very different actions and she makes a distinction between two discrete approaches (Orlikowski, 2000, p. 405):

13

- An approach which posits technology as embodying structures (built in by designers during technological development), which are then appropriated by users during their use of the technology
- An approach based on an understanding in which structures are emergent growing out of recursive interactions between people, technologies, and social action in which it's not the properties of the technology, per se, but through a process of enactment, that people constitute and reconstitute a structure of technology use (Orlikowski, 2000, p. 410).

These distinctions are important for the practice of design because technologies are designed with certain purposes in mind and they embody certain properties and features intended for particular kinds of use. Networked learning environments contain technologies that as a consequence reflect certain understandings of communication, interaction, collaboration, teaching, and learning that are incorporated in their design. These properties of technologies which are the outcome of design intentions are not themselves determinant of the uses made of them, but later we discuss the ways that certain features of technologies can become available as *affordances* in use, and so make certain kinds of practice more available than others.

INFRASTRUCTURE FOR LEARNING

One of the ways in which networked learning environments present themselves to potential users is as an infrastructure. The traditional conception of an infrastructure is something that is already in place, ready-to-use, completely transparent and not requiring consideration such as the water system, the electricity supply, the railway, the mail services and more recently the Internet. Infrastructure though often out of sight comes into sharp focus when it fails. The plight of New Orleans after hurricane Katrina was a classic example of infrastructures failing and as a consequence of that failure immediately becoming highly visible. Infrastructures viewed in this way are arguably a defining characteristic of the modern era and the digital infrastructures of the current period are potentially a defining characteristic of the postmodern. This understanding focuses on infrastructure as an object, something that is built and maintained and then sinks into relative invisibility in the background. In physical universities the lecture theatre with tiered rows of seating is rarely questioned as a form of physical room arrangement, yet it enables and constrains the use of space. Similarly the filing cabinets and memos that surround a university administration are often largely invisible components in the organising and arranging of university activities. It follows from this that the activities around the infrastructure are heavily shaped by its structure. In a way this is exactly the kind of infrastructure we want in an educational setting, something that just works, supporting learning activities and communicative practices.

In order to discuss how something becomes an infrastructure, the design and re-design of infrastructure and the question of how the infrastructure should or could be, we need to focus on the processes of maintenance and development. Edwards (2003) discusses infrastructures as socio-technical systems, which are reliant on complex organisational practices for maintenance and for making the infrastructure meaningful. Edwards makes the point that the way infrastructures reside in the 'background' is in some sense definitional for an infrastructure.

> ... the fact is that mature technological systems – cars, roads, municipal water supplies, sewers, telephones, railroads, weather forecasting, buildings, even computers in the majority of their uses – reside in a naturalized background, as ordinary and unremarkable to us as trees, daylight, and dirt. Our civilizations fundamentally depend on them, yet we notice them mainly when they fail, which they rarely do. They are the connective tissues and the circulatory systems of modernity. In short, these systems have become infrastructures (Edwards, 2003, p. 186).

As socio-technical systems they rely on an integration of artefacts of various scales and kinds with social and organisational features in a constant dialectical process.

The perspective we present on infrastructure draws on the works of Susan Leigh Star and Karen Ruhleder (Star & Ruhleder, 1994; 1996) and it is developed further in Bygholm & Nyvang (this volume) and Guribye & Lindström (this volume). Star and Ruhleder suggest that we interpret information and communication technologies in use as infrastructures that shape and are shaped by practice and in this sense we understand infrastructure as a relational concept, stressing the fact that it is only when artefacts are brought into use and become part of a practice that they become an infrastructure. In order to characterize the relational side of infrastructure Star & Ruhleder suggest eight dimensions:
- Embeddedness (integrated in social structures and practices)
- Transparency (can be used without removing focus from the task)
- Reach or scope (goes beyond individual tasks or processes)
- Learned as part of membership (an inherent part of an organization)
- Links with conventions of practice (shapes and is shaped by practice)
- Embodiment of standards (builds on standards and conventions)
- Build on an installed base (must relate to existing technologies)
- Visible upon breakdown (loses transparency and is drawn into focus when it breaks down) (Star and Ruhleder, 1996, p. 113).

These dimensions are quite general in character and they could be used to characterize phenomena such as language, all of which points to the ambiguity and complexity of seeing infrastructure as a relational concept. They argue that an infrastructure occurs when the tension between local and global is resolved. That is, an infrastructure occurs when local practices are afforded by a larger-scale technology, which can then be used in a natural, ready-to-hand fashion (Star and Ruhleder, 1996, p. 114). Setting up an infrastructure is not a once and for all procedure, it is an ongoing and dynamic process.

In dealing with the balance between practice and technology and the problems that arise in the emergence of infrastructure Star and Ruhleder draw on Bateson's (2000) understanding of communicative systems (For a fuller discussion see Bygholm and Nyvang, this volume). Bateson's approach identifies three levels of communication as relevant for understanding the problems involved in the process of creating and re-creating an infrastructure.

- Level one problems appear as matter of fact problems, such as not knowing how to get a user name, or publish a message in the system or not understanding what is wrong when the server go down.
- Level two problems are concerned with how to use the system properly, for example what kind of messages should be published and to whom. Thus level two is concerned with classifying and with discussion and reflection about the type of problems involved in using, supporting and running the system in the context of use.
- Level three is one further step more abstract, and involves questions such as what kind of learning goals we want to pursue using information and communication technologies or the general politics involved in the choice of platform (e.g. commercial vendor locked or open source). We would say that the issues raised on level three are concerned with the fundamental issues and values of educational practice.

The use of infrastructure in this volume takes a somewhat different approach to the metaphoric use of infrastructure found in Bielaczyc (2001 and 2006) and Lakkala et al. (2008). These authors take a particular stance in relation to the design of aspects of a learning setting to which they apply the term infrastructure. Bielaczyc (2001 and 2006) concentrates on dimensions of social infrastructure including cultural beliefs, practices, socio-techno-spatial relations and interaction with the outside world. In addition Lakkala et al. (2008) introduce what they describe as a 'more comprehensive set of components' including a cognitive infrastructure. They also propose a 'Pedagogical Infrastructure Framework' initially aimed at providing a tool for analysis but potentially offering a tool for design. The location of infrastructure in these accounts is at a local and micro design level whereas the concept if infrastructure used in this volume remains at the macro and meso levels in which infrastructures largely take the form of being given elements of local design and not a part of the day-to-day design process (Jones et al., 2006). This implies a relationship between design and learning in which infrastructures for learning aren't directly designed by the academic staff who are involved in the detailed pedagogic design of courses and programs.

AFFORDANCE

In this chapter we have been using the term affordance without a full explanation of its meaning. However we will argue that this key term needs to be developed through the discussion and critique of its recent interpretations within the field of TEL (Technology Enhanced Learning). We present a different understanding of the concept which we contend is both more in line with the original Gibsonian concept, and permits a more fruitful conceptualization of the design and use of digital networked technologies for learning. This different understanding of affordance is outlined here and is considered in more detail in the chapter by Kaptelinin and Hedestig (this volume) and in our discussion in the concluding section of the book.

The concept of affordance has been applied to technology in the sense that: technologies possess different affordances, and these affordances constrain the ways that they can possibly be 'written' or 'read' (Hutchby, 2001, p. 447).

The concept of affordance, used in this way, allows for the possibility that technologies can have effects on users and that particular technologies can as a consequence constrain users in definite ways. The idea has its origins in the work of Gibson (1977) who was interested in the psychology of perception. Gibson argued for a non-dualist understanding of perception. His main interest was studying perception as an integrated or ecological activity. Affordances in Gibson's view might vary in relation to the nature of the user but they were not freely variable; the affordances of a rock differed from those of a stream, even though different animals might see the affordances of each differently.

Since Norman's application of the term to the design and use of artefacts (Norman, 1988), the concept of affordance has been central to research on human computer interaction. However, beneath the acceptance of the analytical force of the concept lies a disagreement as to the ontological nature and epistemological status of an affordance. Thus, a fundamentally contentious point is whether a distinction should be drawn between 'real affordances' and 'perceived affordances' (Norman, 1999) or between affordances and perceptions (Gaver, 1991; McGrenere & Ho, 2000). Gibson's view is strongly relational and differs in significant ways from the later application of the idea of affordance by Norman (1990, 1999). Norman takes what can be understood to be an essentialist and dualist approach in which technologies possess affordances and users perceive them. Other researchers, most notably McGrenere and Ho (2000), emphasize the need to re-introduce and further develop the original Gibsonian concept of affordance. According to McGrenere and Ho returning to the original Gibsonian notion would mean acknowledging that affordances are "independent of the actor's experience, knowledge, culture, and ability to perceive" (McGrenere and Ho, 2000). This claim has been echoed by Torenvliet, who observed that Gibson's view was that affordance was a characteristic of the environment that exists relative to an object but that it exists independently of perception (Torenvliet, 2003). This discussion is further developed by Kaptelinin and Hedestig (this volume) who argue that culture and experience cannot be separated from affordances and develop this point in relation to activity theory. Elsewhere Derry in a critical commentary on the recent use of the term in educational contexts comments that:

> The leap from ideas originating in perceptual psychology linking perception and action in a non-cognitive relation of organism and environment to an educational context dependent on interactions between humans, is at the very least questionable (Derry, 2007, p. 504).

In light of this the view the interpretation of the term that we propose for understanding networked learning environments and the relationship between technological infrastructure and activity is one that treats affordance as a *relational* property and returns to a broadly Gibsonian and ecological stance. In this way of thinking about affordances, properties exist *in* relationships between artefacts and active agents.

17

We need to be clear that Gibson specifically emphasized that the issue for a theory of affordance is not whether or not affordances exist or are real, but whether or not optical information makes it possible to perceive them (Gibson, 1979). This observation is non-essentialist and non-dualist and affordances in this view could be discerned in a relationship between different elements in a setting whether the potential user of an affordance perceives the affordance or not. As noted by Derry (2007) in networked learning environments we are likely to be concerned with reflexive social relationships. Gibson's understanding of perception still leaves the possibility that the second order nature of meaning is understated. A relational view of affordance would suggest that we could analytically discern features of the setting apart from the perceptions of particular groups of users, but any actual group of users would have varied perceptions and understandings and they could draw out significantly different meanings from the setting. As a consequence designers can only have direct influence over those abstract elements that may become affordances while educators involved in the process might be able to assist participants by suggesting how they might 'read' the affordances.

THE INDIRECT NATURE OF DESIGN

Design is the second key term in our conceptual framework and we choose to use the term because it implies an approach that engages in an activity informed by theory but one also deeply engaged in practice. We do not think of design as a bridging activity *between* theory and practice (See Beetham and Sharpe, 2007). Rather in our view design is immediately both theory and practice; a social practice that is explicitly informed by theory and a form of praxis (DeLaat and Lally, 2003). Design involves a systematic approach, which may involve rules and protocols derived from evidence, and a set of local and context based practices that are dependant on circumstances. As a consequence design is a skilful and creative activity which, although it is not predictable, can be open to improvement and development resulting from the application of research and scholarship.

Design is also related to the introduction of new technologies and the impact of extremely mediated forms of social activity (Suchman, 2007; Beetham and Sharpe, 2007). Design is an activity that is fundamental to discussions about the nature of knowledge in networked societies. Societies in which knowledge is understood to be relational to the way it is used and to its users. University teaching has always involved the use of artefacts, preparation and planning and these can be considered as proto-typical elements of design. The use of all kinds of technologies in the 20th century and the development of digital and networked technologies from the late 20th century onwards implies a greater need for systematic design. Digital and networked technologies require forethought and more explicit representations of the tasks that learners and teachers are expected to undertake. However the take up and use of technologies cannot be guaranteed by design and teaching practices have proved remarkably resilient to technological change (Cuban, 1986, 2001; Suchman, 2007).

The relationship between planning and design in tertiary education and the situated actions in which teachers and students engage has become increasingly problematic. Policy pressures have been added to technological changes with the effect of promoting increasingly formal rational planning approaches to design. In this book we are concerned with practitioners, who are rarely involved in the design of the technological and institutional infrastructures in which they work. We are interested in design as a process of mobilising what are largely given elements to create productive networked learning environments. We argue that learning can never be directly designed, only designed for (i.e. planned in advance). (See also Jones, 2007; Beetham and Sharpe, 2007; Wenger, 1998). Learning itself is only indirectly related to what we design and plan, indeed we argue that it is at least two steps removed. The activities, spaces and organisations that we design rely on being inhabited by the teachers and learners who will 'enact' our designs. Goodyear et al. (2001) have summarised these distinctions as an indirect approach to learning and their relationships are shown in figure 2.

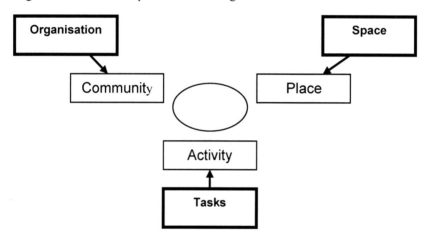

Figure 2. Indirect approach to learning. (Goodyear et al., 2001)

TASK AND ACTIVITY

The distinction between tasks and activities forms part of the broader design philosophy outlined above. Because students constitute their own learning context it should be expected that students' activity will often differ from the task that initiated it. Goodyear et al. following the French ergonomist Alain Wisner, draw a distinction between 'task' and 'activity' (Wisner, 1995). Designers set tasks, prescriptions for the work the students are expected to do, activity on the other hand is what people actually do. Teachers set the tasks but learners then have to interpret the specifications of the task. The subsequent activity of students is a more or less rational response to the task when understood as a part of the student's overall context. Students constitute their setting, their own learning context, out of the technology and infrastructure, parallel tasks they have to conduct at the same time, other calls on their time, their past experiences and their understanding of what their teachers actually value. It is to be expected that the activity students undertake is likely to be different from the task which initiated it.

We would also like to extend and refine the notion of activity found in Goodyear's work by adding to it some of the concepts found in the work of Vygotsky (1978) and under the banner of activity theory. Activity in the Vygotskian theoretical tradition is not simply a series of actions, a state of being active or a string of linked behaviours. Activity is always conditioned by the circumstances in which it takes place, both the circumstances of the person themselves and the external circumstances within which the person acts. Particular actions may become routinized and automatic operations that require little or no intentionality. Even so activities and the actions that combine to form them are more than simply operations because they are intentional and motivated by a purpose with the aim of achieving an objective. For our purposes the relationships we identify as activity are the more or less intentional actions that take place when students engage in tasks set as part of designs for learning in a networked learning environment.

ORGANISATION

In a networked learning environment the way organisation is enacted is often related to a variety of social theories and approaches to learning including 'computer supported collaborative learning' (CSCL) and 'communities of practice'. Goodyear himself suggests that organisation indirectly relates to community. Our approach differs from both of these approaches in that it does not privilege strong relationships such as cooperation and collaboration or the close relations of community. Unlike these approaches the definition of networked learning, provided earlier in this chapter, has the potential to draw attention to relationships based on weak rather than strong ties. (For a further elaboration of this view see Jones, 2004, 2004 b; Jones and Esnault, 2004).

One of the most commonly adopted notions of community, 'communities of practice', has developed from the apprenticeship model proposed by Brown, Collins and Duguid (1989), and the idea of learning as legitimate peripheral participation developed by Lave & Wenger (1991). It is most commonly associated with the work of Wenger (1998). For Wenger, networks are not necessarily in opposition to the ideas of communities of practice. Indeed Wenger suggests that a network with strong ties resembles a community.

> Communities of practice could in fact be viewed as nodes of "strong ties" in interpersonal networks (Wenger, 1998, p. 283)

However, he also stresses the difference in purpose between networks and communities of practice:

> ...but again the emphasis is different. What is of interest for me is not so much the nature of interpersonal relationships through which information flows as the nature of what is shared and learned and becomes a source of cohesion – that is, the structure and content of practice (ibid. p. 283).

In other words, Wenger is not only concerned with the flow of information between nodes, he also emphasizes the differences in what flows across the network.

Communities of practice are characterized by three related structural properties, that of a shared enterprise, mutual engagement, and a shared repertoire (Wenger, 1998, p. 72 ff), while networks are characterized as interconnected nodes (Castells, 1996/2000) or the connections between learners, learners and tutors, and between a learning community and its resources (Goodyear et al., 2004). As such networked learning is concerned both with establishing connections, and defined relationships whereas a learning environment based on communities of practice is concerned with the establishment of a shared practice. An area of common ground between network analysis and communities of practice may be found in the idea of networks of practice proposed by Brown and Duguid (2001) which deals with relationships that are too broad and diffuse to be considered communities of practice.

Networked learning might suggest that strong notions of community ignore the importance of the strength of weak ties. The idea of the strength of weak ties originates in a paper written by Granovetter (1973) in which he argues that previous network theory had implicitly prioritized strong ties that were primarily within small well defined groups. Weak ties he argued would allow for the analysis of interaction *between* groups and for the analysis of social activity that was not confined to primary social groups. Weak ties are in consequence a potentially interesting topic to explore in relation to digital networks and networked learning. Networked learning environments bring together a variety of elements that extend beyond the local or small closely bound group and draw these elements together in organizational units that are large and relatively diffuse in which there may be no clear boundaries.

Granovetter offered the following definition of the strength of an 'interpersonal' tie:

> The strength of a tie is a (probably linear) combination of the amount of time, the emotional intensity, the intimacy (mutual confiding), and the reciprocal services which characterize the tie. (Granovetter, 1973, p. 1361)

It should be born in mind that Granovetter's work preceded digital networks by some years and that the kinds of relationship he discusses are limited by the usual geographical and temporal constraints of a face-to-face environment. Granovetter is also concerned with individuals, and networks in this view are composed of persons who form the nodes and the links are the relationships between these people. Currently networks composed of digital media are more likely to be thought of as comprising nodes of various types, including individuals, small, medium and large organizations, technological artefacts and systems etc. The stance Granovetter takes is also one that tends towards a reductive essentialism, describing networks as collections of individuals, and suggesting that the networks are what individual nodes make of them. This view can be contrasted with a more relational view of networks, which we favour, in which the individual components of networks, whether persons, groups or institutions are themselves emergent in their character, conditioned by their position in the network. Networks in this second view cannot be reduced to the characteristics of the component nodes as the nodes' character is itself dependant on its position and role in the network.

The notion of networked learning and the practical application of the design of networked learning environments raise several questions:
- Should researchers in CSCL and education more generally serve as critical opponents to the overall trends in the networked society as expressed by Castells and stand up against 'networked individualism', or should the design of CSCL and networked learning reflect these trends?
- Which models, networked models or community of practice models, are more productive with respect to the learning of the individual participant and under what conditions? Is it, for example, more productive for busy professionals to be organized through a pedagogical model based on relatively weak ties among the participants, or is it more productive to be organized in accordance with a pedagogical model facilitating the development of the strong ties in a community of practice or perhaps even a blend of both?

SPACE AND PLACE

In a networked learning environment place and space become highly contingent factors. As a consequence they have become a focus of attention for the design of all types of learning environments that are affected by digital networks, whether learners are co-located, distant or in a combination of the two (see, for example, Goodyear et al., 2001; Jamieson et al., 2000; Ponti & Ryberg, 2004). Other authors have noted that we should expect students to customize designed learning spaces and make their own "local habitations" (Nardi & O'Day, 1999) or "learning nests" (Crook, 2002). More generally we argue for a distinction to be made between space, which is understood as a relatively stable and potentially designed environment, and place, understood as contingent and locally inhabited. We argue that fostering a sense of place in networked learning environments is necessary in order to develop a social and emotional context to sustain social interactions and collaboration, whether these interactions are composed of either strong or weak ties.

The idea of space has been developed strongly in relation to network technologies, most particularly in terms of 'cyberspace'. The term cyberspace, originating in the works of William Gibson and particularly in his 1984 novel *Neuromancer*, came into common usage in the 1990s to capture the new sense of something beyond the computer interface that was being developed in the emerging digital networks. This sense of a new kind of space was reinforced with the development of the World Wide Web and the sense that through the use of hypertext and uniform resources locations a spatially referenced environment was developing in which we used *addresses* to visit *sites*. The spatial metaphor has been a powerful force in network development with designers making use of easily understood spatial references for the design of interfaces and in order to explain the move from the computer as s stand alone tool to the computer as one of a number of devices that can be used to access a networked digital environment.

Participants in a computer network whilst they are simultaneously situated at a real point in time and space are also displaced from that physical point in a virtual space configured through the network. Lash (2001) has argued that technology, in particular Internet technology has resulted in an abstraction from place:

> Technological forms of life are disembedded, they are somehow 'lifted out'. As lifted out, they take on increasingly less and less the characteristic of any particular place, and can be anyplace or indeed no place. This lifted-out space of placelessness is a generic space...It is not any particular space, but a generic space. Its context is no context at all. Its difference is indifference...The Internet is a generic space. It is no particular space. Indeed, networks are themselves by definition lifted-out spaces (Lash, 2001, p. 113).

In contrast Hine (2000) points out that despite the generic nature of Internet spaces the local is very much embedded in particular uses of the Internet, e.g., homepages or social networking site profiles such as those on Bebo, Facebook, and MySpace. In practice people using network spaces are never completely disembedded or separated from their off-line activities and spatial locations. Rather offline spaces interpenetrate online netscapes and together they configure new hybrid forms. Moreover the properties of space as experienced offline are used to inform the design of online environments.

Harrison and Dourish (1996) pointed to the way that software designers had exploited the properties of space to provide a spatial structure for people's online activities. They had designed online features that allowed users to orient themselves through an interaction with digital objects and thus understand the configuration of the virtual landscape. As Harrison and Dourish (1996) put it, "space is the opportunity, place is the understood reality". They suggest that the meaning and usefulness of a space increases when people build a history of experiences that allows the space to obtain the richer quality of 'place.' This change involves supporting the development of "appropriate behavioral framing"; that is the emergent patterns of human behaviour and interaction that offer understandings of the space. Harrison and Dourish refer to both physical environments and to media spaces, which would include information spaces, and hybrids of the physical and the virtual. The great flexibility of virtual spaces, with their potential sense of transience and impermanence, requires participants to engage in a process of re-creation of meanings to cope with uncertainty. In so doing, they become involved in a process of place-making, which is necessary in order to appreciate the online environment and to develop conditions for sustained and meaningful social interaction (Lee, Danis, Miller & Jung, 2001). The adoption of the notion of place has theoretical and methodological implications because it influences the range of concerns that are involved in field studies, and the range of methods that are used to relate to the users' lived experience of place in networked learning environments (Ciolfi and Bannon, 2003). We argue that using a concept of place as distinct from space could improve the conceptual development and design of networked learning environments. It is important to understand the way human beings may experience designed spaces and the potentials that exist for users to constitute their own places for the designers to be able to understand the way novel elements could change, interact with and shape the original designed space.

CONCLUDING REMARK

Following this introduction we present twelve case studies which are developed in relation to the framework presented earlier and in the final section of the book we return to discuss the framework in response to the material presented in the case studies. Each of the case studies whilst able to be read in their own right were developed iteratively with the framework and in some ways they therefore formed the basis on which this introduction was written. The process of developing the ideas found in this book should be seen as a collaborative process and an expression of a collective effort, although the authors of the Introduction take sole responsibility for the final formulation. As with all social knowledge the case studies reflect times that have already past or are just passing, because as Hegel remarked, the owl of Minerva spreads its wings only with the falling of the dusk (Hegel, 1820 Preface). In the final section we explicitly address the changes that are currently taking place in networked learning and the wider technological environment, bringing our reflections to a conclusion and linking them with current developments. We argue that this process of reflection on the recent past through the use of case studies is essential if we are not to be driven solely by novelty and a constant re-invention in the wake of each wave of technological change.

ACKNOWLEDGEMENT

This chapter is a collaborative effort based on a range of inputs from all the participants of the Kaleidoscope European Union funded Research Team (ERT) on Conditions for Productive Learning in Networked Learning Environments.

REFERENCES

Bakhtin, M. (1986). *Speech genres and other late essays* (V. W. McGee, Trans., C. Emerson, & M. Holquist, Eds.). Austin, TX: University of Texas Press.

Baerentsen, K., & Trettvik, J. (2002, October 19–23). An activity theory approach to affordance. *Proceedings of the second nordic conference on human-computer interaction* (pp. 51–60). Aarhus, Denmark.

Bateson, G. (2000). *Steps to an ecology of mind: Collected essays in anthropology, psychiatry, evolution, and epistemology*. Chicago: University of Chicago Press.

Beetham, H., & Sharpe, R. (Eds.). (forthcoming). *Rethinking pedagogy for a digital age: Designing and delivering e-learning*. RoutledgeFalmer

Bielaczyc, K. (2006). Designing social infrastructure: Critical issues in creating learning environments with technology. *The Journal of the Learning Sciences, 15*(3), 301–329.

Bielaczyc, K. (2001). Designing social infrastructure: The challenge of building computer-supported learning communities. In P. Dillenbourg, A. Eurelings, & K. Hakkarainen (Eds.), *European perspectives on computer-supported collaborative learning* (pp. 106–114). The proceedings of the first european conference on computer-supported collaborative learning, University of Maastricht.

Brown, J. S., Collins, A., & Duguid, P. (1989). Situated cognition and the culture of learning. *Educational Researcher, 18*(1), 32–42.

Castells, M. (1996, 2000). *The rise of the network society* (2nd ed.). Oxford, UK: Blackwell Publishers.

Castells, M. (2001). *The Internet galaxy: Reflections on the internet, business, and society*. Oxford, UK: Oxford University Press.

Ciolfi, L., & Bannon, L. (2003, December). *Space, place and the design of technologically enhanced physical environments*. Workshop on Space, Spatiality and Technologies, Edinburgh, Scotland, 12–13 December 2003.

Crook, C. (2002). The campus experience of networked learning. In C. Steeples & C. Jones (Eds.), *Networked learning: Perspectives and issues*. London: Springer.

Cuban, L. (2001). *Oversold and underused: Computers in the classroom*. Cambridge, MA: Harvard University Press.

Cuban, L. (1986). *Teachers and machines: The classroom use of technology since 1920*. New York: Teachers College Press.

De Laat, M. F., & Lally, V. (2003). Complexity, theory and praxis: Researching collaborative learning and tutoring processes in a networked learning community. *Instructional Science, 31*(1–2), 7–39.

Derry, J. (2007). Epistemology and conceptual resources for the development of learning technologies. *Journal of Computer Assisted Learning, 23*, 503–510.

Dillenbourg in Strijbos, J.-W., Kirschner, P. A., & Martens, R. L. (Eds.). (2004). *What we know about cscl—and implementing it in higher education*. Boston: Kluwer Academic Publishers.

Edwards, P. N. (2003). Infrastructure and modernity: Force, time, and social organization in the history of sociotechnical systems. In T. J. Misa, P. Brey, & A. Feenberg (Eds.), *Modernity and technology* (pp. 185–225). Cambridge MA: MIT Press.

Engeström, Y. (1987). *Learning by expanding—an activity theoretical approach to developmental research*. Retrieved November 6, 2005, from http://communication.ucsd.edu/MCA/Paper/Engestrom/expanding/toc.htm

Engeström, Y. (1999). Innovative learning in work teams: Analyzing cycles of knowledge creation in practice. In Y. Engeström, R. Miettinen, & R. L. Punamäki (Eds.), *Perspectives on activity theory* (pp. 377–404). Cambridge, UK: Cambridge University Press.

Engeström, Y. (2001). Expansive learning at work: Towards an activity theory reconceptualisation. *Journal of Education and Work, 14*, 133–156.

Flyvbjerg, B. (2001). *Making social science matter—Why social inquiry fails and how it can be succeed again*. Cambridge, UK: Cambridge University Press.

Flyvbjerg, B. (2004). Five misunderstandings about case-study research. In C. Seale, G. Gobo, J. F. Gubrium, & D. Silverman (Eds.), *Qualitative research practice* (pp. 420–434). London and Thousand Oaks, CA: Sage.

Flyvbjerg, B. (2006, July). Making organization research matter: Power, values, and phronesis. In S. R. Clegg, C. Hardy, T. B. Lawrence, & W. R. Nord (Eds.), *The sage handbook of organization studies* (2nd ed., pp. 370–387). Thousand Oaks, CA: Sage.

Gaver, W. W. (1996). Situating action 11: Affordances for interaction: The social is material for design. *Ecological Psychology, 8*(2), 111–129.

Gaver, W. (1991). *Technology affordances* in CHI'91 Conference Proceedings, 79–84.

Gibson, J. J. (1977). *The theory of affordances*. In R. Shaw & J. Bransford (Eds.), *Perceiving, acting and knowing*. Hillsdale, NJ: Erlbaum.

Gibson, J. J. (1979). *The ecological approach to visual perception*. Hillsdale, NJ: Lawrence Erlbaum Associates.

Goodyear, P., Jones, C., Asensio, M., Hodgson, V., & Steeples, C. (2001). *Effective networked learning in higher education: Notes and guidelines*. Lancaster, UK: CSALT, Lancaster University. Retrieved November 6, 2005, from http://csalt.lancs.ac.uk/jisc

Goodyear, P., Banks, S., Hodgson, V., & McConnell, D. (2004). *Advances in research on networked learning*. Kluwer: Dordrecht.

Granovetter, M. S. (1973). The strength of weak ties. *The American Journal of Sociology, 78*(6), 1360–1380.

Harper, R., Randall, D., & Rouncefield, M. (2000). *Organizational change and retail finance: An ethnographic approach*. London: Routledge.

Harrison, S., & Dourish, P. (1996). Re-place-ing space: The roles of space and place in collaborative systems. *Proceedings of CSCW 96* (pp. 67–76). New York: ACM.

Hine, C. (2000). *Virtual ethnography*. London: SAGE Publications Ltd.

Hutchby, I. (2001). Technologies, texts and affordances. *Sociology, 35*(2), 451–456.

Ilich, I. (1970). *Deschooling society*. New York: Harper and Row. Full text available online. Retrieved January 10, 2007, from http://www.preservenet.com/theory/Illich/Deschooling/intro.html

Jamieson, P., Taylor, P. G., Fisher, K., Trevitt, A. C. F., & Gilding, T. (2000). Place and space in the design of new learning environments. *Higher Education Research & Development, 19*(2), 221–236.

Jones, C. (2007). Designing for practice: Practicing design in the social sciences. In H. Beetham & R. Sharpe (Eds.), *Rethinking pedagogy for a digital age: designing and delivering e-learning*. RoutledgeFalmer.

Jones, C., Dirckinck-Holmfeld, L., & Lindström, B. (2006). A relational, indirect, meso-level approach to cscl design in the next decade. *International Journal of Computer-Supported Collaborative Learning, 1*(1), 35–56.

Jones, C., Dirckinck-Holmfeld, & Lindström, B. (2005). *CSCL The next ten years—a European perspective*. CSCL 2005, Taiwan.

Jones, C. (2004a). Network theory and description—The Lancaster ALT Masters programme. In L. Dirckinck-Holmfeld, B. Lindström, B. M. Svendsen, & M. Ponti. *Conditions for productive learning in networked learning environments*. Aalborg: Aalborg University/Kaleidoscope. Retrieved November 6, 2005, from http://www.ell.aau.dk/index.php?id=60

Jones, C. (2004b). The conditions of learning in networks. In L. Dirckinck-Holmfeld, B. Lindström, B. M. Svendsen, & M. Ponti. *Conditions for Productive Learning in Networked Learning Environments*. Aalborg: Aalborg University/Kaleidoscope. Retrieved November 6, 2005, from http://www.ell.aau.dk/index.php?id=60

Jones, C., & Esnault, L. (2004). The metaphor of networks in learning: Communities, collaboration and practice. In S. Banks, P. Goodyear, V. Hodgson, C. Jones, V. Lally, D. McConnell, & C. Steeples (Eds.), *Networked Learning 2004: Proceedings of the Fourth International Conference on Networked Learning 2004* (pp. 317–323). Lancaster, UK: Lancaster University and University of Sheffield. Retrieved November 6, 2005, from http://www.shef.ac.uk/nlc2004/Proceedings/Contents. htm

Kirschner, P. A., Strijbos, J., & Martens, R. L. (2004). CSCL in higher education. In J.-A., Strijbos, P. A. Kirschner, & R. L. Martens (Eds.), *What we know about CSCL: And implementing it in higher education*. Boston: Kluwer Academic Publishers.

Koschmann, T. (2002, January 7–11). Dewey's contribution to the foundations of CSCL Research. In G. Stahl (Ed.), *Computer support for collaborative learning: Foundations for a CSCL community*. Proceedings of CSCL 2002, Boulder, Colorado, USA.

Lakkala, M., Paavola, S., & Hakkarainen, K. (2008). Designing pedagogical infrastructures in university courses for technology-enhanced collaborative inquiry. *Research and Practice in Technology Enhanced Learning, 3*(1), 33–64.

Lash, S. (2001). Technological forms of life. *Theory, Culture & Society, 18*(1), 105–120.

Laurillard, D. (2002). *Rethinking university teaching: A conversational framework for the effective use of learning technologies* (2nd ed.). London: RoutledgeFalmer.

Lave, J., & Wenger, E. (1991). *Situated learning—Legitimate peripheral participation*. New York: Cambridge University Press.

Lee, A., Danis, C., Miller, T., & Jung, Y. (2001). Fostering social interaction in online spaces. In M. Hirose (Ed.), *Human-computer interaction (INTERACT'01)* – Eighth IFIP TC.13 Conference on Human-Computer Interaction IOS Press, 59–66.

Liljenström, H., & Svedin, U. (Eds.). (2005). *Micro, meso, macro: Addressing complex systems*. London: World Scientific Publishers.

McGrenere, J., & Ho, W. (2000, May). Affordances: Clarifying and evolving a concept. *Proceedings of graphic interface 2000* (pp. 179–186). Montreal, Canada.

Nardi, B., & O'Day, V. (1999). *Information ecologies: Using technology with heart*. Cambridge, MA: MIT Press.

Norman, D. (1988). *The psychology of everyday things*. New York: Basic Books.

Norman, D. A. (1990). *The design of everyday things*. New York: Doubleday.

Norman, D. (1999). Affordance, conventions, and design. *Interactions*, 6(3), 38–42.

Orlikowski, W. J. (2000). Using technology and constituting structures: A practice lens for studying technology in organizations. *Organizations Science*, 11(4), 404–428.

Ponti, M., & Ryberg, T. (2004, April 5–7). Rethinking virtual space as a place for sociability: Theory and design implications. In S. Banks, P. Goodyear, V. Hodgson, C. Jones, V. Lally, D. McConnell, & C. Steeples (Eds.), *Proceedings of the fourth international conference on networked learning 2004*. Jointly organized by Lancaster University and the University of Sheffield. Lancaster University, Lancaster, UK.

Säljö, R. (1999). Learning as the use of tools: A sociocultural perspective on the human technology link. In K. Littleton & P. Light (Eds.), *Learning with computers: Analysing productive intervention*. London: Routledge.

Schatzki, T. R. (1996). *Social practices: A wittgensteinian approach to human activity and the social*. Cambridge, UK: Cambridge University Press.

Schatzki, T. R., Knorr Cetina, K., & Von Savigny, E. (Eds.). (2001). *The practice turn in contemporary theory*. London: Routledge.

Stahl, G. (2003). Meaning and interpretation in collaboration. In B. Wason, S. Ludvigsen, & U. Hoppe (Eds.), *Designing for change in networked learning environments: Proceedings of the international conference on computer supported collaborative learning 2003*. Dordrecht, The Netherlands: Kluwer Academic Publishers.

Stahl, G. (2006). *Collaborating with technology: Mediation of group cognition*. Boston: MIT Press. Retrieved from http://www.cis.drexel.edu/faculty/gerry/mit/

Stake, R. (1995). *The art of case research*. Thousand Oaks, CA: Sage Publications.

Star, S. L., & Ruhleder, K. (1994). *Steps towards an ecology of infrastructure: Complex problems in design and access for large-scale collaborative systems*. Paper presented at the of the conference on Computer Supported Cooperative Work.

Star, S. L., & Ruhleder, K. (1996). Steps toward an ecology of infrastructure: Design and access for large information spaces. *Information Systems Research*, 7(1), 111–134

Suchman, L. (2007). *Human-machine reconfigurations: Plans and situated actions* (2nd ed.). Cambridge, UK: Cambridge University Press.

Taylor, C. (1985). *Philosophical papers 1&2*. Cambridge, UK: Cambridge University Press.

Torenvliet, G. (2003). We can't afford it! The devaluation of a usability term. *Interactions*, 10, 12–17.

Vygotsky, L. (1978). *Mind in society. The development of higher psychological processes*. Cambridge, MA: Harvard University Press.

Wellman, B., Quan-Haase, A., Boase, J., Chen, W., Hampton, K., Isla de Diaz, I., et al. (2003). The social affordances of the internet for networked individualism. *JCMC*, 8(3). Retrieved November 7, 2005, from http://jcmc.indiana.edu/issues.html

Wenger, E. (1998). *Communities of practice—learning, meaning, and identity*. New York: Cambridge University Press.

Wenger, E., McDermott, R., & Snyder, W. M. (2002). *Cultivating communities of practice*. Boston: Harvard Business School Press.

Wertsch, J. V. (1998). *Mind as action*. New York: Oxford University Press.

Winch, P. (1990). *The idea of a social science and its relation to philosophy*. London: Routledge.

Chris Jones
Institute of Higher Education
Open University, United Kingdom

Lone Dirckinck-Holmfeld
Department of Communication and Psychology
Aalborg University, Denmark

ANN BYGHOLM AND TOM NYVANG

AN INFRASTRUCTURAL PERSPECTIVE ON IMPLEMENTING NEW EDUCATIONAL TECHNOLOGY

The Case of Human Centred Informatics

Technology changes in steps – practice with technology in organisations evolves over time and across generations of technology.

INTRODUCTION

In this chapter we analyse the implementation of new technology for communication and collaboration in Human Centred Informatics, a bachelors and masters program at the faculty of humanities at Aalborg University. Our focus is on the organisational implementation (meaning that we focus on change in organisations – not on programming software which is another context where you will meet the term). Our aim is to explicate and understand the problems and possibilities in the implementation process at the meso-level. We use the concept of infrastructure as the unit of analysis to focus on the relationship between technology, educational practice, organisation, and knowledge involved in shaping educational practice with technology in organisations. The aim is to understand the variety of problems that are attached to the implementation of new technology within a learning environment that encompasses several hundred people, all with very different roles, tasks and practices.

In a review of research on the application of technology to collaborative learning in higher education, conducted by Resta and Laferrière (2007), six sets of recommendations are identified, one of them being concerned with organisational issues. Thus they state that:

> Research is needed on the organisational issues related to implementing CSCL in higher education to determine the essentials conditions that must be in place for effective faculty use of CSCL (with particular attention to the level of support provided). (Resta & Laferrière, 2007, p. 76)

They furthermore argue that such research will lead to the development of viable designs for adoption strategies within organisations. Jones, Dirckinck-Holmfeld and Lindström (2006) have identified a similar need for research at the meso-level

L. Dirckinck-Holmfeld, C. Jones and B. Lindström (eds.), Analysing Networked Learning Practices in Higher Education and Continuing Professional Development, 29–43.

of collaborative learning. The meso-level is placed between the macro and the micro and is characterized as follows: Meso would identify interactions in and with the settings beyond the small group, but still with a local focus that was open to routine control and intervention (Jones et al., 2006, p. 37).

More generally they suggest that differentiating between macro-, meso-, and micro-level assists us in identifying the details of the learning environment. Moreover, that attention at the meso-level helps us in understanding the basic conditions that allow for collaborative learning and collaboratively driven change at the institutional level. A focus on the meso-level thus implies a focus on the relationship between the basic elements involved in a learning environment.

To emphasise the importance of the relationship between practice and technology is not new to research in information systems, nor is infrastructure the only concept or theoretical construct that pursues this focus. As was commented in Management Information Quarterly (MISQ):

> ...research in the information systems field examines more than just the technological system, or just the social system, or even the two side by side; in addition, it investigates the phenomena that emerge when the two interact. (Lee, 2001, p. iii)

Indeed the significance of focusing on the phenomena that emerge when the social and the technical system interact has been recognised and conceptualised in several ways, as also mentioned in the introduction to this volume. E.g. by distinction between technology as artefact and technology in use (Orlikowski, 2000); by the distinction between affordances per se and perceived affordances (Norman, 1999); by application of activity theory that encompasses both motive, artefact and the social context in order to understand practice (Nardi, 1996); by introducing actor-network theory which links the act with all of its influencing factors producing an network, where elements of any kind may be included: humans, technological artefacts, organisations, institutions, etc. (Latour, 1999); and by using the concept of genre (drawing upon activity theory) to embrace both artefact type and tradition (Spinuzzi, 2003).

With this chapter we aim to carry out meso-level analysis of organisational implementation of technology by means of the concept of infrastructure. Meso-level analysis addresses questions and issues that go beyond the individual or small group learning experience and focuses on the conditions that allow for learning in a specific learning environment. The concept of infrastructure furthermore strengthens the attention on the relationship between the elements involved. In so doing, we identify and label the challenges of organisational implementation of ICT for learning in higher education. Thus in the following section we introduce and discuss the concept of infrastructure, present our case and the analysis and finally conclude in regards to organisational implementation.

INFRASTRUCTURAL PERSPECTIVE

The traditional concept of an infrastructure is something that is just there, ready-to-use, completely transparent and often taken for granted (for example, the water or electricity supplies, the railway, the mail services and the internet). Under this concept there is a tendency to perceive infrastructure as 'hardware' – implying something that is built and maintained and which then sinks into the invisible background, to be noticed only when it breaks down. But as Edwards (2003) points out, infrastructures are socio-technical in nature, meaning that to qualify as an infrastructure a system requires not only hardware but also organisations, socially communicated background knowledge, general acceptance, reliance and near ubiquitous accessibility.

According to Wiktionary (http://en.wiktionary.org) an infrastructure is "an underlying base or foundation especially for an organisation or system" and "the basic facilities, services and installations needed for the functioning of a community or society". This definition points to the fact that for the understanding of infrastructure the development or evolvement of ways to deal with this underlying base is equally important. For example, telephony is possible not only because signals can be transmitted over a distance using electromagnetic waves via electronic transmitters, but also because of the invention of an appropriate appliance – the telephone – which can be used for the purpose of transmission. Importantly, the system is not successful simply because the technology works, but because enough people want to use, own and pay for a phone with which to communicate with others. It works because the whole service is highly organised, making sure that it is possible to make calls to the people you want to talk to. Furthermore it is difficult to separate the development of the 'base' infrastructure from the development of services and regulations that support its functionality. Infrastructures, therefore, includes technologies that are socially co-defined by their use and are always under a process of development or change; they grow through their use, and it is their use that defines whether or not something becomes an infrastructure.

Star & Ruhledger (1996) and Hanseth (2000) (among others) discuss the infrastructural aspects of IT systems. They both suggest different dimensions to characterise an infrastructure. While focusing on use and practice Star and Ruhledger mention eight different characteristics that are: *embeddedness* (integrated in social structures and practices); *transparency* (can be used without removing focus from the task); *reach or scope* (goes beyond individual tasks or processes); *learned as part of membership* (an inherent part of an organisation); *links with conventions of practice* (shapes and is shaped by practice); *embodiment of standards* (builds on standards and conventions); *build on an installed base* (must relate to existing technologies); and *visible upon breakdown* (looses transparency and is drawn in focus when it breaks down). Very much in line with this, but with slightly more emphasis on the technical prerequisite for an infrastructure to function as such, Hanseth (2000) suggests that an infrastructure is *evolving* (evolves continuously); *shared* (must function as a shared resource or foundation for a community); *open* (lack of borders in how many elements it may include, how many users may be using it and also in the sense that there are no limits to who might contribute to its design and deployment, and that the development time has no beginning and no ending); *heterogeneous* (including sub-infrastructures based on different versions of the same standard or different standards covering the same functionality); *builds on an installed base* (backward compatibility, which also means that the existing heavily influences how the new can be designed and that infrastructures are considered as existing already, never having been developed from scratch).

These dimensions suggest "an infrastructure, which is without absolute boundary or a priori definition" (Star and Ruhledger, 1996) and they also point to the fact that infrastructures cannot be understood independently of their use. An IT system, then, becomes an infrastructure in relation to the technical and social elements of an organised practice within which it functions. It is evolving over (a long) time, it does not have a fixed group of users and it is a dynamic, ongoing process with no fixed centre of control. It both forms and is formed by use. The infrastructural perspective places in the foreground the fact that IT systems are never designed from scratch, they always build upon exiting tools and practices. To put emphasis on this dynamic Hanseth proposes the term "cultivation" instead of design, and draws attention to the resemblance to a living organism. In this he is drawing on Dahlbom and Janlert's (1996) distinction between construction and cultivation as two very different ways of thinking of design; construction denoting the process of selecting, putting together and arranging a number of objects to form a system, whereas in cultivating we interfere with, support and control a natural process.

To get a deeper understanding of the sort of problems arising in this natural process Star and Ruhledger turn to Bateson (2000) and his understanding of communicative systems. Communication, in Bateson's terms, is an extensive and far reaching concept referring to the kinds of phenomena that cannot be understood in terms of physical laws. His study of communicative behaviour included problems from very different domains, e.g. schizophrenia, alcoholism and the communicative system of whales and dolphins. Regardless of the particularities in the domain involved, Bateson's focus was on the understanding of the general laws and patterns of communication. Inspired by Bertrand Russell's theory of logical types, Bateson has pointed out that the human communication operates at several levels of abstraction. The levels are organised in a hierarchical structure, such that each level is communication about it's sublevel. The level that is communication about communication is called meta-communication, and the level that is communication about meta-communication is called meta-meta-communication, and so forth. In the distinction between the content and relationship level of a message.the relationship or meta-communicative level is used to classify the content level of the communication, to inform on how to understand the message. Bateson points out that there is a gulf between the meta-message and the message. A gulf that is of the same nature as the gulf between a thing and the word that stands for it, or between the member of a class and the name of the class. Bateson's understanding of learning corresponds to his theory of communication in the sense that learning is communication and, like all communicational phenomena, should be understood as a hierarchy (i.e. having different levels).

The number of levels that are possible to identify in human communication is not fixed, but like Star and Ruhleder we use three; these being relevant to understanding the problems of implementing new technology for communication and collaboration within the educational setting of Human Centred Informatics. Level one problems appear as 'matter of fact' problems, like not knowing how to get a user name, or publish a message in the system or not understanding what is wrong when the server goes down. Level two problems are those of using the system properly, knowing what kind of messages should be published and to whom. Thus, level two is concerned with classifying, with discussion and reflection on the type of problems that arise in using, supporting, and running the system in the use context. Level three is one step more abstract, and poses questions about the values and bases of the work done, like what kind of learning goals are to be pursued, or the general politics of the choice of platform (vendor locked or open source). Issues raised on level three are concerned with the fundamental issues and values of the specific practice.

The above discussion indicates that applying an infrastructural perspective to technology as opposed to regarding it as system or tool, affords an understanding of the complexity of relations between technology and the way it is used. Additionally, the levels borrowed from Bateson help in sorting out, analytically, the types of problems that arise from changing the learning environment as seen from the meso-level. But while the infrastructural levels are useful in labelling implementation challenges and organising them in different categories, they do not support identification of and distinguishing between practices involved. First and foremost, there are two practices that stand out: these are the pedagogical practice of facilitating learning and the practice of supplying ICT in the organisation – research in ICT and learning do tend to focus on the pedagogical use of ICT, including specific designs, and not so much where the technology comes from. Support in relation to both technology and pedagogy is a third process or practice that, as stressed by Resta and Laferriére (2007) and Kanstrup (2005), is crucial in organisational implementation of educational technology. We thus suggest that pedagogy, technology and support are core practices in a learning environment. In reality, pedagogy, technology and support are woven together, but for analytical purposes we suggest they are regarded as separate but interdependent elements of an educational infrastructure.

Having explicated the infrastructural perspective and core practices we want to pursue the overall aim of identifying and labeling the challenges that are part of the organisational implementation of ICT for learning in higher education. More specifically, we want to investigate the following questions:

- Pedagogical practice: how, when, and why does communication change under the new technological conditions?
- Support practice: what kind of support is needed and which challenges do the supporters meet?
- Technology practice: what kinds of problems are involved in acquiring, operating and maintaining new ICT?

In the next section we describe our case and methodology before going into the analysis of the questions.

CASE STUDY

Human Centred Informatics is an educational program within the Faculty of Humanities, offering bachelor (3 years), master level (bachelor + 2 years) and Ph.D. level (master + 3 years) education, and has approximately 500 students. It combines communication, organisation and ICT studies, equipping students with the tools to become critical yet constructive participants in the evaluation and construction of ICT and new media. Human Centered Informatics already uses ICT supported learning, but primarily in educational programs placed off-campus.

The pedagogical foundation of Human Centered Informatics is the variant of problem based learning (PBL) known as problem oriented project pedagogy (POPP) (Dirckinck-Holmfeld, 2002). In practice, students spend approximately 50 per cent of their time on coursework and 50 per cent on supervised, group organised, problem based projects. This means that educational technology must support collaboration and community building involving both students and faculty.

This study is part of a larger action research project that has been divided into three phases, moving from implementation of ICT in a semester with relatively few students (21) and faculty (6) involved, to a semester involving more students (80) and faculty (20), and finally to a full scale implementation. Phase one was used to uncover the practical problems implementing different kinds of ICT, and to study faculty implementing ICT in individual courses with little coordination. Phase two focused on using ICT to improve coherence, flexibility, transparency and quality in teaching and learning. The degree of coordination in the use of ICT was higher in the second phase. Among other things this meant that a common platform was implemented across all courses and activities in the relevant semester. Lotus Quickplace was chosen because of the flexibility it offered in tying all activities together within a common structure, but which could remain open to local re-design by faculty, students or administrators. In the third phase the Quickplace based structure from phase two was refined and expanded and implemented across the Human Centered Informatics program.

This investigation is designed as a case study and was carried out after one semester with full scale implementation (spring 2004). To document the implementation process we monitored the use of the Quickplace environment over one semester and conducted semi-structured research interviews with key figures. A key figure is here defined as a person that seems to have played an important role in the process or showed an above average devotion to the use of Quickplace. We thus selected members of the faculty (3), administrators (2), students (1), Quickplace support staff (3) and system administrators (2) for interviews. In the interviews the discussion was centred on knowledge, competencies and opinions in relation to aspects of practice affected by the implementation of Quickplace.

The transcripts of the interviews were reorganised according to the theoretical framework and according to themes that emerged across the interviews.

ANALYSIS AND DISCUSSION

Analysis and discussion is structured around the analytical framework and research questions presented earlier in this chapter. In our analysis of the pedagogical practice we use data from interviews with faculty, students, and secretaries. Quick-place support staff provided data for our analysis of the support practice, while data for the analysis of technological practice came from the system administrators. We use the levels extracted from Bateson's work on communication, and also used by Star and Ruhledger (1996) to identify and label the different categories of problems involved in each practice.

Pedagogical Practice

In the present case the implementation of new educational technology is closely linked with the emergence of a new pattern of communication within the pedagogical environment. The members of faculty we interviewed were especially concerned with two issues: change in conditions for communication with students, and change in their own work conditions. Thus, one of the interviewed faculty members stressed that good communication no matter if it is verbal or textual is richer than that offered by the new system, which is based on text based asynchronous communication. Being a coordinator of the first semester of Human Centred Informatics she points out that in her opinion good communication and rich social interaction are even more important with new students:

> The first semester presented some completely different problems to others because you [students] have to be integrated into a culture that has yet to be established. But then the question is: what tools do we need to communicate during the first semester and how can we show that we are in a department of communication? (faculty, semester coordinator, line 17–23).

However, this is not the only problem that she experienced during the introduction and use of the new system. Before the system was implemented most of the communication between faculty, students and the coordinator of the semester took place via a secretary who came to know almost everything about the semester. This was about to change because all parties got easier access to communicate directly in the system, with the result that no one really had an overview any longer. At the same time an old discussion about the division of labour between different groups of university employees re-emerged, because the system called for a review of decisions on who does what.

The other faculty members we interviewed, who were coordinators of higher semesters in the same programme, agreed that the possibility for communication and dialog were restrictive in the new system (compared to face-to-face), and added that on-line communication changed their work conditions. The new system made it possible for students to ask questions 24 hours a day, to expect written comments on papers instead of oral responses, and require on-line publication of PowerPoint presentations and lecture notes. Each of those requests may have seemed reasonable, but the faculty members we interviewed argued that this was all part of a transformation of their work conditions and demands. They felt they were forced to take on new tasks, due to the expanded facility for communication online, but did not manage to get rid of any existing tasks by way of compensation. Furthermore, they felt that the system had made their work and communication more visible, transparent and less private in a way that was at times quite troublesome. In general, they had nothing to say against transparency and visibility, but felt that many problems they had regarded as inevitable during the course of a semester were, thanks to the virtual environment, made public in an unreasonable way. In a specific case, complaints from individual students were posted in a shared forum and even though the matter was out of the hands of the coordinators they felt unhappy about the situation – not only because the problem existed, but because the complaints, though unjustified, made them look responsible for it, so causing them loss of face.

To facilitate the kind of rich social interaction they sought to promote, the faculty members advocated the use of a real life classroom, complete with physical teaching aids such as notice boards and paper. If students have to find information e.g. on boards outside the offices of the faculty, then these boards, say the faculty members, become the centre of informal gatherings, where students and faculty staff meet to discuss important issues. In the faculty members' opinion, this kind of informal gathering and interaction is not yet afforded by the new system.

None of the problems pointed out by the faculty members had anything to do with the use of the system, what we call level one problems; that is, gaining access to it, publishing documents etc. This could be because there were no such problems, but it could also be that, for the faculty members we interviewed, second and third order issues were more significant. It may be that some of these problems had more to do with finding the right balance between the forms of communication available, as the use of the new system does not necessarily exclude the use of other media, such as notice board and paper.

While the faculty members focused on the problems of good communication, the role of dialog and their own work load, the secretaries and students were more concerned with the potential of the new system. The student we interviewed argues that one integrated ICT based platform for communication and collaboration will make it far easier to keep track of all relevant information. As for the secretaries, they maintained that the system had actually reduced their work load. The secretaries' responsibility to students is primarily to keep them informed on such matters as class schedules, cancellation, enrolment for exams etc. Once the implementation was complete they could just post all this information on the system and their part of the work was done. In principle, the students could reply and ask questions to at least some of these messages, although the secretaries pointed out that they did not have the time to check the systems for messages and reply to them. They did mention a need for educating the students in actually accessing the information on the system, as a lot of them missed the deadline for exam enrolment, but basically the secretaries were content with the new, predominantly one-way, communication form.

The faculty members, secretaries and students all pointed to different possibilities and problems connected with the use of the system. The students wanted a common on-line structure, giving easy access at anytime and from any place. The secretaries and faculty added that students also want the greatest possible amount of help and service. The secretaries want to reach as many students as possible in as fast and easy a way as possible. The faculty members on the other hand stress that as professional experts in communication they see a need for a more diverse pattern of communication than the virtual environment offers. They also stress that the degree of service and flexibility that students find convenient may not be advisable or possible, from their professional point of view.

It seems that implementation of a new system for communication and collaborating also created a need for renegotiating the communicative practice within the educational setting. During its introduction the faculty members, secretaries and faculty members were all shown how to operate it, but there was no explicit discussion about what the new conditions for communication meant for their respective work practices.

Support Practice

The support team consisted of one full time e-learning consultant (although his time was not 'fully' on this project) and two part time student assistants. The students were enrolled in Human Centered Informatics and were thus students in the program they were supporting as well.

From the beginning of the project the assumption made by researchers, project management and the support staff was that it had to be an iterative project, where evaluations were fed back into the implementation process continuously. That decision was made based on experience, the available literature and prior studies that suggested that implementation of ICT could be understood as a learning process (Nyvang, 2004). The iterative approach was both a solution and a challenge to the support staff. A solution because it also presented a way to develop their knowledge base, and a challenge because learning from iterations is also complicated; the reason being that each iteration throws up many different and contradicting views on the right way to use the system and the right way to support the users. In other words iteration was a level one activity in the support practice, but reflections on how to be iterative and how to learn from iterations were level two and three problems. We do not in our data see simple, easy and unproblematic solutions to these challenges, but as the next paragraphs show, the support team developed a practice that attempted to handle the challenges.

First of all, the support team played a different role in different parts of the process. They started with the design of the structure and went on to the design of interface of the Quickplace environment, based on experience from a pilot project

BYGHOLM AND NYVANG

and their own knowledge relevant to the task at hand. One of the student assistants describes it this way:

> At first we looked at how it had been running so far. I had been in the semester in which it was used [part of the pilot project]. [Student assistant 2] had been a supporter there and then we talked about the things we would like to change, wrote a list and then started on the design; the layout of a page. There were some things that we thought should be done differently. And then we made different models. (Quickplace support staff, student assistant 1 line 103–114)…Regarding the structure and similar issues, we talked to the semester coordinators to find out what their needs were –whether there was a specific need in individual semesters (student assistant 2 line 267–271).

Here we see that the design and support team had a pretty clear idea about how to solve the level two problem of obtaining the specific knowledge needed for designing and implementing a structure within the web-environment. However, they did encounter a level one problem when it came to the implementation of a single sign-on, which was intended to give the users unrestricted access from a single signing in process. Fortunately the server administrators solved this problem.

When the support team had the design in place it was made available to the users prior to the start of a new semester. The top priority of the support team in the next phase – the period just before and immediately after the semester commenced – was to solve or avoid level one problems among the members of the pedagogical practice, as well as the students and administrative staff. This they achieved by answering questions and solving problems for individual users and by offering short courses to groups of users. The courses gave a short introduction to the new platform and practical exercises. This course did not pay much attention to the level two problems of the users – very little was done to introduce proper and efficient use of the platform to the users. The guidance given to individual members of the faculty did pay more attention to the level two issues.

The support team noted several challenges in the way things were done during the implementation of the new platform. First of all, they were in a different organisational unit (a research lab) to the system administrators and felt that the chain of command was unclear. They felt that a clearer division of responsibility could have made some of their work easier because it had enabled them to make faster decisions on some issues. The supporters also underlined that even though the new platform was widely known and widely used in the organisation there was still work to do to on pedagogical and didactical innovation, and on the utilisation of all the features offered by the platform (e.g. the support for collaborative work and learning). The student we talked to supported this statement. He saw a great need for using it in a more innovative fashion in order to harvest some of the real potential benefits.

Level three problems did not seem to be discussed much when it came to support. It turned out to be an underlying assumption that support was something required in a project like this and that the present support was functioning well and assumed to be sufficient in this case. However, we saw an emerging discussion

38

about the definition of flat and hierarchical structures. The design and support team believed they had designed a flat structure, whereas one of the semester coordinators thought it was hierarchical. This was a clear indication of a need to negotiate the meaning of specific words, so as to ensure a better communication across practices. It also indicated a need to negotiate the structural needs across the pedagogical and support practice. We also heard different opinions on the role of the support. Some thought that support should just take care of technical problems while others suggested a more integral approach to technical problems *and* the development of practice with the technology. In the present case the supporters had knowledge about the program they were supporting, as well as in-depth knowledge about the technology and the use of ICT in learning and teaching. With this background in mind we suggest that support is seen as a mediator that promotes the use of new technology by solving actual problems for users and by guiding them towards efficient and innovative use.

Technology Practice

What kinds of problem are involved in acquiring, operating and maintaining new ICT? To illustrate the complexity of the problems we will look at an example from the Human Centered Informatics case from the perspective of the system administrator's office. It is a story that highlights how solving a relatively simple technical problem can become an extremely complex process, involving all sorts of issues – technical and non-technical.

During the first months of its full scale implementation the system went down frequently. This was of course very inconvenient and confusing for the users, many of whom had just started to use the system. Apart from restating the server, which made the system functional once again, the system administrator's office began to investigate the cause of the problem and how to solve it. It had not occurred during the former phases of use and so attention was given to what made this implementation special. In contrast to previous phases, the system had on this occasion been integrated with the general catalogue of users, which was kept in the system administrators' office in order to avoid entering all the names manually. This integration was possible according to the system documentation. Nevertheless, it was thought that the problem had something to do with the system losing contact with the user catalogue, making it impossible to log in. At this point help was sought from the systems' supplier who, as it turned out, had a comprehensive web based support system, which was able to offer a solution. However, access to the online fix was delayed, due to the fact that the university had acquired the Quickplace system through a joint research project with the supplier, and thus did not have the customer ID needed by the online support system. While struggling to obtain a customer ID, the system administrator's office decided as a temporary solution to restart the server every night. They also put up a surveillance system in order to detect exactly when the problem occurred. Eventually it transpired that the supplier knew of the problem and how to solve it.

In the end it turned out to be merely a level one problem, but the process of solving it, getting the right information and installing the fix, involved several investigations at levels two and three. The idea of putting up a surveillance system is an example of a level two decision, thus a consideration on how to act when something is not working. Also, the service and maintenance of the system was brought into question. There was no explicit decision concerning system surveillance outside normal working hours, which meant that if the server went down outside normal working hours it would not be restarted right away. However, it became apparent that there was in fact a need for a round-the-clock watch, because the system was being used at all hours. Should the server go down during the night without being monitored it would not otherwise get re-started before next morning at eight, when the system administrator's office was back at work. Working with the server problem also identified some level three questions (e.g. the discussion on platforms). It was difficult for the system administrator's office to actually work with the problem because they had no access to the system's code (and for a period no access to the supplier either, as mentioned above). They would have preferred an open source system with a large user community, as this would have allowed access to the code and to other users with the necessary technical insight. Besides this there were some organisational considerations concerning, for example, who was going to decide how much to spend on a solution, and how it was to be paid for.

The technology practice had no formalised goals for system functionality, stability, or server surveillance – nor had it a formalised policy for choosing and implementing new systems. It was clearly stated in an interview with the manager of the system administrator's office, though, that the system administrator's office wanted test software before it was rolled out to end users, in order to avoid problems and that they also wanted surveillance systems outside normal working hours to be able to find and solve critical problems as soon as possible. When it came to identifying the most critical problems the answer could not be found within the technology practice because the end users are not there. They are in for instance the pedagogical practice. This again brings us to conclude that considerations and negotiations across more than one practice are needed to identify the most prominent challenges.

FINDINGS AND LESSONS LEARNED

Infrastructure defined as something that is just there, ready at hand and transparent did not emerge in the Human Centered Informatics case. The technology we studied did, however, develop towards representation and support of the work of staff and students, which is another quality of an infrastructure (Star & Bowker, 1995). What is interesting then, on top of our original research questions, is why the infrastructure did not emerge?

The analysis has been conducted under the headings of pedagogical practice, support practice and technology practice. In the matrix below we have grouped the findings in a hierarchy of the three levels suggested by Star & Ruhledger (1996). The matrix[1] points to the fact that the problems and issues involved in accomplishing an infrastructure for networked learning are manifold and of diverse nature.

Table 1. Critical questions and problems linked to the implementation of educational technology in the case of Human Centred Informatics.

	Pedagogical practice	Support practice	Technology practice
Level 1	Lack of ability to sign-on and publish messages.	Lack of single sign-on.	Server breaks down.
Level 2	Which kind of communication is relevant in which media?	On what knowledge base is the support and structure for networked learning designed?	How is the technological stability and reliability ensured?
Level 3	What is the role of dialogue?	What is support and what is the relationship between support and other practices?	Who owns, controls, and has access to the source code of the software? What is technological stability and reliability?

The level one challenges were the most specific. They are also likely to be the most case specific and the easiest to deal with, and in our case they were all solved. However, they were not entirely uncomplicated, because what appeared to be a simple problem on level one is influenced by the values, cultures and knowledge inherent in the levels two and three. It is for instance only a problem that the server is off-line if it is generally agreed that the server must always be on-line. The level two and three challenges were more difficult to deal with, because they were in the form of open ended questions that could only be dealt with through negotiation, alignment and coordination – often across more than one practice. Level two is a good example: The negotiations within the pedagogical practice about relevant communication and media were influenced by design decisions made by the supporters within the support practice. The technology practice and reliability of the software also influenced the media/communication negotiation; the argument being that a medium that is not technically stable cannot be used for important messages. For their part, the members of the technology practice were a little reluctant to throw a lot of effort into stabilising a system with little importance to the users and the organisation. Fortunately, the members of the technology practice understood that the lack of stability was exactly what kept the new system from gaining in importance, and a double-bind across the practices were avoided.

Another argument from a participant in the pedagogical practice was that communication in a physical space had higher value, more validity and more important social side effects in comparison to communication in virtual spaces. That perspective on communication contradicted some of the level two and three reflections made by other members of the same practice, and just as importantly it contradicted the views of the members of the support practice, who worked with the knowledge (and conviction) that communication in virtual spaces has a significant pedagogical potential.

In conclusion, level two and three challenges are the most demanding, since they cannot be solved or handled by solely by individuals within the organisation, only by collectives – if we want an infrastructure with the qualities described by Star & Ruhledger (1996). The success of the infrastructure depended on the way these issues were handled. This brings us back to the question of meso-level analysis and design. The designer has to design for learning by supporting negotiation about the process and goal/value related issues in the organisation. By supporting learning the designer also to supports the fine weaving together of existing practices and emerging new practices in the organisation. Also, the dimensions used by (Star & Ruhleder, 1999; Hanseth, 2000), to characterise infrastructure – the emphasis on embeddedness, on backward compatibility, the embodiments of standards, and the link to conventions of practise – point to the fact that the infrastructural perspective is more about smaller steps of continuous evolution than it is about sudden revolution (Star & Bowker, 2002). Of course, the educational organisation may decide it wants a revolutionary change in technology, but it is hard to imagine the day-to-day emergence of a new infrastructure. The alignment of individual contributions to one or more practices and the handling of contradictions is time and resource consuming. As a general lesson to inform meso-level design the infrastructural perspective puts emphasis on the already existing – and evolving – nature of technology use.

As for the further work with the specific problems elucidated upon in this study, we would like to stress the importance of organisational structures that support not only the use of the technology, but also discussions about the proper use of the technology within its intended context, and discussions about the goals and values. Once again we draw on the work of Kanstrup (2005), who stresses the importance of simultaneous membership of different practices (also called multi-membership) in the educational organisation as a means to mediate between different practices and thus support the emergence of new infrastructures within the organisation. Kanstrup goes as far as to talk about gardening inspired by an ecological perspective. Only by means of a gardener and a gardening approach within the organisation can practice evolve over time. Even though gardening is not a term associated with the original meaning of the word infrastructure we find it useful in supporting our understanding of the emergence of an educational infrastructure.

NOTES

[1]   A former version of this matrix were presented in (Bygholm & Nyvang, 2004)

REFERENCES

Bateson, G. (2000). *Steps to an ecology of mind: Collected essays in anthropology, psychiatry, evolution, and epistemology*. Chicago: University of Chicago Press.
Bygholm, A., & Nyvang, T. (2004). *Creating an educational infrastructure - Experiences, challenges and lessons learned*. Conference ICT and Learning in Regions, June 2003, Aalborg.

Bygholm, A. (2007). Communication across sectors in health care - a case of establishing new infrastructure. In A. M. Kanstrup, T. Nyvang, & E. M. Sørensen (Eds.), *Perspectives on e-Government*. Aalborg: Aalborg University Press.

Dahlbom, B., & Janlert, J. E. (1996). *Computer future, mimeo*. Department of Informatics, Gøteborg University.

Dirckinck-Holmfeld, L. (2002). Designing virtual learning environments based on problem oriented project pedagogy. In L. Dirckinck-Holmfeld & B. Fibiger (Eds.), *Learning in virtual environments*. Fredriksberg, Samfundslitteratur.

Edwards, P. N. (2003). Infrastructure and modernity: Force, time, and social organization in the history of sociotechnical systems. In T. J. Misa, P. Brey, & A. Feenberg (Eds.), *Modernity and technology*. Cambridge Mass: MIT Press.

Hanseth, O. (2000). The economics of standards. In C. U. Ciborra, K. Braa, A. Cordella, B. Dahlbom, A. Failla, O. Hanseth, V. Hepso, J. Ljungberg, E. Monteiro, & K. A. Simon (Eds.), *From control to drift. The dynamics of corporate information infrastructures*. New York: Oxford University Press.

Jones, C., Dirckinck-Holmfeld, L., & Lindström. (2006). A relational, indirect, meso-level approach to CSCL design in the next decade. *International Journal of Computer-Supported Collaborative Learning*, *1*(1), 35–56.

Kanstrup, A. M. (2005). *Local design*. Unpublished Ph.D., Aalborg University, Aalborg.

Lee, A. (2001). Editorial. *MISQ*, *25*(1), iii–vii.

Nardi, B. (Ed.). (1996). *Context and consciousness, activity theory and human computer interaction*. Cambridge Mass: MIT Press

Norman, D. (1999). Affordance, conventions, and design. *Interactions*, *6*(3), 38–43.

Nyvang, T. (2006). *Implementation of ICT in higher education*. Paper presented at the Networked Learning 2006, Lancaster.

Nyvang, T. (2007). *Ibrugtagning af ikt i universitetsuddannelse (Implementation of ICT in Higher education)*. Unpublished Ph.D., Aalborg University, Aalborg.

Nyvang, T., & Johnson, N. A. (2004). *Using activity theory framework (atf) to build an analytic bridge across the atlantic: Two cases of information and communication technology (ict) integration*. Paper presented at the SITE 2004, Atlanta.

Nyvang, T., & Roseeuw Poulsen, C. (2007). Implementation of ict in government organizations - user driven og management driven? In A. M. Kanstrup, T. Nyvang, & E. M. Sørensen (Eds.), *Perspectives on e-government: Technology & infrastructure, politics & organization, and interaction & communication*. Aalborg: Aalborg University Press.

Orlikowski, W. J. (2000). Using technology and constituting structures: A practice lens for studying technology in organizations. *Organizations Science*, *11*(4), 404–428.

Resta, P., & Laferriére, T. (2007). Technology in support of collaborative learning. *Educational Psychology Review*, *19*(1), 65–83.

Spinuzzi, C. (2003). *Tracing genres through organizations - a sociocultural approach to information design*. Cambridge, MA: The MIT Press.

Star, S. L., & Bowker, G. C. (2002). How to infrastructure. In L. A. Lievrouw & S. Livingstone (Eds.), *Handbook of new media* (pp. 151–162). London: Sage.

Star, S. L., & Ruhleder, K. (1996). Steps toward an ecology of infrastructure: Design and access for large information spaces. *Information Systems Research*, *7*(1), 111–134.

***Wentzer, H., & Bygholm, A. Attending Unintended Transformations of Health Care Infrastructure. In *International Journal of Integrated Care* Vol. 7, 14. November 2007 - ISSN 1568-4156 - http://www.ijic.org/

Tom Nyvang
e-Learning Lab. Center for User Driven Innovation, Learning, and Design
Department of Communication and Psychology
Aalborg University, Denmark

Ann Bygholm
e-Learning Lab. Center for User Driven Innovation, Learning, and Design
Department of Communication and Psychology
Aalborg University, Denmark

GIOVANNI FULANTELLI

BLENDED LEARNING, SYSTEMS THINKING AND COMMUNITIES OF PRACTICE

A Case Study

*There is no human activity from which every form of intellectual participation
can be excluded: homo faber cannot be separated from homo sapiens. Each
man, finally, outside his professional activity, carries on some form of
intellectual activity, that is, he is a 'philosopher', an artist, a man of taste, he
participates in a particular conception of the world, has a conscious line of
moral conduct, and therefore contributes to sustain a conception of the world
or to modify it, that is, to bring into being new modes of thought.*

Antonio Gramsci

INTRODUCTION

The aim of the study presented in this chapter is to illustrate an experience of
networked learning and, through its analysis, to reflect on the way that networks
(meant both as technological and social connections) can dramatically influence
and modify not only the way students learn, but also the inner dynamics and
processes of the institution running the networked learning course.

Specifically, the results presented here are based on the experience of the
research team I belong to at the, Institute for Educational Technologies (ITD) of
the Italian National Research Council (CNR), which designed and managed a
1100-hour blended learning course. The course, financed by the Italian Ministry of
Employment, was aimed at 25 young people graduated in technological as well as
humanistic disciplines. The objective of the course was to train experts in online
hi-quality learning processes.

The strength of the reported case lies in the fact that the course, originally
planned according to formal rules and precise constraints (as established by the
financing Ministry), gradually changed into something quite different, as a result of
the face-to-face and online interactions among the people involved. This does not
mean that my research group changed the course structure and organization, even
though the curriculum and the scheduling of in-person and online sessions, which
had been fixed at the design phase, became increasingly flexible as time went on.
Rather, I refer to the course's overall effect upon the relationships between everybody

*L. Dirckinck-Holmfeld, C. Jones and B. Lindström (eds.), Analysing Networked Learning Practices
in Higher Education and Continuing Professional Development, 45–62.*

who contributed to it (including the students), which was both unforeseen and transforming. In practice, the course rapidly turned into something more like a research activity, with outcomes that were as significant for students as for the CNR researchers, who changed their whole approach to it. Similar reactions were noted amongst the teachers of the course (in this chapter, we use the term 'teacher' to refer to academic staff, course subject experts and researchers giving lessons in the classroom or facilitating online sessions), and the course tutors. Finally, as I explain later on, the social dynamics at the CNR were profoundly influenced by the course.

What makes this of such interest is that at the beginning of the course, there were two separate groupings of people, one being a network of researchers, experts, trainers, tutors, technicians and administrative staff, the other being the students. Both groups started working together towards achieving clear didactic goals declared at the beginning of the course. After a while, however, these distinctions all but disappeared, because the level of cooperation both between and within the groups meant that everybody was working to satisfy common learning needs that arose as the course progressed. And, as the barriers separating the groups broke down, the network transformed into a 'Community of Practice' (Wenger, 1998).

Jones (2008), highlights the role of connections in networked learning, as firstly introduced by Goodyear et al. (2004): connections between one learner and other learners, between learners and tutors; between a learning community and its learning resources; connections that are promoted by information and communication technology. I can state that the transformations introduced by the course started as a consequence of the connections depicted by Jones, especially those between people. At the same time, the face-to-face relationships also played a key role in fostering the transformations and influencing the CNR staff.

By quoting Wenger (Wenger, 2005), I could say that the proposed case is exemplary in highlighting the role of connections in "increasing the learning capability of the system and its constituents", where the term system refers to the union of the two originally distinct groups.

Indeed, the interpretation of the course and the modifications produced by it, upon people and processes as a system, was depicted by Fulantelli (2004), within the concepts of the 'Systems Theory'. According to this theory, all biological and social systems can be considered as Open Systems, complexes of interrelated elements, that exchange matter, energy and information with the environment and, because of this exchange, they tend to follow a constant evolution. In recent years the Systems Theory framework has originated the concept of systems thinking (also referred to as systemic approach), defined by Peter Morgan as "a way of thinking that looks at the 'whole' first with its fit and relationship to its environment as a primary concern" (Morgan, 2005, p. 4).

Specific to the case analyzed in this chapter, systems thinking meant to look at the course as a new element within the open system (i.e. the institute of the CNR), and to work on the course (a new sub-system) in the context of all the other activities. In my research group, we were therefore interested in producing inputs for the new sub-system (i.e. all the work necessary to design and run the course) as well as in analyzing the feedback coming from the course, elaborating upon it, and modifying the behaviour of all the other sub-systems consequently.

In this chapter I enrich the interpretation of the blended course described in this study according to the systemic approach, with some reflections inspired by the Community of Practice concept (Wenger, ibid). The application of systems thinking to the course has led, on the one hand, to the elimination of any dualism between community of practices and community of learners and, on the other, to the enforcement of the vision of the CNR as a Learning Organization. Central to this case study is the role of technology in the fulfilment of the research objectives.

The next section describes the theoretical framework of the case study, after which the QFAD blended e-learning course, on which the case study is based, is presented. Finally, the research methodology and some reflections about the course complete the case study. Specifically, we argue that the application of systems thinking to the course has led to conditions for productive learning in a networked learning environment.

THEORETICAL FRAMEWORK

Before introducing the main theoretical perspectives that have informed this case study, it is worth highlighting that the design of the original blended learning course could be reported as an example of networked learning research that did not interrogate explicitly the theory used during the course. This is a typical situation for networked learning research, as noted by de Laat et al. in their paper on the use of 'Theory–Praxis Conversations' to enhance the research evidence base for 'Networked Learning'(de Laat, M. et al., 2006).

However, this does not reflect the lack of a theoretical perspective at the point of design. In actual fact, the course revealed unforeseen issues that produced important theoretical questions during its progress. In order to answer these questions, the structuring of a new theoretical framework has been necessary.

Two bodies of literature were critical for shaping this theoretical framework, as depicted in this section: 'Systems Theory' and 'Learning Organizations'.

This section does not cover all elements of Systems Theory and Learning Organizations; it focuses on the specific items that are essential to provide readers with the author's theoretical perspective to the case study.

Systems Theory, Systems Thinking and Learning Organizations

The general aim of the Systems Theory is to identify answers to complex problems. The theory is based on and integrates concepts from more general theories like the Communication Theory, the Information Theory, Cybernetics, and, above all, the General System Theory (GST). GST is seen as one of the most revolutionary paradigms of science of the 20th century; it was formulated in 1937 by the biologist L. Van Bertalanffy (1962) in order to explain the regulating processes of live beings. Since it was published (only after the end of World War II), the studies on this theory have multiplied in most fields of Science.

According to the Systems Theory, all biological and social systems can be considered as 'open systems'; in GST terminology, systems are complexes of interrelated elements, and they are declared 'open' (as opposed to closed systems) when they exchange matter, energy and information with their environment and, because of this exchange, they tend to follow a constant evolution. Particularly importantly, this evolution comprises a sort of balancing between the internal entropy of the system (a numerical measure directly related to the decrease of the order and to the increase of equivalence between the parts of the system; entropy in thermo-dynamics is defined "the energy dissipated as a consequence of the internal processes of the system and that cannot be used again to produce work"), and the *negative entropy* obtained by incorporating matter, energy and information from the environment.

In closed systems, having no interaction with the environment, there is a prog-ressive tendency to the increase of entropy and, as a consequence, to the rigidity of the system. On the contrary, open systems, by interacting with the environment, tend to achieve a constant state of entropy and consequently increase their internal order, undergoing a progressive differentiation of their parts or elements. However, if the interaction stops (i.e. it does not produce any change in the system), then the system tends to increase internal entropy and, in the case of biological or social systems, it will eventually die.

A key issue arising from the Systems Theory is that not only do open systems interact with the environment, but all the parts of the system have dependencies upon one another (according to a sub-system model), so that changes in one part will have an impact on the whole system. For this reason, every open system should be studied as a whole.

The research work presented in this case study draws on the Systems Theory as a new way of thinking about problems. In this, I reflect on Lazlo's approach, which considers Systems Theory as a new way of thinking about science and scientific paradigms (Lazlo, 1996). Specifically, I am interested in understanding how Systems Theory in general, and systems thinking in particular, can inform educational practice. To do this, I analyse systems theory historically, and consider it as a reaction to Reductionism.

Reductionism has produced educational models that fail to recognize the inter-dependence between groups of individuals, structures and the processes that enable an organization to function. (Schein, 1980; pp. 4–11). In addition, reductionist models tend to ignore the interdisciplinary nature of knowledge, and produce educational paradigms based on the separation between different disciplines. As a consequence, the educational systems grounded in reductionist philosophy suffer, on the one hand, from the problems with the fragmented knowledge, and on the other hand from a model of school separated by daily life (Senge 2000; pp. 27–49).

In recent years, systems thinking has been developed to provide techniques for studying systems in holistic ways to supplement traditional reductionist methods.

In this chapter, I adopt the same vision of systems thinking as Peter Morgan: I consider systems thinking as "a way of thinking that looks at the whole first with its fit and relationship to its environment as a primary concern". (Morgan, 2005; p. 4).

Systems thinking is therefore a perspective, the same that can be found in the original Greek term 'sustema', whose meaning is reunion, conjunction, reassembly. The same perspective can be found in the works of many philosophers beginning in the seventeenth century – Descartes and Leibnitz, amongst others (François, 1999)

Systems Theory and systems thinking have been applied in many fields. The systems framework is also fundamental to 'Organizational Theory', as we can think of organizations as complex dynamic goal-oriented processes. Kurt Lewin was particularly influential in developing the systems perspective within Organizational Theory (Lewin, 1951; Lewin, 1946).

One of the most meaningful examples of systems approach to 'Organizational Learning' can be found in Senge (1990). Senge introduces systems thinking amongst the five disciplines of Organizational Learning. Systems thinking is considered by the author as the discipline that allows people to better understand interdependency and change; consequently, people learn to deal more effectively with forces that shape the consequences of their actions.

The Italian National Research Council, a research institution, has a natural tendency to behave as a learning organization. This influenced my research team when we designed the QFAD blended e-learning course, thus considering the Organizational Learning concept to be central to our course. As researchers, we were therefore interested in understanding how a group of people (the students) collectively enhance their capacities to produce the outcome they really want to produce (Senge, 2006).

Only when we matured the systems thinking approach, did we realize that the Organizational Learning was central to the whole group, including students, researchers, experts, and so on. The rest of the chapter illustrates the result of our chosen approach.

THE QFAD COURSE

As mentioned in the introduction to this chapter, the case study presented is based on a blended e-learning course entitled 'QFAD - Esperti in Processi FAD di qualità' (experts in high quality e-learning processes).

The main objective of the course was to assist young professionals in developing awareness and understanding of the pedagogical and methodological approaches to the design of high quality e-learning courses, as well as in acquiring the technological skills necessary to manage a learning management system and develop online contents. The course was taken by 25 post graduated students, 11 males and 14 females.

Most of the students were from Sicily (4.4 million inhabitants), except for two from Calabria. Even though Sicily and Calabria are separated by the 3 kilometres of the Messina strait, the scarcity of transport infrastructure makes the travel from Calabria to Palermo (the location of the CNR institute) quite long (around 4 to 5 hours by train; 3 to 3 hours 30 minutes by car; no direct flight connections). Most of the students from Sicily had similar mobility problems, so that almost all students had to rent a flat in Palermo in order to attend the face-to-face sessions of the course, moving back to their residential home only during weekends and holidays.

In order to better understand the context of the course, it must be said that, unlike other institutions (e.g. schools, vocational training centres) where the main activity is teaching and/or training, the main activity at the Italian National Research Council is research. The strategic choice of my research group was therefore not to conceive of the course as a one-off event on the fringes of the institute's main activities, but as a process to be integrated with the other research activities.

The Selection

The main objective of the selection was to create a group of students who were highly motivated by the course topics and, at the same time, a group containing as many different educational, cultural and professional backgrounds as possible. This was essential in order to activate, in the group, learning strategies based on experience exchange.

It should be pointed out that e-learning is, in fact, a multidisciplinary subject and can be applied to almost every knowledge field. Experts in e-learning know that the application of a technology rather than a methodology to a specific field requires the fulfilment of needs strictly related to that field. Previous experiences can effectively contribute to the analysis of these needs and to the design of the e-learning solution. Nevertheless, much impetus can be provided through the comparison with experts in the application field.

By looking at the matter from a systemic point of view, I could also say that the selected students tried to overcome the constraints typical of a reductionist approach to education (Senge, 2000).

The selection (amongst 48 candidates) was based on:
- Three questionnaires aimed at testing candidates on informatics, English and general knowledge
- An aptitude test
- A problem solving test (after sharing candidates in small groups)
- An individual interview to assess motivation.

The Course Organization

The course included the following activities:
- Classroom activities: 492 hours
- Online class activities: 138 hours
- Work experience in private and public educational agencies and bodies (called '*stage*'): 450 hours
- Individual meetings with experts in business and enterprise creation: 20 hours.

The duration of all the activities was eight months. An eight-week period of classroom lessons at the beginning of the course was scheduled. Following these, classroom and online lessons were interleaved in a very flexible way.

During the course progress, a national conference (*La Formazione a distanza: Uno strumento a disposizione delle organizzazioni per lo sviluppo delle risorse umane*), an international seminar (*E-learning for SMEs in Europe: 3 case studies*) and a final international conference (*E-learning: New trends and opportunities*) were organized.

In order to illustrate the several disciplinary areas that contribute to the definition and development of e-learning, the course included modules covering the different perspectives on e-learning, as summarized below:
- Psycho-pedagogical aspects of e-learning
- Methodologies and strategies to design e-learning processes
- Technological solutions for e-learning
- Economic issues
- Law and regulations for online courses
- Quality in e-learning processes.

Teachers and Tutors

Teachers (refer to the introduction to this chapter for the usage of the term 'teacher') and tutors were from different public and private institutions and companies, in order to guarantee a real multi-perspective approach to e-learning. I include below the list of institutions and companies whose personnel was involved in the educational process:
- Italian National Research Council – Institute for Educational Technologies
- ASFOR – Associazione Italiana per la Formazione Manageriale, Milan
- University of Pisa, Department of Informatics
- University of Palermo, Department of Mathematics
- University of Palermo, Faculty of Medicine
- University of Palermo, Faculty of Psychology
- Giunti Media Lab, Milan
- Isfol, Istituto per lo Sviluppo della Formazione Professionale dei Lavoratori, Rome
- Istat, Istituto nazionale di statistica, Rome
- Isvor Fiat, the Corporate University of the FIAT Group, Turin
- Open University – Business School, Milton Keynes, UK
- University of Palermo, Policlinico
- Ristrutturazione Organizzazione Industriale srl, Palermo
- Techsystem s.r.l., Palermo.

Some freelance professionals working in the e-learning field at national level were also invited as experts.

It should be noted that all the experts were invited not only according to their relevance to the topic to be illustrated to the class, but also after checking their availability to follow the class, in the role of tutors, throughout the whole educational process (in-class lectures, online sessions, *stage* periods and so on). Actually, the idea was to create connections between students and people from the productive and research worlds; however, this revealed an extraordinary step towards the development of a community of practice.

The Work Experience: the 'Stage'

Similar to the selection of experts and tutors, we invited a mix of public and private institutions and companies involved in e-learning, and let students select the preferred site for their workplace experience. The students' choice was mostly driven by their interest in the specific view of e-learning carried out by each institution or company. In some rare instances, students chose according to the proximity of the institution/company to his/her home town.

We invited each institution/company to present their view of e-learning and the activities to be done by students during the *stage* phase. The following list includes the organizations that were eventually selected for the *stage* activities:
– Italian National Research Council – Institute for Educational Technologies
– Centro per la Formazione Permanente e l'Aggiornamento del Personale del Servizio Sanitario, Caltanissetta
– Didagroup, Roma
– Isvor Fiat, Torino
– University of Palermo, Policlinico
– Proteo, Palermo (Catania site)
– ROI s.r.l., Palermo
– University of Padoa

The preliminary meetings between the CNR staff, the students and people responsible for the training departments at each organization were also extremely important identifying organizations which were the most collaborative to host the students. In fact, the continuity between the educational process and the work experience during the *stage* period could have been compromised by a strongly structured organization where all the activities, included the *stage* ones, were strictly related to the schedule and objectives of that particular organization. To reduce this possibility, we identified collaborative and flexible organizations, and agreed on the activities to be done by students that could meet our educational objectives, the course organization and, above all, the student's interests. While discussing the future activities, we also investigated the organization's attitude to monitoring the course activities beyond the end of the *stage* period. As for the experts and tutors, we were trying to enlarge the community of practice centred on the course.

The Technology

The role of the technology has been extremely important for the course, by contributing to the full achievement of the course objectives.

The main element of the infrastructure was a multimedia classroom connected to the Italian Internet backbone for public research institutions, with 25 computers for the students and one multimedia workstation for teachers and tutors. The multimedia classroom was designed directly by the technicians working at the CNR, according to the course needs, and arranged during the weeks immediately before the beginning of the course.

For the students 25 notebook computers with ADSL connection (or ISDN or GPRS for students living in areas not covered by ADSL) were rented. The necessity for the notebooks arose during the initial weeks of the course, when many of the students complained about the lack of appropriate computer and internet connection at their places of residence. As stated previously, most of them had to rent a flat in Palermo in order to attend the course, and left their personal computers at home. As full internet access was essential in order to participate, the notebooks ensured that every student, including those in the flat, were able to attend every online session.

Indeed, this solution proved to be dramatically important for the whole process, since it allowed students to be connected with a community that was already growing, and during the stage period, to stay connected.

Before signing the agreements with the organizations that were available to host students for the *stage* activities, we checked that each student would get access to a PC connected to the 'net at his/her *stage* site.

Another important element of the infrastructure was the Learning Management System that we adopted for the online sessions. We selected 'Learning Space' by IBM. The reasons for adopting this platform were mainly economic, since we were already using it for an online university course run by our Institute in collaboration with the University of Palermo. Since its activation, Learning Space served the students simultaneously as a repository of learning resources and a virtual meeting place for the enlarged community (students, teachers, and so on). In addition, the use of the platform was extremely important in giving students the necessary confidence to adopt technologies for distance education, becoming active users of e-learning courses, with a positive role to play in designing e-learning courses and processes. I would say that, for this particular course, the selection of a specific LMS platform was not as important as in other e-learning courses. In fact, we did not expect a great performance from the system (e.g., the number of people using the platform was rather small), or functionalities different from the ones that could be found in most of the commercial platforms available at that time. Rather, it was the way the platform was conceived and used that made it an important element of the QFAD course.

Finally, two mailing lists were activated during the course activities. The reasons being that Learning Space soon showed itself to be inappropriate for supporting the communication flow between the students: it transpired that they connected to the Learning Space platform only a few times a week, and preferred using e-mail as their daily communication tool. In addition, some students declared that Learning Space mailing lists began to feel more like using a study tool than a 'simple' communication channel. In addition, mailing lists had to reach even the experts involved in the QFAD course, and they did not like having to access Learning Space just to use the mailing lists. Thus, of the two additional mailing lists, one was made private for the use of students only, the other open – initially at least – for both students and CNR staff. However, we later agreed with students that both the mailing lists would be opened up to other people connected with the course in different roles. These included:

- Teachers
- Tutors
- People responsible for the organizations hosting the students during the *stage* activities
- Speakers invited to the national and international seminars and conferences
- Other students with contacts to the QFAD students during the course (specifically, 24 female students attending a course on e-learning run by a private company in Palermo and 8 PhD students of the University of Palermo, Faculty of Economics, who were interested in financial issues related to distance learning).

Overall, the provision of separate mailing lists proved to be a highly appropriate strategy, giving students the opportunity to communicate with other people and to get to know them. Consequently, we observed a continuous growth of the community.

METHODOLOGY

Given the particular characteristics of the QFAD course, which was originally designed as a higher education course, but almost immediately turned into a research project, it was decided that a 'Participatory Action Research' approach (Dick, 2006; McTaggart, 1991; Wadsworth, 1998) would be a good basis for data collection and analysis of events and experiences in ways that other methods are unable to achieve.

Following Wadsworth (1998), it is very difficult not to conceive research in this sector as a participatory action research. This is reflected in the author's words:

> Participatory action *r*esearch does not conceptualise this as the development of predictive cause-effect theory ('if this, then that'). Instead, as in the slogan: 'the future is made, not predicted', it is more like 'what if we…, then maybe'. *Possibility* theory rather than *predictive* theory. That is, human actors are both wilful and capable of thwarting research prediction, and wilful and capable of selecting and implementing theories or probabilities they want to see manifested! Conventional science sees this as undesirable 'contamination' and 'bias'. Participatory action research sees this as a goal, and the stuff of which 'real life' is made or enacted. (Wadsworth, 1998, The action element section)

The rationale for adopting an Action Research framework as the methodology for our research is also contained in the words of Riel (2007):

> Goals of Action Research include: the improvement of practice through continual learning and progressive problem solving; a deep understanding of practice and the development of a well specified theory of action; an improvement in the community in which your practice is embedded through participatory research. Action research as a method is scientific in that it changes something and observes the effects through a systematic process of examining the evidence. The results of this type of research are practical, relevant, and can inform theory. Action Research is different than other forms of research as there is less concern for universality of the finding and more value placed on the relevance of the findings to the researcher and the local

collaborators. Critical reflection is at the heart of Action Research and when this reflection is based on careful examination of evidence from multiple perspectives, it can provide an effective strategy for improving the organiz- ation's ways of working and the whole organizational climate. It can be the process through which an organization learns. (Riel, 2007, Introduction section).

In the QFAD course, the spiral *stages* that characterise participatory action research were reflected in its organization, as the CNR staff were both involved in the course and also acting directly on it.. In addition, each phase was designed according to reflections made on the results of the previous phase. Finally, each phase was aimed at activating the modifications that were necessary to enable the conditions for productive learning.

In addition, participatory action research reflects the systems thinking approach. In fact, one of the principles of action research is that data collected by researchers can be shared with practitioners (Riel, 2007). This is central to the systems thinking approach to the course, and it is even more important when considering that my research group is part of the whole.

There are also many successful application stories of action research in organiz- ational learning (Dick, 2006, p. 446). Explicit connections between action research approaches and the systems thinking approach can be found in Senge's works (2000), where the influence of Argyris's action science and Forrester's systems dynamics on Senge's theorized five disciplines is evident.

Coming back to the case study presented in this chapter, we at the CNR, posed one important question at the beginning of the course:
– How can we guarantee productive learning in a blended course whose unusual features make it quite different from similar initiatives?

During the course, when the influence of systems thinking began to emerge in the process, and it was becoming clearer and clearer that learning involved the whole group and not only the students, we defined a more precise research question:
– If we apply the systems thinking approach to the organization and management of the course, in what ways will the positive and negative feedback arising from the system help us to promote productive organizational learning?
And finally:
– How should we design the virtual learning environment in order to guarantee productive learning?

The data sources from this study varied during the course. At the beginning, when we started with a very formal approach, the data sources were questionnaires and interviews (some of the interviews were video taped). In one case we were allowed to record the lesson given by an external expert, and the videotape was then used as a source of observations.

After some weeks, when the systemic thinking philosophy started to influence all the participants (especially the researchers), we adopted more informal data sources, such as field observations, oral discussions, together with more formal material such as documents produced by the students.

After the activation of the networked learning environment, during the online sessions and the *stage* period, oral discussions were substituted with written discussions (e-mail, forum, chat) and phone calls.

Finally, after students came back to the CNR for the last part of the course, social occasions and informal talks were the main data sources.

The data sources reported above concern the more traditional side of a course. However, the systemic thinking approach made it necessary to collect data not only concerning the students, but regarding as many people involved in the course as possible. This is also a main principle of action research: in fact, to be successful, the action researchers have to draw an ever widening group of stakeholders into the arena of action (Riel, 2007). External experts, tutors, people responsible for the *stage* periods, as well as other people working at the CNR (researchers, technicians and administrative people) were part of the system, and we needed some kind of information from them too. E-mail and phone calls were the main data sources for people not working at the CNR; briefing sessions and social occasions were the main data sources for my colleagues.

My role in data gathering was greatly simplified by my role in the project. I was involved in most of the activities related to the project's creation: design, planning, reception of the students amongst others. I was responsible for contacting teachers and experts, and agreeing with them on a common study curriculum for the students. I was also involved in the selection of the institutions and companies involved in the *stage* period. Specifically, I had to provide them with training path proposals to suit our students and our research interests, and coordinate with them during the *stage* development.

Therefore, my role was central in establishing the students' educational path, and I was greatly influenced by the students' reactions to the course lectures, by the scientific interests of my institute, as well as by my own research interests.

Thanks to this role, I had the opportunity for direct contact with students almost every day – at the beginning of the day, during some of the lessons and, above all, at the end of each lecture. In this way I received constant feedback from them, which I then fed into all the other elements of the system.

Other than these informal occasions to gather data, we also scheduled meetings with the students every week, which lasted 2 hours on average, in order to formally to their training needs, wishes, hopes and problems.

As a result, data for this study consisted initially of interview transcripts, questionnaires and field notes. Gradually, field notes became more important, together with a log of the meetings I had with the students, where I noted our conversations, the feedback from my colleagues after giving them a report of these conversations, the results of phone conversations and a summary of the e-mail messages exchanged with people external to the CNR.

Data analysis was performed by adopting an hermeneutic point of view, in order to make sense of the whole and the relationships between people, the organization and information technology (Bleciher 1980; Boland, 1991; Lee, 1994; Myers, 2004).

My analysis was triangulated with the interpretations of others, whose feedback, reactions, ideas and responses were woven into the data.

Data analysis and interpretation was an ongoing part of the data gathering practice; according to the participatory action research paradigm it was extremely important to transform the results of reflections highlighted by the data analysis into a new action. The reflections were the result of the system reflection on what had been done and what needed to be done.

DISCUSSION AND IMPLICATIONS

One of the innovative aspects of the QFAD course arises from the fact that it was developed as a learning organization activity. We therefore tried to measure the level of success of the course by using traditional methods (e.g. exam results), but also strategies typical of learning organizations. Following Senge (2006), we asked people how they felt about their 'work'; we asked them if they enjoyed learning together; we observed people in order to see if they were excited about the course; we asked them if they were more effective in solving the real cases that were proposed by the experts but which belonged to everyone. And we saw people passionate in what they were doing. 'People' being the students, the teachers, the experts, the tutors, those responsible for *stage* activities, as well as ourselves, the research team at the Italian National Research Council managing the course.

Online (fully or blended) courses are not innovative by definition; the use of information and communication technologies does not guarantee productive learning. The blended course presented here was originally planned as a traditional higher education course; however, I argue that the systems thinking approach to the course and the natural aptitude of a research institute to become a learning organization, changed it into an exemplary case for the Networked Learning field.

In fact, from the early days of the QFAD course, our research interest brought us to consider the course as a research project on e-learning. Consequently, our first decision was to select a group of students with different university degrees, cultural background and professional experiences, in order to guarantee the multiplicity of interpretations and approaches to e-learning. Actually, this reflects the systemic thinking influence on the interdisciplinary nature of knowledge.

This decision became fundamental for another reason: as Lieberman and Grolnick noted, communities of practice grow as the needs of the members change (1996). Dalgarno and Colgan (2006) report that fundamental change can only occur over time through active engagement with new ideas, understandings and real-life experiences, and through experimentation with new behaviours and ways of doing (Loucks-Horsley et al., 2000). By selecting students with different perspectives on e-learning, we encouraged this change from the beginning of the course. During the first 2-3 weeks, the CNR staff started to share with the students some ideas about the issues that relate to e-learning; sharing ideas is one of the basic mechanisms by which to expand a community of practice (Lave & Wenger, 1991), specially when their participants are attempting to expand the membership through sharing and communicating with colleagues outside the existing community boundaries (Dalgarno and Colgan, 2006). The development of a community of learners during the course, which progressively melted into a community of practice was something absolutely unforeseen, and at the same time it represents the most valuable sign of the success of the initiative, much more valuable than the official evaluation parameters usually required for funded educational initiatives.

Our intention to behave as a learning organization played a key role in this, since we were not only interested in listening to the students needs, but we felt involved in the course as learners ourselves. The systems thinking literature is also consistent with this observation: the system *CNR staff + students* evolved as a whole, as proved by the result of having a single community of practice throughout and at the end of the course.

Role of the Teachers and Tutors

In the QFAD experience, we have tried to involve teachers and tutors in the community of practice. We were not interested in having online tutors that could support us in managing the online sessions; indeed, our interest was in making the teachers feel part of a group of peers. Therefore, it was extremely important to work together with the teachers, even at the emotional level, and lead them to see the QFAD group as the core of an enlarging community. The teachers started to build peer-to-peer relationships with the students, thus blurring the distinction between communities of learners and communities of practice.

In order to facilitate this process, we asked teachers to illustrate real cases of e-learning projects, point out the problems which arose during their design or execution, and involve the students in finding solutions to these problems. To be more precise, each teacher was invited to contribute to the creation of a shared repertoire of e-learning cases and to engage students in their solution. Similarly, students were encouraged to share their own experiences, including those they may have had during previous work with other professionals. In such a way, students and teachers became a community of practice, by sharing a common enterprise (the solution of the real cases), through a mutual engagement and building a shared repertoire of cases and solution (Wenger, 1998).

We met some resistance to this idea, surprisingly, from the students more than from the teachers. Actually, most of the experts declared themselves to be very happy to share their knowledge and experience with the group. In contrast, the students' negative feedback was mainly driven by the unusual approach to the relationship between student-teacher, which is usually more formal than we proposed. After an initial scepticism, however, even the students got the confidence to discuss with experts on a peer-to-peer basis.

Role of Technology

Information and communication technologies (ICT) have been essential to set up the community of practice and connect the students to it, for many reasons.

Firstly, the technology-facilitated communication tools allowed students to overcome the initial scepticism towards the idea of treating the CNR staff and the experts as peers, as reported by many students. A well-known benefit of computer mediated communication (CMC) is the reduction of social distances between the participants within a virtual setting (e.g. chat, forum, mailing list, and so on). Many of the students viewed the mailing lists activated for the course as a valid support to facilitate their informal approach to the experts. Similarly, the experts reacted to the students as peers. However, it is not possible to state to what extent CMC has contributed to the teachers' reaction, since they were asked to consider students as peers even during the face-to-face lectures.

A second fundamental opportunity offered by ICT was to strengthen the previously weak connections between the class and an expert who was leaving Palermo after his/her 3-4 days (on average) of lessons. Through the mailing lists, it was possible to keep the experts involved even after their module ended. This was an important step towards the development of the community of practice. In fact, through the use of the mailing lists, a community of practice which had started with the face-to-face activities, continued to grow during the online sessions.

With the use of the technology-facilitated communication tools during the *stage* period the situation was quite different. For a long time, students were scattered all over Italy for their work experience (sometimes, small groups of students joined the same company or institution). Consequently, the Internet became not only the tool for communicating with each other, but also the virtual meeting place where they could share their experiences. In such a way, students could discuss their work with other students, and also with other experts and with the CNR staff, thus providing new insights for all the participants and, at the same time, receiving important feedback to be used in their work experience.

In addition, the experts had the opportunity to discuss real cases of e-learning projects with other experts (directly or indirectly), thus becoming increasingly involved in the community.

It should be noted that, specifically in this case study, the effect of ICT on productive learning is important but not evident: ICT has strongly supported the social relationships considered essential for effective learning processes. Even though these social relationships started in a traditional setting, during face-to-face activities, it would have been impossible to sustain these relationships without ICT, and to transform them into the basic connections of a community of practice. This reflects the strengths of the infrastructure adopted in QFAD. Following Star's and Ruhleder's suggestion to interpret ICT in use as infrastructures that both shape and are shaped by practice (Star & Ruhleder, 1996), we argue that the QFAD infrastructure has played a central role in the design of productive learning.

In addition, the QFAD case has highlighted the role of the infrastructure as an important element of the whole learning system. The infrastructure has actively contributed to set up and manage the relationships in the network. In a blended course, such as the QFAD course, infrastructures should be as invisible as possible, and act as a transparent support to the communication and learning processes. This requires the use of basic technical tools (e.g. simple mailing list rather than sophisticated communication environments provided by LMSs), and a complex organization that can guarantee the use of the ICT tools, i.e. the establishment of an effective learning infrastructure.

FINAL REMARK

Finally, I wish to conclude by arguing that the main contribution of this case study to the issue of Productive Learning in Networked Learning Environment is the fact that the researchers at my institute have observed the network through the theoretical lens of systems thinking.

Accordingly, we have observed the initial network of students and learning resources, and realized the importance of the relationships with other nodes usually considered external to the network. We have therefore brought these nodes into the network, and conceived the enlarged network as a system.

Consequently, we have changed identity and membership, by considering students, experts, researchers at the same level, and involving everyone in the design of the next phases of the course. We have also changed practice and learning trajectories, and we have enabled experts and students with different backgrounds to collaborate on and solve real cases.

The systems thinking approach has therefore stimulated the changes – amongst all people involved in the QFAD course – which represent the conditions for productive learning (Dirckinck-Holmfeld et al., 2008).

ACKNOWLEDGEMENTS

This chapter is based on a research project funded by the Italian Ministry of Employment. The author would like to thank his colleagues at the Institute for Educational Technologies of the Italian National Research Council for their enthusiasm. Appreciation is also extended to all the people who offered their competences and friendly support to the QFAD team. Finally, a special thank-you to the 25 friends who decided to enrol in the QFAD course, and transformed it into something special.

REFERENCES

Bertalanffy, L. Von (1962). General system theory—A critical review. *General Systems, 7*, 1–20.
Bertalanffy, L. Von (1968). *General system theory: Foundations, development, applications.* New York: George Braziller
Bleicher, J. (1980). *Contemporary hermeneutics: Hermeneutics as method, philosophy and critique.* London and Boston: Routledge & Kegan Paul.
Boland, R. J., Jr. (1991). Information system use as a hermeneutic process. In H.-E. Nissen, H. K. Klein, & R. A. Hirschheim (Eds.), *Information systems research: Contemporary approaches and emergent traditions* (pp. 439–464). Amsterdam: NorthHolland.
Dalgarno, N., & Colgan, L. (2006). Supporting novice elementary mathematics teachers' induction in professional communities and providing innovative forms of pedagogical content knowledge development through information and communication technology. *Teaching and Teacher Education, 23*(7), 1051–1065.
de Laat, M., Lally, V., Simons, R. J., & Wenger, E. (2006). A selective analysis of empirical findings in networked learning research in higher education: Questing for coherence. *Educational Research Review, 1*(2), 99–111.
Dick, B. (2006). Action research literature 2004–2006. *Action Research, 4*(4), 439–458.

Dirckinck-Holmfeld, L., Nielsen, J., Fibiger, B., Danielsen, O., Riis, M., Sorensen, E. K., et al. (2009). Problem and project based networked learning—The MIL case. In L. Dirckinck-Holmfeld, C. Jones, & B. Lindström (Eds.), *Analysing networked learning practices in higher education and continuing professional development*. Rotterdam, The Netherlands: Sense Publishers.

François, C. (1999). Systemics and cybernetics in a historical perspective. *Systems research and Behaviral Science, 16*, 203–219.

Fulantelli, G. (2004). A systemic approach to e-learning as a path towards quality. *Proceedings of the international conference online educa berlin 2004*.

Goodyear, P., Banks, S., Hodgson, V., & McConnell, D. (2004). *Advances in research on networked learning*. Dordrecht, The Netherlands: Kluwer.

Jones, C. (2009). Networked learning and postgraduate professionals: A case study and a comparision. In L. Dirckinck-Holmfeld, C. Jones, & B. Lindström (Eds.), *Analysing networked learning practices in higher education and continuing professional development*. Rotterdam, The Netherlands: Sense Publishers.

Lave, J., & Wenger, E. (1991). *Situated learning: Legitimate peripheral participation*. Cambridge, UK: Cambridge University Publishers.

Laszlo, E. (1996). *The systems view of the world*. New Jersey: Hampton Press.

Lee, A. S. (1994). Electronic mail as a medium for rich communication: An empirical investigation using hermeneutic interpretation. *MIS Quarterly, 18*(2), 143–157.

Lewin, K. (1946). Action research and minority problems. *Journal of Social Issues, 2*(4), 34–46.

Lewin, K. (1951). *Field theory in social science; selected theoretical papers* (D. Cartwright, Ed.). New York: Harper & Row.

Lieberman, A. (1995). Practices that support teacher development. *Phi Delta Kappan, 76*(8), 591–596.

Lieberman, A., & Grolnick, M. (1996). Networks and reform in American education. *Teachers College Record, 98*(1), 7–45.

Loucks-Horsley, S., Stiles, K., & Hewson, P. (2000). *Briefing for the national commission on mathematics and science teaching for the 21st century*. Washington, DC.

Loucks-Horsely, S., Love, N., Stiles, K. E., Mundry, S., & Hewson, P. W. (2003). *Designing professional development for teachers of science and mathematics* (2nd ed.). Thousands Oaks, CA: Sage.

McTaggart, R. (1991). Principles for participatory action research. *Adult Education Quarterly, 41*(3), 168–187.

Morgan, P. (2005). *The idea and practice of systems thinking and their relevance for capacity development*. Retrieved March 12, 2007, from the European Centre for Development Policy Management website Retrieved from http://www.ecdpm.org/Web_ECDPM/Web/Content/Navigation.nsf/index2?Readform &http://www.ecdpm.org/Web_ECDPM/Web/Content/Content.nsf/7732def81dddfa7ac1256c240034 fe65/55508ad7813bc1b7c12570c000496e82?OpenDocument

Myers, M. D. (2004). Hermeneutics in information systems research. In J. Mingers & L. P. Willcocks (Eds.), *Social theory and philosophy for information systems* (pp. 103–128). Chichester, West Sussex, England: John Wiley & Sons.

Riel, M. (2007). *Understanding action research*. Retrieved March 12, 2007, from the Center For Collaborative Action Research website, http://cadres.pepperdine.edu/ccar/define.html

Schein, E. H. (1980). *Organizational psychology* (3rd ed.). New Jersey: Prentice-Hall.

Senge, P. (1990). *The fifth discipline. The art and practice of the learning organization*. New York: Doubleday.

Senge, P. (2000). *Schools that learn: A fifth discipline fieldbook for educators, parents, and everyone who cares about education*. New York: Doubleday Dell Publishing Group.

Senge, P. (2006). *An interview with peter senge*. Retrieved June 24, 2007, from the Society for Organizational Learning website, http://www.solonline.org/organizational_overview/#interview

Star, S. L., & Ruhleder, K. (1996). Steps toward an ecology of infrastructure: Design and access for large information spaces. *Information Systems Research, 7*(1), 111–134

Steiss, A. W. (1967). *Urban systems dynamics*. Toronto, ON: Lexington Books.

Wadsworth, Y. (1998). What is participatory action research? *Action Research International Journal.* Retrieved Sept 23, 2007, from http://www.scu.edu.au/schools/gcm/ar/ari/p-ywadsworth98.html

Wenger, E. (1998). *Communities of practice: Learning, meaning, and identity.* Cambridge, UK: University Press.

Wenger, E. (2005). *Learning for a small planet—a research agenda, version 2.0.* Retrieved January 12, 2007, from http://ewenger.com/research/index.htm

Giovanni Fulantelli
Institute for Educational Technologies,
Italian National Research Council

RACHEL M. PILKINGTON AND KAREN R. GULDBERG

CONDITIONS FOR PRODUCTIVE NETWORKED LEARNING AMONG PROFESSIONALS AND CARERS

The WebAutism Case Study

'The actual quote, "Just having a little chat," occurs at the 138th turn of
conversation in a doctor's waiting room.... the words are spoken as a kind of
excuse to the male doctor.... most remarkable of all is that the "little chat,"
in a few short turns of conversation, has acted as a powerful device for
constructing and sustaining the community....*

Falk & Harrison, p. 610.

INTRODUCTION

The above quotation is not taken from the case study to be discussed here. Nor is it
an observation of electronic discussion, but rather one of face-to-face conversation.
However, it speaks eloquently of the issues that are central to this case study.
Firstly, there is the role of dialogue within the learning process (enabling us to
learn from each other's experience) and in shaping the element of community
(developing our sense of belonging to and being cared for by a community). In
other words, the quote highlights the central way in which cognitive and affective
aspects of learning may be linked through community. Secondly, we get a sense of
the way in which dialogue of this kind is often grossly underestimated. Rather than
building it in as a central component of the learning experience, our schools,
colleges and universities will often marginalise it – banishing it to their corridors
and communal waiting places. Thirdly, by saying the words are 'spoken as a kind
of excuse', the quote also highlights the way in which learners often feel they must
hide this activity from their teachers rather than share it with them, largely because
it is seen not as discourse, and therefore of central importance, but as mere 'chat'.
Tutors may also feel particularly dubious about the value of this 'chat' when it
takes place online, and so fail to appreciate the opportunities for learning that it can
open.

As the above quotation suggests, this case study is primarily concerned with
the factors that affect productive interaction – the kinds of interaction that help

L. Dirckinck-Holmfeld, C. Jones and B. Lindström (eds.), Analysing Networked Learning Practices
in Higher Education and Continuing Professional Development, 63–83.

construct and sustain online learning communities and help make them productive in terms of their formal and informal learning goals.

The case study explores the development of a learning community taking part in a certificated course for professionals and carers who work with children and adults diagnosed with an autistic spectrum disorder (ASD). Students are, primarily, support staff, teachers or parents. They work in a variety of schools, in peoples' homes or for adult services. Some are qualified practitioners and others are unqualified. One of the key admissions criteria for the course is that they have either cared for or worked with people with ASDs for at least two years. They are therefore not new-comers to ASD but start the course already belonging to overlapping formal and informal communities of practice.

In this chapter we discuss processes that are involved in creating a productive online learning community in accordance with the activity system framework proposed by Jones, Dirckinck-Holmfeld and Lindström (this volume and 2006). The issues explored include: the infrastructure, resources and processes required for successful implementation; mediating tools and ways in which the learning space is further customised and used (see Ryberg & Ponti, 2005); the roles of community members and the sharing of goals, activities and tasks; the kinds of learning taking place in part dependent on ethics, trust and social capital (see Rasmussen, 2005). In particular, we discuss the role of interactive processes in building a sense of community, co-constructing knowledge through community and transforming practice.

At the end of the chapter we consider what might be particular to the WebAutism case study and what might be issues for Networked Learning in a more general sense. Research questions addressed through the case study therefore include:
– Do students become a learning community in any meaningful sense?
– Do the infrastructure and affordances of the networked learning environment support student learning?
– Is there evidence of interactions in the networked community resulting in a transformation of existing practice in the boundary communities of family, school and the workplace?
– What are the roles of students and tutors within these processes?

The data collection and analysis methods are mainly qualitative. We looked for evidence of discourse patterns which previous work (Kneser, Pilkington & Treasure-Jones, 2001; Pilkington, 2003) suggested were indicative of deeper engagement. We also looked for emerging themes using interpretive techniques and Nvivo modelling software. We found evidence of community building and patterns of interaction that were related to the nature of the task such that both the nature of the task (what is discussed) and the quality of the discussion suggest a developmental process; one which shifts the learner away from simple reproduction toward the potential to transform practice. We reflect upon the implications for an emerging understanding of productive networked learning.

THEORETICAL PERSPECTIVES

The underpinning theoretical framework for the analysis is based on socio-cultural and activity theory (Engeström, 1987 and more recent developments of the theory by the Helsinki School). We adopt the notion of an activity system (figure 1 shows an example representation) that may be used to describe activities at different levels of granularity, as suggested by Jones, Dirckinck-Holmfeld and Lindström (this volume and 2006). Theoretical perspectives on developing learning communities derive from several socio-cultural perspectives and the study of discourse (Cole & Wertsch, 1996; Lave & Wenger, 1991, Bakhtin, 1981). Some have looked at the concept of a discourse community (Swales, 1990) and the defining characteristics of such communities. Others (Lave & Wenger, 1999) have looked at what might be meant by communities of practice. Common to both is the suggestion that to be a community, a community should show evidence of mutual engagement, joint enterprise toward shared goals and shared repertoires or mechanisms for inter-communication. However, a 'learning community' further suggests a shared commit-ment toward co-construction of knowledge (Garrison & Anderson, 2003; Mercer, 1995). Online learning communities may therefore differ in some key respects from other communities, much as Computer Supported Collaborative Learning environments may differ in key respects from Computer Supported Collaborative Working environments. In particular, what is meant by productive in the two different scenarios may differ (the former may emphasise productivity in terms of evidence of change within participants whilst the latter may emphasise productivity in terms of output or artefacts). Anne Edwards also talks of the transformative power of discourse communities to change institutions/systems, or other boundary communities (Edwards, 1999). Tutors participating in this case study saw it as an objective that learning should have the potential to change practice. Thus, if a community is a learning community we might expect evidence of progress toward ways of communicating and representations of the communication that themselves can help mediate the transformation process (Lave & Wenger, 1991, 1999).

Activity theoretical frameworks have extended Vygotskian theory (Engeström, 1987; Jones, Dirckinck-Holmfeld and Lindström, 2005) to include the concept of a community of interacting individuals within activity systems that also feature differentiated roles or a 'division of labour' and rules concerning who may engage with what tools, in what ways and to what purpose. These ideas have been instant-tiated in figure 1 for the case of the Virtual Learning Environment (see figure 1 'VLE tools', 'rules', 'interaction with others' and 'roles'). An individual's goals within the community may therefore have varying degrees of overlap with the objectives of the activity system (and it is reasonable to ask the question 'whose objectives are they anyway'. In other words, conflict or contradiction concerning the ownership of objectives is a legitimate aspect of the study of an activity system. Moreover, the relationships between students in online networks, their processes of constructing individual identities within this community and within the boundary communities of practice in their field of study, will in part determine the transfor-mative power of the community (see e.g. Stacey et al., 2004).

To the extent that the WebAutism course design team had a broadly socio-constructivist perspective, the course is predicated on some theoretical assumptions, such as that meaningful learning is constructed out of experience and that the sharing of experience through discussion is a stimulus for reflection that can impact on practice (Kolb, 1984; Schön, 1987; Mercer, 1995; Garrison & Anderson, 2003). The diagram in figure 1 illustrates a possible instantiation of the activity system for the case.

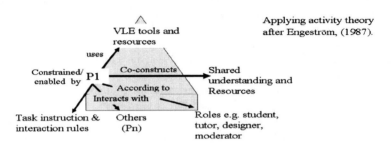

Figure 1. The activity system triangle for our networked learning community

The approach captures the ways in which productive outcomes are dependent on a number of different factors including: the nature of the task (Mason, 1991; Fung, 2004); the rules concerning who may act on what aspects of the task and their access to tools to help them (Benzie, 2000); the ways in which these tools – through their affordances (physical and culturally interpreted) either enable or constrain performance on task (Jones, Dirckinck-Holmfeld & Lindström, 2005) and the affective and social relationships between individuals (Macdonald, 2003; Guldberg & Pilkington, 2006). The representation in figure 1 is limited in a number of respects, for example it does not represent:

– The relationship of the individual to other communities, i.e. cyber communities and face-to-face communities
– The ways in which interaction in other communities/systems affects the joint constructive activity of the represented system
– The ways in which the understanding and ownership of objectives by individuals varies
– The ways in which the community itself is dynamic – not static – in its aims, membership and activity
– The Virtual Learning Environment (VLE) is not just one tool but a number of tools in complex combinations that relate to multiple activities, and have different access privileges/rules of engagement and affordances.

Importantly, participants can change their degree and level of participation over time, alongside changes in their sense of ownership of the community (Lave & Wenger, 1991). Moreover, communities need time to develop and can manage some activities more effectively as they develop (Tuckman, 1965; Salmon, 2000 and 2002; Guldberg & Pilkington, 2006). Thus the notion of 'legitimate peripheral participation' and the shift by individuals from peripheral to central participation over time suggests that communities are not static but dynamic. There may also be multiple overlapping systems and communities to which individuals belong.

For example, Ekeblad (1998) discusses the typical e-mail distribution list and uses three nested activity system triangles to represent how different individuals take responsibility for different aspects of achieving community goals: technically supporting the communication channel itself; managing the academic community; and contributing to the academic content.

ORGANISATION AND INFRATRUCTURE

In this section the aim is to discuss organisational and course design processes for the case study at what Jones, Dirckinck-Holmfeld & Lindström (2006) have called the meso level.

In 2002 the WebAutism course at the heart of this case went 'live', with its first students learning together online. The course is administered as one of a set of programmes within Continued Professional Development (CPD) in the School of Education at Birmingham University and leads to the award of the University Certificate (1 year course) or Certificate of Higher Education (2 year course). The target student group is comprised of non-traditional students – typically mature, many are parents or carers of people with Autistic Spectrum Disorder (ASD) and for many the course will represent re-entry into formal education after many years of no formal study. The course uses web-based technologies so that students who are dispersed over large distances within the UK and abroad no longer need to regularly travel to the university. However, the course team felt it was essential that students should still be able to work in small groups involving reflective discussion-based activity based on their beliefs about how students learn.

The course is offered as a flexible and blended course with online module activities supported by face-to-face workshops, online tutorials and discussions. Each student belongs to a regional tutor group headed by a regional tutor who acts as a facilitator of online discussion.

In this section it is important to distinguish between the activity systems involved in the design and delivery of the programme through the chosen VLE (WebCT), including the customisation/personalisation of the VLE. It is also important to understand how labour is divided between these systems. There are problems in using a simple three-triangle representation similar to that of Ekeblad (1998) for representing the case, i.e. a system for managing the VLE, a system for managing course content and a system for delivering/participating on the course. To represent our case study we need to distinguish:

– Central and local technical support teams who split roles for maintaining WebCT servers, managing access privileges, VLE induction, monitoring student use, customizing the VLE and developing electronic resources
– The regional tutors, lecturers and teaching support staff who have different roles and responsibilities for creating content resources, setting and marking assignments, helping students with course enquiries and facilitating discussion

– Individual students belonging to overlapping communities, including a subset of participants who share membership of some practitioner communities with their tutors.

In the WebAutism case study we can therefore distinguish multiple overlapping activity systems involved in the design of the environment, its ongoing customisation and the management/delivery of activities within it. Since the main focus of this paper will be on the role of dialogue interaction in developing and sustaining the learning community, activity systems at more macro and meso levels can not be considered in detail through the analysis of presented data. However, these systems clearly either serve to support or threaten activity in the micro system, and in some instances, activity in these systems may be considered pre-requisite for a successful outcome at the micro level. In other words, interaction at the micro-level must be "designed in" at the meso level – and activity at the macro level must not overly conflict with or threaten activity at meso and micro levels.

For the WebAutism project there is a core design team which itself is composed of two distinct communities – academics with teaching experience and relevant knowledge of ASD, and the local (within department) e-learning support team with knowledge of the VLE as well as expertise in electronic resource creation. It was felt absolutely essential that these two groups of staff were brought together in a core design team that also included key administrative support staff. However, these groups also communicate in overlapping communities related either to autism or e-learning as an academic subject, or to administrative groups, e.g. CPD.

As part of the project a content management system (CMS) was developed to help manage large volumes of course content and to support authoring by academics.

To create the CMS the team drew on the expertise of the university's Centre for Education Technology and Distance Learning (CETADL), to which the School of Education subscribed as a member department. At an early stage of the project CETADL hosted the course on its servers and provided some technical support to develop bespoke solutions in relation to the CMS, but it wasn't possible to call on this resource indefinitely. At a later stage the university made a central commitment to WebCT as the institutional VLE for the whole campus. Responsibility for hosting WebCT on servers then transferred from CETADL to the central Information Services (IS) e-learning team. This marked a change in the perception of the use of WebCT, from 'innovative' to 'mainstream' (a perception perhaps reflecting an aspiration for the future rather than any large change in the actual numbers of lecturers using WebCT at that time).

Updating to new versions of WebCT was now the responsibility of IS, whilst local e-learning members of the core design team continued to manage technical induction and remained the first point of contact for student enquiries. Technical support was therefore split for a time between three different activity systems on three different sites – CETADL, IS and the local e-learning team. Consequently, the complexity of communication processes increased, and to customise the environment also required more negotiation and some loss of control by the local team.

One of the positive aspects of centralised support was was the availability of a help-desk that students with technical questions could contact during their evenings and weekends. Unfortunately, the support it provided was felt to be inadequate in a number of areas. There is no doubt that students would have preferred the person answering their enquiries to have had knowledge not only of the local area network or WebCT in general but the particular content of their course. Students have difficulty in determining their problems sufficiently enough to put their questions in the right vocabulary. Thus, the inevitable need to forward requests to the right person causes delay. It is equally clear that the only way to address some of these tensions is to develop communication procedures that include guidance to students, tutors and technical staff from different teams to help target support efficiently.

Face-to-face induction sessions, quick start paper guides so you 'don't need to log in to find the log in instructions', and the telephone number for a local departmental helpdesk. These are all aspects of support that have continued to be provided by the local departmental e-learning team, who are able to answer local contextual questions. Moreover, a member of the local team monitors participation and contacts students who appear not to have accessed WebCT in order to complete activities. This helps students get started and can be particularly helpful in identifying a further layer of problems associated with accessing from home via their own network-service provider.

The lessons learned may seem obvious, but complex organizations need to structure their technical support in ways that ensure a very high standard of reliability (i.e. very low unscheduled downtime), but which still make sense in terms of cost (i.e., staff, hardware resources and systems that are easy for students to use). The organisational learning involved is by no means trivial.

AFFORDANCES OF THE VIRTUAL LEARNING ENVIRONMENT

In this and the next section we look at the properties of the VLE that enable or constrain learning activity in our case study. Tensions emerge in relation to the selection of tools. There is debate concerning alternative approaches that institutions should take – should they buy into what many call 'monolithic' systems, like WebCT, or should local design teams gather a number of inexpensive 'low hanging fruit' (Ellaway, 2006). Such technologies can perhaps be selected at a finer level of granularity and integrated to form environments better suited to specific purposes. An analogy might be made between buying a ready meal from the supermarket and buying the separate ingredients for a meal from a number of specialist shops. There is convenience in the ready meal but you can't choose only those ingredients that you want. Shopping in specialist outlets may result in good quality ingredients, but skill and effort are required to make them work effectively together.

So what ingredients are we looking for? The concept of affordances has often been rather narrowly applied to the concrete features of technology, and the potential IT offers has often been argued on the basis of these features alone. This may in part be responsible for the 'hype' that some writers (e.g. Reynolds, Treharne & Tripp, 2003) suggest is the fault of technology enthusiasts. An emphasis on affordances as features suggests that IT has the power to revolutionise learning in a way that ignores issues in the integration of technology with existing practice. This does not do justice to the concept of affordance. As John and Sutherland (2005) point out, Gibson's (1979) original idea was to describe actionable properties from the user's perspective (Rasmussen, 2005).

Thus, technologies are designed with purposes in mind – features that from the perspective of the designer will be effective but often require a change in the cognitive constructs of the user (the teacher or learner) or other aspects of their local environment before they are actionable. It is often difficult for the designer to see the tool from the perspective of the teacher or learner since they do not immerse themselves in the the local context during the design phase. This means the design often embodies an abstract or generalised perception of the user or fails to understand the activities the user wants to perform, their support requirements or the constraints placed on them by the local organisation. This highlights the importance of user-centred design, in which real users are members of a local design team and learning is two-way: designers learn the requirements of administrators, teachers and students whilst administrators, students and teachers learn the practical limitations of designing with particular technologies. However, the division of responsibilities in large organizations can leave tutors feeling remote from such decisions. As one tutor put it:

> 'As a tutor there is little point in my evaluating MOODLE .... my institution will not purchase an alternative VLE for a good number of years and when they do they won't ask my opinion.' (tutor, University of Birmingham).

At the University of Birmingham, since the choice of VLE is taken at the level of the institution, it is this centralisation of the decision making regarding the choice of technology and the availability of training for it that means that one system must take account of the needs of tutors wanting, on the one hand, to assess medical students through banks of MCQs and, on the other hand, WebAutism students discussing the care of children with special needs.

The teaching and learning philosophy behind the WebAutism course is a socio-constructivist one. It has been argued that the philosophy underpinning WebCT is traditional. Evaluation of WebCT seems to reveal the activities expected of the student to be mainly read–review–test. With earlier versions of WebCT, in particular, it was difficult to use the tool for collaborative group activity.

For example, WebCT initially allowed only one discussion board per course, making it difficult to break the cohort down into smaller discussion groups that could still access content material through one common gateway. This didn't enable a good fit between the WebAutism model of one course and the many regional tutor groups. The local design team initially worked hard to overcome this by creating courses that contained only a discussion board and linking these to the master course with its dynamically generated content from the CMS. More recent versions of WebCT have made the management of different groups of students within a single course much easier. It is also now easier for students to upload their original material, and in a greater range of media. For example, a recent addition to WebCTs tool kit includes a blog that enables students to edit their own pages (to a limited degree).

However, customisation remains a cumbersome process for the average tutor, and there is less scope for students to construct and personalise the content – to metaphorically 'rearrange the furniture'. As Winograd and Flores (1986) put it, we are really only conscious of the tool when it gets in the way. However, simply providing a default WebCT course without specialisation would not be productive. Moreover, it is time consuming for the average tutor to customise WebCT to meet their course needs and most will want support from someone with a specialist technical knowledge, both at the design stage and throughout the course for general problem solving.

SPACE-PLACE – CUSTOMISING THE VIRTUAL

We have seen, from the last two sections that it is critical to the design process to bring together in one team those people who are familiar with the physical properties of the tools and those who understand the pedagogic and cultural requirements of the course.

Ryberg & Ponti (2005), in discussing the concepts of space and place, note the need to personalise learning environments to meet the needs of the individuals who will inhabit them. As has been demonstrated in the above discussion, instantiating the 'space' of the VLE to form a 'place' of study is not always easy and in this case study has required a core design team consisting of tutors with specialist knowledge in ASD and local e-learning specialists.

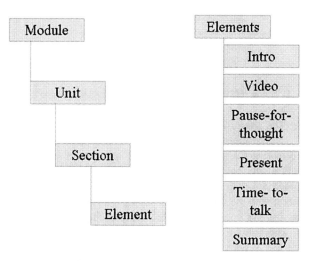

Figure 2. Course template based on Guldberg & Pilkington (2006).

Key decisions concerning the local customisation of the space at the design stage involved determining the structure of the course, the content units and associated resources, linked multimedia activities, problems and tasks and how these were to be integrated with discussion questions. Arguably, one of the most innovative aspects of the WebAutism online course has been the integration of these components. Audio and visual material is integrated with reflective tasks (pause-for-thought) and discussions (time-to-talk). Content authors work to a structural template with which students become familiar. Each multimedia content section follows the same framework of elements, with six sections making up a unit and each section bounded by a time-to-talk (see figure 2).

The integration of content structure with the discussion timetable ensures that there is always a critical mass of students discussing the same topic within a given two-week period. The structure particularly helps first year students pace their study but is also designed to encourage students to participate in discussion and help them overcome isolation. In year two the six-section unit is replaced with four less formal workshops encouraging more personal research and collaboration.

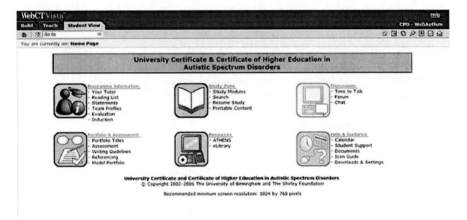

Figure 3. The WebCT space instantiated as WebAutism place

Figure 3 illustrates the WebCT space populated with WebCT tools such as the content pages and asynchronous discussion board. Elements of customisation include use of the e-learning team's own icon set and the labelling of these to represent the elements of the course. Some tools like the calendar and quick start guides are brought together under a 'guidance' section with the question mark icon. The 'time-to-talk' section with the speech bubble icon guides students to asynchronous discussion boards, whilst the book icon guides them to the study zone containing the content sections. The content sections display multimedia material and embed pause-for-thought tasks. When video material is provided on a separate CD ROM there is an indication in the online text. There is also instruction to go to the discussion board when time-to-talk is reached – here an initial posting from the tutor details the discussion topic and task, to which students are invited to reply.

GOALS ACTIVITIES AND TASKS

As indicated at the end of the last section, discussion tasks work across and link the spaces (real and virtual) in which students act. In the case study example, discussion questions serve to link the content space (the study zone) with the discussion space (time-to-talk) through the activity of message board posting that is aimed at sharing experiences and reflecting on practice. The nature of the discussions and how these are managed needs careful consideration (Salmon, 2002; Desanctis & Gallupe, 1987). In addressing the question of how we support the development of networked learning communities we need to consider:

- Equitable and ethical rules concerning how joint activity is managed
- Ways of managing relationships between members of the community to ensure the community remains welcoming to new participants
- A shared language or repertoire (or at least enough common ground to develop one)
- Facilitation roles (increasingly shared with students) that reflect the focus of activity and make adjustment toward common goals (reflexivity)
- Developing student self-regulation in identifying and affirming effective practice whilst challenging less effective practice.

Researchers have found that the nature of the task influences the kinds of collaboration that takes place (Henri 1992). Moreover, Fung (2004) notes that discussion tasks can fail if the discussion question is not focused at the right level. In the case study reported here time-to-talk questions were designed to give students the opportunity to reflect on personal experience and relate this to issues emerging from the pause-for-thought reflective activity embedded in content material. Discussion questions that gave students the opportunity to reflect on practice more generally and less personally tended to encourage more debate. For example, a time-to-talk discussion topic on whether an eclectic approach to intervention was to be preferred over universal adoption of one particular approach to intervention produced lively debate. Chains of interaction occurred in which students replied, challenged, countered or reinitiated (by asking each other new questions in processes which served to elaborate and refine the content being generated). In contrast, pre-set discussion topics that gave students the opportunity to share personal experience often created longer, more monologue-like contributions. Replies were few and brief. For example, a time-to-talk that set students the task of observing a conversation and reporting the non-verbal communication it produced did not stimulate similar chains of interaction indicative of debate, since no one could easily form an alternative point of view concerning a conversation they had not seen themselves. However, many of these contributions suggested a deepening awareness of what it might be like to be a person with an ASD, which suggests that sharing individual experience without debate can still provide powerful learning opportunities.

DEVELOPING COMMUNITY

Garrison and Anderson (2003) argue that meaningful learning is a two-fold process, beginning with the construction of meaning from a personal perspective and then refining understanding collaboratively through sharing experience within a community. However important this is for shaping understanding, social as well as cognitive interaction is also important for effective collaboration since the social climate impacts on motivation, confidence and engagement (McConnell, 1994; Edwards & D'arcy, 2004).

Structure also seems necessary for productive debate. Discussion is likely to be more productive when someone monitors discussion, facilitates interaction and summarises outcomes (Berzsenyi, 1999; Veerman, Andriessen & Kanselaar, 2000; Goodyear, 2001). Research suggests that the tutor needs to create conditions for friendly and constructive debate by establishing ground rules and encouraging students to adopt responsible roles (Pilkington, 2003; Pilkington & Kuminek, 2004). In the remainder of this section we will consider factors affecting the development of community amongst learners and explore the emerging sub themes of identity, empathy and trust, criticality and transformation. A fuller discussion of the data presented here can be found in Guldberg & Pilkington (2006).

IDENTITY

During the induction week of the course (i.e. when students were learning to use the discussion board and before any time-to-talk task) students were asked to introduce themselves to each other. When observing this we saw students negotiating identity by sharing information with each other about where they lived and worked, and in doing so discovering intersecting relationships with other communities to which they each belonged (see table 1 and Guldberg & Pilkington, 2006).

Table 1. Establishing inter-relationships, locations and roles in induction chat.

VD	Hi EI, Yes I work at Squarefield, I don't know any of the staff at Putham House tho. Did you work with any of the ex Gillhamington staff we have at Squarefield? VD
OE	Hi I'm OE and I work at Putham House, I know CM well. I also go to Squarefield every other Friday to go swimming. I know some staff and children at Squarefield. Maybe we could all meet up? Look forward to hearing from you soon. OE

In this discussion a further four participants introduce themselves as parents, including CC, who identifies as both parent and practitioner and who establishes with MO that their children go to the same school. They also discuss meeting and sharing travel to face-to-face meetings. Although two main sub-groups are identified (practitioners and parents) a range of working and caring roles and relationships are also shared across groups.

EMPATHY AND TRUST

Participants seek, through conversation, to establish how much experience is 'safe' to risk being 'shared' (Preece, 2000; Reeves & Forde, 2004; Rasmussen, 2005). By asking questions participants discover shared interests, values and expertise. These discoveries give them confidence to share more personal experiences. In this tutor group the tutor welcomed and reassured everyone after their first post and this is also likely to have helped participants gain confidence. As the participants disclosed their personal experiences, practitioners who were not parents could be seen gaining new understandings of what it was like to be a parent and a person with ASD (see table 2 from time-to-talk 1).

Table 2. Parents share experience around the importance of diagnosis.

CC	.... due to my own son not being diagnosed till 19 years of age he was totally misunderstood by friends, family and school and virtually became an outcast. We have literally been to hell and back.....
RI	CC, I feel so sorry for your situation, it's so unfair. My son is a high functioning autistic and he was diagnosed when he was 4 years old, and therefore got a statement immediately. Along with the diagnosis and the 'autistic label' came the special school with wonderful special needs teachers, speech therapists, specialist doctors etc that he wouldn't have been entitled to without the diagnosis. But more importantly, we had a reason why our lives had turned into such a nightmare......
CC	Hi TO, my son had a boy in his class at juniors who has Asperger's syndrome. My son came home and told me he had worked it out himself through knowing a lot of the traits his brother has! His teacher asked to borrow information from me so she could read up more on the subject. The other students were not aware of his condition but he was known by many as a naughty boy. I know which "label" I would prefer. CC

CRITICALITY

Time-to-talk 1 asked students to debate the importance of early diagnosis. As well as generating powerful personal experience that ultimately would help to build empathy and trust, this topic also generated long reinitiating sequences typical of debate. There was evidence of a degree of contention not occurring in subsequent discussion. After several participants agreed on the importance of early diagnosis an alternative viewpoint was raised. Although it is difficult from the transcripts to be certain of the extent to which this contention is later resolved, it appeared that practitioners who were not parents had some initial doubts about diagnosing very young children because of the possible effects of early 'labelling'. However, as tables 2 and 3 show, parents strongly favoured early diagnosis because of the access to resources and the new understanding it gave them of their child.

Table 3. Contention in time-to-talk 1.

EI	Hi everyone Please, please don't think that this is my point of view but it seems that these are views held by some people still. I have been chatting with my teacher.... She reported that in some areas children who where given a diagnosis of Asperger's were placed into the EBD school and not into the mainstream school system.... The teacher in the area felt the children would have been better off without a diagnosis and left in mainstream school where people accepted them as they were.... Please, no offence to any of the parents on this course, but another view expressed was that some parents would see the label and not the child. I have experienced one parent who only lists what her child can't do because he has Autism rather than what he can do.... EI
RI	Hi EI, you said in your message above, 'perhaps children could be left in mainstream and be accepted for who they are', unfortunately they don't get accepted. If a child was in a wheel chair or even downs syndrome they are more easily accepted and protected by their peers but someone who has no fashion sense, does and says embarrassing things and just doesn't fit in has a terrible time.

Table 4. Tutor summing up of debate in time-to-talk 1.

PD	I enjoyed following your discussion around the issue of diagnosis. It seems that all of you, from either personal or professional perspective, see diagnosis as a positive starting point to developing understanding and awareness both for parents and professionals. The examples you gave about the change of attitudes and perspectives after the diagnosis (from "that child" or "the child with behavioural problems" to the "child who needs understanding and support") are very illustrative and reflect your own experience as parents/professionals. Many of you also drew attention to the importance of early diagnosis and intervention. Some concern was expressed that the amount of support available to the child and parents depends on the 'geographical location'. Some of you raised a very important issue of necessity of training. Very often staff in mainstream schools lack knowledge and experience of meeting needs of children with ASD. I liked the way quite a few of you came back to the points to clarify the issue. It was good to see you responding to each other's comments – this is an important aspect of the Time to Talk discussions. This Summary indicates that the topic is closed and it is time to move on to the next discussion – Time to Talk 2 (based on Sections 3 & 4). Good luck, PD

The strength of feeling from parents appears to lead the group as a whole toward the view that early diagnosis is important. This debate seemed quite pivotal for the development of the group as a community: the taking of alternative viewpoints by identifiable subsets within the community brings issues into the open, and as parents and practitioners move toward a new consensus the group achieves a new social cohesion, which may enable them to collectively challenge wider institutional practice. The tutor summarises at the end of the time-to-talk in table 4.

The role of the tutor was to set the discussion in motion, ensure students knew what was expected of them and were familiar with general guidance for participating in discussion. Provided that students were not obviously needing direction, tutors would not then generally intervene until summarising at the end of the discussion. Summaries provided the main opportunity for tutors to scaffold discussion. As students developed in confidence tutors tended to comment less on individuals' contributions – validating comments were directed more toward the group than the individual, and students were encouraged to engage more with alternative points of view.

TRANSFORMATION AND EMPOWERMENT: EVIDENCE OF CHANGING PRACTICE

As students engage in discussion there is some evidence of them supporting each other in changing the practice of their workplace and therefore, transforming boundary communities. In table 5 NI responds to RI with suggestions to help her effect change in the school that her child attends. This practical exchange is just one of the reasons why students valued the network and wanted to continue to access it at the end of the course.

Table 5. Participants help each other change practice in time-to-talk 17.

RI	The 'home/school' diaries that O mentioned are a lifeline…. This year in secondary school I don't get any messages or information and it's a worry. Perhaps they think that secondary school children should be more independent. I am forever sending in letters and faxes and emails, but he doesn't have just one teacher through the day, so I suppose it's different. RI
NI	Hi all I just want to ask RI, has your secondary school given you a named person to contact to keep up to date with your son or daughter's progress? Some of our secondary schools are better than others at this. One school has appointed a teaching assistant to work specifically with students with ASD's and she speaks to the parents once a week by phone. Maybe this could be something your school could consider? NI
RI	Hi NI Sorry it's taken so long for me to reply….. I found when I was new, emails got overlooked and so did the little blue communications book, so I started sending faxes - this isn't always possible for other parents. I think I will ask the school if your idea of a named person, that people know they can contact at a certain time with problems, would work for them. Thanks for that. RI

As the students continue to develop they begin to generate new questions to explore for themselves (see table 6).

Table 6. Generating new questions to challenge practice – time-to-talk 13.

OE	One thing that has occurred to me when I have been reading and learning from this module and looking at my practice and others is are we really preparing our children for the real world? If they go to work in an office or wherever they are going to work how can we guarantee that there is not going to be a sound in the background they don't like, fluorescent lighting, distracting posters on walls or the structure they have got used to. Having good lighting no distractions etc may work in the classroom but what happens when all that has gone? Will the world as they know it come crashing down leaving them even more lost and confused? .....

These questions are challenging and suggest an increasing maturity in their ability to reflect upon practice that has the potential to be transformative, not only of individuals but in the wider field.

DEVELOPING COMMUNITY REVISITED

This section began with the desire to look in detail at the discourse of one tutorial group. This was to investigate whether patterns of interaction and content themes could generate insights into processes of development as a learning community. The case study is predicated on a philosophy of learning that is highly structured yet designed to support learners in developing ownership of their own collaborative processes, since the tutor offers only light scaffolding of discussions. Opportunities for the tutor to scaffold development occur mainly through summarising, as in table 4. Evidence of a developing sense of ownership came from a desire for continued access to the discussion board once the course had ended. Students set up their own discussions on MSN messenger and have continued to stay in community using this technology.

The discussion task was found to influence the nature of the interaction. Tasks producing the most monologues and the least debate were most likely to ask students to reflect on personal experience. However, these tasks could be powerful in helping them to gain insights into what it is like to be a person with an ASD. Topics producing more debate tended to pose a specific question for which arguments on both sides could be suggested.

Analysis of discussions further confirmed a developing sense of community identity that could be likened to Tuckman's (1965) stages of group development (from Forming through to Norming and Storming to Performing). As students became more confident, through establishment of identity, they felt increasingly safe to share personal experiences. Later, more challenging questions emerged and the group was able to define at least some common values, from which point they could turn their focus to challenging practice in boundary communities. There was some evidence of attempting to help each other bring an organisation's ways of operating more in line with the values of the group. The data presented here are discussed further in Guldberg and Pilkington (2006).

THE CAUSAL COMPLEX, THE PARTICULAR AND THE GENERAL

Revisiting the causal-complex of factors (see Rasmussen, 2005) likely to affect productive engagement in networked learning, we are now finding a number of issues that do seem to affect many collaborative contexts (Pilkington & Bennett, 2000; Pilkington & Walker, 2003; Guldberg & Pilkington, 2006), and which are also emerging from the Networked Learning field in general (Preece, 2000; Salmon, 2000, 2002). Some of these factors are seen in the WebAutism case, and include:
- A design and development team that has both course tutors and e-learning specialists working closely together as one team
- Reliable networks with adequate bandwidth and technical support procedures that ensure students get online and stay online
- Clear early induction in the use of tools and task requirements
- Customisation/personalisation of the default VLE to mirror the structure of the course – through vocabulary, iconography and navigational routes
- Clear linking of discussion tasks with other content resources and tasks within and without the online environments
- Ground rules to help ensure ethical and equitable participation
- Tutors who give students plenty of time-to-talk, as well as supportive and reassuring comments to build trust between students and tutor
- The selection of appropriate discussion tasks and questions to meet the stage of development of the group and the course aims.

In addition to these factors, this particular case study has some more specific properties, such as collaboration as discussion (as opposed to, for example, joint collaborative construction of a resource or joint problem solving). The functionality required of the VLE to meet these goals differs. A further, more specific property of this learning context relates to the value placed on a development of empathy for the person with ASD through the sharing of experience. This changes the kinds of task and the sorts of contribution that are valued; e.g. narrative is valued as much as argument.

Furthermore, there are some properties of the student constituent that are very specific within discussions. These include the authentic focus on reflective practice, the very personal and affective nature of the discussion topics that require particular sensitivity, and the authentic need to communicate through the VLE due to the wide dispersal of students. Students are also unusually mature given the academic level of the course. It is likely that any reduction in authenticity or less mature and motivated learners could affect how easily or quickly constructive discussion emerges.

CONCLUSIONS

On the dimension of affordances (or – from an activity theoretical perspective – the role of technology as a complex of mediating artefacts) we evaluated WebCT and its customisation from space to place. WebCT's underlying design pedagogy is based (largely) on a traditional approach to teaching which posed some contradictions for the course design team. Thus, the customisation process made no use of some of WebCT's features (such as the quiz) whilst making special use of others (such as the discussion board).

On the social and ethical dimensions, analysis suggested that development of a community was a stage-like process, dependent upon the development of relationship and trust: once students had got to know and trust each other they felt it was safer to share experience. Later we felt the community had developed the potential to transform practice in the home or workplace.

As facilitators, tutors in early dialogues used the summary at the end of discussion activities to reassure and affirm students. Later there is more emphasis on synthesis and comparing and contrasting of alternative viewpoints. It is also possible to see this as indicative of a kind of scaffolding toward more critical and transforming forms of dialogue.

However, as far as goal, activity and task dimensions were concerned, we also found that some discussion questions were better than others at either helping students share experiences or in provoking more critical debate. A question that students were ill-prepared for could mean that even in later dialogues there was less insightful discussion. Based on our findings we believe that conditions for productive networked learning include:
– Customising the online space in ways that enable linking of resources to discussions with clearly related foci, structured and scheduled activity
– Developing trust through induction tasks that enable students to identify, establish and build relationships
– Tutor facilitation strategies that initially welcome, affirm and validate participants, so encouraging the sharing of experience
– Later, as students become more confident (i.e. when foci are sufficiently familiar to students to enable them to engage), tasks and tutor feedback help shift the dialogue toward reflective and critical contributions.

ACKNOWLEDGEMENTS

We wish to thank all the students and academic tutors who have given us permission to conduct research on their contributions, and all those who have been involved with the project over several years, including: WebAutism course tutors and administrative staff; the e-learning team at the School of Education and colleagues at CETADL and IS for their technical support; the Shirley Foundation and University of Birmingham for funding this project.

REFERENCES

Bakhtin, M. M. (1981). *The dialogic imagination* (C. Emerson & M. Holquist, Trans.). Austin, TX: University of Texas Press.

Benzie, D. (2000). *A longitudinal study of the development of information technology capability by students in an institute of higher education.* Exeter, Devon: University of Exeter.

Berzsenyi, C. A. (1999). Teaching interlocutor relationships in electronic classrooms. *Computers and Composition, 16*, 229–246.

Cole, M., & Wertsch, J. V. (1996). Beyond the individual—social antimony in discussions of Piaget and Vygotsky. *Human Development, 34*(5), 250–256.

Desanctis, G., & Gallupe, R. B. (1987). A foundation for the study of group support systems. *Management Science, 33*(5), 589–609.

Edwards, A. (1999). Research and practice, is there a dialogue? In H. Penn (Ed.), *Theory, policy and practice in early childhood services.* Buckingham: Open University Press.

Edwards, A., & D' Arcy, C. (2004). Relational agency and disposition in sociocultural accounts of learning to teach. *Educational Review, 56*(2).

Ekeblad, E. (1998). *Contact, community and multilogue—electronic communication in the practice of scholarship.* Paper presented at the Fourth Congress of the International Society for Cultural Research and Activity Theory (ISCRAT 1998), 7–11 June, Denmark.

Engeström, Y. (1987). *Learning by expanding: An activity-theoretical approach to developmental research.* Helsinki, FL: Orienta-Konultit Oy.

Ellaway, R. (2006). Constructive alignment and integrating e-learning into the curriculum. Workshop presented at *SMILE 2006 symposium on medical interactive e-learning*, 13–15th September, Sestri Levante, Italy.

Falk, I., & Harrison, L. (1998). Community learning and social capital: "Just having a little chat." *Journal of Vocational Education and Training, 50*(4), 609–627.

Fung, Y. Y. H. (2004). Collaborative online learning: Interaction patterns and limiting factors. *Open Learning, 19*(2), 135–147.

Garrison, D. R., & Anderson, T. (2003). *E-Learning in the 21st century.* London: RoutledgeFalmer.

Gibson, J. J. (1979). *An ecological approach to visual perception.* Boston: Houghton Mifflin.

Goodyear, P. (2001). *Effective networked learning in higher education: notes and guidelines,* Deliverable 9 (Vol. 3) of the Final Report to JCALT. Lancaster, UK: Networked Learning in Higher Education Project (JCALT).

Guldberg, K., & Pilkington, R. (2006). A community of practice approach to the development of non-traditional learners through networked learning. *Journal of Computer Assisted Learning, 22*(3), 159–172.

Henri, F. (1992). Computer conferencing and content analysis. In A. Kaye (Ed.), *Collaborative learning through computer conferencing: The Najaden papers* (pp. 117–136). Berlin: Springer-Verlag.

Jones, C., Dirckinck-Holmfeld, L., & Lindström, B. (2005). *CSCL the next ten years—a view from europe.* Paper presented at CSCL 2005: Learning 2005: the next ten years, Taipei, Taiwan.

Jones, C., Dirckinck-Holmfeld, L., & Lindström, B. (2006). A relational, indirect, meso-level approach to CSCL design in the next decade. *Computer Supported Collaborative Learning, 1*(1), 35–56.

John, P., & Sutherland, R. (2005). Affordance, opportunity and the pedagogical implications of ICT. *Educational Review, 57*(4), 405–413.

Kneser, C., Pilkington, R., & Treasure-Jones, T. (2001). The tutor's role: An investigation of the power of exchange structure analysis to identify different roles in CMC seminars. *International Journal of Artificial Intelligence in Education, 12*, 63–84.

Kolb, D. A (1984). *Experiential learning.* New Jersey: Practice Hall.

Lave, J., & Wenger, E. (1991). *Situated learning: Legitimate peripheral participation.* Cambridge, UK: Cambridge University Press.

Lave, J., & Wenger, E. (1999). Learning and pedagogy in communities of practice. In J. Leach & B. Moon (Eds.), *Learners and pedagogy*. London: Paul Chapman Publishing.

Macdonald, J. (2003). Assessing online collaborative learning: Process and product. *Computers and Education, 40*, 377–391.

Mason, R. (1991). Evaluation methodologies for computer conferencing applications. In A. R. Kaye (Ed.), *Collaborative learning through computer conferencing*, (pp. 105–117). Berlin: Springer-Verlag.

McConnell, D. (1994). *Implementing computer supported learning*. London: Kogan Page.

Mercer, N. (1995). *The guided construction of knowledge*. Clevedon, Avon and Philadelphia: Multilingual Matters.

Pilkington, R. M., & Bennett, C. L. (2000). Evaluating CHAT seminars within a WebCT networked learning environment. In M. Asensio, J. Foster, V. Hodgson, & M. McConnell (Eds.), *Proceedings of the second international conference on networked learning 2000 Lancaster 17th–19th April* (pp. 28–37). Lancaster University and Sheffield University.

Pilkington, R. M., & Walker, S. A. (2003). Facilitating debate in networked learning: Reflecting on online synchronous discussion in higher education. *Instructional Science, 31*(1–2), 41–63.

Pilkington, R. M. (2003). Reflecting on roles: Using synchronous CMC to develop a knowledge-building community amongst post-graduates. *International journal of continuing engineering education and life-long learning (special issue on technological support for new educational perspectives), 13*(3/4), 318–335.

Pilkington, R. M., & Kuminek, P. A. (2004). Using a role-play activity with synchronous CMC to encourage critical reflection on peer debate. In M. Monteith (Ed.), *ICT for curriculum enhancement* (pp. 83–99). Bristol, Avon: Intellect.

Preece, J. (2000). *Online communities: Designing usability supporting sociability*. Chichester, West Sussex: John Wiley & Sons.

Rasmussen, A. (2005). Case: Productive learning processes and standardisation. In Dirckinck-Holmfeld & B. M. Svendsen (Eds.), *Report on theoretical framework on selected core issues on conditions for productive learning in network learning environments*, Kaleidoscope Deliverable 24.3.1. Denmark: Aalborg University.

Reynolds, D., Treharne, D., & Tripp, H. (2003). ICT the hopes and the reality. *British Journal of Educational Technology, 34*(2), 151–167.

Reeves, J., & Forde, C. (2004). The social dynamics of changing practice. *Cambridge Journal of Education, 34*(1), 85–102.

Ryberg, T., & Ponti, M. (2005). Constructing place: The relationship between place-making and sociability in networked environments. In Dirckinck-Holmfeld & B. M. Svendsen (Eds.), *Report on theoretical framework on selected core issues on conditions for productive learning in network learning environments*, Kaleidoscope Deliverable 24.3.1. Denmark: Aalborg University.

Stacey, E., Smith, P. J., & Barty, K. (2004). Adult learners in the workplace: Online learning and communities of practice. *Distance Education, 25*(1).

Salmon, G. (2000). *E-Moderating*. London: Kogan Page Ltd.

Salmon, G. (2002). *E-tivities: The key to active online learning*. London: Kogan Page.

Schön, D. A. (1987). *Educating the reflective Practitioner*. San Francisco: Jossey-Bass.

Swales, J. M. (1990). *Genre analysis: English in academic and research settings*. Cambridge, UK: Cambridge University Press.

Tuckman, B. W. (1965). Stages of small group development revisited. *Group and Organizational Studies, 2*, 419–427

Veerman, A. L., Andriessen, J. E. B., & Kanselaar, G. (2000). Learning through synchronous electronic discussion. *Computers and Education, 34*(3/4), 269–290.

Vygotsky, L. (1978). *Mind in society*. Cambridge, MA: Harvard University Press.
Wenger, E. (1998). *Communities of practice: Learning, meaning, and identity*. Cambridge, UK: Cambridge University Press.

Rachel M. Pilkington
School of Education,
The University of Birmingham, UK

Karen R. Guldberg
School of Education,
The University of Birmingham, UK

JUDITH ENRIQUEZ

GENRE ANALYSIS OF ONLINE POSTINGS: COMMUNICATIVE CUES DO EXIST ONLINE

GENRES AS ANALYTICAL LENS

The manner in which we have communicated over the past 20 or 30 years has changed significantly with the introduction of communication technologies, particularly that of e-mail. Exchanges online are usually referred to as written speech (e.g. Elmer-Dewitt, 1994), written conversation (e.g. Wildner-Bassett, 2005), electronic discourse (e.g. Davis & Brewer, 1997) or 'netspeak' (e.g. Crystal, 2001; 2004). Electronic discourse reads as if it is being spoken – as if the sender is 'writing talking' (Davis & Brewer, 1997).

To what extent can we 'write talk' online given a keyboard and a screen? In a forum, online texts are commonly organised into discussion threads. Each thread is intended to visually depict a particular topic of conversation. However, as we know in oral conversation, in the process of communication, the conversation flows not because a particular topic is sustained, but because the interlocutors are able to refer to other related topics and able to repair breaks in the exchange.

In a learning situation, Salmon (2000) indicated that good threading facilities in a conferencing system assist in structuring the knowledge construction of students' messages. Kear (2001) hypothesised that a visual representation of threading would help students to engage in more clearly structured discussions. This chapter argues that structuring tasks and threads online is important, but that we have to understand these in relation to existing and emerging communicative practices, in disembedded fashion. As the following pages will evoke, there are online cues that assist in structuring tasks and threads online.

Language is rarely taken seriously. The focus has always been on the communication medium or tool, but never communication. This chapter presents an occasion to consider language alongside a communication tool through genres (cf Erickson, 2000; Orlikowski & Yates, 1994; 2002). Genres are patternings of communication shared by members of a community. They have identifiable form and purpose. These provide interlocutors with cues for electronic discourse.

We need to understand the convergence of speech and writing online. To do this we need to be clear about the nature of each and differentiate between them. In short, we have, inevitably, to turn our attention to and draw upon linguistics[1].

In this chapter I turn to David Crystal, who is a well known Irish linguist, and I refer the reader to a table summary he provided on the main differences between speech and writing derived from the various editions of *The Cambridge*

L. Dirckinck-Holmfeld, C. Jones and B. Lindström (eds.), Analysing Networked Learning Practices in Higher Education and Continuing Professional Development, 85–102.

Encyclopaedia of the English Language, of which he was the editor (see Crystal, 2001, pp. 26–28). More recently, he produced a glossary of 'netspeak' and 'textspeak' (i.e. Crystal, 2004). Let it also be noted that it has been long known and established that there is no absolute difference between spoken and written language (see, Crystal & Davy, 1969; Baron, 2004). However, it still proves illuminating and a useful heuristic to be clear of the features that typically separate them when we find ourselves either talking or writing, or more often talking in writing over the Internet. In a snapshot, according to Crystal (2001), "speech is typically time-bound, spontaneously face-to-face, socially interactive, loosely structured, immediately revisable, and prosodically rich" (p. 25), while "writing is typically space-bound, contrived, visually de-contextualized, factually communicative, elaborately structured, repeatedly revisable, and graphically rich" (p. 28).

How does online talk match up to these characteristics? On the whole, an online posting is better seen as written language which has been pulled in some way in the direction of speech, rather than as spoken language that has been written down. In electronic exchanges, a discussion or a chat ultimately come to an end, but the text remains. This pushes the linguistic exchange towards the direction of writing as encountered in articles or books and other 'permanent' literature (Crystal, 2001). However, we do recognise that electronic text does not solely rely on the characteristics of writing. It belongs to both.

In this light, this chapter intends to elucidate on how online forum participants adopted and adapted conventions of oral and written strategies and structures for their individual communicative needs. Communication in these forums is seen as an organising process and not as a mere carrier of information or content. It structures what gets said and done and by whom. Furthermore, the structures that emerge and are maintained become themselves additional resources, strategies and communicative cues for further organisation in communicative actions or practices (cf Crystal, 2001; Davis & Brewer, 1997; Orlikowski & Yates, 1994).

Genres are used as the analytical lens of this chapter to further understand the complex layering of online text. It intends to show two things: first that there is a frame or structure that is at work in online environments, which is worth exploring in terms of genres, instead of the imposition of structures that do not fit the emerging communicative practices of those involved. The structures of netspeak are identified using genre analysis in the complex relationship, first, between the medium and the communicative practice of speech and writing, and secondly, between the medium and the activity that involves netspeak. Secondly, the exploration of the linguistic effects of the electronic medium on the communicative practices adapted in an online task provide further insights into how discussion boards may be effectively used for productive networked learning.

The idea of using genres to study communication is not new. It has a rich tradition within the field of literary analysis (cf Bakhtin, 1986), and is emerging as a useful way to explain social action in cultural studies (cf Brown & Duguid, 1991). More than a decade ago it was applied to the notion of organisational communications and specifically to online communications (e.g. Orlikowski &

Yates, 1994; Orlikowski, et al., 1995; Yates, Orlikowski, & Okamura, 1999) and, most recently, in terms of weblogs (e.g. Herring, Scheidt, Bonus, & Wright, 2005).

In this chapter, there are three different aspects of electronic discourse or netspeak that are brought to our attention: 1) what do genres tell us about the communicative practices of students; 2) where do the genres used by the students come from, and 3) what are the factors that facilitate the use of particular genres found in the forums.

In the following sections, the communicative practices of participants in three task based forums address these three aspects and provide similar evidence found in prior studies: 1) that participants employ genres that accomplish the task at hand, and the absence of certain genres provides information about their perception of the context of their interaction (e.g. Orlikowski & Yates, 1994); 2) that the genres used are initially and implicitly imported from the communicative practices used in other contexts (e.g. Orlikowski & Yates, 1994); and 3) that there are key participants who are able to explicitly shape or change the genres initially used (e.g. Yates et al., 1999).

In my discussion, I refrain from referring to postings as 'discussions' or 'messages', nor is there a strong emphasis on the level of participation in terms of the number of postings recorded by the virtual learning environment (i.e. Blackboard) for each participant. Consequently, postings are not assumed to be conversational, nor are their purposes those of discussion. Instead the emphasis is on the emergent nature of structure through the repetitions and regularities of *purpose* and *form* in terms of genres used in the forums.

GENRE: PURPOSE AND FORM

According to Orlikowski and Yates (1994; 2002), a genre is identified by its socially recognised purpose and common characteristics of form. Or in the words of Erickson (2000),

> A genre is a patterning of communication created by a combination of the individual, social and technical forces implicit in a recurring communicative situation. A genre structures communication by creating shared expectations about the form and content of the interaction, thus easing the burden of production and interpretation (p. 2).

First of all, a genre is not individual and private. It is socially constructed and shared (e.g. a discussion about assessment). Its form refers to its medium (e.g. discussion board), its structural features (e.g. letter format) and its linguistic features (e.g. level of formality, or graphic devices). The heart of the matter is that a genre has a recognisable form, but the form is what best enables a purpose. So in focusing on its form, the question is 'what purpose is being fulfilled?' This purpose may be multiple.

In different situations, participants draw from existing genre norms to accomplish a communicative action. The example provided by Yates and Orlikowski (2002) is that of choosing a letter template rather than an informal note genre for composing an e-mail message that is addressed to an unfamiliar international correspondent. In short, genres provide a template for interaction between members of a community. The particular genre template of a community is an important resource in facilitating efficient communication. In an online environment, individuals may draw on different genre norms out of habit and base genre norms on previous experiences to facilitate a communicative act.

Secondly, genres are context dependent. They shape, but do not determine the relational cues influenced by the technological environment, task design, previous genres used and the social relationships of those involved. People participate in genre usage rather than control it. One genre exists alongside others and is influenced by them. Even though genres are dynamic entities that adapt to a change of circumstances, they develop regularities of form and substance. These regularities become established conventions and begin to influence all aspects of communication. In short, there are genres that serve as foundation blocks, but there are those that are specific to practice situations. If certain genres are the foundation of the genre templates for communicative interaction in an online environment, then it is rather important that these are supported at the very start of a course or activity. If other genres are important in a certain context of use only, then it is relevant for the tutor to know which contexts these might be. It is also relevant to know that genres are interdependent, that is, coordinated and combined to accomplish a specific purpose or communicative act (e.g. Mulholland, 1999; Orlikowski & Yates, 1994).

The students in this study had not used the virtual learning environment, Blackboard, before. So how did each of them decide which genre to use online? Organisational studies suggest that people fall back on what they already know, that is, their existing genre repertoire, when they are faced with something new (Orlikowski & Yates, 1994). In an educational institution, the genres would include lectures, course programmes, assignments (essays), exams, etc. Thus, in this case, the students would be likely to fall back on education-related genres and communicative practices based on the use of electronic media (e.g. email, chat, text messaging) that have been a common part of their daily lives.

NETWORKED COURSE AND ITS PARTICIPANTS

In the academic year 2004–2005 there were 21 teacher trainees (18 females, 3 males, coded as H1–H21) with an average age of 24, in a postgraduate certificate programme for the secondary school teaching of History.

Course Content

The aim of the course was to prepare trainees to teach History in secondary schools. The teaching on the course focused on the how's and why's of teaching History (e.g. classroom management, lesson planning, assessment).

The trainees were expected to develop their knowledge of the subject itself and how it could be effectively taught in schools. Continuous assessment was practised throughout the course. There was no examination as such. To pass the course, each student must follow the course satisfactorily by attendance, participation, and completion of set work; by meeting the set passing mark/standard in written assignments and in practical teaching, and by demonstrating that the requirements of Qualified Teacher Status were met.

Structure of the Course

The course ran for 36 weeks from September 2004 to June 2005, and was substantially school based, with 24 out of the 36 weeks being spent in schools. The course had two 'distance' phases (A and B). For each of the phases the trainees worked in school placements for 10–11 weeks. They returned to the university campus for the final week of the course.

The Online Forums in Blackboard

According to the course tutor, the structure of the course was a key influence on the introduction and use of forums in Blackboard. The postings were shaped and triggered by the course structure, the thread structure of Blackboard and the tasks in the forums.

There were a total of 13 forums in this course. Three of these are described as primary source of data for the genre analysis of this study. The three forums were History, Schools and Society (HSS), Assessment (AS) and Teaching Bilingual Pupils (TBP) with a total of 56, 66 and 52 postings, respectively.

HSS Forum. HSS was one of the forums introduced within an induction workshop on how to use Blackboard during the first week of the course. It had two main threads. The first thread explicitly structured the required content and the way in which the forum may proceed and develop. The requirements of the task were identified as follows:
– Summary of views
– References (citing sources that helped views)
– Argument why History should be part of the core curriculum
– Review of initial statements (or earlier postings) on the board
– Comments on the postings of others (if in agreement).
These clearly defined what may constitute a posting in relation to the task at hand. It is also important to note that this (task) thread made it quite explicit that:
– Posting of views, though permanently recorded, does not mean they may not change
– Students may revisit and review their postings
– Students may comment on points of view on which they agree.
These set the ground rules of engagement within the forum. These are very pertinent to the general content and form of the postings that emerged in this forum and those created afterwards, as is elaborated later.

AS Forum. The AS forum was also task based, with a series of questions relating to assessment matters. The first three threads initiated by the tutor were articles to be read. These were intended to assist the students in planning their teaching and assessment of pupils when went to their schools in three weeks time. A link between the articles on assessment and the students' assessment of their placement school pupils had been subtly established here. The students were asked to answer questions and react to the articles in the light of what they themselves were about to embark upon.

Furthermore, aside from the rules of engagement made explicit in the HSS forum above, another board rule was introduced in this forum. The tutor made it clear that all forums created would be accessible throughout the year (i.e. course duration).

TBP Forum. In the TBP forum, the students were divided into four groups (A, B, C and D). Each group had to choose two articles to read, from which they had to summarise the important points relating to their teaching of History. From a task in HSS to an article in AS, by the time this forum was created a thread had become something else – a group.

Unlike the first two forums already described, the students were, in this forum, grouped by the tutor to perform a collaborative task of choosing and reading two articles from the NALDIC website (i.e. http://www.naldic.org.uk/docs/resources/). As with the AS forum, they had questions to answer in relation to the articles read. This time the forum was not just a task, but a task allocated to specific members of a group and the students were not expected to engage with everyone in the forum.

Consequently, exchanges were limited within each group. The task did not allow explicit messages outside the defined membership within a given group. No new threads were created, that is, no other group was created aside from those set up by the tutor.

METHODOLOGY

The primary data for this particular analysis consisted of a subset of the 498 messages posted in 13 forums. Three of these forums were chosen for this genre analysis. The choice was based on the total number of messages posted in each at the end of the course. The average number of postings was 58 (a total of 174 messages). This average number gave the analysis sufficient amount of data for the form and purpose of the genres in each forum to emerge, and for regularities to be identified.

The messages were analysed qualitatively at two levels: first, by looking at the general structuring of the each message, based on the two identifiable dimensions of genre (i.e. purpose and form) discussed above; and secondly, by reading within the structure of the message and following referential links to other places and situations outside the online forum. The second level of analysis was enacted through the relationships within and between the structuring of threads in Blackboard: 1) of the task posted by the tutor in each of the forums; 2) of the course as briefly described above; and 3) of the communicative practices of the participants based on their other institutional engagements, as well as their personal habits and idiosyncrasies.

Each of the forums were analysed to identify recognisable purpose and common features of form. The coding of the *metastructuring* of the online transcripts was assisted with some of the categories that Firth (2002) used in his study. Table 1 presents the general purpose and form of postings that were found in the forums, and whose analysis is discussed in the following sections of this chapter.

Table 1. Genre Coding Category (Adapted from Firth, 2002)

Coding Category	Definition of Coding Category
PURPOSE	
Individual Comment (IC)	Personal comment to an individual
Individual Response (IR)	Personal response to an individual
Individual Solicitation (IS)	Personal question/suggestion to an individual
Group Comment (GC)	Personal comment to a group
Group Response (GR)	Personal response to a group
Group Solicitation (GS)	Personal question/suggestion to a group
FORM	
Greeting to all/group	Presence of a salutation or greeting phrase
Personal Greeting	Presence of greeting to an individual/s
Closing	Presence of valediction and/or name
Iconics	Presence of text items representing graphics
NO Valediction or Salutation	Absence of a greeting or closing remarks

Form is always defined by the purpose(s) being staged by the writer, depending on what he/she ultimately wants to leave behind in the forum for others to read. Furthermore, we find that the form categories relate to social factors, and therefore a form category is in some ways a purpose in itself. Therefore, purpose is not solely found in the content of the postings, but also in the orderings (e.g. genre categories) that are outside the medium.

Most of the codes in Table 1 are easily identified in the forums. For example, the codes under the heading of Form were quite obvious in a lot of ways. However, the Purpose codes were not as straightforward and as clear. The codes were not solely defined and identified within the content of a posting. For example, the thread structure of the forums facilitated the identification of who is responding to whom without having the name of the recipient explicitly mentioned:

Author: [H3]

Date: 12-07-2004 17:20

Subject: Re: The importance of Grades

Hi everyone

What both you and [H5] have said really makes sense and i thought I'd add my tuppence worth! (bold added – ed.)

In H3's posting above, it was the thread structure that made it quite obvious that 'you' was H21, as it was threaded to H21's posting. The same is true for H1's posting below. 'You' refers to H5 who mentioned the DfES (Department for Education and Skills) document and to which H1's posting was threaded.

Author: [H1]

Date: Sun Feb 06 2005 13:25

Subject: Re: Access and Engagement in History

Hi Guys

Sterling effort so far!

I will take a look at the DfES document **you** have mentioned; as it seems, from what you have said, to raise some useful points.

… (bold added – **ed.**)

In short, the thread structure assisted in coding, and the reply button facilitated individual response.

On the other hand, the thread structure made a group response less obvious. For example, there are just three explicit group responses in the forums. In general, we may say that any posting is a group response as it has had the potential of being read by all or the majority who had accessed to the forums. However, this is not always the case, as there were postings that were obviously meant for a specific individual in the group or to both, as in H1's posting above.

Group response is a rather elusive and inaccurate code because of the implicit structuring that Blackboard permits and assumes, in terms of access, and which is nevertheless not quite clearly defined within its thread structure. That is, threads establish links between *individual* postings alone.

The reader has to bear in mind this less clear cut aspect of coding and how the thread structuring of the forums acted on how the postings were structured within threads and how the coding process was influenced by the threads. Furthermore, although tables of numbers are produced in the following pages, the focus and emphasis is not the quantity (i.e. how many) of post segments falling into each code. Instead, they elucidate and describe the structuring of online communication as they emerged in three Blackboard forums as initiated by a particular task.

For each forum, the regularities and repetitions identified in postings revealed the genre structuring adapted by the participants in their online talk. The cues found in subject heading changes and timing of postings are described in the following sections.

STRUCTURING ONLINE TALK

In all three forums, the task threads were the focus and purpose of the students' postings. The main threads in the forums were not messages. They were tasks to be done. The students maintained an essay format in their task responses. The form of the forums was shaped by the repetitive use of rhetorical questions, changes in subject headings and the presence of acknowledgments through individual and group comments/responses and solicitations. There were students who were able to follow the rules of engagement and shift away from simply performing the task.

The summary of the purpose and form of the forums is shown in Table 2.

Table 2. Genre structuring in the forums

	HSS	AS	TBP				
			GrpA	GrpB	GrpC	GrpD	Total
PURPOSE							
Individual Comment	14	15	7	0	7	3	17
Individual Response	6	15	3	1	10	2	16
Individual Solicitation	2	3	1	0	2	0	3
Group Comment	6	6	2	0	4	0	6
Group Response	0	2	0	0	0	0	0
Group Solicitation	19	9	10	2	5	12	29
FORM							
Greeting to all/group	1	1	6	0	1	11	18
Personal Greeting	0	0	0	1	3	0	4
Signature (Name)	5	10	6	3	7	11	27
Valediction/Closing	3	2	1	0	2	2	5
Presence of graphic element (e.g. 'x', ':0')	1	3	0	0	2	5	7
No salutation/ valediction	53/51	61/60	8/13	8/9	7/9	4/11	z27/52

In general, the students kept within the content cues of the tasks that were posted. The content of the postings was defined within the requirements of the task as outlined above. For example, in the HSS forum a summary of views was provided. Questions found in the postings were mostly rhetorical, not intended to solicit a response, but rather to make a point. There were a total of 19 rhetorical questions found in this forum, and 12 news article references as required. Individual comments and responses were found to acknowledge and show agreement to the postings of others.

However, as with every rule, there is, or, in this case, are exceptions. There were three students (e.g. H11, H1 and H3), who did more than just respond to the task. For example, the last message from H1 read very differently. That is to say, it conversed. It may not have begun with a greeting, but it definitely had a valediction and it was also the first one to have one. It read as follows:

> Without wishing to sound (too much) like a proponent of the 'New Right', I did read an, admittedly slightly 'alarmist' article by Chris Hasting and Julie Henry in the Sunday Telegraph (30/05/04). ...

> No? Well, ok, but a valid point arises from this. While none of us, I'm sure, would wish to go back to the dry delivery of dates and battles, ...

> Regards,

> [H1]

Most of the postings did not have any salutation or valediction. This is, firstly, because their structure was mostly based on the genre of essay writing, and secondly, one could argue that of the few that did 'converse', they were written as if they were being spoken out loud; when conversing face-to-face we do not begin by saying "Dear ..." or "Hi ...", nor do we finish by saying the words "Regards, ..." or "Yours sincerely, ...".

The form of the forum reveals a genre that is not orientated towards letter writing. Yet, in adapting essay writing structure, the participants excluded personal greetings while including (in some instances, at least) individual and group comments and solicitations (although group response to these was quite difficult to detect, as already pointed out). This demonstrates how genres are combined to accomplish a particular task. Examples of this may be found in three sections of a typical posting: at the beginning, as acknowledgments before the writer provides his or her answer; in the middle, as references within the body of the 'essay'; or at the end, as closing remarks.

In the AS forum, as in the HSS forum, the students kept within the content cues of each assigned article. The content of the postings was about the articles they had read. There were 31 rhetorical questions in total. And, there were still some news article references. in this forum, albeit just three.

School placements became an additional trigger for student postings, with 11 references. Perhaps this was a referential link to what they were about to do, or were doing, within the time frame of this forum (i.e. three weeks before they went for school placement).

In the TBP forum, where threads were groups, the postings became more message-like. They did not appear to be written in the genre structuring of an essay. Instead, they were more like informal notes or letters with salutations and valedictions. This forum had the most instances of group solicitations, and more instances where students placed their name at the end of their postings.

Additional communicative strategies were produced in a group task online. The postings were generally negotiated and kept 'open' for dialogue with postings that included 'what a member has done', 'what he/she thinks', 'what she/he would proceed to do for the group'. In short, in this structuring the posting was never finished, rather, it was always left 'to be continued'. This somehow stretched the temporal flow of the exchanges. For example, the structuring that was maintained by three members of Group A, albeit very briefly, was that of group solicitation and response in terms of 'what I have done', followed by 'what I think', including individual comments on preceding postings, then 'what I will do' and/or 'what do you think', which kept the exchanges flowing. These elements emerged as communicative strategies, adapted to the written word by those involved, in order to complete a collaborative task online: in this case, selecting two articles to read.

CHANGING SUBJECT HEADING

Regularities and repetitions of greetings, comments, responses and solicitations in the postings content are further demonstrated in online forums by changing the subject heading. The subject heading had been used in various ways in the forums, mainly, as a headline that provided the reader with brief information of what the posting is about. It also signalled interruptions, such as a break, a closure or a topic change - a way of picking out a more specific topic derived from earlier postings.

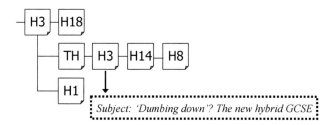

Figure 1. 'Dumbing down'

In total, there were 30 subject heading changes (8 in the HSS forum, 8 in the AS forum and 14 in the TBP forum). Two of them are described in this section. The manner in which such a change was prompted or initiated in the threads is quite interesting. For an illustration of how a subject was changed, sections of postings within the above mentioned thread (Figure 1) are described:

H3 posting (the first one in Figure 1) put forward a rhetorical question reacting to an article she had read in the Guardian:

Dare one say that if the history GCSE took such a vocational course it would be **'dumbed down'**, prioritising cross-curricular and employable skills over historical content and methodology? (bold added – **ed.**)

H18's posting made the following comment in response:

I don't think history would be '**dumbed down**' by looking at it this way (bold added – **ed.**).

TH also picked up 'dumbed down' with an individual comment to H3:

I don't know about anyone else but [H3]'s posting make me want to jump back into the classroom and get on with history for history's sake!. The debate over the new 'Hybrid' GCSE in history - with a vocational element will rage on. Its creator... is not willing to sacrifice historical standards for a **dumbing down** ... (bold added – **ed.**)

TH finished her posting with the question "Does it pose a threat of dumbing down?" The next posting by H3 changed the subject heading to 'Dumbing down'? The new hybrid GCSE' (see Figure 1).

In the TBP forum, it is interesting to note that the groups (i.e. A & D) with the most salutations and group solicitations, and which used the communicative strategies of 'what I did' and 'what I will do', had the most number of subject heading changes. In this forum the focus of the exchange is not on the task or what was said in the content, but on threads that were enacted either as groups or individual members and what they said facilitated a different structuring of the written conversation. The changing of subject heading became a turn-taking strategy and a posting became a turn in a manner that resembles face-to-face conversations; that is, a turn may or may not elaborate or pursue a topic at hand.

The subject heading was used to prompt group members about the particular topic or question. In general, the subject heading was changed to the title of the article that had been read as part of the group task. Furthermore, in the second example, the subject heading becomes a trigger for starting a posting:

Author: [H11]

Subject: More advanced learners of EAL at Key Stage 4 and post 16

I am aware that **this** is a different article from that which we agreed to read, however, this article grabbed me as I was interested in approaches to EAL at post-16 as I had four pupils at AS level with EAL at my last placement (bold added – **ed.**).

Author: [H9]

Subject: finding a common language

I found **this** one a bit more difficult to get my head around. (bold added – **ed.**)

The demonstrative 'this' was used as a deictic word to refer to the article which was the subject heading.

The subject heading was mostly used to change the current topic. The only link between postings was a temporal sequence which was established by clicking the reply button, at which point the relationship between topics was broken.

The act of changing subject headings had multiple relational effects in the forums. Firstly, they interrupt – virtually closing down or dismissing the topic initiated in a thread. Secondly, they emulated turn-taking. It was an attempt on the part of the receiver to acknowledge the most recent interlocutor before 'taking the floor' to write talk.

TEMPORAL STRUCTURING

Consecutive postings in the forums facilitated conversational exchanges in the threads of the postings. Apart from the fact that these kinds of postings were generally shorter in word length, they were more likely to have individual and/or group comments and responses.

However, this was not always the case. It also depended on the nature of the task in the forum. For example, in the AS forum, consecutive postings did not produce conversational structuring. Instead, when a participant's posting was followed by another one or two, each one was a direct response to a different article thread (see Table 3).

Table 3. Consecutive Postings in Assessment Forum

Date/Time	Student	Thread
13/10/2004 13:10	H11	Butler's article
13/10/2004 13:31	H11	Cottingham's article
13/10/2004 16:41	H17	Cottingham's article
13/10/2004 16:55	H17	SPAG
13/10/2004 17:41	H20	Cottingham's article
13/10/2004 17:48	H20	SPAG
13/10/2004 21:58	H9	Butler's article
13/10/2004 22:14	H9	Cottingham's article
13/10/2004 22:27	H9	Harrison's article
13/10/2004 22:32	H9	SPAG

Table 3 further demonstrates how the students were accessing the forum with a clear purpose of responding to the task.

COMMUNICATIVE CUES ONLINE

This chapter has produced sufficient evidence to argue that online cues can that structure online exchanges. In the online forums, participants were not able to read body language or facial expressions. They were not able to modulate their tone of voice as they would normally do in a face-to-face conversation. However, they were able to modify some features of their writing.

In this chapter, the form and purpose of individual postings were not solely analysed in themselves, but in relation to the medium being used, the task requirement, the particular thread and the posting responses it elicited from the others. The object being to understand how the netspeak flows and gets interrupted when there is no turn-taking. There are no interruptions, overlaps or granting of the floor in the forums. Each participant was writing a monologue (Davis & Brewer, 1997). It only became a dialogue after it had been time stamped in the order it was received by Blackboard, not in the order in which it was uttered in writing or threaded to another posting.

In each forum, there was a particular relational frame and certain online cues that the participants had to work with – the tutor's instructions, the articles related to the task, changes in subject heading, rhetorical questions, references, resources, questions, expectations, time of day, their location and preoccupation, thread structure, comments or replies from other students.

The main threads - the tutor,- prompts, were mandatory. They required responses from all students. The purpose and the requirements of the task provided the students with an initial structure to work with, using the familiar academic writing format of an essay. Repetitions produced regularities in the form or structure of the postings found.

Repetition

There is repetition in the forum postings. Students repeated key words, phrases, names and grammatical structures. They adapted discourse strategies based on the familiar genres, such as those used in the articles they were assigned to read including the writing styles used by their peers and also from their own experience. For example, in responding to a reading task, they adapted the academic genre of an essay in general.

As in any normal conversation, they used repetition as a means of sustaining the discussion of particular ideas in order to show agreement, express opinions and feelings related to materials they had read, to acknowledge other's postings, and to expand each other's arguments.

In general, the overall genre structuring of the forums were largely dominated by the following elements or patterns:
– Valediction or salutation
– Response to the tutor-prompt or main thread with an assertion or claim followed by some form of justification or example to warrant the claim, which had been asked or required by the tutor herself as the manner in which to post
– Personal values or opinions
– Personal knowledge
– Rhetorical questions evoked from shared experience or knowledge
– Embedded narrative of personal experience
– Agreement/acknowledgement of others' postings.

In short, repetitions structure the exchanges of particular topics or concerns. It preserves the shared purpose of the participants and it facilitates the *flow* of the written conversation.

Rhetorical Questions

Students drew from their own experiences in oral and written discourse to respond to articles and texts created both by their fellow students and the forum tutors. In particular, they adapted the strategy of using rhetorical questions.

A rhetorical question is an illocutionary act that does not require an answer. Instead, it is a declarative statement that is used to persuade or to emphasise one's arguments or opinions. In academic writing, students are generally discouraged to use rhetorical questions. They are said to be inappropriate, as the point being made may be misunderstood. In fact, students must be 'up front' in their meaning, making statements with clarity.

However, in written conversations, academic or otherwise, rhetorical questions are crucial. They make the written text 'converse'. They provide openings for the reader to participate in or connect with – to agree/disagree in what has been declared in writing.

In the forums discussed, the rhetorical questions were obviously not questions (cf. Fayh, 2003), but a device for proving their claim or assertion, and for getting their purpose and meaning across to the others. They were not assertions intended to close down any further discussion. Instead, they were invitations – what I would call *written pauses* – that provided an opportunity for an interruption, though only in a delayed sense, much as we create oral talk.

Subject Heading Change

The flow of talk does not merely depend on uninterrupted exchanges, nor by a single coherent topic of conversation. Conversations are made up of interruptions and topic changes. In the online setting these are executed through subject heading changes. Initially, subject headings were tutor's prompts to begin a particular online task. They presented a specific topic of discussion. Throughout the life of a forum subject headings were changed to repeat or focus on a specific topic that had been 'uttered' in the online text. They were mostly derived from a word, a name or a phrase from a posting or reference.

Subject headings present cues to the reader about what to expect. Like newspaper headlines, they have an indexical function in that they suggest to the reader the gist of the posting. They serve as signposts that tell the participants both 'what' and 'where' they are in a forum. And they could literally begin anywhere – at any topic, thread, or with any individual posting. The start of a forum is unique to each participant every single time he/she accesses it. Therefore, subject headings serve multiple roles. For instance, they could help a participant guess, predict or anticipate what the posting is about and to frame his/her reading strategy accordingly, will he/she read and/or respond to the topic of which this is the 'headline'?

Temporal Attribute of a Posting

There are several notions of time that are associated with asynchronous conferencing. These include conference duration (the length of time that a conference is open for participation); conference frequency (the number of times that participants access the conference); and individual duration (the time spent in reading and writing each time a person's enters the forum during the time it is open). All of these temporal traces are established post-hoc and provide very little clues to understand the effect of time on how a participant proceeds to read and write during the life of the forums.

The analysis in this chapter discovers that there were occasions when participants threaded their individual postings to the most recent posting at the time of access, though there was no obvious link (i.e. relevance) to this posting in anyway, except that of a temporal sequence. This occurred at the change of subject headings.

CLOSING

Genres were used as an analytical frame for a meso-level analysis of written talk. Communicative cues were identified in order to elicit a kind of content analysis based on the purpose and form of genres using the code categories of Firth (2002). The analysis was not only framed within the technological environment or forum structure of Blackboard. The patterns of communication were read in relation to the institutional context where Blackboard was located, as well as within a particular course structure and specific task requirements.

In enacting genre analysis, I acknowledge the problems in reading postings that took place in my absence, and which only give traces of each exchange. My reading is directed by left to right indentation of successive threads. This does not in anyway replicate the interactivity of the exchanges between the participants (cf Davis & Brewer, 1997).

In the forum, when reading postings within a thread or topic, one could go in any direction: up and down, sideways or on to an old or new posting, and then up and down again. The student could move from one posting to another, from one thread to the next. There were moments when the normal linear conventions of text and the temporal sequence of postings were suspended while the students were using thread structures, subject headings and previous postings as navigation cues to 'stage' a new posting. These were all left un-traced.

The repetitions found in the form of forum content, the emulation devised in changing subject headings and the presence of rhetorical questions became artefacts when the 'life' of the forums was 'over'. The online postings were read differently: reading the artefact or traces demanded a topical orientation which was not always sequential. Overall, the remains of the written utterances (at least those discussed) included responses to the task requirements that were posted by the tutor.

In the forums, we find the participants drawing on their genre repertoires of oral and written discourse strategies. The postings have the immediacy characteristics of speech and the permanence characteristic of writing. Their written features seem to be more like texts in the genre of personal and formal letters and academic essays.

In the above analysis the postings were mostly independent (declarative) statements. They were not intended to respond to a sender or interlocutor. They were mostly intended to accomplish a task. This emphasises the fact that the online task is a major structuring frame. It defines the purpose of the postings. And within this frame students proceed to import their own communicative strategies, which are primarily based on an essay form. However, for the TBP forum, where a thread was enacted as a group, another textual form emerged, which included 'what I have done' and 'what I will do' (e.g. Group A).

There were referential moves that present links to the tutor-prompt, to self-writing, to the postings of the other students and to threads where there were no real links, except that which was established by the 'Reply' button in the forums.

Whether you call it electronic discourse, netspeak, CMC, or written conversation, it is like any other form of language performed by people who are interacting for the purpose of making or sharing meaning, and it is replete with formula; that is, repetition of words and phrases, the replication of patterns in subject headings, and the emulation of strategies such as rhetorical questions.

The main point of the relational effects (i.e. affordances) presented in this chapter is to suggest that written talk must be understood both within and outside the technological environment and the design of the specific task. Writing talk is a confluence of many streams of activity, richly equipped with tools, materials, experiences and purposes, enacting communicative cues that structure productive networked learning.

NOTES

[1]   I am no linguist and have very scant knowledge in the area of linguistics. This study was my first attempt to engage in a very limited way with the various manifestations of 'online talk', mainly through genres discussed in the next section.

REFERENCES

***Bakhtin, M. M. (1986). *Speech genres and other late essays*. In C. Emerson & M. Holquist (Eds., V. W. McGee, Trans.). Austin, TX: University of Texas Press.

Brown, J. S., & Duguid, P. (1991). Organizational learning and communities-of-practice: Toward a unified view of working, learning, and innovation. *Organization Science, 2*(1), 40–57.

Crystal, D. (2001). *Language and the internet*. Cambridge: Cambridge University Press.

Crystal, D. (2004). *A glossary of Netspeak and Textspeak*. Edinburgh: Edinburgh University Press.

Crystal, D., & Davy, D. (1969). *Investigating english style*. London: Longman.

Davis, B. H., & Brewer, J. (1997). *Electronic discourse*. Albany: State University of New York Press.

Elmer-Dewitt, P. (1994). Bards of the internet. *Time Magazine, 4*(7), 66–67.

Erickson, T. (2000). Making sense of computer-mediated communication: Conversations as genres, CMC systems as genre ecologies. *Proceedings of the 33rd Annual Hawaii International Conference on System Sciences, 3*, 3011.

Fayh, P. J. (2003). Indicators of support in online interaction. *International Review of Research in Open and Distance Learning, 4*(1), 1–16. Retrieved from http://www.irrodl.org/index.php/irrodl/article/view/129/600

Firth, D. R. (2002). Emergent online communities: The structuring of communities of practice over the internet. *Proceedings of the 23rd International Conference on Information Systems (ICIS)*, Barcelona, Spain. Retrieved from http://www.business.umt.edu/faculty/firth/

Herring, S., Scheidt, L., Bonus, S., & Wright, E. (2005). Weblogs as a bridging genre. *Information Technology & People, 18*(2), 142–171. Retrieved from http://www.emeraldinsight.com/0959-3845. htm

Kear, K. (2001). Following the thread in computer conferences. *Computers & Education, 37*(1), 81–99.

Mulholland, J. (1999). Email: Uses, issues and problems in an institutional setting. In F. Bargiela-Chiappini & C. Nickerson (Eds.), *Writing business: Genres, media and discourses* (pp. 50–84). London: Longman.

Orlikowski, W. J., & Yates, J. (1994). Genre repertoire: The structuring of communicative practices in organizations. *Administrative Science Quarterly, 39*(4), 541–574.

Orlikowski, W. J., & Yates, J. A. (2002). It's about time: Temporal structuring in organizations. *Organization Science, 13*(6), 684–700.

Orlikowski, W. J., Yates, J. A., Okamura, K., & Fujimoto, M. (1995). Shaping electronic communication: The metastructuring of technology in the context of use. *Organization Science, 6*, 423–444.

Salmon, G. (2000). *E-moderating: The key to teaching and learning online*. London: Kogan Page.

Wildner-Bassett, M. E. (2005). CMC as written conversation: A critical social-constructivist view of multi identities and cultural positioning in the L2/C2. *Calico Journal, 22*(3), 635–656.

Yates, J. A., & Orlikowski, W. (2002). Genre systems: Structuring interaction through communicative norms. *The Journal of Business Communication, 39*(1), 13–35.

Yates, J. A., Orlikowski, W. J., & Okamura, K. (1999). Explicit and implicit structuring of genres in electronic communication: Reinforcement and change of social interaction. *Organization Science, 10*(1), 83–103.

Judith Enriquez
Department of Learning Technologies
University of North Texas, USA

FRODE GURIBYE AND BERNER LINDSTRÖM

INFRASTRUCTURES FOR LEARNING
AND NETWORKED TOOLS

The Introduction of a New Tool in an Inter-Organisational Network

People who study how technology affects organizational transformation increasingly recognize its dual, paradoxical nature. It is both engine and barrier for change; both customizable and rigid; both inside and outside organizational practices. It is product and process.

Star & Ruhleder, 1996, p. 111.

INTRODUCTION

In this chapter the introduction and use of a web-based portal for the support of knowledge sharing and learning in an inter-organisational network is analysed. We introduce the notion of *infrastructures for learning* as a way to understand and analytically approach the technological and social arrangements of networked learning practices. The case study focuses on how a particular tool was integrated into an existing infrastructure for learning. The analysis concerns the participation structure and how the network activities relate to local work practices, and how the introduction of the web-based tool contributed to changing the activities in the network.

With the emergence of the Internet and networked learning environments, a focus on information and communication technology (ICT) as stand-alone artefacts can miss some crucial characteristics of such networked environments. In this paper, we put forward the notion of *infrastructures for learning* (Guribye, 2005) to deal with the interconnectedness of artefacts and of how such artefacts are themselves intermeshed with other technological, institutional and social arrangements. This notion is used here as a backdrop for the analysis and as a way of making certain aspects and questions relevant in the presented analysis.

The adoption and use of groupware have been studied extensively in the field of Computer Supported Cooperative Work (e.g., Grudin, 1988; Grudin & Palen, 1995; Orlikowski, 1992; Bradner, Kellogg & Ericson, 1999). The focus is often on why such applications fail or why they are not adopted as they were supposed to have been. A common conclusion is that to understand the adoption process it requires a focus both on technical features, and on social context and the culture of

L. Dirckinck-Holmfeld, C. Jones and B. Lindström (eds.), *Analysing Networked Learning Practices in Higher Education and Continuing Professional Development, 103–115.*

the workplace in which the groupware is introduced. In this paper we look at the introduction and use of a web-based tool that was intended to support the practice of an existing inter-organisational network. While similar to many of the studies of the adoption of groupware, this particular study focuses on the integration of a tool into an existing infrastructure for learning.

The case study is relevant in several respects when it comes to understanding both networked learning and the relation to supporting infrastructures as it is addressed in this book (see the introductory chapter this volume, also Jones, Dirckinck-Holmfeld, & Lindström (2005)). In one sense this case illustrates how networked learning is concerned with new social ties between members of networks. It should be pointed out though, that in this case the social ties are those of a collegial network. This network is supported by certain technological, organisational and communicative structures and focus is set on the transformation of these structures in relation to the practice and participation in the network.

The chapter starts with an introduction of the notion of infrastructures for learning. Then a description of the case is given, with emphasis on the organisational frame-work, including a short presentation of the web-based tool. This is followed by a description and analysis of the practice within the network and how this related to the infrastructure for learning. In particular, we look at the asymmetric particip-ation structure in the network, how the network activity relates to local practices, and how the introduction of the tool changed the mode of participation within the network. Finally, some concluding remarks are made.

INFRASTRUCTURES FOR LEARNING

In their article *Steps Toward and Ecology of Infrastructure*[1], Star & Ruhleder (1996) present an analysis of infrastructure as fundamentally relational and ecological: "It becomes infrastructure in relation to organized practices ... not as a thing stripped of use" (p. 113). Infrastructure means different things in different situations and for different people, and its boundaries cannot be *a priori* defined. With this under-standing, infrastructure is seen as an ecology of tools, action and built environment. It is not simply 'a technology', but is interwoven with and is inseparable from social and other non-technical elements. As such, an infrastructure is part of the technological, material and social conditions of organised practices.

Hanseth (2000) offers a similar description of infrastructure where infrastructure, in addition to being enabling and socio-technical in character, emerges as "*an evolving, shared, open and heterogeneous installed base*" (p. 60, italics in original)[2]. This understanding of infrastructure draws on actor network theory (e.g., Latour, 1987) and infrastructure is seen as a heterogeneous actor network. Hanseth & Lundberg (2001) distinguish between what they call universal service infrastructure and work oriented infrastructures. In principle, the first provide services to all citizens, while the latter have the same characteristics as the first, but at the same time they are developed to support specific work tasks and work practices (p. 365).

In a similar sense it is possible to analytically identify *infrastructures for learning*[3]. We offer the following definition:

An infrastructure for learning is a set of resources and arrangements – social, institutional, technical – that are designed to and/or assigned to support a learning practice.

As such, infrastructures for learning can, for analytical purposes, be seen as having the same characteristics as infrastructures in general, but they are at the same time relational to practices that are aimed at learning and knowledge development. In parallel to how Kling (1992; see also Jewett and Kling, 1991) sees computing infrastructure as a set of resources that support working computational arrangements, infrastructures for learning can be seen as a set of (institutional, technical and social) resources and arrangements that support a certain learning practice. It is in this sense, not necessarily just the technological resources that are included, but also other institutional arrangements, the physical locations etc.

An illustrative example can be taken from a typical educational institution. In a university, the teaching and the students' activities are commonly supported by a number of resources, such as administrative routines, a telecommunications network, a learning management system, and physical locations (lecture halls etc.), that together make up an infrastructure for learning. These arrangements are interconnected and when analysing such practices the infrastructure for learning must be understood in broad terms and with a focus on how it appears in relation to these organised practices.

In this paper we try to shed some light on how the introduction and use of ICT can transform existing organisational arrangements, especially in relation to arrangements meant to support the exchange of knowledge and learning processes. The way this is approached is by viewing the introduction of the web-based tool as an effort of making a networked tool a part of an infrastructure for learning. The tool is thus seen as a part of a set of interrelated resources and arrangements to facilitate and support a learning practice.

CASE STUDY – BACKGROUND AND ORGANISATIONAL FRAMEWORK

In 1987 a few companies, acknowledging that they might benefit from each others' knowledge in different areas, established an inter-organisational network called Industrinettverket for Sunhordaland [The industrial network of Sunhordland – a region in the south west of Norway] (IFS). In 2000 IFS comprised 17 industrial companies, with representatives from the various companies working together to pool their competence development efforts and to arrange courses and seminars. The member organisations differ in size (from 15 employees to approximately 1600), with respect to what they produce, and in the respective production processes. For an overview of the events in the network's history, see Table 1.

Previously (from 1995) the IFS had engaged in a project to strengthen the member companies' position in their respective markets and enhance the quality of their end products through total quality management, continuous improvement, internal control and partner collaboration. Work groups were established consisting of executives, employee representatives and other members of the companies' staff. They met twice a year in conferences as part of a competence development forum. Some of the companies were already in a vendor-customer relationship with each other, but for many, these were the first formal meetings with the representatives of the other companies. Relationships between the participating companies were initially established at both inter-organisational and inter-personal levels. To accommodate the exchange of information and experiences, and to facilitate discussion between members, it was decided that the participants from the different companies should be organised into a number of subject groups. These groups were set up according to professions or subjects (e.g., an information technology group, a marketing group, a quality assurance group).

In this study one of the subject groups was followed closely for a year (2000)[4]. This case study is based on an ethnographic inquiry. The material gathered consisted of documents that plot the history of the network, strategy documents, annual reports and minutes from meetings in the subject group. Many of these documents were available through the web-portal. Five of the members of the subject group were also interviewed (in depth, open-ended interviews), one of which was the project leader for the work with the new portal. In addition, the head executive of the network was also interviewed. The data collection also included fieldwork comprising of participation in meetings and seminars. The data gathered have been subject to a qualitative analysis with a focus on understanding events and activities in their context. For the purpose of this chapter we first give an overall description of the case and the setting, then we have chosen a number of aspects that appeared in the analysis and which we found relevant for discussing the topic at hand. The citations from the interviews and documents have been selected to serve as illustrative examples of key aspects of the activity.

The group chosen was the quality assurance group, (KS/HMS[5]) which is pre-occupied with quality assurance and issues related to health, security and the workplace environment in general. From 1995–2000 the group met in face-to-face meetings four times a year, but they also had more regular distance communication using the established communication infrastructure of telephone, fax and e-mail.

Being organised into a subject group was seen as a fruitful way of extending the participants' social network and providing them with a forum in which they could discuss problems and raise issues that they were facing in their work. The group had a flat membership structure, in that all participants carried equal status. They did, however, elect a leader for the group. With this role came the responsibility of setting up meetings and writing minutes from these meetings. Participation was also considered voluntary, meaning that no member company was obliged to contribute personnel for every group.

From 1998 to 2000 the network participated in another project (the NIN-project) whose aim was to improve ICT competence within each member company, to the point where they all might actively use ICT tools in their network activities. During the first year many of the employees (especially managers and other key personnel) participated in ICT courses and seminars. The network's information technology group was chosen to steer the project and one of its members was hired as the project leader. Another important element was the implementation of a web portal to support the network's activities. To test the portal the KS/HMS group was selected as a pilot, with special emphasis on the discussion forum that was implemented as part of this solution.

At the time, all member companies had Internet connections and used e-mail systems, while some also had teleconferencing systems. With the increased use of ICT that the project brought about, IFS started to consider possible ways in which ICT could support the network's core activities. Another network (in a neighbouring region, with which IFS had some cooperation) had already implemented a web-based environment and had reported positive experiences with it, which prompted IFS to buy a prototype of the system.

Table 1. A sketch of events in the network's history

Period	Event
1987–1992	Establishing the network
1995–2000	Initial project -
	Inter-organisational arrangements
	Subject groups, regular meetings
1998–2000	NIN-project
	Training staff in ICT (courses and seminars)
	Starting the preparations for the first version of IFS Online, KSM/HS group selected as the pilot group
January 2000	First version of IFS online delivered by the external vendor
January – May 2000	Testing the use of the new system
	Experiencing technical problems
May – August 2000	Decided to abandon the current solution
	Negotiating a new deal with a local vendor
August – November 2000	The local vendor develops a new version of IFS Online
	Members of the subject group provide input to the design of the new portal
November 2000	The new version of IFS Online launched
	KS/HMS group starts to use the discussion forum
	Several discussions about KS/HMS topics

THE DEVELOPMENT OF IFS ONLINE

In January 2000 IFS implemented the first version of the web portal (IFS Online). This was supposed to function as a web portal for the network's member companies, with a news board on the main page for publishing information about the network's activities, a user discussion forum and a document archive. It also included a notification service, so when a new message was posted by one member, an e-mail notification was automatically triggered to all other members.

An external vendor delivered the first version of the web-based portal in January 2000. With great enthusiasm the network members tried out the new system, but many experienced technical problems. It simply did not function as it should. The portal had an unacceptable low response time, and many of the standard browsers[6] employed throughout the different companies did not display the java applet menu properly. The external vendor of IFS Online, however, did not experience the same type of problem when testing the system in their environment, thus they did not consider it of great importance, and gave it a low priority. This situation eventually led the IFS administration to consider other potential vendors. During the summer of 2000 one of the member companies took responsibility for developing a new version, and in November 2000 this was implemented and made available for all network participants. This new version relied on different technological solutions, and although it was based on the earlier, vendor solution, it had been modified specifically to avoid the problems that had been encountered with that earlier version.

As soon as the new version of IFS Online was up and running the KS/HMS group keenly tried it. For a period of 20 days the system was used frequently, culminating in a discussion about an interpretation of the law regulating the working environment, where five of the members participated actively. Several discussions took place simultaneously, from which emerged a communication pattern. However, after a few weeks the KS/HMS group virtually stopped using the discussion forum[7]. The only postings were a few meeting notices and minutes from meetings that were saved in the document archive

THE INTRODUCTION AND USE OF IFS ONLINE

When the tool was introduced an orientation towards the tool's use emerged, which stood in sharp contrast to the way the KS/HMS group had been working the previous years. When they had met regularly and in face-to-face meetings they had specific issues to discuss. Members would present certain challenges they were facing in their workplace, with regard to their specialism of quality assurance, and these issues would be taken up for discussion during the meeting. In addition, the meetings were used by the group members to report on relevant changes that had been implemented in their respective organisations.

Asymmetric Participation Structures

The collaboration within the KS/HMS group was originally organised around four seminars a year, where the members met face-to-face, presented topics of interest and discussed problems and developments in their respective companies. There was diverging interest in the chosen topics, but this did not seem to be of major importance. In various respects, the implementation of ISO-standards within the large and small companies had become quite demanding, many of the problems only bearing similarity on the surface. To some extent these meetings reflected this situation from the outset. Group participants from the larger companies wanted to have longer discussions about their company's issues and more less set the agenda for the meetings. However, this asymmetry in the participation structure was not of major concern, and the members from the smaller companies still felt that they benefited from attending the meetings and listening to the discussion, even though they weren't taking a particularly active role. Still, not all were completely satisfied with the way the meetings were organised.

Extract 1:

Maybe it is their understanding of my problem – they live in their world and I live in mine, and my experiences after having been in contact with them is that I do not gain very much from it [...] We operate in different industries and it is not always easy to learn from the experiences others have made.

This extract illustrates how the participants sometimes found others' contributions and discussions of little relevance to their own work situation and that others' experiences were not easily transferable to their own practices.

Extract 2:

There are companies at different levels, and if we [the group members representing his company] talk too much about process organisation and related issues, then I am not sure the other companies really know what we are talking about. Unless such issues are of concern to them I do not think they are willing to take part. And it is obvious that these smaller companies have their hands full in simply performing their daily tasks.

In the above extract the interviewee points to an important aspect of the difference in their knowledge interests. The member companies are organised in different ways[8]. Members from the larger companies often did not see the value in taking part in the group work simply to help the other members. In the larger companies they were mostly concerned with total quality management systems, often based on a process-oriented view of production. The smaller companies, on the other hand were commonly occupied with solving smaller, more concrete problems related to their production based on procedures that prescribed in detail how to carry out a specific parts of production. As is suggested in the extract 1 these differences translate into the way that the individual company representatives participate in the subject group's work. Interestingly, these differences had not been very apparent during the early phases (before introducing IFS Online).

Network Activities and Local Practices

Another issue that is touched upon in extract 2 above is the relationship between the participants' daily work and the activities within the network. The network was intended to be a vehicle by which member organisations could share different competencies, via their group representatives, and so become a supplement to each company's internal training programme. IFS Online was supposed to help integrate this sharing process into the normal working day of each member. It was an issue that was addressed in one of their reports, which dealt specifically with the role that IFS Online should perform:

Extract 3:

Development and implementation of an information network (mainly Internet based through IFS Online) will provide the tool for the member companies to use. At the same time it is important that the content of the information network is directly related to topics that are of interest to the member companies, and that it as much as possible is integrated as a part of the daily work (IFS-report, 1/1999).

It was difficult, however, to maintain a balance between the daily working routines within a company and the activities within the network. Some viewed the work demands of the network and those of the member organisations as being in conflict with one another. The manager of the project gave this reply when asked about how he saw the difference between working for the network (managing the project) and working for his company.

Extract 4:

There is a substantial difference [between working for IFS and for the particular member organisation], because in [our company] you can order people to do certain things ... if we are upgrading something within IT, then we do it. Nobody can deny us that. In the network [IFS], however, you are dependent on some sort of voluntariness. I can't force anyone to do anything in the network.

In this answer it is suggested that there exists, for this employee, a clash of loyalties, between his IFS activities and those of his actual job, as demanded by his employer. This might be seen as an inherent contradiction or tension in the organisation of network activities. The demands of the network are a secondary and voluntary activity for the employees in the member organisations, and compete for the time they would normally allocate for they're real jobs of work. Another member of the KS/HMS group spoke in even more explicit terms when he gave an account of the relationship between the activities in the network and the work he does for his own company:

Extract 5:

You have to prioritise between different things, and it might be that you give a lower priority to this [the work in the KS/HMS group]. It is just the way it is – the most important task you do is the one that gets you your salary! You have to do the job there first. This network comes as an addition.

This illustrates how members viewed the relationship between the daily duties at their place of work and those required of the network. The reason, reportedly, was that many of them had rather heavy workloads at their respective companies. Collaboration in the network was regarded as important to increase skills in the area of KS/HMS. For the most part, however, the members said they did not have enough time to take part in these activities, as daily work had to take priority.

Online Participation

Online discussions constituted a different mode of participation in the group's activities. First, the need to articulate issues in terms of posting a message on IFS online, presents challenges for the participants in that their contributions need to be written out in statements that are persistent and visible to the other members.

IFS Online allowed the users to follow the events of the discussion forum without actively engaging in the discussions. This phenomenon is often referred to as 'lurking' (e.g., Hine, 2000). One of the participants, who posted no messages to the forum, said that he occasionally browsed it to keep himself updated on the ongoing discussions. Some of the members also said they did not actively take part in the discussions because they did not want to ask questions that others might think of as foolish.[9] Another said that because the discussion forum was open and everyone could read his submissions he did not want to post questions[10]. For these members, lurking was a way to participate in the activities, without having to express their views or risk asking the 'wrong' questions.

Still, reading or browsing the discussions in the forum was not visible to the other members in the group. In the face-to-face meetings some of the members were quite passive as well, attending these meetings without contributing to the discussions, mostly listening to what was being said and this way keeping up to date on the various topics. As attending the face-to-face meetings was emphasised, the passive role taken by some of the members was not considered a problematic issue. In a discussion forum, however, the lack of postings can easily be interpreted as not participating.

DISCUSSION – INTEGRATION OF THE TOOL

In the case being studied, the arrangements made to support the practice of the network and the communication between the members in the subject group can be considered an established infrastructure for learning. It consisted of the communications infrastructure, including the use of tools such as telephones, email, fax, and the communication network. In addition, items such as notebooks and projectors, and even buildings they're in, are part of the infrastructure that underlies and transparently supports the practice of the subject group's work. The infrastructure also includes the personnel that work to keep these arrangements up and running.

Trying to introduce the web-based tool, IFS Online, as part of this working infrastructure involved making changes at different levels. Both at the technical level (such as implementation of the software on the server) and at a human resource level (such as having staff to run the necessary services), changes were made to ensure that the process would be as easy as possible. Yet despite these efforts, as it has been illustrated, the introduction of this computerised tool into the established work practices had unforeseen consequences for the way the group members perceived their work. There was a clear shift of focus from subject matter (KS/HMS work) to the technical specificities of the new tool. In other words, the set of resources that were introduced remained *focal* resources rather than *supporting* resources (Kling, 1992) in the group's work. In projects that try to implement and integrate a new set of tools or technologies into an existing practice, such a focus can be expected. Having such a phase in projects, where the technological tools are in focus, can be seen as common to any adoption process. It is a process of naturalization of artefacts (see Bowker & Star, 1999, pp. 298–300).

The introduction of the new tool seemed to reinforce existing differences in the participation structure. Although the members already had to cope with participating in the network activities along with doing their regular job, they usually found the time to participate in the face-to-face meetings. Introducing the discussion forum was intended as a way to have the members participate in the activities of the network on a more regular basis. This, however, also involved spending more time on these 'secondary' activities, and thus they got a lower priority. In addition, differences in their knowledge interests, and difficulties in seeing how the topics under discussion had any relevance to the practices in their own companies, it seems, contributed to this reinforcement.

Implications

This case is an illustrative example of how it can be quite futile to 'dump' a technology into an existing set of work practices with no clear idea of how it will contribute to the current communication channels and infrastructure. In such cases a thorough understanding of the key elements of an existing practice can be crucial. As in this case, the value of the structure provided by the regular face-to-face meetings was probably underestimated. These meetings gave the activity structure by providing rhythm and regularity, but also by having a defined agenda and a division of labour for each meeting. This structure probably helped to overcome issues of asymmetric participation and different knowledge interests. In addition, the regularity (and the low frequency) of the meetings gave a dedicated and circumscribed amount of time to use on this activity. When the web-based tool was introduced there were no clear limits on how much or little time the use of the forum should occupy. In this way it is easy to give less priority to tasks that are considered secondary to the day-to-day tasks. A participation model based on voluntariness can be very fragile, and it is easy to give less priority to these kinds of activity than those that are part of the actual day job. These challenges could perhaps have been addressed by assigning specific tasks to the participants and allocating time that could be dedicated to this activity.

CONCLUDING REMARKS

The adoption of IFS online involved aligning it with the existing communication and computing infrastructure – the installed base. In other words, making it compatible with existing technologies such as the PCs and browsers already in use. This task required negotiations with various parties (e.g. the vendors, a neighbouring network, the members, and the network administration). The process of aligning the technology with the existing infrastructure is as much a process of negotiation of responsibilities, resources and tasks, as it is a question of technological feasibility.

Analytically, these issues are not understood within a narrow focus on the particular features of the web-based tool. Rather, a wider focus on the various aspects of the infrastructure for learning: the existing arrangements for supporting the activity of the members; the resources available; the institutional framework; and how this is related to the particularities of the participation structure and the differences in the knowledge interests, were key dimensions identified in the analysis.

Designing an infrastructure for learning is different from designing a technological tool. It is not only a question of designing single-standing artefacts, but pedagogical and organisational arrangements. Following Wenger (1998) design can be understood as "the systematic, planned, and reflexive colonization of time and space in the service of an undertaking. This perspective includes not only the production of artefacts, but also the design of social processes such as organizations or instruction" (p. 228). This view of design can also be taken into account when looking at infrastructures for learning. As Wenger is looking at communities of practice as the arena for learning, he further asserts that "*learning cannot be designed* but that it can only be designed *for* – that is, frustrated or facilitated" (p. 229, italics in original). The notion of infrastructures for learning implies such a relation between design and learning. With regard to Goodyear's (2002, see also the introductory chapter in this book) model of indirect design, the notion of infrastructures for learning implies that the actual infrastructure cannot be designed, but the supporting resources and arrangements can be tended to. What the actual consequences of such arrangements will be in practice is dependent on the realization of the infrastructure for learning.

In this chapter we have discussed an empirical case study of an effort to incorporate a networked tool into an infrastructure for learning. As it is illustrated in the case it is important to pay attention to how social and technological arrangements fit together. Understanding such arrangements as an infrastructure for learning – a set of social, technical and organizational arrangements and resources – contribute to paying attention to exactly such interconnections.

NOTES

[1] See also Bowker, Timmermans, & Star, 1996; Bowker & Star, 1999; Star, 1999.

[2] See also Hanseth & Monteiro, 1997; Hanseth, Monteiro & Hatling, 1996.

[3] For a full overview and discussion of the theoretical and historical background of the concept see Guribye (2005). The notion of infrastructures for learning was first discussed in a paper by Guribye and Netteland (2003).

[4] The data collection was done by Geir André Bakke. The analysis presented here is a reworking of the analyses presented in Guribye & Bakke (2001), Bakke (2002), Guribye, Lindström and Bakke (2005) and Guribye (2005). For further details on the data collection and analysis see Bakke (2002) and Guribye (2005).

[5] The acronym will be used throughout the paper referring both to the group and to the subject of the group's work. In Norwegian the letters denote Kvalitetssikring/Helse, Miljø og Sikkerhet [quality assurance/health, environment and security].

[6] In particular this was problematic for those running earlier versions of MS explorer and Netscape Navigator.

[7] After December 2000 there was one discussion in February 2001 with five answers to the original submission. Subsequent to this (and until September 2004) there have been four postings by the same author in the discussion forum with one or zero answers, all of which were posted in 2002.

[8] E.g., depending on what they are producing – some of the companies mainly engage in large projects, such as building an oil platform yard, and others in mass production of a single product. The latter is what the informant refers to by the term 'process-organisation'

[9] Star & Ruhleder (1996) made a similar observation (see pp. 123–124). In his study of the Answer Garden, Ackerman (1994) reported that the possibility to ask questions anonymously was seen as a way to lower the threshold for posting contributions.

[10] Only members of the network have access to read the content of the messages.

REFERENCES

Ackerman, M. (1994). Augmenting the organizational memory: A field study of answer garden. In *Proceedings of CSCW'94* (pp. 243–252). Chapel Hill, NC: ACM Press.

Bakke, G. A. (2002). *Computer mediated collaboration in an industrial competence network: An ethnography of inter-organisational learning.* Unpublished Research Masters thesis, University of Bergen, Norway.

Bowker, G. C., & Star, S. L. (1999). *Sorting things out: Classification and its consequences.* Cambridge, MA: MIT Press.

Bowker, G. C., Timmermans, S., & Star, S. L. (1996). Infrastructure and organizational transformation: Classifying nurses' work. In W. J. Orlikowski, G. Walsham, M. R. Jones, & J. I. DeGross (Eds.), *Information technology and changes in organizational work* (pp. 344–370). London: Chapman & Hall.

Bradner, E., Kellogg, W. A., & Erickson, T. (1999). The adoption and use of "babble": A field study of chat in the workplace. In *Proceedings of ECSCW'99* (pp. 139–158). Dordrecht, The Netherlands: Kluwer Academic Publishers.

Goodyear, P. (2002). Psychological foundations for networked learning. In C. Steeples & C. Jones (Eds.), *Networked learning: Perspectives and issues* (pp. 49–75). London: Springer.

Grudin, J. (1988). Why CSCW applications fail: Problems in the design and evaluation of organizational interfaces. In *Proceedings of CSCW'88* (pp. 85–93). New York: ACM Press.

Grudin, J., & Palen, L. (1995). Why groupware succeeds: Discretion or mandate? In *Proceedings of ECSCW-95* (pp. 261–277). Dordrecht, The Netherlands: Kluwer Academic Publishers

Guribye, F. (2005). *Infrastructures for learning – ethnographic inquiries into the social and technical conditions of education and training.* Doctoral thesis, University of Bergen, Norway.

Guribye, F., & Bakke, G. A. (2001). Motivation and contradictions in an industrial competence network: An empirical study of ICT-support for inter-organisational collaborative learning. In S. Bjørnestad, A. Mørch, & A. L. Oppdahl (Eds.), *Proceedings of the 24th information systems research seminar in Scandinavia.* Bergen, Norway.

Guribye, F., & Netteland, G. (2003, August). *Representations of knowledge in infrastructures for learning.* Paper presented at the EARLI 2003 Conference, Padova, Italy.

Hanseth, O. (2000). The economics of standards. In C. Ciborra, K. Braa, A. Cordella, B. Dahlbom, A. Failla, O. Hanseth, V. Hepsø, J. Ljungberg, E. Monteiro, & K. A. Simon (Eds.), *From control to drift: The dynamics of corporate information infrastructures* (pp. 56–70). Oxford [England]; New York: Oxford University Press.

Hanseth, O., & Lundberg, N. (2001). Designing work oriented infrastructures. *Computer Supported Cooperative Work, 10,* 347–372.

Hanseth, O., & Monteiro, E. (1997). Inscribing behaviour in information infrastructure standards. *Accounting, Management & Information Technology, 7*(4), 183–211.

Hanseth, O., Monteiro, E., & Hatling, M. (1996). Developing information infrastructure: The tension between standardization and flexibility. *Science Technology & Human Values, 21*(4), 407–426.

Hine, C. (2000). *Virtual ethnography.* London; Thousand Oaks, CA: SAGE.

Jewett, T., & Kling, R. (1991). The dynamics of computerization in a social science research team: A case study of infrastructure, strategies, and skills. *Social Science Computer Review, 9*, 246–275.

Jones, C., Dirckinck-Holmfeld, L., & Lindström, B. (2005). CSCL - The next ten years – A view from Europe. In T. Koschmann, D. Suthers, & T.-W. Chan (Eds.), *Computer supported collaborative learning 2005: The next 10 years!* (pp. 237–246). Mahwah, NJ: Lawrence Erlbaum Associates.

Kling, R. (1992). Behind the terminal: The critical role of computing infrastructure in effective information systems development and use. In W. W. Cotterman & J. A. Senn (Eds.), *Challenges and strategies for research in systems development.* New York: John Wiley & Sons Ltd.

Latour, B. (1987). *Science in action: How to follow scientists and engineers through society.* Milton Keynes, England: Open University Press.

Orlikowski, W. J. (1992). Learning from notes: Organizational issues in groupware implementation. In *Proceedings of CSCW'92* (pp. 362–369). New York: ACM Press.

Star, S. L. (1999). The ethnography of infrastructure. *American Behavioral Scientist, 43*(3), 377–391.

Star, S. L., & Ruhleder, K. (1996). Steps toward an ecology of infrastructure: Design and access for large information spaces. *Information Systems Research, 7*(1), 111–134.

Wenger, E. (1998). *Communities of practice: Learning, meaning, and identity.* Cambridge, MA: Cambridge University Press.

Frode Guribye
Department of Information Science and Media Studies
University of Bergen, Norway

Berner Lindström
Department of Education
Gothenburg University, Sweden

CHRIS JONES

NETWORKED LEARNING AND POSTGRADUATE PROFESSIONALS

Comparing Course Designs

The developed world is in the midst of a paradigm shift, both in the ways in which people and institutions are actually connected. It is a shift from being bound up in homogenous 'little boxes' to surfing life through diffuse, variegated social networks. Although the transformation began in the pre-Internet 1960s, the proliferation of the Internet both reflects and facilitates the shift.

(Wellman, 2001)

INTRODUCTION – DESIGNING FOR NETWORKED LEARNING

Castells (2001) writes about the relationship between emerging technologies and social forms and following Wellman he describes the form of networked society as one of "networked individualism" (1996, 2001). He claims that digital networks and the Internet are especially effective at maintaining weak ties and that in relation to strong ties networks assist in their maintenance at a distance. The linkage between a networked ½ and forms of networked learning is still unclear; however, the term 'networked learning' has become one of several now in popular use to describe learning within a society that is dependant upon digital networks for its social organization. The Centre for Studies of Advanced Learning Technology (CSALT) at Lancaster University is associated with the following definition of networked learning.

> Networked learning is learning in which information and communication technology (C&IT) is used to promote connections: between one learner and other learners, between learners and tutors; between a learning community and its learning resources. (Goodyear et al., 2004)

The central term in this definition is *connections*. The definition takes a relational stance, in which learning takes place in relation to others and also in relation to learning resources. Networked learning differs from CSCL and Communities of Practice as it does not privilege relationships such as cooperation and collaboration or the closeness of community and unity of purpose. Unlike CSCL and communities of practice this definition of networked learning draws particular attention to the place of learning resources in relational terms. The idea of networked learning has

L. Dirckinck-Holmfeld, C. Jones and B. Lindström (eds.), *Analysing Networked Learning Practices in Higher Education and Continuing Professional Development*, 117–137.

been explored from this perspective by Jones (2004), Jones and Esnault (2004) and Jones et al. (2006).

This chapter begins with a case study of an MSc in Advanced Learning Technology at Lancaster University (ALT MSc), which was designed and taught by some of the same people who were responsible for the definition of networked learning quoted above. It then goes on to compare this course with a Masters in Online and Distance Education at the Open University in the United Kingdom (MA ODE). The case studies and comparisons are aimed at the level of course design, on the ways in which academic staff organise and structure modular courses in terms of the tasks set for students, on the allocation of technological support and resources and finally on the conceptions of how students will organise themselves to carry out the work set. The case studies do not explicitly reference the student experience, which would warrant a chapter of its own. The topic of this chapter is important, not least because the case studies report on the pedagogical structure of programmes that are developing the next generation of professionals in the field. The programmes are examples of Masters level education that reflexively teaches about networked learning whilst simultaneously making use of networked learning technologies and practices.

The ALT MSc, until its recent replacement by a networked learning PhD, was a long standing and successful programme. The degree was selected to provide a case study because it was designed by a team that described its own design principles in terms of networked learning, and because the author of this chapter was already working on the programme in an academic capacity. Comparisons are then drawn with the MA in Online and Distance Learning at the Open University. This second programme was chosen partly for the same opportunistic reason – that the author was an academic involved in the programme – and partly because the Open University is the largest distance learning provider in Europe. The programme also happens to offer a good basis for comparison because it was not guided by the same pedagogical design principles. It grew out of an Open University pedagogical tradition described as Supported Open Learning (SOL), which reflects the distilled experience of a large distance learning university. By contrast, the ALT programme is a largely distance learning programme in a university whose operations take place in a single location.

The areas of particular interest that emerge from this chapter resonate with many of those to be found throughout this volume. Recurring themes can be seen, for instance, in the way that the design focus in both Masters programmes is focused on individual learning in a social setting (networked individualism), in the task driven nature of the designs (indirect design) and in the way that the technological and institutional infrastructures affect teaching and learning (institutions and infrastructure). The chapter also offers a comparison and contrast with case studies in other chapters, in particular those of Dirckinck-Holmfeld *et al*, Pilkington and Guldberg and Vines and Dysthe. The comparison with Dirckinck-Holmfeld *et al* is centred on the similarities in recruitment from busy professionals, and the contrast with this case lies in the underlying philosophies that inform the programmes of study reported here, in particular concerning the focus on resources. Pilkington and

Guldberg offer a comparison and contrast to the formal educational setting presented here, with their example of networked learning located in a situation beyond formal education. Finally, the chapter by Vines and Dysthe offers a comparison with the ways in which a technological infrastructure interacts with course design by enabling and constraining certain kinds of activity.

THE ADVANCED LEARNING TECHNOLOGY PROGRAMME

The author of this case study was deputy director of the ALT programme until October 2005. Original research at Lancaster was conducted as part of the course evaluation, in which the author was assisted by Dr Maria Zenios and Vanessa Watts, an intern student from Texas A&M, USA with no connection to the ALT programme. The case study relied upon formal course documentation including the documents developed for validation and accountability as part of the university and UK system of quality assurance. Specific research was conducted to track one module taught in 2004, ALT 04 *Learning Technology: methods of research and evaluation*, and to analyse the pattern of student intake to the programme.

The ALT programme embodies a set of views on networked learning that have been set out in a number of documents over the years. One of these documents was a book, *Effective networked learning in higher education: notes and guidelines* (Goodyear et al., 2001), the result of a two year research project into students' experience of networked learning. The book was written for teachers who might be thinking of implementing networked learning, and included a summary of the perceived strengths and weaknesses of networked learning, set out under the following headings.

Table 1. Strengths and Weaknesses (Goodyear et al. 2001)

Claimed Strengths	Claimed weaknesses
Interactive, but flexible	Lack of expressive richness
Promotes active engagement	No immediacy
Reflective, aiding 'deeper' processing	Prolonged decision making
Permanent record	Requires technical access and competence
New opportunities for group working	A different style of communication
Social interaction	Levels of discourse may be at odds
Ease of access to global resources	De-personalising effects (more analytical/judgmental)
Under-represented groups	Need for shared goal(s) to sustain activity
Changing relationships in learning	

It can be seen immediately that the strengths and weaknesses in this list are not simply features of the technologies; rather they suggest a complex interaction between the technologies as they are deployed, and the work of mobilizing the technologies within particular settings. I will take one example from each column to illustrate this point.

Permanent Record

The discussions that take place within a networked learning environment can leave a more or less permanent trace. This feature can be thought of as an affordance of digital technologies. This can be contrasted with face-to-face discussions that require special measures, such as the keeping minutes or making audio recordings to provide a degree of permanence. However the realisation of the possibility of a permanent record still requires the social organization of the traces the technology enables to ensure that they are maintained and made available to participants and others.

A Different Style of Communication

The different forms of communication in digital networks can lead to changes in communication patterns. In asynchronous text communication the delay built into the system is often attributed as the cause of either beneficial changes, such as leading to more considered replies, or difficulties, such as the anxiety felt when a message receives no timely response. Such patterns of communication are a complex interplay between technological and social features such as the organization of the group and its interactions, and the expectations that users of the system have in terms of the behaviour of others.

The ALT Modules and Programme

The ALT programme was designed to allow study for a diploma or a full masters level degree, and also carried the option for individual modules to be taken separately without the need to register for the full programme. Approximately one third of the students registering for modules did not initially register for the programme. Some of these registered later, but the fraction one third gives a sense of the proportion between registrations for the full programme and individual modules. The programme was designed primarily for part time study and generally took between 30 and 48 months to complete. The minimum period of registration was 24 months but it was very rare for the programme to be completed in two years. The programme was cost-efficient at quite low numbers and the modules that ran in the final years of the programme had registrations of less than 20 students at any one time. These cohort numbers were unusually low because the MSc/diploma programme closed to new entrants in 2006, as the ALT programme was due to be replaced by a taught PhD in the same academic area. The modules for the ALT programme were organized into a two-year timetable that allowed students to join the programme at the start of any module. In effect this meant they could join at three points in any one year.

Students' performance on this programme was assessed by their coursework for each module, plus a final project report for those intending to complete at masters level. Course work assignments were negotiated between students and tutors on an individual basis, although in each case there remained a strong connection between the module and the student's own work setting. Each assignment was submitted at the end of the module and during the module students were expected to participate in online discussions of assignment ideas, draft assignments and associated activities. The assessment for a module was equivalent to a 6,000 word assignment (18 M level credits) or a 12,000 word assignment (36 M level credits). The distinction between the assignments graded at 18 or 36 M credits was considered to be both qualitative and quantitative. The final project was equivalent to a maximum of 18,000 words (54 M level credits). As an example of the final profile of credits to obtain a standard ALT masters level degree, candidates would have to complete 6 modules, five of which would be single weighted and one double weighted, as well as completing the final project.

Technology

The ALT programme had a simple web page that provided links to programme documentation, the university library (including digital resources specifically for the programme normally accessed through the library), and the current and previous module discussion spaces. The discussion platform was provided using Lotus Notes and the overall design of the Lotus Notes environment was provided using a locally supplied template. Each module had a separate discussion space that was used for discussion and to post updates and materials.

There was a synchronous text-based chat tool that was part of the Lotus Notes platform, which was used in some modules as part of the module activity and which students could access independently at any time. In addition, the students had been introduced to Sametime, a Lotus Notes-based environment that was not part of the standard platform, allowing audio and video conferencing, shared documents and whiteboard. Sametime was only used for demonstration purposes on the modules and the activities conducted in Sametime were not essential in any of the modules. The ALT programme was supported by the university library and digitized texts (book chapters and online journal articles) were provided online via links from the course and home pages. Each module still provided hard copies of readings, which included journal articles, book chapters and, in some cases, complete books. Overall, the technology was robust rather than rich. A major consideration in this regard was that it had to support distance students from all over the world.

Recruitment to the course

Recruitment to the ALT programme and to individual modules came primarily from among teaching professionals in post-compulsory education, training in a business environment and consultancy. Between 2001 and 2004 14 of the 64 participants were from outside the UK. Of these, ten were from countries outside Europe (one from

Malta – then an accession state), including Brazil, China (PRC), India and several Middle Eastern states. Of the non-European participants a significant number (approximately 50 per cent) were expatriates from European home countries. The career background of all students recruited over the same three years reflected the course criteria. Approximately half (31 students) were from educational institutions, the remainder were from a variety of public bodies, including the BBC and government ministries and from private sector businesses including large corporations and small to medium size businesses. Three were independent consultants and a further two students were consultants working in small companies.

The ALT programme aimed to support continuing professional development (CPD) for busy working professionals who already have some connection to adult education and training. The programme was aimed at people who were "involved in the design, development, use or evaluation of ALT systems"; "Involved in training, and in higher, further or adult education" but it was explicitly "*not* oriented towards schools" (ALT home page). The course was intentionally designed to allow for study in a flexible way, in terms of both time and distance, by limiting face-to-face and synchronous contact. The structure of the programme was a mix of distant/ independent study, social engagement supported by ICT, and non-compulsory short intensive residential periods.

> The ALT programme is seen as a place in which participant's work related interests come together with our research based knowledge. The goal of the programme is to find fruitful ways of combining these two. (ALT course validation documentation 1999)

To achieve this the programme explicitly built on the idea that participants brought to valuable prior experience to their studies. The social process of the course was built on an engagement with the participants' own experiences in a relationship to the programme resources which were brought to the modules by active research staff.

THE OPEN UNIVERSITY

The Open University's pedagogical model, Supported Open Learning (SOL), was developed in the context of a large and diverse student intake. The model is constructed upon a number of key factors:
- Distance or Open Learning
  - Learning 'in your own time'
  - Reading, undertaking set activities and assignments
  - Possibly working with others
- Resources
  - Printed course materials, set books, audio and video cassettes, CD/DVD materials, home experiments, course and programme web sites (previously broadcast TV programmes)
- Systematic support

- A course tutor, a regional network of 13 centres, central library and technical support
- Tutorial held within regions, day schools and online tutorials (previously and optionally e.g. languages, summer schools).

When reviewing SOL in relation to Learning Design, McAndrew and Weller (2005) wrote that the "roots of this approach" were in the use of high quality media with tutorial support for students in form of day schools, telephone and formative commenting on assessments. However the OU had become "one of the largest providers of online education" and this change of focus to online provision had been accompanied by adjustments in the models (ibid 2005, p. 281). SOL is not a static approach but has altered alongside the increasing use of internet technologies for distance education.

The workforce at the Open University is not like that of a standard university, as it is largely a core-periphery model. A central course team based in Milton Keynes is responsible for the production of course materials and laying out an overall plan for the students' activity, typically specified in a course guide, which explains how the student is expected to study and includes a timetable of progress through the course activities and assessment. Tutor support is provided by part time associate lecturers who are supported by full time staff at regional centres. The associate lecturers include some full time Open University staff, as well as faculty from other universities working additional hours and retired academic staff. The students are expected to move through the materials and activities as a cohort and the timetable is enforced through assessment deadlines. Across the university a typical tutor group would involve approximately 20 students who are assigned to an associate lecturer. The division of labour at the Open University separates teaching into a number of functions so that course production (involving the design of a course or programme, preparation of resources and media for presentation) is done centrally in teams, whereas day to day contact and tutoring is conducted through regional centres and part time associate lecturers.

The OU Masters in Online and Distance Education (MA ODE) Modules and Programme

The MA ODE programme was launched in 1997 and initially offered a single 60 M level point course (H801 *Foundations of open and distance education*). Two further 60 M level point courses followed (H802 *Applications of information technology in open and distance education*, and H804 *the implementation of open and distance learning*) and an optional dissertation gaining 60 M level credit points. It was early 1999 before the programme was able to offer the full 180 credit points needed to complete the MA in Open and Distance Education. With the 180 points representing a minimum of three years' study, the first students graduated in late 2000. Within the full range of courses currently available (see below) successfully completing sixty points results in a Postgraduate Certificate in Open and Distance Education and 120 points successfully completed results in a Postgraduate Diploma in Open and Distance Education.

The programme design allows for variations in course descriptions, and in addition to dealing with very different content matter each of the courses adopts a model for teaching and learning that, whilst broadly reflecting the SOL model, varies considerably in its detail. This is perceived by the course teams as a particular strength of the programme in providing the ability to adapt and experiment with pedagogical forms broadly in line with SOL. Students are allocated to online tutor groups where they are encouraged to work in a collaborative way with other students, contributing to computer conferences and working both individually and in groups with the support of a tutor.. Tutors have their own online area and they are supported by a member of the central academic staff, who acts as course chair. There are no face-to-face activities programmed into this degree because all support is provided through other media. The teaching and learning are described as guided and resource-based, using a mix of media including print.

The profile of the courses has altered over the years and currently the programme is in transition from largely 60 M level points per course to a range of shorter 30 M level point courses, with a single 60 M level point capstone course. This allows students to begin modules at two points in the year, September and February, and to take on a lower commitment with each module registration. The current range of courses is as follows:

- H800: (60 points): *Technology-enhanced learning: practices and debates*(first presentation in Feb 2009, last year of course 2014 or 2016)
- H804: (60 points): *Implementing online, open and distance learning* (last year of presentation 2008)
- H806: (60 points): *Learning in the connected economy* (last year of presentation 2008)
- H807: (30 points): *Innovations in elearning* (last year of presentation 2011)
- H808: (30 points): *The elearning professional* (last year of presentation 2011)
- H809: (30 points): *Practice-based research in educational technology* (last year of presentation 2013)
- H810: (30 points): *Accessible on-line learning: supporting disabled students* (first presentation Sept 2008, last year of presentation 2013).

Student assessments are based on their course work in the form of tutor-marked assignments (TMA) which are designed to support the programme by providing both formative and summative assessment. TMA assessment tasks range from traditional essays to practical web-based tasks and reflective writing. The final assessment of each module is in the form of an 'examinable component' (ECA). This is not an examination in any usual sense because it is a longer piece of work than the TMAs earlier in a module but it is generally similar in format and is submitted and assessed in a different and more centralised manner.

Technology

Over the period of ten years the MA ODE has been supported by a variety of technological platforms. The first platform was specially designed for the ODE programme itself, and was not part of the wider university technical platform. The eBBS (electronic Bulleting Board System), as it was called, was an effective platform but following some technical problems that required a robust support system it was decided to move to the web version of the Open University's First Class conferencing system. This was to alleviate the difficulties that had arisen with the eBBS system which only had limited local technical support rather than being supported by the full institutional system. From 2006 the OU VLE (Open University Virtual Learning Environment) has provided an integrated suite of services, with Moodle as the core platform, available to all course teams over the Web. There has also been a significant institutional effort to prepare staff to re-design their courses appropriately for the new networked environment

Currently, all MA ODE courses are fully online, with all materials, student, and tutor and course team interactions taking place through the OU VLE and associated online environments, such as blogs, wikis, podcasting, an e-portfolio system. The OU VLE will shortly introduce Elluminate for synchronous online interaction, replacing a previous in-house system called Lyceum. All assessment is conducted online and the final ECA is submitted using the Open University's own eTMA system and MyStuff, an in-house system for e-portfolio work.

Recruitment

The Online and Distance Education (ODE) postgraduate programme aims to recruit from a wide range of educational professionals, as described on the ODE programme web site:

> You could be working in a variety of post-compulsory educational contexts, including lecturers, teachers, trainers, support staff, educational technologists, media specialists, learning systems managers, librarians, learning centre advisory staff, etc., from a range of knowledge domains.
> (http://iet.open.ac.uk/courses/postgrad/ode/index.cfm)

The ODE programme is not a standard OU programme because it runs with smaller numbers of students than many OU courses and it has a more flexible approach to some elements of the standard SOL model, for example the use of resources. The OU Supported Open Learning model relies on the central production of high quality course materials including set books by the OU course team. The ODE programme has moved away from this towards resources that are externally produced and already available, e.g. journal articles and chapters from existing books.

The market for the MA ODE courses largely comprises professionals in tertiary level educational institutions both in the UK and elsewhere. There are significant but smaller groups, such as managers and administrators in non-educational settings. Overall the majority of students are recruited from the public rather than the private sector. The gender of students is evenly split and the age profile is heavily biased to the over 40s, with only 12.6 per cent being under 40 at graduation and 9.1 percent being over 60. The programme was designed from the start as a global programme, so that students can register from anywhere in the world. Approximately one third are resident outside the UK (34 per cent). The largest group of non-UK students (18 per cent) are resident in other EU countries, but a significant proportion (16 per cent) are from a wider global area, including China (PRC Hong Kong and Taiwan), Japan, USA, Australasia and the UAE.

COMPARISONS OF COURSE DESIGNS

The Principles of the Course Design

The design of the ALT programme was developed over a long period and the principle elements of design reported here are those identified in the final years of course documentation. Nevertheless, they reflect this long development and are not revisions of basic principles. Equally, the MA ODE has developed over a ten year period and has undergone a number of revisions. Its overall framework reflects the OU approach to Supported Open Learning, though unlike the ALT programme the MA ODE modules show a degree of pedagogical variation, and overall the programme is not as uniform in its approach as the ALT programme. Despite this there are some strong similarities, and like the ALT programme the MA ODE has a broadly constructivist and collaborative approach to learning. On the other hand the emphasis on a resource based approach is more marked in the MA ODE than the ALT programme, even though the ALT programme had a set of readings prescribed for each module. This section does not cover all elements of course design, but focuses on three specific areas: individual learning in a social context, pedagogical organisation through tasks and activities and the role of course resources and the provision of a technological infrastructure.

Individual Learning in a Social Context

Both programmes recruited students from a layer of busy professionals who were only able to study part time. They also aimed to recruit worldwide, and although in both cases students were largely from the British Isles and mainland Europe, some were recruited from locations further afield. Both of these recruitment patterns placed an organisational constraint on the use of synchronous and collaborative work. Synchronous work was not ruled out but constrained by the problems of integrating students across time zones. This constraint was obviously made worse by the small number of students outside mainland Europe, whose times zones were particularly different. For collaborative work to take place it was necessary to build in a sufficient prior warning of events that would require synchronisation with others, and to allow flexibility for students whose work commitments conflicted with course priorities. For postgraduate professionals recruited from the greatest distances there are structural constraints that place limits and restrictions on their use of collaborative methods.

The ALT programme was interested in placing individual learning in a number of specific social contexts.

The Lancaster University Advanced Learning Technology (ALT) programme has a strong interest in individual learning, though it is usually individual learning *in a social context*. (Handbook p. 7)

One of the ways in which the individual role is emphasized was in relation to the setting of assignment tasks:

The individual learner's centralized role, especially in negotiation of the assignment tasks, ensures that they are pivotal in defining appropriate tasks that help the development of their working knowledge and professional practice. (Handbook p. 19)

The social contexts explicitly referenced in ALT course documentation emphasize a form of boundary crossing in which knowledge has to be disembedded from one social setting and re-embedded in another. Discussion of this type of process can be found in both Wenger (1998) and Brown and Duguid (2001) and it's related to the ideas of constellations of practice and networks of practice respectively. Wenger explicitly identifies the export of styles and discourses which, whilst not practices themselves, provide resources that can be used in the context of practice.

The ALT programme regards this particular process, which is part of communities of practice thinking, as central to networked learning (Wenger, 1998). Communities of practice involve a process of relatively close engagement between members of a community whose focus is on the sharing of practice. Shared practice in turn requires members to have the time and space to collaborate. The idea of a community of practice has been translated into the ALT programme in the following way.

A 'community of practice' is a way of describing a set of people who share work related interests and who recognise each other as valuable co-members. Part of what we are trying to do through the ALT programme is create and support such a community in the field of ALT. (ALT Handbook p. 17)

The design of the ALT programme does not seek to create a community of learners, rather it tries to manage the organizational forms and tasks of the programme such that it may nurture the kinds of learning community which the programme values. It is an indirect approach to community that assumes the participants already have work based and professional communities of their own. In this context the ALT programme functioned as an additional site for community development rather than providing the core community. From this perspective the ALT programme resembles the idea of a constellation of practice developed by Wenger (1998).

Some configurations are too far removed from the scope of engagement of participants, too broad, too diverse, or too diffuse to be usefully treated as a single community of practice. (Wenger, 1998, p. 126)

ALT programme participants are from a broad range of work and professional backgrounds and their interests are diverse. The engagement in the programme is temporary and part-time, and so their central loyalties remain elsewhere.

The community aspect of the MA ODE, however, is less explicitly developed. For example, each MA ODE module has a course guide that sets out the module's aims. The general tenor of the guides can be seen in the following description of the approach in H804: *Implementing Online, Open and Distance Leaning*:

> As for the course's teaching approach, you will find it is designed to encourage learning that is student-centred, resource-based, 'constructivist' and collaborative... It means that within the framework we have set up, we expect you to take considerable responsibility for deciding which aspects of implementing ODL you want to concentrate on, to choose and use suitable resources, to develop your own perspectives, and to contribute to making your group a strong learning tool.

> The success of this depends on collaboration between students. What you get out of it will depend chiefly on what you and your colleagues put into it – especially into the online forums. (H804 Course Guide)

The course guide for H806: *Learning in the connected economy* has the following section which explicitly addresses the kinds of reasons leading to this approach and the limiting of collaboration and community aspects:

> Individual and group activities

> One of the advantages of being connected is the ability to communicate with peers. There are many approaches to learning that focus on dialogue or collaborative tasks, and these can be very beneficial. They also come at a price, however. They result in some loss of freedom and independence, since the learner is reliant upon the interaction of others to fulfil the learning outcomes. We have thus tried to maintain a balance in this course, providing a number of group activities where appropriate, but with the majority of activities being individual. (H806 Course Guide)

However, despite the change of emphasis in each module the idea of working alone as part of a tutor supported group is common to all of the MA ODE modules. The course guides have a common feel and they are usually drafted with reference to previous course guides and the guides of the other courses running in parallel on the programme. Nevertheless there is, unlike the ALT programme, a degree of flexibility that allows for quite distinct module forms in the MA ODE.

The designers of the MA ODE and ALT programmes are both aware of the problems of coordinating students with different work rhythms often across time zones and the programmes reflect differences in their relative scale and in the employment patterns of the their cohorts of students. The small scale of the ALT programme, with a single cohort forming a sole conferencing unit, allowed for a degree of flexibility and personalisation to meet student requirements. On the other hand the MA ODE, though a small programme by OU standards, is still large enough for students to be divided amongst a number of tutor groups. As 'a consequence the course requires a standardised approach to ensure that all tutor groups are treated in a similar manner. This formalisation of processes is also due to the fact that the programme relies on part time tutors who have not been involved in course design. In the case of the ALT programme the course designers are generally the tutors, and there is direct day to day negotiation with students about the progress of the course. In the MA ODE the process is indirect and formalised, because the course was set out by the central course team and any day-to-day negotiation takes place between tutors and students or between tutors and the course team rather than directly with the course designers.

Pedagogical Organisation through Tasks and Activities

Both programmes are organised as a series of activities, around which the students' structure their learning. However, the programmes organise using activities in different ways. On the ALT programme students received a summative assessment at the conclusion of the module and grades were received by students after the module had concluded. Formative assessment took place across the programme as a whole and progression to subsequent modules was expected to take place only after completion of the previous assignment. The internal structure of the ALT programme was that each module fell into three sequential phases. During the first phase students were asked to work on several short tasks individually and to post their responses into the discussion space. The design at this stage was oriented around the tasks and the individual and the coordinated activity of posting contributions only took on a collaborative aspect later, when students were asked to reflect on each other's postings. Prior to the second phase there was a short two day residential school. Students who attended the residential were involved in intensive face-to-face activities and developed a strong group sense. On their return it was noticeable that the energy and online activity of residential students often contrasted sharply with that of the students who had not attended the residential school. As a consequence organisational measures were adopted to help to overcome the different levels of activity, including the distribution of videos of the residential sessions and the formation of mixed groups comprising students who had attended the residential with others who had not.

In the second phase of the modular design students were told to expect greater online activity and the tasks assumed that they would engage in online discussion or, in the case of some modules, group collaboration. It was nonetheless possible to complete this phase in a relatively individual way. Participation was uneven between students and in relation to the same student on different modules. The third phase of each module involved students completing the negotiation with their tutors of a topic for their assignment. For those attending the residential the discussion would have begun with a one-to-one meeting with a tutor while they were at the residential. The agreed topic and an outline were posted to the online space at the close of the second phase, from which point onwards the students largely worked alone to produce their assignments. Interaction between students over the whole module was uneven. In the ALT 04 module in 2004 the low levels of participation in both phase 1 and phase 2 tasks suggested there was a particular problem in that year. However, a comparison with the same module in 2002 suggested this was not the case, and that neither the volume nor the quality of participation in 2004 were noticeably lower. This raises a question about the general level of interaction on the ALT programme and whether this affected the learners' experiences or programme outcomes.

By contrast, assessment on the MA ODE is continuous within each module, with tutor marked assessments inserted throughout, usually coinciding with the completion of blocks of work. It should be pointed out that in this sense, 'blocks' do not correspond to the 'phases' of the ALT programme. Although there is a sense of progression within the modules on both programmes the blocks in the MA ODE are not as distinct in character as the phases of the ALT programme, although it is usual to have an introductory block and a block at the end of the module that allows students to prepare their examinable component submission without being disturbed by online activities. A typical arrangement for assessment on the MA ODE would be as follows:

Table 2. Assignment Guide (H807)

Continuous assessment	Word length	Weighting	Cut off date
TMA01	1300	16%	3 March 2008
TMA02	2000	34%	7 April 2008
TMA03	3000	50%	12 May 2008
The examinable component			
Project	4000	100%	7 July 2008

The MA ODE TMAs are marked summatively by the tutor and provide formative feedback as the module progresses. As noted earlier each module also has a final examinable component (ECA). Typically, this is not a traditional examination and involves work of a similar character to the TMAs, although it is graded differently and does not allow for late submission other than in exceptional circumstances. The ECA is submitted using the OU's electronic tutor marked assessment system (eTMA) and the administration of the ECA adheres to central university procedures, so it is outside the direct control of the course team.

Designing Tasks and Activities

The pedagogical organisation of both programmes manages students' work by setting a series of tasks or activities throughout a course module. This sub-section considers the thinking behind such tasks and activities and compares the ways in which the two programmes managed students' work by relating local practices to the wider institutional framework of the respective universities.

The ALT programme had a pedagogic focus on the design of learning tasks. A learning task in this view was a specification for learner activity. Its design drew on what was known about how people learn, on the tutoring team's knowledge of the academic subject matter and/or their knowledge of vocational competences, and on knowledge of the characteristics of the learners. Examples of learning tasks would include essays, or the development of courseware and the building of relevant artefacts. To be effective it was considered that a task needed to be well-specified, at least to the extent that the chances of a learner engaging in unproductive or unrelated activities are kept within reasonable limits. Its specification was also thought to need a degree of openness that would allow for variability in learner's needs and to encourage a creative response from the students. The tasks for the students in the ALT programme replicated this understanding of design, which originated with the course designers.

Goodyear (Goodyear et al., 2001) one of the originators of the ALT programme makes reference to the distinction between 'task' and 'activity'. In this view tasks are what designers set; they are prescriptions for the work that students are expected to do. Activity is what people actually do. Teachers set the tasks but learners then have to interpret the specifications of the task. The subsequent activity of students is a more or less rational response to the task when understood as a part of the student's overall context. Students constitute their setting, their own learning context out of all the other tasks they have to face, the other calls on their time, their past experiences and their view of what their teachers actually value. It is to be expected that the activity is likely to be different from the task that initiated it. The ALT programme relies on students taking responsibility for their own learning and making their own interpretations of learning tasks. The programme also recognizes that they are busy people and that learning is only one of the things they have to fit into their day.

As discussed by Jones and Dirckinck-Holmfeld (Chapter 1) and Goodyear *et.al* (2001) the distinction between tasks and activities forms part of a broader design philosophy that also informed the ALT programme. The distinction between task and activity is associated with two further distinctions, those between space and place and between organization and community. Together, these three distinctions are referred to as an indirect approach to learning (see Figure 2 Section 1 this volume). In contrast, the MA ODE is built around the idea of activities which are identified by Open University practice as a set of tasks, roles and resources. The word 'activity' is used throughout the course module documentation but it is rarely, if ever, given a formal definition or further development. It is an unwritten assumption of the course documentation that the idea of an activity is well understood and this usage flows directly from the idea of Supported Open Learning.

A review of Supported Open Learning (SOL) in 2004 summarised the state of the practice at the Open University in this way:

> SOL (as it will be referred to in much of the paper), is both a set of practices and a set of ideas and ideals. Its iconic status in the University has meant that conceptions of SOL have to some degree departed from practice. (Swann, 2004)

SOL whilst ultimately aimed at students is focused directly on the associate lecturers – the part time staff contracted to work with students – as opposed to the course team. Associate lecturers were until recently issued with a guide to SOL in their first year of employment, as well as SOL reference files. However, the SOL idea is influential at all levels – 'iconic', as Swann describes it – and it informs the practice of course teams. In the usual pattern of OU courses and modules, activities are non-assessed suggestions for the work that students should do, and they are embedded throughout course materials. Though not assessed themselves activities can be related to later assessments and vary in their scale. For example, on H808: *The e-learning professional* the following activity was set in the fifth unit of the course:

Core Activity 6.1: eLearning as a profession

1. Spend some time (1–2 hours) examining the links provided in the resources section below. Look for and read closely the definitions of elearning professionals or the specifications for education and training courses aimed at elearning professionals. Make notes comparing these specifications with your own education and training, and with the education, training and/or experience mentioned by the members of the H808 course team in the Unit 1 podcast.

2. Read the chapter by Perkin and write a short comment (max 500 words), in your blog or on the course forum, on whether you think his view of modern society is justified. How does Perkin's view compare with alternative descriptions of modern society that you are aware of? (For example, the 'information society', the 'network society' or the 'risk society'.)

3. Read the article by Warrior and use her thoughts on education as a profession to help you in framing your own thoughts with regard to elearning. Write your own preliminary and brief definitions of 'profession', 'elearning' and 'elearning professional' based on your reading, and post them to your blog or the forum.

The level of detailed organisation indicating what a student should do is much higher in the MA ODE than in the ALT programme, which is structured as a process over time but is much less prescriptive about how the work should be carried out. This choice of task specification has consequences, but ones that are not easy to evaluate. Students succeeded in both programmes and produced work that was ratified by external examiners as being of Masters standard, yet one programme provides a great deal more scaffolding than the other and it is not clear from the outcomes whether this is necessary for its success or leads to higher quality.

Technology Infrastructures and the Place of Resources

Both programmes depend upon a central provision of a technological infrastructure around which the course can be devised. Both rely on VLEs provided by the university, a VLE built a Lotus Notes base for the ALT programme and built on a Moodle base for the MA ODE. Though each programme can specify how the technological infrastructure is deployed, the basic systems are centrally controlled and the decisions about major developments in the technological infrastructure are not controlled by the respective course teams. The central provision of the techno-logical infrastructure has some interesting results in terms of a convergence of organizational forms at the programme and course levels. For example, both programmes are organized into course teams that devise the outline of the individual courses, in terms of the resources required and the calendar of events and activities. The course teams reflect a division of labour at an institutional level beyond the control of programme or module designers. The course team structure was reinforced on the ALT programme by the inclusion of representatives from the library and the central Learning and Technology team. At the Open University the course team structure reflects a long tradition in terms of a division of labour and the inclusion of various central units onto course teams.

The ALT programme provided paper based resources which were mailed to all participants. Readings included journal articles, book chapters and for some modules complete books. The use of paper based resources was maintained for a number of inter-related reasons.

- The cost of bespoke digitization and copyright clearance for digital resources has been greater than the cost of paper copies and postage
- The problem for distance part time students in obtaining effective off site access to digital resources
- The problems of integrating digital resources with the existing VLE platform
- Resistance by existing students to entirely digitized materials.

Within UK higher education there is an agreement on copyright that means paper copies can be made at no additional cost to the university and department running a programme. To provide electronic versions the cost of copyright clearance and digitization for journal articles and book chapters was still carried by the university so that it was cost effective to retain paper distribution.

Towards the end of the ALT programme the Heron service was introduced, which digitizes materials and secures copyright clearance (http://www.heron.ingenta. com). Heron began as a national service in the UK which had been developed by the Joint Information Systems Committee (JISC) and is now part of Ingenta, an online publisher. Once digitized, the materials are retained in their digital form so the cost of the process is only borne once by the first user in the UK higher education sector. The ALT programme employed the Heron service to provide digitized reading materials for each module, although paper copies of the materials were also supplied. In part this was a response to the novelty of digitized course texts and the displacement of printing costs onto the students when providing electronic copies. This form of digital delivery has been replaced in the OU by the integration of its library services, so allowing a transition in course delivery to fully networked access of digitised resources.

The MA ODE has now moved away from the delivery of books and articles in paper form to a fully online service. This has been enabled by the above mentioned integration of library services and the development of a single log-in, which authenticates users across a range of services. The single log-in was an important step, as the ALT students had to use their university log-in and password to access the main ALT areas, followed by another password to access materials from the library catalogue. If they wished to access materials from an external (non university) network they needed a further 'Athens' password, which allowed access to a range of digital resources for all UK registered students. The single log-in for MA ODE students, whether taking a single module or the full MA ODE programme, was an essential development towards enabling fully online programmes. For the Open University as a whole this marked a significant development in the SOL model, because the university had previously been associated with the in-house production of high quality resources that were used widely in higher education. The MA ODE has moved towards a light and rapid production model that makes use of resources that are already in the public domain rather than developing bespoke resources for the programme. The Open University faces a choice in the near future in terms of the costs associated with producing bespoke course resources and the potential benefits such course materials have for enhancing the universities reputation.

The Open University VLE programme has set out to create a level of service integration that puts the university fully online. Despite some difficulties during development it has marked a significant shift towards a 'digitally native' institution, which suggests that technological infrastructure is now a key to pedagogic design in individual programmes. Without the type of institution-wide project and invest-ment made by the Open University the kind of course developed for the MA ODE would not have been possible, just as the lack of a similar set of solutions restricted the development of the ALT programme.

One of the claims of networked learning is that it allows relative ease of access to learning materials and resources. The ALT programme shows how complex the process of providing good access can be in practice. The technology does not present itself as a simple artefact rather the technology is immediately a socially mediated form. Resources are enmeshed in a legal framework of ownership that has more to do with property rights than any technological imperative. Access to materials and resources for teaching and learning is not a simple matter. Some materials such as conference papers and articles appear freely on the Web. But these are often ephemeral settings, with links that move or disappear on a regular basis. In order for them to exist in a properly secure setting they need to be embedded in a social and organizational infrastructure that takes on some of the roles, such as preservation, that libraries have hitherto fulfilled. Once this has been achieved these resources often disappear from the publicly accessible Web and become hidden behind password protection and within database structures. The creation of single log-on authentication and a public 'commons' for educational materials was therefore a political, legal and social process well beyond the control of a single educational programme.

CONCLUSIONS

A common feature of the ALT and ODE programmes is that they are both based on student relationships that are not strongly collaborative though they emphasise a social view of learning. The ALT programme, though it drew on the idea of a community of practice consciously tried to incline students to engage with their external professional and work communities at least as strongly, if not more strongly, than the programme itself. At any one point the students were an uneven mix of novices and experienced participants. On average three or four new students joined the programme at each module start. The new students did benefit from being able to model their participation on more experienced students but as there was no fixed cohort there was only a limited chance of community development within either the module or the full programme. The MA ODE programme is similarly modular in structure, geared primarily towards registration for individual courses, although many students do complete the full programme. Like the ALT programme, the participants in each module will, at any one time, comprise a mixture of those who have already completed other modules and those completely new to the pro-gramme. However being conducted entirely at a distance, it does not have the periodic residential sessions of the ALT modules, so there is even less opportunity to develop a programme based community.

Both programmes appear to fit the description of a system that includes the possibility for weak as well as strong ties forming the basis of a network. The MSc ALT programme ran successfully from the late 1980s until being replaced by a Doctoral programme in January 2008. It has had good outcomes and was explicitly mentioned in the teaching quality assessment audit of the department, which obtained a maximum 24 score in the review. The MA ODE programme is still developing after 10 years and is also recognised as having a consistently high quality. Both programmes are cooperative in the sense that the tutors and students work together to accomplish the sequence of activities during each presentation. This cooperation clearly involves students and tutors in extensive negotiation of meaning about the module content and how it can be understood. It also involves making sense of the module documentation and what the tutors' intentions might be in organising the activities in the way that they have.

However, I think it is apparent that both programmes have a focus on flexibility and the needs of individuals in relation to their learning. The first phases of the ALT modules were largely individual tasks in which the students interacted for the most part with course texts and only used the online facility to post their responses. The work and professional setting of the student provides the social context for this individual activity at least as much as it is provided by the ALT programme itself. These relations between students and the programme resemble those described by Wenger as a constellation of practice and by Brown and Duguid as a network of practice (Wenger, 19989, Brown and Duguid, 2001). The relationships amongst students and between tutors and students can be thought of as weak links. Students on the course remain largely in their work place communities and they are expli-citly encouraged to elaborate this experience in relation to course materials and activities.

Both programmes illustrate the ways in which the design and development of a networked learning programme is constrained by institutional and infrastructural arrangements beyond the course itself. A striking difference between the two programmes is the way the programmes are staffed and how the staffing reflects the wider institutional patterns of the universities. The MA ODE programme reflects the OU core and periphery workforce in having a core course team and associate lecturers responsible for the most of the day-to-day contact with students. The ALT programme, in contrast, follows a model in which the staff who conceive the course are then involved centrally in the tutoring/moderating and assessment processes. In these ways both programmes reflect institutional patterns in their organisation. Despite their different institutional origins it is striking that both programmes have come to a similar system for registration with a programme structure that allows for individual course/modular registration of students.

A key feature of both programmes is the organisation of student activity through the allocation of tasks. These tasks are closely related to the learning resources supplied for each course or module. As distance learners the students are highly dependent upon easy access to a wide range of course and supplementary materials. The systems allowing such access are only partially under the control of the programme teams. Some of the bodies supplying digital resources, such as the library, are based within the institutions. Other suppliers are part of a national or international framework supplying both infrastructure and services, for example JISC and various publishers. The nature of the supply of digital resources for teaching and learning suggests the relationships can be best understood in terms of networks because a networked understanding, as the experience of the learner and the capacity of the programme team depend heavily on a particular coming together of a set of loosely coupled elements.

ACKNOWLEDGEMENTS

This chapter was written with the assistance of the ALT programme team at Lancaster University and the MA ODE team at the Open University. I would like to thank Vanessa Watts, who carried out the research on the ALT 04 module and course recruitment as part of the CHEXIT EU-USA exchange scheme, and Dr Maria Zenios, who has assisted in the development of the ALT case study. Some materials for the case study of the Open University MA were provided by Simon Rae, who's help with the case study was greatly appreciated.

REFERENCES

ALT Handbook. (undated). Lancaster, UK: CSALT Lancaster University. Retrieved April 30, 2007, from http://www.lancs.ac.uk/fss/courses/edres/alt/

Brown, J. S., & Duguid, P. (2001). Knowledge and organization: A social-practice perspective. *Organization Science, 12*(2), 198–213.

Castells, M. (1996). *The information age: Economy, society and culture volume 1. The rise of the network society.* Oxford, UK: Blackwell.

Castells, M. (2001). *The internet galaxy: Reflections on the internet, business, and society.* Oxford, UK: Oxford University Press.

Goodyear, P., Jones, C., Asensio, M., Hodgson, V., & Steeples, C. (2001). *Effective networked learning in higher education: Notes and guidelines.* Lancaster, UK: CSALT, Lancaster University. Retrieved April 30, 2007, from http://csalt.lancs.ac.uk/jisc/

Jones, C. (2004). Networks and learning: Communities, practices and the metaphor of networks. *ALT-J, The Association for Learning Technology Journal, 12*(1), 82–93.

Jones, C., Dirckinck-Holmfeld, L., & Lindström, B. (2006). A relational, indirect, meso-level approach to CSCL design in the next decade. *International Journal of Computer-Supported Collaborative Learning, ijCSCL, 1*(1), 35–56.

Jones, C., & Esnault, L. (2004). The metaphor of networks in learning: Communities, collaboration and practice. In S. Banks, P. Goodyear, V. Hodgson, C. Jones, V. Lally, D. McConnell, & C. Steeples (Eds.), *Networked learning 2004: Proceedings of the fourth international conference on networked learning 2004* (pp. 317–323). Lancaster, UK: Lancaster University and University of Sheffield.

McAndrew, P., & Weller, M. (2005). Applying learning design to supported open learning. In R. Koper & C. Tattersall (Eds.), *Learning design: A handbook on modelling and delivering networked education and training* (p. 412). Berlin: Springer-Verlag.

Swann, W. (2004). *Supported open learning: Reflections on a dynamic system.* The Open University.

Wellman, B. (2001). Little boxes, glocalisation and networked individualism. In T. Ishida (Ed.), *Digital cities 2* (pp. 3–15). Springer-Verlag, Berlin. Retrieved May 20, 2008, from http://www.chass.utoronto.ca/~wellman/publications/littleboxes/littlebox.PDF

Wenger, E. (1998). *Communities of practice: Learning, meaning, and identity.* Cambridge, UK: Cambridge University Press.

Chris Jones
Institute of Higher Education
Open University, UK

OLA BERGE AND ANNITA FJUK

OPERATING OUTSIDE REGULAR OPENING HOURS

Learning Design and Institutional Change

"To program is to understand"

Kristen Nygaard[1]

INTRODUCTION

This paper presents and discusses networked learning courses that operate outside the regular hours of traditional institutional offerings. The learners in this particular case were adults, committed to their daily jobs of work, but nevertheless fully motivated to expand their competencies in the area of computer technology known as object-oriented programming and modeling. The anticipated outcome for each individual taking part was either an improvement in their daily work place performance or the attainment of a new work position. In this case then, productive learning is very much related to the practical relevance of the course to each of them. In line with the basic argument of this volume, i.e. learning can never be directly designed (Dirckinck-Holmfeld, Jones & Bernström, this volume), the challenge was to organize a networked environment in which both the teacher and the learners were all operating productively, in accordance with the objective of learning object-oriented programming.

The organization of productive networked environments is, however, a particular challenge when the courses are offered as an add-on to an institution's existing administrative and technological infrastructure. Such offerings may often lead to substantial extra work for the teachers of the course because some of the usual support functions and institutional routines are not in place (Fjuk, 1998). Arguably, to organize for productive learning environments when the administrative infra-structure has not been adjusted accordingly, requires mechanisms that make it easy to reuse experience and knowledge across semesters (Berge, 2006). In this chapter we suggest that the specification IMS Learning Design (LD) is one approach to meet this challenge. IMS LD (Koper, 2005) aims at promoting exchange and interoperability of digital learning content, with a particular focus on the reuse of teaching strategies and educational goals. IMS LD makes it possible to reify understanding of what constitutes a productive learning environment, and so carries much potential for ensuring that such an environment maintains adequate flexibility (Berge, 2006).

L. Dirckinck-Holmfeld, C. Jones and B. Lindström (eds.), Analysing Networked Learning Practices in Higher Education and Continuing Professional Development, 139–154.
© 2009 Sense Publishers. All rights reserved.

By means of the case study, this chapter explores the challenges of reusing learning resources across two semesters in a networked course on object-oriented programming, and the potential of IMS LD to assist institutional change through such reuse. The meso-level analysis of the empirical data is conducted with the help of cultural-historical activity theory.

The subject of the course that provides the case study is presented first, followed by a section on the research method. The subsequent section presents findings from the empirical study. Then the IMS Learning Design specification is presented, followed by a section discussing how issues identified in the study can be addressed with the help of IMS LD. The chapter ends with a section for concluding remarks.

THE CASE: INTRODUCTORY OBJECT-ORIENTED PROGRAMMING

The course discussed in this chapter was established as part of an initiative to enlarge the constituency of university-level programs in information technology in western Denmark. This initiative, IT University West, is an educational network of four universities established in 1999. IT University West offers programs for both full- and part-time students, the latter targeted at people seeking continuing education. The course 'Introduction to object-oriented programming' (IOOP) was adapted from a campus-based course that had been offered by Aarhus University, part of the IT University West network, for more than a decade. IOOP was first offered as a part-time, networked course in the spring semester of 2003.

Learning Objectives and Pedagogical Approach

The knowledge domain addressed in the course, object orientation, denotes a specific approach to software construction. It is a way of understanding complex phenomena through the analysis and design of executable computer programs (Madsen et al., 1993). In line with the Scandinavian heritage of object orientation, the principal focus of the IOOP course is a systematic and conceptual way of modeling (Knudsen & Madsen, 1990). That is, the emphasis is on constructs that describe concepts and phenomena, rather than on instructions for computers or on the management of program descriptions. Given this view, a central objective is to learn systematic ways of implementing general models and obtain a deeper understanding of programming processes. Hence, it is considered important that the students achieve hands-on experience and develop practical skills, as well as abstract knowledge on the basic object-oriented concepts.

Driven by the needs of the target group and the learning objectives of the course, the pedagogical approach in IOOP was informed by facets of apprenticeship learning (e.g. Nielsen & Kvale, 1997). This pedagogical approach focuses on the learner's participation in a community of practitioners, where the teacher or a more experienced peer legitimizes the skills and knowledge of the individual learner. Mastery does not reside in the teacher alone, but in the community (of which the teacher is a part) and on the structuring of the community's learning resources. Furthermore, the apprenticeship-inspired approach requires good communicative conditions for reflection- in-action and for making the actions of the teacher visible and a source of identification (Nielsen & Kvale, 1997). For example, the teacher should be allowed to articulate and think aloud in terms of both natural and scientific language, as well as in showing the pragmatics of programming.

Course Organization and Learning Resources

The IOOP course was organized as a distributed, networked course. Most activities in the course were structured around mandatory assignments designed as programming exercises. These assignments, together with other learning resources such as course readings, examples, exercises, and video material, were collected in weekly memos. These were published on the course web site for 12 of the 14 weeks of the semester.

The students were expected to work individually or in self-organized groups during the week. In addition to this, an online meeting was conducted each week. The intention of the course design was to treat topics based on the individual student's experiences in solving the weekly assignment in these meetings.

The online meetings were mediated by real-time video streaming from a part of the teacher's PC monitor. Using the Windows Media Player, the students could see the teacher's PowerPoint presentations and text documents, his actions in various programming and modeling applications, etc. There was a corresponding audio stream relaying the teacher's voice. In order to support interactions among the participants, a text-based Instant Messaging (IM) conference was set up in conjunction with the real-time audio and video streams. The IM sessions were set up as private conferences, where the students were invited to join at the outset of the meetings. A teaching assistant also participated in the meetings; her role was to set up and maintain the IM conference, and conduct private IM sessions with the teacher (to provide reminders, for example) and with students who were experiencing technical problems. The video and audio streams from the meetings were captured, indexed with time stamps according to topics, and made available to the students on the course website.

In addition to the networked activities, the students met physically for three 2-day seminars during the semester. These weekend seminars were conducted on the University of Aarhus campus.

METHOD

The primary aim of the study of IOOP was to investigate how learning resources were used and reused in the course, and what the experienced challenges were regarding this issue. In order to understand this practice, we found it important to gain insights into the rationale behind the course design, how teachers implemented the design principles into their teaching, and how the learners used the learning resources in their learning processes. Furthermore, in order to explore the potential benefits of using standards and specifications facilitating learning resource reuse in this situation, we were interested in obtaining an understanding of why these practices occurred and how the design rationale was implemented across semesters of the course. Against this background, the study was designed as an embedded case study

(Yin, 2003), comprising two constituent studies IOOP 03 (autumn 2003) and IOOP 04 (spring 2004).

The IOOP 03 Case Study

The IOOP 03 course was organized as part of a Masters program in software construction. Some of the learners participated as a part of their Master's degree, others attended only this course. Most of the learners had prior knowledge in programming (not necessarily object-orientation) and stated clearly that their motive for participating in the course was related to daily or future work practice. The teacher was one of the two people who designed the course, which was first offered during the spring of 2003. The autumn 2003 course started with a weekend seminar and ended with the final examination. Twelve weekly memos were published.

Different types of data were gathered. The focus of this chapter is institutional aspects of learning resource reuse. Therefore, the interviews with the teacher and teaching assistant constituted the primary source of data, together with the analysis of the learning resources. The other data was used as background for the interviews, observation of online activities (including 10 of the 14 weekly online meetings), and reading of postings on the discussion board. Documents and learning resources available on the course web site were also gathered for analysis. In addition, data was collected by observing one weekend seminar out of the three given, which included video recordings of some events. Finally, in-depth interviews with nine learners, the teacher, and the teaching assistant were carried out just after the final examination. In addition, one interview with the teacher took place early in the semester, focusing on the course design and its rationale. In this instance of the course 22 learners attended. There was one teacher and one teaching assistant. Both authors carried out the case study.

The IOOP 04 Case Study

The IOOP 04 course was organized as part of a Masters program in multimedia design. As with the previous semester, some of the learners participated in the course as a part of their Master's degree, while others attended only this course. The primary motivation for many of the learners was to gain insights into how a programmer works and not necessarily to become a programmer themselves. While the teaching assistant was the same as in the previous semester, the teacher was new to the course.

As with the IOOP 03 case, the course started with a weekend seminar and ended with a final examination. Twelve weekly memos were published. Four face-to-face weekend seminars were held during the semester, the last one a one-day event for a question and answer session and summarization of the subject matter. This seminar was arranged three weeks before the final examination. Twelve learners attended this semester of the course.

In a manner similar to that in the preceding case study, data was collected by observation of online activities, primarily the online meetings (10 of 14) and postings to the discussion forum. Additionally, the weekend seminar was observed by passive participation. In-depth interviews were carried out with four learners, the teaching assistant, and the teacher. The data gathered also included documents and learning resources available on the IOOP web site. As with the IOOP 03 study, our findings in this chapter are primarily based on data from the interviews with the teacher and teaching assistant. The first author carried out this case study.

Analytical Framework

The theoretical framework for our analysis is cultural historical activity theory (Engeström, 1987; Engeström, Miettinen, & Punamäki, 1999), which is founded on a sociocultural perspective on human activity (Leontiev, 1978; Vygotsky, 1978, 1986; Wertsch, 1991). Our analysis is based on a careful search for contradictions – or experienced challenges and areas of tension – in the events and processes we observed as well as in the in-depth interviews conducted.

The concept of contradictions is a powerful analytical instrument for studying reuse in a perspective of institutional change. In an activity theoretical perspective, contradictions are the engine of change and development as well as a source of conflict and stress (Cole, Engeström, & Vasquez, 1997). Contradictions are not necessarily the same as conflicts. Rather, they are historically accumulating, structural tensions (Engeström, 2001). "Activity theory sees contradictions as sources of development; activities are virtually always in the process of working through contradictions." (Kuutti, 1996, p. 34). Contradictions are inevitable features of activity, and "new qualitative stages and forms of activity emerge as solutions to the contradictions of the preceding stage of form." (Engeström, 1987, p. 91). In searching for areas of tension, we were interested in problems, ruptures, breakdowns, and clashes concerning reuse of knowledge and experiences across semesters. Furthermore, the identified tensions were driving forces for suggesting improvements or developments connected to making the networked environments productive.

FINDINGS AND DISCUSSION

In line with an activity theoretical framework, the presentation of data is focused on illustrating experienced challenges – with respect to the reuse of learning resources across the two semesters of IOOP, and on issues that might be particular to the organization of the course to accommodate part-time students.

The teacher of the IOOP 03 course stated that he found it important to not require the students to purchase software licenses in order to participate, as this would represent a barrier for enrolment. This concern was given weight when he selected mechanisms for operationalizing the course design. One example of this is the constellation of applications selected for conducting the online meetings. Commercial groupware like Centra or Macromedia Breeze would accommodate the requirements posed by the online meetings, but the licensing fees were prohibitive. He therefore had to find other solutions. The Windows Media Player is a standard part of the Windows operating system, and did not require any extra installations for the students. The instant messaging application, Yahoo! Messenger, was available for download without license fee. However, selecting client software that was easily available for the students did not mean that the software required for arranging the online meetings from the teachers' side was easily accessible. The application Windows Media Encoder was used in conjunction with the Windows Media Server for creating and publishing the live video stream from the teachers' PC, and the set-up for establishing the video stream was far from straightforward. Commenting on his experiences with this in the interview conducted after the completion IOOP 03, the teacher said:

> [There are] some technical issues that ... I would never imagine that I would concern myself with whether I have a fixed or dynamic IP address at home, how I could ensure that my PC have the same internal and external IP address, and other such issues.[2]

The Windows Media Encoder and Server was not part of the regular technical infrastructure at the University of Aarhus, which meant that the teacher had limited support in setting up the software correctly. "There are some support areas that are not there, areas you as an educator are confronted with and have to deal with", the teacher remarked on the process of preparing the technology for the online meetings.

When asked if there were any parts of creating IOOP as a networked course that he regarded as more time consuming than creating a co-located course, the teacher expanded on the problem regarding technical support:

> It is clear that there are some issues, when thinking about what is more time consuming, some technological problems you don't run into when creating a traditional course. If you want to use application sharing, so that the students can see what's going on, and it doesn't work: what do you do then, who do you ask, and so forth? And you spend some time, that you don't have to spend time on in a traditional course, where you can just tell the IT staff 'we would like to have BlueJ and Java SDK' and whatever you might need to have installed on all the student PCs – and it gets done. Then you don't have to worry more about that. There were not many places we could go to get help for what we wanted.

Because some of the applications chosen for operationalizing the IOOP 03 course design were not part of the established institutional technological infrastructure, institutional mechanisms for supporting set-up of these were lacking. In addition, lack of alternatives to the technology during the progress of the course made the issue of support even more problematic:

> It is a stress factor that one is so dependent on technology. One night [during an online meeting] things went down for me, and that was a stressing experience, if I may say so. Where in a traditional world, one has many more things one could do [...] If it were a traditional lecture, what would I do if the lights went out? I would have found another room, sent ten students out to buy candles, or something. Then you always have some more or less good

back-up solutions. We are much more dependent on that everything works – and there are many things that do not work.

Here, the teacher emphasizes that the participants were dependent on the technology for carrying out the online meetings; a technological breakdown has more significant implications in a distributed setting than in a co-located setting. But the teacher also pointed out some challenges regarding the co-located meetings. He attributed these challenges to characteristics of the target group:

It is a challenge for universities to move from having only the traditional full-time students to also relate to adult students that also are working. This does not have to do with courses being offered as distance education, this has something to do with the target group. Their demands are different, they have some other expectations – with respect to service, for example – and they have different opening hours.

The IOOP 03 teacher expanded on the organizational challenges with respect to the students' 'opening hours', using examples from the weekend seminars that took place on the university campus on Friday afternoons and Saturdays.

If you arrive [on campus] and the doors are locked, it is not easy to have someone come to let you in. And if there are some PCs that are not working, you must ask some students to share computers. This has of course something to do with... if this were a traditional course, there would always be some kind of back-up – if it had been within regular opening hours, so to speak. Then I could have phoned the staff and said 'this is not working', and it would have been fixed in two minutes. You cannot do that, when you are outside regular opening hours. And 'outside regular opening hours', that is starting to mean something. [...] When we are having lunch [during the weekend seminars], why do we have to send all those people down to [the shops] to buy something to eat? There are signs that must be put up, I have to remember to ask a secretary to put them up. So there are lots of organizational and administrative problems to be addressed by doing it this way.

In summary, the IOOP 03 teacher pointed out a number of issues arising from operating outside of established institutional practice. These are related both to the use of technology that was not part of the university's established portfolio, and to conducting seminars outside the university staff's regular working hours. The new practices introduced by IOOP were necessary to accommodate requirements of the new target group: adults engaged in day-time jobs. Thus, the challenges that confronted the IOOP 03 teacher can be seen as tensions grounded in the institutional change of including the adult work-force in the constituency of the university.

In studying the reuse of learning resources across the IOOP 03 and 04 semesters, we found that one of the resources reused by the IOOP 04 teacher was the online meeting construct, which we see as reuse of a course design component (Berge & Fjuk, 2006). Like the teacher before him, the IOOP 04 teacher found it demanding to get the video stream up and running, even though he phoned the IOOP 03 teacher for advice:

It was really hard to get the video streaming to work. There was no end to how many times I had to change the set-up in order to get the video stream through, and then I could not be sure if they actually could hear what I said, if they could receive it, and all those things. So that has dominated large parts of the course, all those things have just given me problems and worries.

It was vital that this particular constellation of ICTs worked properly because of its central position in operationalizing the online meetings and lack of alternatives in case of break-downs. Furthermore, no support from the university's staff was available. We therefore argue that the IOOP 04 teacher would probably have benefited from having the configuration of the video server, as well as the client PC, documented.

The conditions for teaching in a networked environment such as the IOOP online meetings are different from traditional lectures. The IOOP 04 teacher was new to this form, and he had little time for preparing for the course. Due to low enrolment, the decision to arrange the course was taken only two weeks before the scheduled start. In the interview after the end of the course he stated "I was thrown into it, and uncharacteristically for me, I was quite unprepared." A few months before the course, he had an informal two-hour discussion with the IOOP 03 teacher about the course. However, as it was not yet decided if he was going to teach the course, they did not go into details about conducting the online meetings.

One important didactical technique employed by the IOOP 03 teacher was to 'think aloud' during the online meetings. That is, he made a point of verbally reasoning about his actions when working in the BlueJ programming tool. The ability to do so was one of the reasons for selecting the particular constellation of ICTs for conducting online meetings (Bennedsen, Berge, Fjuk, & Caspersen, 2004). In the interview with the teaching assistant, she noted that this was an issue that the two teachers probably had not discussed. She observed that the IOOP 04 teacher did not 'think aloud' in the first online meetings, and she found this problematic. After the online meetings, the teacher and the teaching assistant usually had a telephone meeting where they discussed their experiences from the meeting and planned the week ahead. The issue of 'thinking aloud' was one of the topics they took up. "One of my tasks", the teaching assistant said, "was to convey some of the ideas, why things were as they were, what the idea behind it was." Later on in the interview she stated that "I have become more aware of my role as a carrier of culture, it was not something I had expected to be as extensive as I have come to realize."

The teaching assistant's role during the online meetings included setting up and inviting all students to the IM session, conducting private IM sessions with students having technical difficulties, and to support the teacher by providing reminders etc. This latter task was done by conducting a private IM session with the teacher in a separate window. "I soon realized", she said, "that the messages I wrote to him in that window did not get read". Reflecting on the teacher's situation, she continued:

It is not easy, if you haven't done it before. You should think aloud, you should do it [the programming], and you should manage the whole thing. It also has something to do with how you organize your windows.

Reusing the course design component for online meetings involves the acquisition of operational skills for teaching under the conditions constituted by this form. This includes such apparently trivial issues as finding an adequate layout of windows on the desktop, as pointed out by the teaching assistant. Issues pertaining to operational skill, didactical techniques, and parts of the design rationale were not fully communicated across the two semesters between the teachers. In IOOP 04, one important function maintained by the teaching assistant was to pass on knowledge about 'best practice' from earlier semesters.

In our study of IOOP learning resource reuse (Berge & Fjuk, 2006), we also found that the IOOP 04 teacher reused a variety of learning materials from the previous semester, such as examples, exercises, assignments and instructional videos. However, locating much of this material was not easy. "I had to sift through literally hundreds of files to find what I wanted", he stated in the interview. All the material was stored on a university server, but it was poorly structured and located together with a large amount of unused material, according to the IOOP 04 teacher.

In this section we have identified a number of challenges that an institution traditionally concerned with co-located, full-time students, is likely to meet when conducting a networked course for geographically distributed adult workers. The focus has been on issues concerning the online meetings, but the discussion also includes practical concerns regarding co-located meetings. Moreover, we have identified problematic aspects with reusing some of the learning resources across two semesters. In the following, we will discuss how IMS Learning Design might help alleviate these problems.

REUSING LEARNING RESOURCES

One of the essential aspects of creating productive learning environments is the maintenance of good practices established through earlier experiences. Such culturally developed insights on how students' learning activities can be structured and supported are reified within the computer systems used in the learning environments. Our study, however, includes organizational aspects of productive learning environments. These issues often go beyond what is captured in the various ICT-applications used in the learning situations, and we will therefore discuss alternative mechanisms for expressing experience on what constitutes productive learning environments.

Our approach in this chapter is to discuss such a process in terms of learning resource reuse.

IMS Learning Design

Early work on the reuse of digital learning resources focused on learning content, in the form of learning objects. Learning objects are educational resources that are modular units, which can be assembled to form larger constructs, such as lessons or courses (Wiley, 2000). The primary purpose of learning objects is to facilitate reuse, where the basic idea is that a learning content component can be part of various courses (Downes, 2004). McCormick (2003) states that "efforts to build into Learning Objects (LOs) a definite pedagogy are doomed to failure. Past experience of the development of LOs indicates that low-level and unsophisticated views of learning are encapsulated in them." (Ibid, p. 2). McCormick argues that the pedagogy should be put elsewhere in the learning environment constructed by the teacher. IMS LD (IMS, 2003a, 2003b, 2003c) was designed to facilitate the reuse of such contexts. More specifically, the specification was created to promote exchange and interoperability of e-learning materials, with a focus on the reuse of teaching strategies and educational goals. A key task of the working group behind IMS LD is "the development of a framework that supports pedagogical diversity and inno-vation" (IMS, 2003b, p. 4).

One of the fundamental ideas with IMS LD is to associate educational content with information describing its instructional strategy. This information can then be used for adapting the educational content to a pedagogical approach different from the one for which it was designed. "By labeling the strategy and the components of the strategy in a common, machine-readable manner, the context of a learning opportunity can be managed separately from the content itself" (IMS, 2003a, p. 4).

This does not represent a rejection of the concept of learning objects. "It is important to reuse learning objects, but we must bear in mind that they are not courses; they are the resources needed to perform learning activities. Reusing a learning resource in a new course still requires us to integrate the object into the course activities and method." (Koper, 2005, p. 12). IMS LD represents an approach where learning resources are referred to in the learning design, meaning that learning objects can be replaced without altering the learning design. Learning resources are understood to be both digital and non-digital learning objects, as well as services needed during the teaching-learning process. Services can be discussion forums, chat rooms, monitoring tools, search facilities, etc.

The objective of IMS LD is to provide a containment framework of elements that can describe any design of a teaching-learning process in a formal way. This is achieved by providing a 'meta-language' which can be used to describe a wide range of pedagogical approaches. This meta-language is based on an extensive examination and analysis of many pedagogical approaches carried out by the Open University of The Netherlands (Koper, 2001). In the meta-language, a relatively small vocabulary is used to express, in clear terms, what the various pedagogical approaches ask of the learners and support staff. Generally, a learning design describes the way that "people in specific groups and roles engage in activities using an environment with appropriate resources and services" (Oliver & Tattersall, 2005, p. 21). The IMS LD is based on the metaphor of learning design as the script of a theatrical play. A person gets a role in the teaching-learning process, which can be a learner or a staff role. The person works towards certain outcomes by performing activities within an environment. The environment consists of the appropriate learning objects and services to be used during the performance of the activities. Methods specify the dynamic aspects of the learning design. A method is designed to meet learning objectives, and presupposes certain prerequisites. The method consists of one or more concurrent play(s); a play consists of one or more sequential act(s) and an act is related to one or more concurrent role-part(s) (IMS, 2003b, p. 11).

The IMS LD specification is complex, and it requires a substantial supporting framework of components and services if it is to transform the experience of learning technology (Wilson, 2005). Two of the key architects of the specification state that "the principles and standards are defined, but most of the tooling still has to be developed" (Koper & Tattersall, 2005, p. vi). Because IMS LD is a quite recent specification, there is not a large body of empirical evidence supporting that it actually solves pressing problems in educational practice. Our study explores one possibly important application area of the specification – that of open continuing education programs.

The IMS LD is one of many possible realizations of the more general concept of learning design. Three key ideas in learning design are that people are engaged in learning activities, learning activities may be structured in learning workflows, and learning designs might be recorded for sharing and reuse (Britain, 2004). The complexity of IMS LD, the lack of proven tools, and the work involved in creating designs, all represent barriers to adoption of IMS LD (McAndrew & Goodyear, 2007). An alternative approach to documentation of good practice, facilitating reuse of learning designs, is pedagogical patterns. The intent is to summarize expert knowledge of practice in a compact form and communicate this to those who need it (Eckstein, Manns, Sharp, & Sipos, 2003). Pedagogical patterns often formulate didactical strategies, providing practical guidelines for teachers on issues such as motivating students or arranging seminars. McAndrew and Goodyear see patterns as "something that will not be reused directly but can help informed teachers build up their own range of tasks, tools or materials by drawing on a collective body of experience." (McAndrew & Goodyear, 2007, p. 94). Further, they state that patterns are different from the IMS LD paradigm, "in which the design must be specified tightly enough to be implemented within a player: the pattern is *not* intended to supply a complete solution but rather to give enough guidance to support human intervention and variation in each reuse." (p. 94).

A learning design specified with IMS LD can be regarded as a plan for a learning process. When dealing with open-ended and ill-structured problems, it is neither possible nor desirable to prescribe the students' course of action in detail, in advance. Suchman (1987) argues that every course of action depends in essential ways upon its material and social circumstances. In accordance with this view, "learning can never be wholly designed, only designed *for* (i.e. planned in advance) with an awareness of the contingent nature of learning as it actually takes place." (Beetham & Sharpe, 2007, p. 8). Thus, we see learning as only indirectly related to designs and plans (see also Dirckinck-Holmfeld & Jones, this volume). We are attentive of the issue of 'over-scripting' students' learning processes (Dillenbourg, 2002), and we do not advocate teachers' reuse of IMS LDs as complete solutions for setting up courses. We are, however, interested in exploring how institutions can accumulate experience on creating productive learning environments, and how the IMS Learning Design specification can be used for creating *resources* for teachers in their planning.

From an institutional perspective, it is important that knowledge gained through the experience of conducting a course in one semester can be used in consecutive semesters. When the teacher of the course is replaced, some kind of knowledge transfer is necessary. Such a process can take place through personal communication and documentation. The examples from IOOP (described in the previous section) indicate that such knowledge management might be especially important in situations where the courses are part of an institutional transformation, because some of the usual support functions and institutional routines are not in place. In addition, the issue of knowledge management was elucidated by the short notice given to the IOOP 04 teacher before the course started, which left little time for preparation. Despite the discussions about IOOP between the 2003 and 2004 teachers, and the continuity represented by the teaching assistant, some hard-learned lessons from IOOP 03 were lost. We suggest that documentation pertaining to a number of the issues we raised in the previous section would be beneficial for both the IOOP 04 teacher and students. Moreover, we will discuss how IMS LD can be an appropriate framework for creating a structured documentation of the IOOP course.

One of the major issues identified in the previous section was the challenge of establishing the technology to enable online meetings. We have argued that this issue is of particular importance because the online meetings could only be conducted with the help of the technology and that there was no institutional technological support for this constellation of ICTs. The configuration of the Microsoft Media Encoder could have been documented as part of an IMS learning design. The initial set-up of the online meetings could be defined as an activity of the type support-activity, allocated to a person in the role of 'staff', to be performed once before the first online meeting. Detailed instructions on how to set various parameters in the Media Encoder application and the operating system on the teacher's PC would be specified in a web page, referenced to by the activity-specification element of activity.

Naturally, there is little to be gained for using IMS LD for specifying this activity only. But regarded as part of a larger whole, where the technical set-up of the online meetings is one of a sequence of activities to be performed in preparing and conducting the course, a learning design could be an appropriate mechanism for documentation. Our study indicated that practical facilitation of the co-located meetings, for example, also could be streamlined by the help of a learning design. One activity could be defined for room reservation, notifying a staff member to put out signs giving directions to the off-campus students, making lunch arrangements, etc.

One important aspect of IMS LD is that it allows course designers to be explicit about the pedagogical model underlying the design (e.g. Koper, 2003). The specification provides mechanisms for describing the rationale for the course design. In the previous section we described how the IOOP 04 teacher did not employ the 'think aloud' technique in the first online meetings. It was only after he discussed this with the teaching assistant that he became aware of the importance of using this didactical technique. We therefore propose that documentation of this approach in an LD activity description of the online meetings would constitute a more robust mechanism for sustaining productive practices with respect to the online meetings. The activity description could contain the rationale for organizing learning activities as online meetings, as well as a description of which didactical techniques were suggested for operationalizing them. New teachers would then be better equipped to make informed choices about which techniques to use, and might inspire them to try new approaches. New teachers could thus enrich the body of knowledge contained in the learning design by documenting their experiences using other approaches.

We have also seen that teaching under the new conditions formed by the online meetings requires new operational skills, including seemingly the mundane, such as the arrangement of windows on the teacher's desktop. Tips and 'how-to' instructions regarding practical matters in managing online meetings can also be included in learning design activity descriptions.

In our study of learning resource reuse between IOOP 03 and 04, the 04 teacher also pointed out difficulties in locating the physical files of the learning materials that he wanted to reuse from IOOP 03. These resources can be regarded as learning objects. In order to alleviate such problems the learning materials to be reused could be furnished with metadata and referenced in the learning design. More specifically, an activity in a learning design can reference an environment which in turn contains references to the learning objects used in that activity. This illustrates one of the strong features of IMS LD compared to other approaches to learning objects. The learning design provides a containment framework for learning objects; a model for expressing the semantic relationship between different types of learning objects in the context of specific educational settings.

In summary, we have discussed how constructs provided by IMS LD can facilitate reuse of various elements of a course, ranging from practical arrangements and configuration of software to didactical techniques and learning materials. However, documentation of learning designs requires extra work. It might be difficult for educators to find the time and resources for creating learning designs as part of their everyday work processes. Moreover, such documentation is inherently subject to "Grudin's Dilemma" – who does the job and who gets the benefit. That is, the learning design might be of limited benefit for the course designer who creates it – it is people who make use of it in later courses who will probably benefit the most. In activity theoretical terms, the challenge is to facilitate situations where the creation of learning designs is part of the object of the activity. The networked course IOOP was created by the help of project funding through the IT University West program, and has been a part of Aarhus University's operations after the initial establishment. One opportunity to create learning designs is in situations like this, where institutional change is initiated by project funding.

CONCLUDING REMARKS

We have discussed the reuse of networked learning course design as a meso-level activity in this chapter. This discussion is motivated by desire to understand the conditions needed for sustainable deployment of networked learning systems in educational institutions. We have approached the discussion by micro-level analysis of learning resource reuse in the collaborative networked course, and discussed this practice in relation to the IMS Learning Design Specification.

The IOOP course was part of an effort to include open continuing education in the offering from the university, and can as such be regarded as part of an institutional change program. IOOP thus operated partly outside established institutional practice, particularly with respect to technology and 'regular opening hours'. This situation resulted in a number of challenges for the teachers, as there was a lack of institutional support and routines in those areas. We have argued that documentation of the course design, including its rationale, would alleviate the work of teachers reusing (parts of) the course design and the learning resources accompanying it. We have explored the creation of learning designs conforming to the IMS LD specification as a feasible approach to documentation of the course design.

In conclusion, we suggest that the potential of IMS LD for creating artifacts that support the transformation of educational institutions' practice is worth pursuing. Documentation in the form of learning designs is especially important for sustaining innovative networked learning environment designs and new institutional practices, because critical institutional support for teachers might be lacking when these are introduced.

NOTES

[1] http://en.wikiquote.org/wiki/Kristen_Nygaard
[2] All quotes are translated from Danish by the authors

REFERENCES

Beetham, H., & Sharpe, R. (2007). An introduction to rethinking pedagogy for a digital age. In H. Beetham & R. Sharpe (Eds.), *Rethinking pedagogy for a digital age* (pp. 1–10). London: Routledge.

Bennedsen, J., Berge, O., Fjuk, A., & Caspersen, M. (2004). Learning object-orientation through ICT-mediated apprenticeship. In Kinshuk, C. Looi, E. Sutinen, D. Sampson, I. Aedo, L. Uden, & E. Käköen (Eds.), *Proceedings of the 4th IEEE international conference on advanced learning technologies* (pp. 380–384). Los Alamitos, CA: IEEE Computer Society.

Berge, O. (2006). *Reuse of digital learning resources in collaborative learning environments.* Unpublished PhD, University of Oslo, Oslo.

Berge, O., & Fjuk, A. (2006). Reuse of learning resources in object-oriented learning. In A. Fjuk, A. Karahasanovic, & J. Kaasbøll (Eds.), *Comprehensive object-oriented learning: The learner's perspective* (pp. 131–155). Santa Rosa, CA: Informing Science Press.

Britain, S. (2004). A review of learning design: Concept, specifications and tools [Electronic Version]. *JISC Project Report.* Retrieved from http://www.jisc.ac.uk/uploaded_documents/ACF83C.doc

Cole, M., Engeström, Y., & Vasquez, O. (1997). Introduction. In M. Cole, Y. Engeström, & O. Vasquez (Eds.), *Mind, culture, and activity. Seminal papers from the laboratory of comparative human cognition* (pp. 1–21). Cambridge, UK: Cambridge University Press.

Dillenbourg, P. (2002). Over-scripting CSCL: The risks of blending collaborative learning with instructional design. In P. A. Kirschner (Ed.), *Three worlds of CSCL. Can we support CSCL* (pp. 61–91). Heerlen, the Netherlands: Open Universiteit Nederland.

Dirckinck-Holmfeld, L., & Jones, C. (2009). Issues and concepts in networked learning. In L. Dirckinck-Holmfeld, C. Jones, B. Lindström (Eds.), *Analysing networked learning practices in higher education and continuing professional development*. Sense Publishers.

Downes, S. (2004). Learning objects: Resources for learning worldwide. In R. McGreal (Ed.), *Online education using learning objects* (pp. 21–31). London: Routledge.

Eckstein, J., Manns, M. L., Sharp, H., & Sipos, M. (2003, June 25–29). *Teaching from different perspectives.* Paper presented at the Eighth European Conference on Pattern Languages of Programs, Irsee, Germany.

Engeström, Y. (1987). *Learning by expanding: An activity-theoretical approach to developmental research*. Helsinki: Orienta-Konsultit.

Engeström, Y. (2001). Expansive learning at work: Toward an activity theoretical reconceptualization. *Journal of Education and Work, 14*(1), 133–155.

Engeström, Y., Miettinen, R., & Punamäki, R.-L. (Eds.). (1999). *Perspectives on activity theory.* Cambridge University Press.

Fjuk, A. (1998). *Computer support for distributed collaborative learning. Exploring a complex problem area*. Unpublished Dr. Scient Thesis, University of Oslo, Oslo, Norway.

IMS. (2003a). *IMS learning design best practice and implementation guide. Version 1*. Retrieved October 6, 2005, from http://www.imsglobal.org/learningdesign/ldv1p0/imsld_bestv1p0.html

IMS. (2003b). *IMS learning design information model. Version 1*. Retrieved October 6, 2005, from http://www.imsglobal.org/learningdesign/ldv1p0/imsld_infov1p0.html

IMS. (2003c). *IMS learning design XML binding. Version 1*. Retrieved October 6, 2005, from http://www.imsglobal.org/learningdesign/ldv1p0/imsld_bindv1p0.html

Koper, R. (2001). *Modeling units of study from a pedagogical perspective - the pedagogical meta-model behind EML*. Retrieved October 5, 2005, from http://hdl.handle.net/1820/36

Koper, R. (2003). Combining reusable learning resources and services with pedagogical purposeful units of learning. In A. Littlejohn (Ed.), *Reusing online resources: A sustainable approach to E-learning*. London, Sterling: Kogan Page.

Koper, R. (2005). An introduction to learning design. In R. Koper & C. Tattersall (Eds.), *Learning design. A handbook on modelling and delivering networked education and training* (pp. 3–20). Berlin: Springer.

Koper, R., & Tattersall, C. (Eds.). (2005). *Learning design. A handbook on modelling and delivering networked education and training*. Berlin: Springer.

Kuutti, K. (1996). Activity theory as a potential framework for human-computer interaction research. In B. A. Nardi (Ed.), *Context and consciousness. Activity theory and human-computer interaction* (pp. 17–44). Cambridge, MA: The MIT Press.

Leontiev, A. N. (1978). *Activity, consciousness, and personality*. Englewood Cliffs: Prentice-Hall.

McAndrew, P., & Goodyear, P. (2007). Representing practitioner experiences through learning designs and patterns. In H. Beetham & R. Sharpe (Eds.), *Rethinking pedagogy for a digital age* (pp. 92–102). London: Routledge.

McCormick, R. (2003). Keeping the pedagogy out of learning objects. *EARLI 2003*. Retrieved July 6, 2005, from http://www.eun.org/eun.org2/eun/Include_to_content/celebrate/file/KeepingPedagogy OutOfLOs3v2.doc

Oliver, B., & Tattersall, C. (2005). The learning design specification. In R. Koper & C. Tattersall (Eds.), *Learning design. A handbook on modelling and delivering networked education and training* (pp. 21–40). Berlin: Springer.

Suchman, L. A. (1987). *Plans and situated actions. The problem of human machine communication.* Cambridge: Cambridge University Press.

Vygotsky, L. S. (1978). *Mind in society*. Cambridge: Harvard University Press.

Vygotsky, L. S. (1986). *Thought and language*. The MIT Press.

Wertsch, J. V. (1991). *Voices of the mind: A sociocultural approach to mediated action.* Cambridge: Harvard University Press.

Wiley, D. (2000). Connecting learning objects to instructional design theory: A definition, a metaphor, and a taxonomy. In D. Wiley (Ed.), *The instructional use of learning objects* (pp. 1–35). Bloomington, IN: The Agency for Instructional Technology and AECT.

Wilson, S. (2005). Architectures to support authoring and content management with learning design. In R. Koper & C. Tattersall (Eds.), *Learning design. A handbook on modelling and delivering networked education and training* (pp. 41–62). Berlin: Springer.

Ola Berge
Telenor Research & Innovation
InterMedia
University of Oslo, Norway

Annita Fjuk
Telenor Research & Innovation
InterMedia
University of Oslo, Norway

LONE DIRCKINCK-HOLMFELD, JANNI NIELSEN, BO FIBIGER,
OLUF DANIELSEN, MARIANNE RIIS, ELSEBETH K. SORENSEN,
BIRGITTE HOLM SØRENSEN AND WINNIE RITTERBUSCH

PROBLEM AND PROJECT BASED NETWORKED LEARNING

The MIL Case

*Complex social networks have always existed but recent technological
developments in communications have afforded their emergence as a dominant
form of social organization.*

Barry Wellman

INTRODUCTION

The Masters in ICT and Learning (MIL) is a postgraduate study programme for
professionals in this field, drawing on the principles of problem and project based
learning. In this chapter we discuss processes involved in using MIL to create a
productive networked learning community. In so doing we refer to the framework
proposed by (Jones & Dirckinck-Holmfeld, 2008; Jones, Dirckinck-Holmfeld, &
Lindström, 2006). The chapter focus on:
– How to understand productive learning within an academic masters course for
  professionals
– Identifying the challenges in getting a networked learning infrastructure to support
  productive learning?
   MIL demonstrates best practice for a research based masters program. A survey
(MIL, 2008) of the average exams results shows that the students are doing excellent.
So far, 398 people have fulfilled the course examinations with an average result of
10,0 on a grade scale from 00,0 to 13,0 (10,0 means excellent, while 8,0 is average).
It is therefore assumed that it will provide valuable insights for understanding issues
related to the design of productive learning environments to look closer into MIL.
   We begin by giving some background on MIL including the overall pedagogical
design. This is followed by a discussion of the two main issues: productive learning
and infrastructure. At the end of the chapter we consider the issues that are particular to the MIL case and what may be issues for networked learning more generally.
   The presentation and discussion of the MIL learning environment builds on data
from the authors' long term engagement as researchers, managers, and teachers and

*L. Dirckinck-Holmfeld, C. Jones and B. Lindström (eds.), Analysing Networked Learning Practices
in Higher Education and Continuing Professional Development, 155–174.*

from previous studies using primarily a qualitative approach. The insider-relation to MIL has strengths and limitations. The strengths are in-depth firsthand experiences with the learning environment, while the direct involvement may also provide blind spots, which may limit the critical scope of the analysis.

PRESENTING MIL

The Masters programme in ICT and Learning (MIL) is a postgraduate study programme for professionals. To enter the program requires at least two years of relevant practice and the academic requirements of a bachelor degree or similar formal competencies. The students have a very diverse background. Approximately two thirds of the students come from educational practices (all levels) and one third from business (human resource, ICT and software development). The distribution between men and women is fifty-fifty. The students come from all over Denmark (including the Faroe Islands and Greenland) and some from neighbouring countries such as Norway and Sweden. The programme is provided in Danish.

MIL was established in 2000, a unique programme within Danish higher education. It is the result of collaborative (and ongoing) development between five of the country's universities: Aalborg University, Aarhus University, Copenhagen Business School, The Danish University School of Education, and Roskilde University under the umbrella of IT West[1] (Danielsen, Dirckinck-Holmfeld, Sørensen, Nielsen, & Fibiger, 1999; Fibiger, Dirckinck-Holmfeld, Nielsen, Sørensen, & Danielsen, 2000, 2. eds.) The rationale behind the collaboration is multi-faceted: to create a joint masters program provides volume; it increases the diversity of the learning environment, engages students with different and leading research environments and provides a framework within which the founders can work together. Furthermore, it gives an opportunity to explore – on a long term basis – the strengths, the challenges and the weaknesses of a virtual organization, and of networked learning.

Pedagogical Design

A networked learning environment for problem and project based learning is not an assembly of software and computers (Tolsby, this volume). A networked learning environment is a lived practice made up of: People working together on formulating and solving problems, a curriculum to be studied, an organization, a learning infrastructure, including software and computers, and a pedagogical design to tie all this together. Inspired by Winograd's notion of design (Winograd, 1996), MIL may be described as bringing the users, the context and the system together by the organising principles of problem and project based learning.

Problem and project based learning (POPP/PBL)[2] builds on principles of productive learning through joint project work, shared meaning construction and object orientation. ICT as infrastructure, tool and artefact plays a central role in the mediation of communication, collaboration and learning. POPP/PBL borrows ideas from production practices as described by Friedrich Engels: "The tool specifically symbolizes human activity, man's transformation of nature: production" (Marx and

Engels, Selected Works, 1953 p. 63, quoted in John-Steiner & Souberman, (1978)). The core principle of POPP/PBL is that the students learn and acquire knowledge when transforming a problem area by using contemporary tools and resources. This is not restricted to the transformation of nature, but certainly directed towards social and psychological activities as well.

POPP/PBL is a dynamic pedagogy where participants bring new problem areas to be studied. The problems to work with are not pre-defined by the curriculum or faculty, but brought in by the students and further elaborated in discussions and negotiations between peers, faculty and external stakeholders. In most cases the problems to be investigated are related to students' own work practices. It is especially the problem formulation, in conjunction with problem solution that brings dynamics to the learning environment. Students are forced to critically rethink the problems to be studied: What is the problem? Who has the problem? When did the problem become a problem? Why is it a problem? How can the problem be solved?

MIL is based on a pragmatic concept of POPP/PBL and ICT – a networked version of POPP/PBL. The MIL model (see below) incorporates a series of integrated didactical principles: problem formulation, enquiry of exemplary problems, participant control, joint projects, dialogues, interdisciplinary approaches, and action learning (Dirckinck-Holmfeld & Fibiger, 2002). Furthermore, it stimulates students and faculty (facilitators, supervisors, lecturers, professors) to engage in a shared enterprise around the research problems, (the problem/and the thematic framework for the semester), and to develop a shared repertoire of concepts, theoretical and methodological approaches through course work. The model enhances the opportunities to develop a community of practice because it is adaptable to the engagements of the participants, while at the same time it creates interdependencies among them. Further more; it also supports the individual's construction of meaning through the construction of shared understanding, and through negotiations, confrontations and engagement in relation to the long-term development and change of (professional) identity (Dirckinck-Holmfeld, 2002; Fjuk & Dirckinck-Holmfeld, 1997). The basic structure is illustrated below (fig. 1).

A Flexible and Blended Learning Environment

MIL is organised as a flexible and blended learning environment with online module activities supported by on-campus seminars and workshops. There are four course modules, one project module and the thesis – a total of 60 ECTS points. Most students study part time over two years, although it is possible to enrol as a full-time student or even to take single modules at a time. The online learning environment is supported by face-to-face interaction in three on-campus seminars, a one-day project seminar on-campus, and one day on-campus for the final examinations. (The face-to-face seminars are represented by the stapled lines in Figure 1). These seminars are hosted in turns by the partner universities in Jutland or in the Copenhagen area[3].

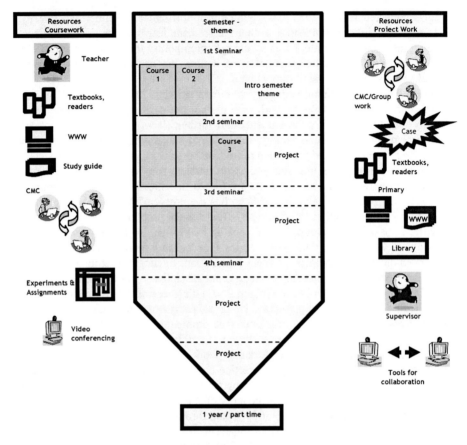

*Figure 1. MIL – a problem and project based networked learning environment
(first presented Dirckinck-Holmfeld, 2002)*

The overall design of the learning environment reflects some of the principles for dramaturgy as suggested by Laurel (1993). It has a clear marking of start and end, a clear rhythm instantiated through the face-to-face seminars and tasks (Dirckinck-Holmfeld, Sorensen, Ryberg, & Buus, 2004), and there is explicit guidance and expectation of the roles played by coordinators, faculty/supervisors and students.

Networking the environment enables students to form groups according to interests and which are not restricted by geographical or temporal boundaries. With respect to the concept of networking, MIL is a combination of strong and weak ties[4] (Granovetter, 1973). Students are organized in big groups with 40–50 students in each year group. At the big group level, the students connect occasionally with each other and share experiences, ideas and information, while those in the project group work closely together based on strong ties. The relationships among the students in the big group can be seen as a network of interest (Brown & Duguid, 2000), while we would argue that the project groups are kinds of communities of practice (Wenger, 1998), sharing a common enterprise; i.e. the problem and the project, a mutual engagement both academic and social, and a shared repertoire of theories and ways of working.

Within MIL, collaboration is the overall approach to learning, not because of ideological reasons but because we find the approach productive in the process of learning, knowledge acquisition and meaning making. This is especially true for the first year project and the final thesis. However, course modules are also based on smaller tasks and case-work, to stimulate collaborations, discussions, and integration of theory and practice. Further more the students are not only working on their own in the groups, but they have close contact to faculty and supervisors throughout the processes, who are facilitating and critically supporting the inquiry process and the shaping of the project.

MIL applies different methods in the various courses. Some courses are built around a dialogue approach (Sorensen & Takle, 2003) in which students are asked, in groups in the asynchronous environment, to present and discuss the course literature and relate to own experiences. These courses are very important in training the students in virtual asynchronous dialogues, within a kind of boundary-crossing laboratory situated between academia and practice. Other courses are informed by a socio-constructionist approach asking the students to develop a product together, and in other instances by a case-oriented approach asking them to investigate a real problem, for example from their professional life. In general, all courses use a flexible approach in the sense that the students themselves introduce the problems, cases, and examples to be studied. In the spring semester they form groups and produce a research/action learning project, integrating and going beyond the various course activities.

The traces for a collaborative environment can be found in the number and quality of postings, the length of the treads, and in the students' project reports. These are documented in a number of articles and theses (Dalsgaard, 2007; Dirckinck-Holmfeld et al., 2004; Fibiger, 2005; Fibiger et al., 2004; Sorensen & Takle, 2003).

PRODUCTIVE LEARNING

In the previous section we defined productive in relation to the Marxist conception of production and the use of tools as transforming nature, social and human issues. In the following we will follow this definition by looking at productive learning as transformation and change of the learners' identity. In a previous article (Dirckinck-Holmfeld et al., 2004) within MIL we discuss transformation and change of identity in relation to four criteria:
– Change of practice
– Change of competences
– Change of membership

- Change of trajectory.

The discussion is based on an open questionnaire given to the students after they have fulfilled the MIL programme (Ritterbusch, 2003). We are presenting a summary of the results below.

Table 1. Student evaluation 2003

- As a whole the study must be said to have fulfilled all my expectations to the education
- Very large benefit... - beyond comparison that of my different educations from which I have gained the largest professional/personal benefit
- To me MIL has to a very large degree been a process of formation – for good and worse :-)
- I have benefited very much from the education that has been very relevant and close to practice
- It has certainly been an education that has moved me forward. I have gained insight in working methods at an academic level and thereby I have overcome my educational feeling of inferiority (in the daily life I am associated with a lot of academics). I have become ready to take on tasks that I would never before MIL have dared to accept (e.g. doing a presentation on Problem Based Learning)
- The study area of my thesis has meant something to my future career
- Beneficial
- Exciting assignments/projects
- Good comradeships
- Good well functioning arrangements
- Great planning (possibility for improvisation a big strength)
- Beneficial with teachers very rich on initiative and from various institutions
- Extremely good with seminars
- Good that groups were formed from the start
- Possibility of working in depths with the different subjects
- Possibility for networking
- Good theoretical teaching and foundation
- Great variety in the study
- Good mixture between theory and practice
- The structure of the subjects – the modules supplement each other well – both professionally and pedagogically
- The cross-institutional structure means (contrary to other educations) that one gets 'hands-on' experience with educational cultures
- Good possibilities for testing out theories in practice
- The exemplary structure of many of the courses e.g. when we work with portfolios we do so in a portfolio environment
- Fellow students with different experiences make the shared 'database' big and increase the value of discussions, group work etc.

> - Freedom of choice in relation to assignments/projects ensures that everybody can select something that is relevant to them
> - The education is based on collaboration
> - The dynamics between process and product was – seen in large perspective – very beneficial

Change of Practice

Coming from business and education, public and private, higher education and primary education, being designers, teachers and system administrators MIL consists of a complex pattern of interwoven professional identities and memberships in a diversity of practices. Through the engagement in course discussions, project work and assignments the students are confronted with this mixture of professional identities, while new methodologies and approaches urge them to negotiate and renew their current practices and experiences. "Fellow students with different experiences make the shared 'database' big and increase the value of discussions, group work etc." (Ritterbusch, 2003)

The professional identity is challenged in a number of ways. Students with a college background is thrown into an academic culture; students coming with a technical or science background are exposed to humanistic and social science approaches and vice-versa for the students coming with a humanistic background.

Change of Competencies

Theoretical work in connection with the first hand experiences offered by MIL develops a social and technological imagination in the application of ICT and learning. "The exemplary structure of many of the courses e.g. when we work with portfolios we do so in a portfolio environment" (Ritterbusch, 2003). Furthermore, problem formulation and flexibility give the students methodological skills, which are applicable in their professional practice. "Freedom of choice in relation to assignments/projects ensures that everybody can select something that is relevant to them" (Ritterbusch, 2003)

Change of Membership

In order to change their identity and membership, students are urged to be involved in academic activities beyond those they encounter as normal study activities. They are invited, for example, to familiarise themselves with academic contexts such as conferences, international research projects and publishing. In this way they gradually become members of the academic community. "It has certainly been an education that has moved me forward. I have gained insight into working methods at an academic level, and thereby I have overcome my educational feeling of educational inferiority (in my daily life I associate with a lot of academics). I am now ready to take on tasks that before MIL I would never have dared to accept (e.g. giving a presentation on Problem Based Learning)" (ibid. p. 1).

MIL is also engaged in current social and political realities, and seeks to strengthen critical, democratic and change oriented values and awareness in relation to ICT and learning. Many students bring this on to their professional practice. "To me MIL has to a very large degree been a process of formation – for good and worse :-)" (ibid p. 2)

Change of Trajectory

The above examples illustrate that the learning trajectory created by the course's pedagogical design offers an inherent potential for change of identity. However, pedagogical design apart, the changes in student identity and trajectory are also due in no small measure to the level of engagement, by both students and teachers, in course discussions and project work.

Following (Goodyear, Jones, Asensio, Hodgson, & Steeples, 2001), we argue that learning can never be directly designed, only designed *for,* (see also Wenger, 1998). Learning is only indirectly related to what we design and plan. The activities, spaces and organisations that we design rely on being inhabited by others, the particular teachers and learners who 'enact' our designs. (Goodyear et al., 2001) have summarised this as *an indirect approach to learning* (see fig. 2 in Jones & Dirckinck-Holmfeld, this volume). Goodyear et al. argue that we can design the tasks, the organisation and the space, in which learning may take place, however we can't be sure how the tasks are carried out, organisation becomes community or spaces become places. Following Goodyear et al. (2001) we can say that learning in principle is ungovernable. However, we also find that it is possible to create more insights into what works, in order to stimulate and facilitate for productive learning, for example through case studies as in this book. Using MIL as a point of departure, the concept of productive learning has been elaborated as transformation and change of identity in relation to four criteria: Change of practice, change of competences, change of membership and change of trajectory. In that optic, a productive masters' learning environment for professionals goes beyond acquiring specific competencies, and is a comprehensive and unified process related to the notion of change of identity.

THE LEARNING INFRASTRUCTURE

Building MIL up as a networked learning environment in virtual space, between universities that are widely geographically dispersed, requires a very robust and lively learning infrastructure. For MIL and other networked masters programmes, the virtual environment *is* the primary infrastructure – not the buildings.

Bygholm & Nyvang (this volume) reflect on learning infrastructures. In common usage 'infrastructure' refers to the generally subordinate and relatively permanent parts of an undertaking. In a city we might think of the sewerage system, the water supply, the electricity or gas utilities and the communications systems, such as roads and telephony, as infrastructures.

Bygholm & Nyvang draw on the works of Star and Ruhleder and suggest that we interpret ICT *in use* as infrastructures that both shape and are shaped by practice. They go on to propose that we understand infrastructure as a relational concept. "Thus we ask, when – not what – is an infrastructure" (Star & Ruhleder, 1996). In line with this approach Guribye & Lindström (this volume) suggest that infrastructure should be understood as relational and as an ecology (see also Nardi & O'Day, (1999)), while Jones & Dirckinck-Holmfeld (this volume) propose that infrastructures are complex environments rather than singular tools or artifacts.

The MIL infrastructure serves as a good example of a complex learning environment. The complexity in tools, background organisations and support staff is described in table 1:

Table 2. MIL infrastructure

Infrastructure elements	Background organisation	Support staff	Comments
Overall access to the learning environment takes place through the web page: www.mil.aau.dk	e-Learning Lab, which is a research lab, has an experimental server making services available on an experimental basis, e.g. Typo3. Hum-IKT, which is the operating ICT office maintains the server	MIL secretary, e-Learning Lab secretary, and Hum-IKT	The web page is designed in Typo3. External consultants have provided the basic design. Web design and updates are carried out by the MIL secretary. Structural web-design changes are supported by e-Learning Lab, while Hum-IKT maintains the server
Asynchronous VLE-system, FirstClass Collaboration Suite	ELSA, which is the operating e-learning office maintains and makes the overall design of the VLE-system, FirstClass Hum – IKT maintains the server MIL secretary and the teachers make the specific design of the MIL learning environment	MIL secretary ELSA Hum-IKT	FirstClass is the basic infrastructure for MIL. All information related to the programme, all course activities and communication with supervisors take place in FirstClass. All participants are expected to use FirstClass on a regular basis.
Synchronous video, Adobe Acrobat Connect Professional	A national organisation 'Forskningsnettet' within the Ministry of	Forskningsnettet MIL secretary	Used by students in their project work, and for course activities. Some teachers also use

	Science, Technology and Innovation provides relevant shared ICT services for the Danish universities and research institutions.		Connect Professional in the supervision.
Peer-to-peer tools and web 2.0: Skype, Windows Messenger, Google Docs, Blogs, ELGG	Students bring in tools to use. MIL secretary supports and give hands on courses to teachers. Some of the tools are also an object for the module on ICT tools	Students MIL secretary Teachers related to the ICT module	The students (and teachers) use a number of peer-to-peer tools and web 2.0 tools to support their collaboration and communication.
Other communication and collaboration tools: Centra, Moodle, Quickplace…	Students' work place	Students and students' workplace e-Learning Lab	The students bring in tools from their work place and make them also available for the other students. The tools are used to support the students' project work as well as they are used to design prototypes of learning environments.
Tools to support project- and coursework: Camtasia, reference tools, word processing….	Students workplace MIL secretary/MIL ICT-course Aalborg University Library	Students MIL secretary Teachers related to the ICT module	Students are expected to use a number of tools in relation to the course- and project work. MIL provides some of the tools for a cheaper price. The library provides other tools, for example reference tools
Streaming video of selected face-to-face course activities	Video streaming service Hum-IKT	Video streaming service	Aalborg University has a facility that offers a video streaming service. The service has to be paid for by the hour. Video

			streaming is used to record many of the face-to-face activities to be re-used by the students in the virtual periods, or by the students who can't attend the face-to-face activities
Administrative ICT, student registration, examines, economic system	AAU - administration	AAU administration MIL secretary	The administrative system is primarily used by the MIL secretary. Students use it in relation to registration, enrolment for examinations etc.
Library resources, library repositories, national and international databases, help desk,	Aalborg University Library	Aalborg University Library - specific MIL-service with online help	Regular services, online help, materials are sent free of charge
Thesis repository	Aalborg University Library	MIL secretary	All student theses are uploaded to a repository and can be used for free by other students and the public.
Archive (FirstClass)	MIL secretary Hum-IKT	MIL secretary	Students, teachers and administrators get access to archived FirstClass environments in order to reuse and learn from previous experiences.
Student counsellor (telephone, skype, e-mail, FirstClass & Second Life)	MIL secretary, Student counsellor, Office for Conti-nuing Professional Education, & IT West	Office for Continuing Professional Education, & MIL secretary	Student counselling takes place through virtual and physical means. The student counsellor – a former MIL-student can be met in Second Life.
Physical ICT laboratories	Administrative offices at the five partner universities, ICT operational offices, MIL	Building department ICT – operational offices. MIL secretary	To run the face-to-face seminars in different physical locations pre-requisites a huge

	secretary. At Aalborg University seminars are located at the library, who also takes care of some of the needed technologies, except FirstClass.		effort of the MIL secretary and the local organisers. The universities have different administrative rules, provide different service level, and are also very different regarding support and flexibility.
Physical seminars, food etc.	External provider, MIL secretary	MIL-secretary	Not all the university canteens or refectories can be used outside regular opening hours. MIL therefore organises lunch and dinners through an external provider
Physical seminars, cleaning	Five partner universities	Building-control-department MIL-secretary	Not all partner universities have a cleaning service outside regular opening hours. The secretary therefore also has to do some clean-up

INFRASTRUCTURE, AN ORGANISATIONAL ISSUE

Building this kind of infrastructure is linked closely to organisational issues. Its composite character makes it complex to handle, and it's fair to say that universities as systems are not yet ready to handle this on a routine basis. In the case of MIL, the management at all partner universities have been very supportive, but the respective administrative systems are in general not yet geared up to support and maintain this kind of complex learning infrastructure.

To address the complexity it is valuable to use the activity system model as developed by Engström (Engström, 1987, 2004). The model can be used to illustrate the different objectives, rules etc. that govern the different groups and background organisations involved in developing and maintaining the learning infrastructure (see also Nyvang & Bygholm; Pilkington & Guldberg, this volume). There are different activity systems involved in realising the infrastructure for a networked learning environment such as MIL, each having different objects, rules, norms etc. The main activity systems to be identified from a learning point of view are those involving teachers, coordinators and students, who are dependant on all parts of the infra-structure. But then there are also a number of other actors involved, particularly in the realisation and maintenance of the infrastructure; for example, Hum-ICT, the library, the MIL secretary and external agencies. To illustrate the complexities of such a system we can contrast the activity system of Hum-IKT and MIL.

A potential conflict between MIL (teachers, students, coordinators) and Hum-IKT is easy to identify. First and foremost, the role of the infrastructure related to the objective of the activity system is different. For students and teachers, the VLE and the homepage make up the most important part of the infrastructure. Without access to these systems, via a productive functionality and an intuitive interface, the students can not interact with and participate in most of the learning activities. Previous research within MIL has shown the following patterns in the student use of the VLE system:

> *Enthusiasts* make up around 15 percent of the students. They go for all infor-
> mation and are very active in conferences on nice-to-know information. They
> are on the VLE daily, often in more than one session, and also at the weekends.
> They have read all the contributions to the conferences and are very active in
> meta-conferences and social activities on the web. *The pragmatists* also make
> up around 15 percent of the students. They go for need-to-know information,
> and are only on the VLE once or twice a week. They focus on the obligatory
> course conferences and participate only in debates as part of the curriculum.
> The rest of the students: *the main streamers* make up around 60–70 percent.
> They are on the VLE nearly every day, depending on their need for information
> and their activities in civil and professional life. They are involved in the
> course conferences and the meta-conferences. From time to time they can be
> involved in conferences with nice-to-know information, but it is not a must
> and many of these conferences are unread (Fibiger et al., 2004)

But for Hum-IKT to provide a suitable infrastructure for MIL is only one among many other competing tasks. The objective of the infrastructure also varies within the different activity systems. For Hum-IKT issues such as security and stability, easy administration and accessibility have higher priority, while among students and teachers/coordinators the interface and pedagogical functionality are the prominent considerations. Moreover, from a pedagogical point of view there is a continuous stream of new systems and software to integrate, which need support and maintenance, which is in conflict with the policy of many institutions, who only support and maintain one learning management system.

In the case of MIL, the collaboration with Hum-IKT has been exceptional, and due to flexibility and goodwill from both organisations the online infrastructural services have fitted well with the needs of MIL. Often both partners have gone beyond the call of duty and have developed services that go far beyond their routine practice. In that sense, MIL has also served as a form of a test bed for new software and infrastructure solutions for Hum-IKT.

The different elements in the infrastructure (see Table 2) play different roles and are designed with different purposes. The VLE activities are, generally speaking, designed from an academic perspective focusing first and foremost on providing the necessary tools for the students' interaction and collaboration. Tools for supporting written communication and scholarly dialogues have been given particular priority. This may explain why 85 percent of students primarily use the online learning environment for strict scholarly purposes whilst only 15 percent use it as a nice place to 'hang out'. However, when we look at the physical seminars we see they are designed from a holistic perspective, giving the learning environment an agreeable balance of quality, terms of aesthetics, room functionality, the food, community, conviviality etc. and the academic performance.

This situation can be explained by the different metaphors that have informed the design. When using a tool metaphor it makes sense to regard the online infrastructure as subsidiary to the central activities of interaction, dialogues and mutual construction of knowledge – in that sense it should be as invisible as possible. However, when we design for community building, engagement, shared enterprise and mutual knowledge construction, and apply an ecological perspective, then much more complex issues are at play about which metaphors to use to guide the design of the virtual learning environment regarding the functionality, the aesthetics and the experiences to be provided for. In MIL it seems as if both kinds of design values have been incorporated. The tool perspective is dominating the VLE infrastructure, while the physical infrastructures have to a greater degree, built-in values of pleasure, conviviality, enjoyment and aesthetics along with the academic activities, and in that sense the learning environment is balanced. However, it raises such questions as: what will happen if more of the activities are moved to the VLE and the physical seminars are reduced? What will happen when the generation of students who have grown up with 3D games (e.g. Second Life) enter the programme? Will they be satisfied with a primarily text-based virtual learning environment?

For networked learning the focus on infrastructures for learning is important in order to understand the productivity of a learning environment. And in relation to this is the conceptual discussions on what is an infrastructure for learning, how to design and organise very important issues. The MIL case has provided insight into the complexity of the learning infrastructure in form of tools, background organisations and support staff. This has been a big eye-opener for our self to realise the composite nature of the infrastructure, and it supports very well the view that infrastructure are complex environments rather than singular tools or artifacts. The study also question the general view, that infrastructures are subordinate and relatively permanent parts of an undertaking (Bygholm and Nyvang, this volume). Rather the study supports a relational and an ecological approach suggesting that the infrastructure should be viewed as an active part of the learning environment affording the diverse practices. The study has especially made us aware that the dominating tool-perspective may be should be questioned in a networked learning environment for professionals, and instead new metaphors based on more holistic experiences mirroring the concept of productive learning as transformation of identity should guide the design.

THE PARTICULAR AND THE GENERAL

The MIL case has some specific properties, which has to be considered in order to generalise the findings. One specific property is the organizational arrangement to enable five universities to collaborate. This arrangement enriches the learning environment to the benefit of the students, teachers and coordinators. Another specific finding is the strength of the specific PBL-approach for continued professional development, providing an appropriate balance between shared commitment and freedom, focused and peripheral engagement, work-based anchoring and theoretical and conceptual work. Furthermore, the MIL design has realised a delicate balance of a number of elements that help the learning community flourish: diversity, problem orientation, collaboration through projects, construction, access to expertise, relationships, shared enterprise, community cultivation, flexible participation, open ended and engaged conversations (see also (Wenger, White, & Smith, in preparation).

Some of the findings from the case study on MIL are specific to the constellation of participants under observation, and maybe also to the overall Danish cultural context for MIL. However, we will suggest that a number of the findings are general for networked learning environments:

- Virtual learning environment tools also make virtual organizations possible. However, realizing them is a complex matter implying organisational, pedagogical and technological challenges
- Infrastructures are complex and must be carefully designed to afford both the virtual and physical activities in accordance with the overall values and objectives of the learning community. Re-use of learning activities and reifications of traditions and practices are important aspects of learning infrastructures
- The design rationale of socio-emotional (aesthetics) and cognitive-academic (rational) values must interact with and correspond to the objects of the learning community
- A productive and flourishing learning environment for professionals implies balancing: diversity, problem orientation, collaboration, construction, supervision, academic challenges, relationships, shared enterprise, cultivation, sponsorships, flexibility, open ended and engaged conversations, coordination, negotiation and inter-dependencies. POPP/PBL may serve as an organising pedagogical model for this
- Productive learning for professionals focus on transformation of identity. This transformation concerns change of practice, change of competencies, change of memberships, and change of trajectories.

CONCLUSIONS

The MIL case study has focused on the conditions for creating a productive and flourishing learning community. The attention has been on the meso-level aspects of designing for productive learning. We have not looked in detail at the single teaching and learning activities, but focused on MIL at an activity system level with a special interest in the learning infrastructure, the pedagogical principles and the notion of productive learning.

In MIL, the students, teachers and the steering committee form a learning community, sharing the enterprise to investigate and conduct experiments with ICT and learning. The learning community is diverse, and participants have a flexible relationship. During some periods they are deeply engaged, and MIL is in the front of minds, while in other periods, such as when the pressure of professional work is more demanding, MIL is sent to the back. In addition, the different tasks and activities within MIL call for different levels of engagement from the students. The collaboration and commitment, which constitute the core principle of POPP/PBL, afford a shared engagement, but also imply a big effort of coordination work in the project groups, while the engagement at the global MIL level is more fluid. Furthermore, the learning community is not static or stagnated, but is continuously under creation and recreation as a reaction to the engagement and actions of the participants. The flourishing development is dependant on a number of orientations with such elements as diversity, problem orientation, collaboration, construction, supervision, academic challenges, relationships, shared enterprise, cultivation, sponsorships, flexibility, open ended and engaged conversations, interaction between theory and practice, analysis and transformation, coordination work, and a supportive and engaging infrastructure as important design focus.

In the section on infrastructure we asked: what is a learning infrastructure? We found out that the MIL infrastructure is rather complex and we wanted to address the importance of this issue. When designing for networked learning environments, designers are very concerned with which LMS or VLE to implement. However, when taking MIL as an example it becomes obvious that learning infrastructures are much more complex environments, where technical, organisational and pedagogical elements must be considered. As such, infrastructures are the meeting point between the macro – institutionalized university policies, technological design values etc. – and the micro – the way that students, teachers and managers are enacting the infrastructure processes.

The case study raises the question: should a learning infrastructure be as invisible as possible and act as a kind of a subsidiary for the interaction and collaboration, and/or should it serve as a more active means for being and belonging; allowing for rich, aesthetic and experience-based learning activities? Using the metaphor of a learning ecology, we should regard the infrastructure as an active part of the learning community, and the way that it interacts with the participants and learning activities should be in accordance with the overall values and objectives of the learning community. In some communities a minimalist, functional online infrastructure fits well, while in others the requirements and expectations are much richer and demanding.

In line with a socio-cultural perspective, our focus on productive learning has been on the productive aspects of learning. However, opposite of main-stream socio-cultural perspective (for example Engeström's expansive learning (Engeström, 1987) we have focused less on the societal aspects, and more on the transformative aspects of learning related to the professionals in the form of change of identity. Indications of transformative learning as change of identity has been change of practice, change of competencies, change of membership and change of trajectories. The findings in this case study are tentative, and should be explored more systematically in relation to professionals and networked learning. A first step may be to implement the concepts into MIL's own quality control systems.

The final question is the one of the role of the pedagogical principles. POPP/PBL does not have a causal effect in relation to the learning outcome. However, POPP/PBL fits well with the professional students' interests in, and their opportunities to participate in, continued professional development. The mixed mode learning environment, with online work and a few physical seminars offers a good blend of rhythm, flexibility, mutual dependencies and commitment. More specifically, the POPP/PBL model fits with the students' interest in combining theory and practice, and to work on open ended problems from own practice. Moreover it provides a practical approach to the development of academic methodological skills and insights into knowledge of science. The networked version of PBL/POPP further more prepares the students to be active participants in networked practices.

ACKNOWLEDGEMENTS

We wish to thank all the MIL students and teachers who have enriched the MIL learning community through out the years. Furthermore, we want to thank our fellow institutions: Aalborg University, Aarhus University, Copenhagen Business School, The Danish University School of Education, Roskilde University, and not least IT-West. Through their engagement and flexibility they have provided the organisational and financial background for MIL. Special thanks go to Hum-IKT at Aalborg University for the overall ICT support and the very positive commitment far beyond traditional operation(s).

NOTES

[1] IT University West is an educational network between the four university institutions in the West of Denmark; Aarhus School of Business, University of Southern Denmark, Aalborg University and University of Aarhus. IT University West was established in 1999 with the purpose of strengthening education and research within ICT in Denmark. IT University West offers graduate studies and further education within a broad range of the field of information technology.

[2] The term Problem Based Learning was originally coined by Don Woods, based on his work with chemistry students in McMaster's University in Canada. However, the popularity and subsequent world-wide spread of PBL is mostly linked to the introduction of this educational method at the medical school of McMaster University in the 1960s (de Graaff & Kolmos, 2007). Search within Google for problem-based learning gets more than 1.180.000 hits. Search for project-based learning gets about 154.000.000 hits (Google, 2007) meaning that both problem-based and project-based learning seem to be quite widespread concepts. We use the term POPP (Problem Oriented Project Pedagogy) as our special pedagogy of linking problem orientation, projects and technology (Dirckinck-Holmfeld, 2002)

[3] The organisation of seminars in different physical locations (universities) have provided a number of unexpected advantages: equal recruitment from East and West Denmark, better insights into the culture of the different partner universities, special opportunities (guest lectures, facilities, resources) and visibility at the host institution.

⁴ Following Granovetter: "the strength of a tie is a (probably linear) combination of the amount of time, the emotional intensity, the intimacy (mutual confiding), and the reciprocal services which characterize the tie" (Granovetter, 1973, p. 1361)

REFERENCES

Brown, J. S., & Duguid, P. (2000). *The social life of information*. Boston: Harvard Business School.
Bygholm, A., & Nyvang, T. (2009). An infrastructural perspective on implementing new educational technology - The case of human centred informatics. In L. Dirckinck-Holmfeld, C. Jones, & B. Lindström (Eds.), *Analysing networked learning practices in higher education and continuing professional development*. Rotterdam: Sense Publishers.
Dalsgaard, C. (2007). *Åbne læringsressourcer - mod en sociokulturel teori om læringsressourcer* [Open-ended learning resources - towards a sociocultural theory of learning resources]. Aarhus University, Aarhus.
Danielsen, O., Dirckinck-Holmfeld, L., Sørensen, B. H., Nielsen, J., & Fibiger, B. (Eds.). (1999). *Læring og Multimedier* (2nd ed.). Aalborg: Aalborg University Press.
de Graaff, E., & Kolmos, A. (Eds.). (2007). *Management of change: Implementation of problem-based and project-based learning in engineering*. Rotterdam: Sense Publishers.
Dirckinck-Holmfeld, L., & Fibiger, B. (Eds.). (2002). *Learning in virtual environments*. Frederiksberg: Samfundslitteratur Press.
Dirckinck-Holmfeld, L., & Jones, C. (2009). Issues and concepts in networked learning - Analysis and the future of networked learning. In L. Dirckinck-Holmfeld, C. Jones, & B. Lindström (Eds.), *Analysing networked learning practices in higher education and continuing professional development*. Rotterdam, the Netherlands: Sense Publishers.
Dirckinck-Holmfeld, L., Sorensen, E. K., Ryberg, T., & Buus, L. (2004). A theoretical framework for designing online master communities of practice. In *Proceedings of the networked learning conference*. Lancaster: Lancaster University http://www.shef.ac.uk/nlc2004/Proceedings/Contents.htm.
Engeström, Y. (1987). *Learning by expanding - an activity theoretical approach to developmental research*. Retrieved 060803, 2003, from http://communication.ucsd.edu/MCA/Paper/Engestrom/expanding/toc.htm
Engeström, Y. (2004). New forms of learning in co-configuration work. *Journal of Workplace Learning*, *16*(1/2), 11–21. Retrieved from www.emeraldinsight.com/1366-5626.htm
Fibiger, B. (2005). Videndeling i læringsforløb - Erfaringer fra undervisning på Masteruddannelsen i It og læring. *Tidsskrift for Universiteternes Efter- og Videreuddannelse* Retrieved from http://www.unev.dk/view.aspx?artikel_id=486(5).
Fibiger, B., Dirckinck-Holmfeld, L., Nielsen, J., Sørensen, B. H., & Danielsen, O. (Eds.). (2000). *Design af Multimedier* (2nd ed.). Aalborg: Aalborg University Press.
Fibiger, B., Nielsen, J., Riis, M., Sorensen, E. K., Dirckinck-Holmfeld, L., Danielsen, O., et al. (2004). Master in ICT and learning - Project pedagogy and collaboration in virtual e-learning. *The Electronic Journal of e-Learning*, *3*(1), 15–20. Retrieved from www.ejel.org
Goodyear, P., Jones, C., Asensio, M., Hodgson, V., & Steeples, C. (2001). *Effective networked learning in higher education: Notes and guidelines*. Lancaster: CSALT, Lancaster University.Lancaster: CSALT, Lancaster University. Retrieved from http://csalt.lancs.ac.uk/jisc/
Google. (2007). Retrieved April 30, 2007, from http://www.google.dk/search?hl=da&q=problem-based+learning&meta=, http://www.google.dk/search?hl=da&q=project-based+learning&meta=
Granovetter, M. S. (1973). The strength of weak ties. *Americal Journal of Sociology*, *78*(6), 1360–1380.
Guribye, F., & Lindström, B. (2009). Infrastructures for learning and networked tools - The introduction of a new tool in an inter-organisational network. In L. Dirckinck-Holmfeld, C. Jones, & B. Lindström (Eds.), *Analysing networked learning practices in higher education and continuing professional development*. Rotterdam: Sense Publishers.

John-Steiner, V., & Souberman, E. (1978). Afterword. In M. Cole, V. John-Steiner, S. Scribner, & E. Souberman (Eds.), *Mind in society*. Cambridge: Harvard University Press.

Jones, C., & Dirckinck-Holmfeld, L. (2009). Introduction. In L. Dirckinck-Holmfeld, C. Jones, & B. Lindström (Eds.), *Analysing networked learning practices in higher education and continuing professional development*. Rotterdam: Sense Publishers.

Jones, C., Dirckinck-Holmfeld, L., & Lindström, B. (2006). A relational, indirect, meso-level approach to CSCL design in the next decade. *International Journal of Computer-Supported Collaborative Learning, 1*(1).

Laurel, B. (1993). *Computers as Theatre*. Addison-Wesley Publishing Company.

MIL. (2008). *Master i IKT og Læring: 2000–2007 status og udfordringer*. Aalborg: Aalborg University.

Nardi, B. A., & O'Day, V. (1999). *Information ecology - Using technology with heart*. USA: MIT Press.

Pilkington, R., & Guldberg, K. (2009). Conditions for productive networked learning among professionals and carers - The WebAutism case study. In L. Dirckinck-Holmfeld, C. Jones, & B. Lindström (Eds.), *Analysing networked learning practices in higher education and continuing professional development*. Rotterdam: Sense Publishers.

Ritterbusch, W. B. (2003). *Student evaluations from MIL 2003*. Aalborg: Master in ICT and Learning (MIL) Aalborg University.

Sorensen, E. K., & Takle, G. S. (2003). *Learning through discussion and dialogue in computer supported collaborative networks*. Paper presented at the Society for Information Technology and Teacher Education International Conference 2003(1), [Online]. Retrieved from http://dl.aace.org/ 12261

***Star, S. L., & Ruhleder, K. (1996). Steps toward an ecology of infrastructure: Design and access for large information spaces. *Information Systems Research, 7*(1), 111–134.

Tolsby, H. (2009). Virtual environment for project based collaborative learning. In L. Dirckinck-Holmfeld, C. Jones, & B. Lindström (Eds.), *Analysing networked learning practices in higher education and continuing professional development*. Rotterdam, the Netherlands: Sense Publishers.

Wenger, E. (1998). *Communities of practice - learning, meaning, and identity*. New York: Cambridge University Press.

Wenger, E., White, N., & Smith, J. (in preparation). *Technology and communities*. Book Surge Press.

Winograd, T. e. a. (Ed.). (1996). *Bringing design to software*. New York: Addison-Wesley Publishing Company.

Lone Dirckinck-Holmfeld
Department of Communication and Psychology
Aalborg University, Denmark

Oluf Danielsen
Department of Communication
Roskilde University, Denmark

Bo Fibiger
Department of Media and Information Studies
University of Aarhus, Denmark

Janni Nielsen
Center for Applied Informatics
Copenhagen Business School, Denmark

Marianne Riis
Department of Communication and Psychology
Aalborg University, Denmark

Elsebeth K. Sorensen
Department of Media and Information Studies
University of Aarhus, Denmark

Birgitte Holm Sørensen
Department of Pedagogical Anthropology
The Danish School of Education University of Aarhus, Denmark

Winnie Ritterbusch
Department of Communication and Psychology
Aalborg University, Denmark

ARNE VINES AND OLGA DYSTHE

PRODUCTIVE LEARNING IN THE STUDY OF LAW

*The Role of Networked Technology in the Learning Ecology
of a Law Faculty*

*To the extent he can make a voice of his own, or a range of voices, he will
find that he has avoided becoming a 'stereotyped lawyer'. He will have
learned to work as an independent mind in his own way.*

*James Boyd White
(From expectation to experience. Essays on law and legal education, 1999)*

INTRODUCTION

In this chapter we examine how the introduction of a virtual learning environment
(VLE)[1] affords 'productive' learning practices in a law programme. We take the
view that productive learning requires more than individual mastery of a subject
matter, although mastery is important. Rather, we feel that productive learning
must be understood in relation to wider aspects of the learning ecology (Barron,
2006), such as the institutional learning design and technological infrastructure, as
well as the students' learning experiences, interactional processes and identity
transformation. Here, we report on a pedagogical case study of an innovative
Norwegian law faculty, where a VLE has become an integrative part of a radical
change in the teaching and learning environment. We shall analyze the VLE's
effects on a range of intertwined conditions: historical, cultural, institutional, and
pedagogical. Our discussion focuses on the VLE's ambivalent role, which in this
case is that of a powerful tool for creating a social setting in which students can
conduct authoritative discourse, while simultaneously allowing for more transparent
and collective-oriented learning processes. The double edged function of the
networked technology, as well as the law faculty's overall learning design, is discussed
from a sociocultural learning perspective and in regard to the question of what
constitutes 'productive' in contrast to 'reproductive' and 'counterproductive' learning
practices.

*L. Dirckinck-Holmfeld, C. Jones and B. Lindström (eds.), Analysing Networked Learning Practices
in Higher Education and Continuing Professional Development, 175–199.*

THE CONTEXT

Characteristics of the Study of Law

Law is a traditional discipline, generally not known for pedagogic innovation (Munro, 2001). Instead, legal education is associated with procedural and fixed knowledge, intense reading, the pursuit of high marks, individual aptness, and the high stakes of final exams that separate the wheat from the chaff. These are common characteristics, found in academic law communities across epochs (e.g. Friedland, 1996; Karseth & Solbrekke, 2006; Kennedy, 2003; Kissam, 2003; Pihlajamäki & Lindblom-Ylänne, 2003; Twining, 1994; Åkvåg, 2000). Studies on law education in Norway have reported that law students are more competitive, spend more time on reading, and are more focussed on curriculum than most other students in other disciplines (Jensen & Nygård, 2000; Karseth & Solbrekke, 2006; Strømsø, 2003).

Moreover, law is an argumentative science, where students need to develop oral, written and argumentative skills. Essential for learning in general, these skills are especially crucial for the field of law. Bernt and Doublet (1999) underline the importance of learning the oral and written genres that are used by the professional communities which law students aspire to join. Writing and talking are thus central to the practice of the discipline, in addition to being tools for acquiring disciplinary knowledge. This implies training in how to analyse, discuss and solve contentious issues of law.[2] From a sociocultural learning perspective, we argue that law students need to learn how to produce knowledge, not just to reproduce set opinions from authorities such as textbook authors, professors, statutory provisions and legislators.

THEORETICAL APPROACHES

Sociocultural perspectives on learning, communication and knowledge production form the theoretical rationale for this study (Bakhtin, 1981, 1986; Lave & Wenger, 1991; Vygotsky, 1962, 1978; Wenger, 1998; Wertsch, 1991, 1998). We perceive knowledge as socially constructed, mediated and distributed between persons, artefacts, traditions and time. It is transferred through, and simultaneously shaped by the language we use and by participation in communities of practice.

In our discussion of the role played by the VLE in an academic law community, we will employ Wertsch's (1991, 1998) concept of 'cultural tools' or 'mediational means', which derives largely from the writings of Vygotsky and Bakhtin. According to Wertsch, mediated action concerns the basic claim that human action and mind are fundamentally shaped by the cultural tools that individuals and groups employ. He underscores the ambivalent effects that new cultural tools can have on existing forms of mediated actions, in terms of affordances and constraints:

> When trying to develop new cultural tools, the focus naturally tends to be on how they will overcome some perceived problem or restriction inherent in existing forms of mediated action. However [...] even if a new cultural tool frees us from some earlier limitations of perspective, it introduces new ones of its own (Wertsch, 1998, p. 39).

In order to understand more of the dynamic interplay between technology and other infrastructures for law students' learning in a networked learning environment (Jones, Dirckinck-Holmfeld & Lindström, 2006) we have chosen to view the law faculty as a community of practice (Wenger, 1998). Seen in this way, law study involves enculturation processes where students have to learn how to think, argue, write and talk in ways that are accepted in this professional culture. These are complex, social and situated activities that cannot be learned in isolation from the subject content (Prior, 1998; Russell, 1993). Further, we will discuss our empirical findings to elucidate upon Wenger's conception of 'learning design', which advocates the need for social infrastructures that foster learning. Essentially, Wenger argues that there is no straightforward relationship or linearity between a learning design and learning in practice, because "learning happens, design or no design" (1998, p. 225). This line of reasoning resembles Illeris' (1999; see also Lave & Wenger, 1991, p. 97–98) criticism against those who expect concurrence between what is taught and what is learned. In a fairly similar way, we oppose an increasing tendency to equate the notion of 'community of practice' and productive learning practices, i.e. the assumption that knowledge and skills are easily and inevitably produced because people cooperate. As Nystrand (1986) has warned: "authentic questions, discussion, small-group work, and interaction, though important, do not categorically produce learning" (p. 72). The quality of students' dialogic interactions varies and influences how and what knowledge is produced in problem-based learning environments (Innes, 2006). Ultimately we will discuss how and to what degree the overall learning design in our case promotes and impedes diversity, dissent and dialogic relations (Bakhtin, 1981, 1984) between students, teachers and teacher assistants (TAs). Consistent with Bakhtin's theory of dialogic discourse, differing voices can contribute to improved facility for critical thinking, in contrast to reproductive consensus-based approaches which essentially seek uniformed, standardized, and homogenous solutions to any problems. Central to the dynamic processes of meaning creation and identity transformation is the tension between what Bakhtin (1981) has termed the 'authoritative' and the 'internally persuasive' discourse. This tension provides a powerful lens for us to analyse power, authority, and learning discourses within the academic law community. In the analysis of these issues we consider the applied technology as an essential constituent.

BACKGROUND FACTORS CONTRIBUTING TO CHANGE

Radical pedagogical changes are rare in higher education, particularly in universities with their tradition of lecture based teaching, individual study strategies and reproductive final exams. The transformation of the teaching and learning environment that has taken place in the faculty of law at the University of Bergen has therefore gained attention. In 2004 the law faculty was awarded a prestigious national prize for innovative change by the Norwegian Agency for Quality Assurance in Education. Before giving a description of the changes, we will briefly discuss five factors we have identified that contributed to the faculty's restructuring: 1) An unacceptably high failure rate during the 1990s; 2) a diagnostic study of the learning environment; 3) international trends in the teaching of law; 4) the availability of a VLE; 5) the Quality Reform of higher education in Norway, effective from the academic year 2003–04.

The Bergen law faculty was formally established in 1980, although law studies originally started in 1969. During the 1990s failure rates were unacceptably high, particularly in year 3 and 4. Teaching was still primarily lecture-based, and students relied on rote learning in order to reproduce what was learned from course literature at the final high stakes exam, even though student evaluations over the last two decades had shown dissatisfaction with the exam system and more writing and small group seminars had been suggested. Many students failed repeatedly, causing some of them immense personal problems (Raaheim & Hauge, 1994). Two educational psychologists from the Programme for Research on Learning and Instruction were hired in 1993 to map the learning environment and produce a diagnostic study, including a survey among all the students. The researchers were clear in their final recommendations for the changes:

– Compulsory written assignments each semester
– Marks given on mandatory written assignments should count towards the final grade
– Regular feedback on seminar tasks
– One teacher follow same group of students for 2 semesters
– Carefully designed assignments, tied to lectures
– Organized, student led groups, supported by a contact teacher
– Change of assessment system
– Introduction of regular student evaluation (Quality Management System) (Raaheim & Hauge, 1994, pp. 13).

These recommendations sketched a complete transformation of the study of law. The immediate follow-up, however, was piecemeal. The infrastructure and pedagogical tools to manage such a deep restructuring of the teaching and learning environment were still lacking. The availability of a VLE was therefore a major factor in making the restructuring possible. A climate of change, however, developed over time, influenced by both internal and external factors. International trends in law education contributed to change, particularly the shift in how the university law studies were organized and taught in Scandinavia (cf. Pihlajamäki & Lindblom-Ylänne, 2003; Wilhelmsen & Lilleholt, 2003). A growing number of law faculties had introduced a problem-based learning approach with student-centred instruction, change of obsolete exam traditions and more formative assessment. The role of feedback as the key to better learning was recognized, but because the Bergen law faculty was significantly understaffed it had to establish a corps of teacher assistants (TAs). This action was economic and gave the most ambitious students a challenging opportunity for broadening their professional qualifications. The responsibility for organizing, instruction and follow-up of the 70 TAs involved was chiefly assigned to a full-time professional pedagogue, who was hired to prepare the pedagogical ground for the implementation of the national Quality Reform and, subsequently, to ensure the pedagogical quality assurance and internal standards of teaching and learning.

The consequence was that when the Quality Reform of Norwegian higher education was announced, the ground was prepared for reform of the study of law at the University of Bergen.[3] Several case studies and reports have documented the radical pedagogical, technical and structural changes that have taken place over the last five years at the law faculty (Lian, 2003; Møller-Holst, 2006; Pedersen, 2005; Wilhelmsen & Lilleholt, 2003; Östergren, 2006).

RESEARCH QUESTIONS AND METHODOLOGY OF THE PRESENT STUDY

Our research study focuses on productive learning processes in the study of law and how extensive use of a virtual learning environment became a basic prerequisite for pedagogical changes, without which they would be impossible to implement. To understand the pedagogical role played by technology, we need to investigate how the VLE relates to the context specific infrastructures for learning, and the prevailing instruction and assessment practices of the academic law community.

Our overarching research question is: What role does Classfronter, a Norwegian version of a VLE, play in the learning ecology at the law faculty and how does it contribute to productive learning? More specific questions are:

– What changes in the infrastructures for learning have taken place? How are these changes interrelated and related to technology?
– What indications are there of a more productive learning environment, and what has been the effect of technology?

Data were collected through participatory observation of a range of student learning activities, in-depth interviews of five small group participants, one graduate student and three members of the administrative staff, document studies and electronic diaries written by 20 undergraduate students in the period from January 2005 to August 2006. The diary instructions were quite open, aimed to give the researchers in-depth information of the learning experiences of undergraduate law students, on campus as well as outside it.[4] Interviews and group meetings were recorded and transcribed before analysis. Access to the complete collection of student drafts, with comments in Classfronter, from all four first-year courses, adds an important data source. All written materials have been transferred to Nvivo 2.0, a specialised software programme for qualitative data analysis, to support coding and analysis.

THE STORY OF INFRASTRUCTURAL CHANGE AND THE ROLE PLAYED
BY TECHNOLOGY

The comprehensive learning environment reform was essentially a top-down faculty response to deal with the problems of high failure rates and low student achievement. Classfronter was introduced in all undergraduate courses, two years prior to the Quality Reform, in order to deal with the increased amount of writing, teacher- and peer-feedback. The study structure, however, was changed as a direct result of the Quality Reform. The master programme in law requires five years of full time study. Each year consists of modularised courses (most courses are 10 or 15 credits), with exams after each course. The following description of the study structure is based on the first year programme, but year 2 and 3 are fairly similar.

First year students start with two introductory courses, followed by courses in administration law, family and succession law and contract law. Legal method is integrated in all courses. As before the reform, weekly lectures build the content knowledge backbone of the course, but mandatory group work and writing assignments have been added as new elements. All courses are managed by a course coordinator whose main responsibility is to plan, follow up and evaluate the course as well as to instruct and follow up the group leaders (TAs).

Assessment has changed Dramatically

Instead of one major exam at the end of 3 years, each course module has a two-tier exam: 1) a take-home exam (5–7 days), where students are allowed to collaborate with peers, but hand in papers individually. Besides assessing the papers as pass/fail and ranking them in a high, middle or low category, the assessor writes comments in the margins of each paper. Students can also request additional oral feedback. 2) A traditional sit-down exam two or three weeks later, which is graded (ABCDEF). The home exam gives students an overview of the course content and makes them better prepared for the final high stakes exam. In order to register for the final exams, the student must have attended a minimum of 75% of the small group meetings and also passed the take-home exam. Students who do not fulfil this requirement are excluded from the group and their Classfronter password is suspended. As a whole, students' study rhythm is strictly structured, as shown in fig. 1, below.

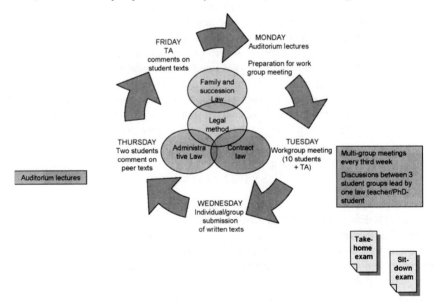

Figure 1. Students' weekly study rhythm in year 1

Normally, students attend one or two auditorium lectures per week. In our case, most lectures were held by the course coordinator. Because one lecturer was given the total responsibility for the course (including formulation of group tasks and examinations, compilations of instructions for TAs, follow-up meetings with the TAs, guidelines for the marking of exam papers, and writing up a final evaluation report), there was established a valuable and coherent alignment of the curriculum and its intended outcomes with the assessment forms (Biggs, 1999).

In between lectures, students prepared for group work by reading relevant law sources and specialist literature and making a written outline of preliminary arguments needed for the assignment. During the group discussion the participants discuss the concrete assignment in detail. Usually the assignment is divided into four or five sub-questions, and the groups discuss all of them. Students then write drafts, individually or in groups of two or three.

Consequence of the New Study Model: Increased Student Interaction

Several organisational and structural measures are taken to ensure that students participate in interactive learning arenas. Most important is the organization and extensive use of mandatory group work and feedback system. Groups of ten students are led by a paid teacher assistant (TA) who is an advanced student in year 4 or year 5. TAs must apply for the position and go through a comprehensive in-house and credit-giving training programme led by an experienced educationist in company with one experienced law professor. TAs are for the most part recruited amongst A and B candidates. They have regular meetings with the course coordinator in order to prepare for the given assignments, and they have also a draft of every weekly writing task, written by a professional, to support them in their tutoring of the group. Despite being given this tool, the TAs are instructed to act as facilitators and not as substitute lecturers. Their primary task is to guide the undergraduate students and lead the group discussion so that the group will keep 'on track'. Although the group work is centred on case based tasks constructed by experienced law professors, the role of the TAs as knowledge brokers (Wenger, 1998) should not be underestimated because they are in position to act as "individuals who provide connections between communities of practice, transfer elements of one practice into another, enable coordination, and through these activities can create new opportunities for learning" (Wenger, 1998, p. 109).

Triple-group meetings, led by a professional law teacher or a PhD student, take place every second or third week and focus on similar assignments. Students are expected to be active participants, raise questions and argue for and against different solutions. This expectation necessitates prior preparation, and immediately after the group meetings, students are required to write their draft. The VLE is tightly inter-woven in this weekly study structure, and since the model is implemented in all undergraduate courses, students are socialised into a consistent pattern of studying that affords certain learning processes which they have to follow for three years.

After the law faculty introduced problem-based learning groups, students were expected to share and construct their knowledge with each other in a far more systematic and transparent way than has been custom amongst law students (Wilhelmsen & Lilleholt, 2003).

Mixed Findings

The productive aspect of conflict, resistance, arguing and exchange of meaning between different voices is a finding that emerges from the student diaries, group observations and interviews. For the students themselves, however, this is partly overshadowed by negative experiences with 'free riders' who do not contribute constructively to discussions or offer feedback. All of which affects students' strategic personal considerations of how much to share with peers who give little in return.

One negative consequence of the lack of structural variation in the compulsory study is that third year students, especially, experience increased problems with motivation for group discussions and writing, even though they still find writing and commenting very useful for their learning process.

> Students tend to be very tired of the compulsory elements after two years. They do not want to attend group meetings. They do not want to prepare for them. They do not want to write the assignments, even though the assignments are very useful for learning (Rosemary's diary, year 3).

Students report that interaction patterns in the face-to-face groups are established early and are incredibly difficult to change. First year student Jonas says he likes and learns a lot from his group, but: "A pattern has evolved where Ann [peer] starts the discussions and the others follow up. This pattern has been stable even though we have got to know one another quite well" (Interview, Jonas, year 1).

We observed that many students were silent most of the time, and some left the group session without uttering a single word, except during the breaks. Often, the TA used much of the group's time to ask direct, pressing questions and to comment on how specific tasks could be understood and dealt with. The TA also typically tried to help students ask 'precise' questions relating to each text fragment in the given task. The law students' reluctance to speak in the groups was, according to our informants, a symptom of their fear of making fools of themselves. Frank, one of the conscientious freshmen we interviewed, points out that because of this, he tends to hand problematic reasoning over to the authoritative voice of the TA:

> I feel very stupid if I mention a legal basis that turns out to be wrong. The easy way out is to wait for the group leader to say the right answers and then we can include it in our written essay (Interview, Frank, year 1).

Still, remaining silent and hiding behind others' leads were not options when students had to think and write for themselves. Third year student Katherine describes her dilemma in her diary just before submitting her assignment into Classfronter:

> I feel that my essay is very poor quality and I actually felt embarrassed submitting an essay for peer feedback that I was dissatisfied with. But I don't have a choice (Katherine's diary, year 3).

As this quote reflects, the technology was disciplining in two ways. First, it required students' compliance and participation: it reflected and reified a strong learning design that colonized students' time and space for reflection and explorative learning activities. Second, it provided an experience authentic to the professional discipline: it provided an environment for students to learn how to deal with appropriate critique from other knowledgeable persons, which professional lawyers must do daily.

PRODUCTIVE LEARNING IN WRITING AND FEEDBACK PRACTICES

Each peer group is divided into three 'commentator teams' to ensure that every assignment will be commented on by different persons throughout the semester. These teams alternate according to a list posted in Classfronter. The whole process is strictly regulated: students' drafts are due at 08 AM on Thursday, peer comments must be posted by Friday at 08.00, and the group leader comments on about half of the texts every week, by Monday at 16.00. Some students write close to 30 drafts per year. The recommended length of the draft is 700 words, though many drafts are considerably longer. The study structure forces the student to work through the same assignment in five overlapping phases:

Self-study → Group discussion → Draft writing → Giving peer feedback → Reading comments

This repetitive learning cycle becomes the students' main orientation point for their study and study progression, and it disciplines the students to work steadily and with focus from the very beginning.

Jonas thinks he has "learnt to become more disciplined" and he underscores the importance of attending the group in order to learn the subject content and do well at the exam:

Group work constitutes the kernel in my learning in the various disciplines. This knowledge is what I remember. This is what sticks. It is noticeable at the exam, and if you get a problem similar to one we have dealt with in our group, your heart beats faster (Interview, Jonas, year 1).

Though interviews with students reveal that they would prefer to have their own choice of attending a group, they are unquestionably very satisfied with the study support they get from the well structured group work and close follow up, especially with what they learn from written feedback mediated through the VLE. Jonas is convinced that direct feedback is very effective because:

It helps you review. I very often look at other students' texts and the group leader's comments because he gives very thorough feedback. He may use an hour commenting on one essay, and there is a lot to be learnt. It is so useful – maybe the best part of the whole study programmes (Interview, Jonas, year 1).

In legal education institutions there is a long tradition of providing students with accurate model texts (e.g. guidelines for the marking of exam papers) and examples of good and less good examination papers.[5] This tradition is still kept up. But the

VLE also provides students with opportunities to learn from unfinished and less excellent texts. From our theoretical perspective this may have a more productive learning effect than model texts, because students come closer to real life difficulties when they must deconstruct and co-construct meanings from unfinished texts and thus create their own internally persuasive words which are "half-someone else's" (Bakhtin, 1981, p. 293–294). The fact that students are not required to revise their texts, however, makes it harder to trace the effects of the peer and TA's feedback.

There is clear evidence in our data that the VLE is a significant collective and discursive arena where students can experiment and discover their own and other students' use of adequate legal methods:

> Writing provides a different kind of learning than reading. It is indispensable, particularly for the study of law. [Writing in law], is a very peculiar genre; if it can be called a genre. (…) It is very much like method, method! I absolutely believe that this has to be learnt through writing (Interview, Frank, year 1).

Another important feature of the VLE has to do with its capacity to store and map student texts, and to make them available independent of time and place. Students use the stored samples of commented texts as a virtual reference book. In preparation for exams the VLE represents an important source of knowledge for many students:

> Read all the group assignments in Classfronter from Family Law. Reading through the essays I and my fellow students have written and the feedback for each one of them is actually an excellent way of reviewing the course content. It also helps me reviewing the methods part before the exam (Elise's diary, year 1).

> I have mainly reread in Classfronter the old essays I and the rest of my group have written. […] This has been an excellent way of preparing for the exam because then I see what are the typical mistakes, and I get ideas of for instance interpretations and sources that I have not seen myself (Martha's diary, year 1).

Comments from TAs have more credibility than from peers, and students value the more advanced knowledge of their group leaders:

> Group leaders [TAs] know what is right and wrong. They are supposed to have the competence and the big overview and be able to tell us when we have done something strange, and what to do and write instead (Interview, Oscar, year 1).

> I have noticed how much I learn from reading fellow students' essays and comments […] It is annoying when people just write 'good' or 'superb' or 'agree'. It is particularly annoying when I spend time on giving constructive feedback and try to do a thorough job of it (Jane's diary, year 1).

Students tend to see TAs as having the necessary knowledge and authority, while they do not always trust comments from peers, largely because they consider such feedback to be lacking in substance. This latter point is empirically supported in a comprehensive content analysis of the written feedback (Vines, forthcoming), showing that TAs give longer and qualitatively better feedback than peers.

Jonas shares with many the problematic experience of having to comment on good quality texts, and he blames it partly on the conformity that is intrinsic to the group-based writing process:

> It is difficult to give constructive comments when we have got the same input, all of us have worked hard, and more or less written the same essay (Interview, Jonas, year 1).

A female third year student elucidates the strong standardizing effect that group leaders can have on the construction of students answers, as compared to the self driven group work in the third year of the law study:

> The TA had such great influence on the work we did that our papers became very much alike. Therefore my experience is that it was difficult to give feedback (Amanda, summary meeting of the diary project).

This quote indicates that undergraduates' writing style and discourse depend crucially on the presence (or absence) of a TA and, hence, how the TAs practice their pedagogical mandate and authorative position within the group they are set to lead. We will discuss this aspect in more detail in the discussion part of this chapter.

Finally, although group discussions and subsequent writing are core elements in the students' knowledge production and learning activities, 'the backwash effect' of the assessment comes into play as none of the many assignments that students write during each course are graded. In the build up to exam periods, where students prioritize reading and repetition, the obligatory assignments and commenting easily take second place.

CHARACTERISTICS AND EFFECTS OF A VIRTUAL LEARNING ENVIRONMENT

Classfronter was built into the learning architecture two years before the implementation of the Quality Reform; according to key academic and administrative staff members they saw no other feasible way to handle the increasing number of written student assignments and feedback. At present more than 1000 written assignments are distributed through the shared VLE every week. One of the professors stated:

> Copying assignments and distributing student drafts as well as teacher and peer comments without Classfronter would have created major practical difficulties. ...Previously, when only 10–15 percent of the students actually handed in assignments given a few times per semester, we could handle it, but today a paper based system would break down when students write every week (Pedersen, 2005, p. 60–61).

This quote points directly to the main benefit of using a VLE, that is to distribute a massive flow of written and commented assignments, through all undergraduate courses. Another major benefit is that the VLE reduces the time that teachers and

TAs spend on writing a lot of comments. The most important and widely used tools in the VLE are the writing and feedback devices, which are essentially a simple text editor and an easy commentary function, as shown in fig. 2 below.[6]

In Classfronter comments can only be inserted at a paragraph level, and not at a sentence level. When students forget to split up their text in small units the commentators' work gets more difficult, as this requires more text references in their comments, which can then easily become too general. Comments from the TA are usually given at the end in order to capture the totality of the argumentation. This reflects an adoption of a long standing practice carried out by the law professors.

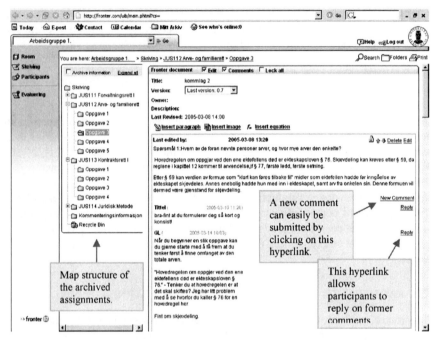

Figure 2. Screenshot of the Classfronter interface

An important feature of the VLE is that the length of comments is not restricted, as distinct from handwritten teacher comments on home exam papers. These are limited by rather small open fields in the margins of a piece of paper and so are inevitably followed by a cover sheet. In this sense, the design of technology has opened up space for extended responses on students work.

There have been enduring problems with Classfronter, and sometimes students have lost their texts because of technical breakdowns. Consequently most users write and save their texts in Microsoft Word and then copy and paste them into the VLE in several steps. Even though the law faculty has been dissatisfied with Classfronter for these and other reasons[7], which we will not elaborate on, administrators have been reluctant to introduce a new learning management system because of the danger of serious breakdown problems when introducing a new technology tool. As such, this exemplifies the severe and almost irreversible effects that such a technology can have if it has been into any faculty's core administrative, teaching and learning practices on a large-scale.

In our analysis of the role played by the VLE in the learning ecology, we follow Salomon's (1995) distinction between 'effects with' and 'effects of' technology. Effects of technology are the long-lasting effects that are a consequence of the intellectual partnership of using mediational tools such as networked computers, while 'effects with technology' occur while the learner is working with particular computer software. Our data allows us to say little of the latter effects. We will here list the most significant effects of this technology:

- The VLE provides the framework for a more complex interaction between a large numbers of students, and between students and more knowledgeable teachers and TAs
- The use of this electronic mediational tool affords varied ways of dealing with the course content. This has been shown to have a motivating effect on the students (Lian, 2003)
- The VLE mediates written co-construction of knowledge and meaning making through its capacity to store vast amounts of data, the opportunity to insert comments on submitted drafts and the password protected access to all group members' writings. This triple function affords 'transparency' of the students' meaning making processes (Lave & Wenger, 1991) and 'knowledge sharing' between the participants that would have been very difficult without support from the VLE. In addition, teachers and course managers get more insight into students' writing and learning processes
- The compulsory and VLE-mediated writing activities structure students' learning processes, and make these processes more visible to themselves as well as the teachers. This has both positive and negative aspects, the positive being the disciplining effect of the structure that helps all students progress and potentially succeed (the reduced failure rate testifies to its efficiency). The negative effect is the high degree of control and possibly over-socialization of students. We will discuss this dilemma later
- The strict structure and time limits are easy to maintain using a VLE, and it can be argued that it would be nearly impossible without such technology. The VLE makes commenting and text sharing more efficient and time saving, and therefore people are willing to do it. At the same time, the learning design challenges the students' sense of responsibility, their promptness in responding to assignments given by the teachers, as well as the expectations built into the system
- The VLE features used in this programme provide a detailed log of every student's study behaviour, and so differ from synchronic chat forums and face-to-face meetings. The positive aspect of this is that it is possible for students and teachers to go back and analyze the strengths and weaknesses of any submitted assignment. Indeed the mandatory requirements of writing, group participation and electronically mediated peer commenting make it difficult for any student to

avoid the hard work of formulating their emerging understanding of the subject matter

– Students are engaged in writing different text types. The VLE supports this emerging knowledge of genres by making easily available model texts in the form of high quality student answers, complemented by detailed comments from the TAs

– The unusual amount of writing required of the students in this study programme, efficiently administered through the VLE, increases their communication skills and socializes them into the genres and way of writing and arguing in the discipline of law

– The text records in Classfronter represent an important reading source for exam preparation

– Assignments and subsequent peer comments can easily be submitted to and read in the VLE from sites that are either off or on campus, and on a 24/7 basis. This is an important feature of the technology, because there are a limited number of computers on campus and the web based technology thus makes it possible for students to work from home or elsewhere

– From an organisational perspective the faculty reduces its total teaching budget through the use of a VLE, which needs to be achieved in order to finance such close follow up, through written feedback, as the law study programme intends.

In different ways, the effects we have listed shape and influence student learning activities. However, in order to determine to what extent the effects of the technology are educationally productive, we need to conduct a closer discussion of how our mixed findings relate to the infrastructures for learning at the law faculty, our theoretical framework, and previous research.

DISCUSSION OF FINDINGS

In this section we will return to our overarching research question and discuss what role Classfronter plays in the learning ecology at the Bergen law faculty and how it contributes to productive learning. We will look at different conceptions of 'productive', and show how different factors contribute or counteract learning.

'Productive' in the Production of Successful Students?

This law faculty has undoubtedly become more effective and 'productive' as a result of the pedagogical reform, in the sense that there has been a dramatic reduction in student failure rate. In this respect the faculty has fulfilled the expectations of the Quality Reform and thus attracted national attention. The strict study cycle that every student has to follow, frequent writing and systematic feedback combined with close monitoring of their work, has reduced the risk of failure and clearly ensured student progression and better exam results. As shown in the previous section, the electronic tools make it much easier to manage the system of group based learning and individual feedback.

The other part of our overarching research question, focusing on how technology contributes to productive learning is, however, more difficult to answer unequivocally, partly because 'productive' is a slippery concept, and partly because it is notoriously difficult to determine what factors influence individual learning and how. The design of this study has provided findings that allow us to discuss this from an organizational and more general educational point of view, but not to draw conclusions about individual cognitive changes.

In the following we will discuss some of the potentially positive and negative factors for productive learning in this particular learning environment, as seen from a socio-cultural perspective, when 'productive' is contrasted with 'unproductive' and 'reproductive' learning (Lillejord & Dysthe, 2008). The role of the TAs in supporting productive as opposed to unproductive learning is particularly in focus.

Positive and Negative Aspects of the Strict Structuring of Students' Learning

One clearly positive aspect of the structured approach is the systematic way that students in this study programme learn legal problem solving through group based text production and peer feedback. It is well documented that systematic use of process oriented writing including teacher- and peer response promotes learning (e.g. Barton, 1994; Clark & Ivanic, 1997; Nystrand, 1986; Prior, 1998).

Asynchronous communication tools give students access to drafts and comments written by peers. Several research studies have shown that students find this useful (e.g. Boud, Cohen & Sampson, 2001; Oldervoll, 2003). In our case the undergraduate law student goes through an extremely well structured and time consuming writing process. What is characteristic of this system is the sheer quantity of text that is produced and the fact that student writing covers the most central parts of the curriculum. We found, for example, that in one particular course a single group of 10 students submitted a total of 18 individual and group assignments into the VLE, amounting to a total 17662 words. The written feedback amounted to an additional 15119 words, almost as extensive as the assignments themselves. This indicates that the response is an important part of the writing and learning activity. The fact that approximately 80 percent of the written comments are from group leaders indicates the same asymmetric pattern as observed in oral communication. Students seem to accept and value the authoritative words from teachers and TAs. The question, in light of Bakhtin's insistence on the importance of developing the 'inner persuasive word', is what kind of identity students are allowed to develop. This adherence to authority may be connected to the strict structuring of the students' learning, which from a sociocultural learning perspective may be unproductive, as it can thwart students' engagement, originality and creativity and hence their ability to develop alternative identities. It can be argued, though, that individual, authoritative discourse creates the most comfortable situation to be in, for instance, for students in modularized courses, who are given clear direction on the most important knowledge and skills they must obtain within a limited time.

Peer Tutoring – a key to Students' Identity Development and Success

TAs can be seen as the gatekeepers of a smoothly run system for learning design within the law faculty, and therefore deserve attention. According to Bruffee (1999), most tutoring programs are a mixture of two main categories, or prototypes, of peer tutoring. The 'monitor type' denotes "direct, centralized, monitor-like tutoring that mobilizes undergraduates as institutional manpower for prevailing institutional ends" (p. 96). In this way the peer tutors act like surrogate teachers. Their peer status is compromised by the fact that they are selected and superior students "who for all intents and purposes serve as faculty surrogates under faculty supervision" (ibid., p. 97). In contrast, the 'collaborative model' denotes "a kind of collaborative learning: indirect, polycentralized tutoring that mobilizes interdependence and peer influence for broadly educational ends" (ibid., p. 96). In this prototype of peer tutoring, the tutor sees the institution from the same perspective as the tutees. Both types can be very effective to student learning, but they produce different kinds of learning and identities. Bruffee's characterisation of the two types of peer tutoring resembles Bakhtin's distinction of the authoritative versus the inner persuasive discourse. Students' knowledge acquisition process is as much dependent on the overall infrastructures for learning (e.g. the peer tutoring model; discursive patterns; cultural tools) as on their individual aptness and academic qualifications. From our case study we have seen strong indications that the way in which TAs intervene in the electronically written communication has an immense impact on how the undergraduate law students construct texts; what they write and what they do not write; and how they develop their identity as legitimate participants in the legal academic community. Moreover, in this context the VLE represents an enculturation arena where the presence and involvement of the TAs serve several purposes, associated with control and authority as well as scaffolding and guidance.

Technology-Mediated Textual Knowledge Production

VLE technologies are not designed as specific tools for learning and collaboration, but are more commonly used for administrative purposes (e.g. to file and distribute administrative information, support structured delivery of teaching materials, convey multiple-choice tests, monitor students' learning process, and so forth). In this case the VLE has been adjusted to be a tool for assignments and feedback, although it cannot be characterised as a specialised pedagogical tool for academic writing. The subject content is created by the law students as a response to faculty designed law cases. Structured feedback from the teachers and TAs allows for productive learning to take place. The networked technology opens up a virtual space for advanced interaction, personal communication and knowledge distribution. Furthermore, it embodies an important account of the learning history of individuals, which they can use actually see and learn from their own and their peers' earlier mistakes. From a dialogical point of view this feature can afford productive learning processes to take place in the future, since:

Each text we write is a speech act, and the success of that text is in the consequences of what follows after, how the text creates a landmark of something done that needs to be taken into account in future utterances (Bazerman, 2004, p. 62).

All texts and comments are made visible to all group members by the VLE, and because participants can view the progress of each others' learning, the law students' interactions with their peers have changed. Just knowing that someone other than the TA/instructor is able to see a text will affect the way students approach any given task.

We are cautious not to make strong claims about the effectiveness of technology in improving students' learning and performance. The important consideration of any new technology is its potential to transform the way in which people communicate knowledge and skills and how information is organised (Säljö, 2003). In this case, comprehensive writing and feedback, combined with the opportunity to discuss collaboratively with peers and a more experienced law student on a regular basis, has obviously facilitated law students' learning. But we have also shown that it facilitates conformity and provides little room for alternative identity construction. The danger is 'over-socialization' (Christie, 1997), a situation where students come to distrust their ability to make independent judgements, and which therefore fosters reproductive forms of learning.

Indications of Productive versus Reproductive and Counterproductive Learning Practices

Through our investigation we have come across a number of tensions and contradictions between the well structured learning design and intended and unintended response patterns in terms of law students' actions. We will contrast these discrepancies in a matrix.

Table 1. Relationship between planned design and student responses

	Intentions of the faculty's learning design	Indicators of productive learning practices (l. p)	Indicators of un- and counter- productive l. p
Study Structure	Strict learning structure defined by a mix of obligatory group and self-directed study activities	Steady study progression Learning is fostered through social infrastructures	Time shortage: constant conflicts between self-study versus obligatory joint activities
	Modularized courses and frequent examinations	Reduction in student failure rate and a higher throughput of students	Much energy spent on preparing and learning the 'right' techniques

	Close follow-up of student learning progression	Persistent study support through close follow up and monitoring.	Gradually decreased student motivation for comprehensive obligatory activities
		Student satisfaction	
Learning method	Problem-based learning	Students learn to articulate and explore different law genres in an authentic way	Predefined and teacher-given problems leave little room for independent writing/thinking
	Face-to-face group discussions	Students share knowledge and learn from multi-voiced perspectives	The authorative word of TAs dominates group discourses
		Students get to know each other and develop a social network	Difficult to create passionate group discussions, and to change established communicative patterns
Knowledge construction	Knowledge sharing through joint problems and collaborative/ cooperative efforts	Student knowledge is socially constructed in an environment of knowledgeable peers	Very high degree of dependency on authorities
	Process-oriented writing and feedback	Learning of legal methods integrated with contents through extensive writing exercises and electronic feedback	Great differences in the quality of assignments and peer comments
	Self-study		'Free riders'
TAs' role	Facilitators: ask open questions, lead discussions, give proper feedback.	Role models for freshmen, and 'brokers' between communities of newcomers and experts	Instructors/teachers substitutes/ authorities: ask precise questions, give the right answers
Teachers' role	Course providers/task constructors/ coordinators/lecturers/ examiners	More responsibility for different phases of students' learning processes	Control student study behaviour, e.g. through tasks, exam and feedback

VLE	Classfronter is used for administrative and economic purposes, as well as pedagogical	Time-saving for admin. Efficient and economic tool for organising a large number of texts	Very demanding and risky to change from one VLE to another system
	Classfronter is used for pedagogical purposes	Affords a joint arena for knowledge sharing and knowledge on a 24/7 basis Offers teachers and students deep insight into student/peer learning process through transparent electronic feedback	Functions as a disciplining tool; colonizes students' time and offers a limited space for reflection and exploration of different solutions
	Archival system	Student assignments and comments represent an important reading resource in preparation for exams	May result in stereotyped ways of solving legal problems
Assessment	75% obligatory attendance in groups Must pass a take-home exam before registering for final sit-down exam	Involve a reduced risk of failure; ensure student progression and better exam results	Still much focus on traditional exams Time-consuming written assignment, but no exam credit

Table 1 shows that the overall learning design at the law faculty has managed to elicit social infrastructures that foster students' learning in many respects, but also that there are tensions in the system design that counteract productive learning. We have tried to identify the 'cracks' (see below) in the learning design at the faculty and what constitutes productive in contrast to reproductive and counterproductive learning practices. The final part of our discussion is an empirically informed sociocultural analysis of what counts as a productive learning environment, and the effect of technology. Wenger's understanding of a learning design will serve as our starting point: "a systematic, planned, and reflexive colonization of time and space in the service of an undertaking" (p. 228). Moreover, many of the contradictive elements in the above matrix echo Wenger's (1998) statement that learning is not a result of an intended design, but a reaction to it, because: "Ultimately, it belongs to the realm of experience and practice. It follows the negotiation of meaning, it moves on its own terms. It slips through the cracks; it creates its own cracks. Learning happens, design or no design" (p. 225). The learning design at the law faculty can be described in terms of a strong procedural script and 'well-oiled processes'

(Crook, Gross & Dymott, 2006) which in many instances has led to a productive learning environment. The law faculty has experimented with new teaching and learning methods, assessment practices and new technology in a competent and well administered manner, under constant pressure from inside and outside forces. It has managed to implement demanding changes initiated by the Quality Reform, and it has furthermore challenged and transformed a long-lived lecture and book-centred learning culture. But as this study indicates, via socio-cultural analysis, there are reasonable arguments for raising a further critical discussion about the role and effects of Classfronter, and to what extent the technology as an intrinsic part of the learning ecology has afforded more productive learning practices.

Authoritative versus Inner Persuasive Discourse

The tension between conformity and divergence is conspicuous in our analysis of the overall learning design at the law faculty, and it is further connected with power and authority. This tension is reflected in what Bakhtin (1981) categorises as "a sharp gap" between the 'authoritative discourse' and 'internally persuasive discourse':

> The authoritative word demands that we acknowledge it, that we make it our own; it binds us, quite independent of any power it might have to persuade us internally; we encounter it with its authority already fused to it. The authorative word is located in a distanced zone, organically connected with a past that is felt to be hierarchically higher. It is, so to speak, the word of the fathers. Its authority was already acknowledged in the past. It is a prior discourse. It is therefore not a question of choosing it from among other possible discourses that are its equal (p. 342).

In contrast to authoritative discourse, "the inner persuasive word is half ours and half someone else's" (ibid.). Matusov (2007) explicates Bakhtin's conceptualisation of internally persuasive discourse as "critical stance to a text: he [Bakhtin] talked about experimenting with the text, questioning the author, imagining alternatives, evaluation of diverse discourses, and challenging the text" (p. 230). From our empirical analysis we will argue that the law students do a lot of this in their written communication and feedback processes, but because the authoritative word of the TAs and the teachers are valued much more than the their own words, they develop a learner identity based on a transmission view of what law education is about. It can also be argued that students are not being given opportunities to explore and experiment with anything other than the authoritative discourses. This argument is supported by our observations of face-to-face groups as well as by student diaries, where alternative approaches are not evident. The fact that the modified problem-based learning model used at this faculty does not involve students in defining meaningful problems themselves, further affirms an image of a dominant authoritative discourse.

From a Bakhtinian perspective, "the creativity and productiveness" of inner persuasive discourse "consists precisely in the fact that such a word awakens new and independent words, organizes masses of our words from within, and does not remain in an isolated and static condition. It is not so much interpreted by us as it is further, that is, freely, developed, applied to new material, new conditions [...] More than that, it enters into an intense interaction, a struggle with other internally persuasive discourses" (1981, p. 345–6).

There are indications that the development of students' inner persuasive discourse is obstructed by the authorative word and by a strict learning design that does not leave much space for experimentation and reflection. We do not view this as an intentional effect. One particularly aspect, however, is the law students' experience of continual conflict between the demand to absorb new information and the expectation to demonstrate their own intellectual development. Students are not asked to revise their work in response to feedback and this can also have a reproductive effect. If students had to revise, they would have to rely more on their peers and recognize the value of good comments. Research on text revision has shown that revision is far more demanding than mere proofreading and can lead to deeper and more reflective learning approaches.

CONCLUSION

As a step toward a more comprehensive understanding of the long term effectiveness of a virtual learning environment upon disciplinary writing and knowledge production in a traditional university subject, we believe that it is important to consider the socializing effects that can be created and maintained by networked technologies upon the participants of a structured networked learning environment. Even though it is well documented that systematic use of process oriented writing, including teacher- and peer response, promotes learning, this study indicates that educators should concern themselves with the subtle boundary between the socializing of students into an academic community and its discourse, and fostering their ability to develop and trust their own 'voices'. Accordingly, university learning designers would do well to bear in mind Crook et al.'s (2006) admonition that a proceduralised and well-oiled system for student assessment and feedback can easily, though unintended, become educationally counterproductive. This is especially so if it leads students "to expect proceduralisation of the creative activity itself" (p. 111). With these cautionary perspectives in mind, we will argue that networked technology is a "double-edged sword". On one hand, it may fortify extensive disciplinary control. One the other hand, it can open a dialogic space in which the student is given the opportunity to blossom out as an independent critical thinker and writer in the discipline. In any case, as we have demonstrated in this study, the potential learning benefits of networked technology are deeply constrained by its very groundedness in the broader cultural, historical and social context.

The design of this case study implies that the findings should be interpreted with care, and our findings do not allow us to make general statements about the whole population of law students. Further research on electronic peer feedback, whether relating to law or other academic disciplines, would be particularly useful in order to understand more of the productive mechanisms between the overall learning design and the discursive, textual practices at the micro level.

NOTES

[1] We use the term 'virtual learning environment' (VLE). In the United States it is more common to use the term 'learning management system' (LMS).

[2] Norwegian law students are principally trained in two distinct written genres. 1) Practical tasks (praktikum), which are constructed on basis of a given case where the problem to be addressed is pre-defined by a detailed description of litigants' claims and allegations. The student is provided with a limited set of legal facts, and in order to solve the legal problem at issue the student is normally expected take the perspective of a judge and applying various and relevant sources of law. The main challenge for the student seems to be to identify and formulate one or more precise judicial problems derived from the available task information. 2) Theoretical tasks (teori), which (often) require the student to give an account of valid law within a more or less defined legal area. This may imply to discuss boundaries and condition of law applications, central legal conceptions, legal effects, or how rules of law are put into practice.

[3] This reform was a direct follow-up of the Bologna Declaration (European Higher Education Area, 1999). Norway, although not a member of EU, has been in the forefront of implementing the Bologna principles. The Quality reform, introduced in 2001, represents an attempt to achieve a higher degree of efficiency through stronger leadership, improved pedagogy and increased internationalisation and quality assurance (www.nokut.no). One noticeable consequence of the implementation of the Bologna Declaration was the introduction of the European Credit Transfer System (ECTS) of credits and the ECTS Marking Scale with grades from A to F. One year of full-time study amounts to 60 credits.

[4] The Diary Project included four 2 hour summary meetings during spring term 2006 where the first author (Vines) and a senior executive from the Law faculty invited the writers to discuss preliminary findings based on what they had written in their diaries up to each meeting. 20 participants volunteered for the project, including students from the three first year of the professional law.

[5] Examples of so-called «outstanding» exam papers with examiner's comments are printed in *The Injuria Law Journal*, a student run journal at the Faculty of Law at the University of Bergen.

[6] In this chapter we will limit ourselves to the specific functional tools in Classfronter that are used in our site. Lian (2003) reports some serious problems and shortcomings with the interface when users submit comments on the original student drafts. Pedersen (2005) has further analysed some unfortunate practical consequences of similar technical problems from a teacher perspective.

[7] Lian (2003) has elsewhere described and analyzed the technical functionality of Classfronter in her study of the implementation of Classfronter at the Law faculty at the UoB.

REFERENCES

Bakhtin, M. (1984). Discourse in Dostoevsky. In C. Emerson (Ed.), *Problems of Dostoevsky's Poetics* (C. Emerson, Trans., pp. 181–269). Minneapolis: University of Minnesota Press.

Bakhtin, M. M. (1981). Discourse in the novel. In M. Holquist (Ed.), *The dialogic imagination: Four essays by M. M. Bakhtin* (C. Emerson & M. Holquist, Trans., pp. 259–422). Austin: University of Texas Press.

Bakhtin, M. M. (1986). The problem of speech genres. In C. Emerson & M. Holquist (Eds.), *Speech genres and other late essays* (V. W. McGee, Trans., pp. 60–102). Austin: Univiversity of Texas.

Barron, B. (2006). Interest and self-sustained learning as catalysts of development: A learning ecology perspective. *Human Development, 49*(4), 193–224.

Barton, D. (1994). *Literacy: An introduction to the ecology of written language*. Oxford: Blackwell.

Bazerman, C. (2004). Intertextualities: Volosinov, Bakhtin, literary theory, and literacy studies. In A. F. Ball & S. W. Freedman (Eds.), *Bakhtinian perspectives on languages, literacy, and learning* (pp. 53–65). Cambridge: Cambridge University Press.

Bernt, J. F., & Doublet, D. R. (1999). *Juss, samfunn og rettsanvendelse. En introduksjon til rettsvitenskapen* [*Law, society and the application of the law. An introduction to jurisprudence*]. Oslo: Ad Notam. Gyldendal.

Biggs, J. (1999). *Teaching for quality learning at university: What the student does*. Buckingham: Society for Research into Higher Education & Open University Press.

Boud, D., Cohen, R., & Sampson, J. (Eds.). (2001). *Peer learning in higher education. Learning from and with each other*. London: Kogan Page Limited.

Bruffee, K. A. (1999). *Collaborative learning: Higher education, interdependence, and the authority of knowledge*. Baltimore: John Hopkins Press.

Christie, N. (1997). Four blocks against insight. Notes on the oversocialization of criminologists. *Theoretical criminology, 1*(1), 13–23.

Clark, R., & Ivanic, R. (1997). *The politics of writing*. New York: Routledge.

Crook, C. K., Gross, H., & Dymott, R. (2006). Assessment relationships in higher education: The tension of process and practice. *British Educational Research Journal, 32*(1), 95–114.

European Higher Education Area. (1999). *The Bologna Declaration of 19 June, 1999*. [Electronic version]. Retrieved January 11, 2007, from http://www.gom.cg.yu/files/1185285842.pdf

Friedland, J. L. (1996). How we teach: A survey of teaching techniques in American law schools. *Seattle University Law Review, 20*(1), 1–28.

Illeris, K. (1999). *Læring – aktuel læringsteori i spændingsfeltet mellem Piaget, Freud og Marx* [Contemporary *Learning Theory in the Tension Field between Piaget, Freud and Marx*]. Frederiksberg: Roskilde Universitetsforlag.

Innes, R. B. (2006). What can learning science contribute to our understanding of the effectiveness of problem-based learning groups? *Journal of Management Education, 30*(6), 751–764.

***Jensen, K., & Nygård, R. (2000). *Studentidentitet og samfunnsmoral. Søkelys på høyere gradsstudenters norm- og verdisettingsmønster* [*Student identity and societal moral issues. On graduate students' norms and value structures*]. Innsatsområdet Etikk, Skriftserie 4. Oslo: Universitetet i Oslo.

Jones, C., Dirckinck-Holmfeld, L., & Lindström, B. (2005). CSCL The next ten years – a view from Europe. In T. Koschmann, D. Suthers, & T.-W. Chan (Eds.), *Computer supported collaborative learning 2005: The next ten years!* (pp. 237–246). Mahwah, NJ: Lawrence Erlbaum Associates.

Karseth, B., & Solbrekke, T. D. (2006). Characteristics of graduate professional education: Expectations and experiences in psychology and law. *London Review of Education, 4*(2), 149–176.

Kennedy, D. (1982). Legal education and the reproduction of hierarchy. *Journal of Legal Education, 32*(4), 591–615.

Kissam, P. C. (2003). *The discipline of law schools. The making of modern lawyers*. Durham, North Carolina: Carolina Academic Press.

Lave, J., & Wenger, E. (1991). *Situated learning – legitimate peripheral participation*. Cambridge: Cambridge University Press.

Lian, T. G. (2003). *IKT og Juss. Et etnografisk studie av IKT-mediert samarbeid i juridisk utdanning* [ICT and law. An ethnographic study of ICT-mediated collaboration in legal education]. Hovedfagsoppgave [master thesis] ved Institutt for informasjonsvitenskap. Universitetet i Bergen.

Lillejord, S., & Dysthe, O. (2008). Productive learning practice - a theoretical discussion based on two cases. *Journal of Education and Work, 21*(1), 75–89.

Matusov, E. (2007). Applying Bakhtin scholarship on discourse in education: A critical review essay. *Educational Theory, 57*(2), 215–237.

Munro, G. (2001). *Outcomes assessment for law schools*. Institute for Law School Teaching, Gonzaga University Press.

Møller-Holst, K. (2006). *Syn på egen læring: en studie av jusstudenters syn på egen læring, basert på erfaringer med gruppeveiledning på Det juridiske fakultet ved Universitetet i Bergen* [*"Views on their own learning": a study of law students' views on their own learning, based on experiences with group supervision at the law faculty at the University of Bergen*]. Masteroppgave [master thesis] ved Institutt for Utdanning og Helse, Universitetet i Bergen.

Nystrand, M. (1986). *The structure of written communication. Studies in reciprocity between writers and readers.* Orlando, FL: Academic Press.

Oldervoll, J. (2003). Portfolios in writing-based education. Experiences from Intermediate Level History. In O. Dysthe & S. Engelsen (Eds.), *Portfolio evaluation as a pedagogical tool: Perspectives and experiences* (pp. 295–310). Oslo: Abstrakt forlag.

Pedersen, M. K. (2005). *Pedagog eller teknogog? Ein kvalitativ studie av kva studiestøttesystemet Classfronter har å seie for læraren som rettleiar og tilretteleggar for læring* [*Pedagogue or technogogue? A qualitative study of the consequenses of using Classfronter, a virtual learning system, with regard to the teacher as supervisor and facilitator of learning*]. Masteroppgave [master thesis] ved Institutt for Utdanningsvitenskap, Universitetet i Bergen.

Pihlajamäki, H., & Lindblom-Ylänne, S. (2003). Adjusting law teaching to social change: A historical perspective to legal education. *Retfærd. Nordisk juridisk tidsskrift, 26*(2), 5–19.

Prior, P. (1998). *Writing/disciplinarity: A sociohistoric account of literate activity in the academy.* Hillsdale, NJ: Erlbaum.

Raaheim, A., & Hauge, H. (1994). *Ressursgruppen - et aksjonsrettet tiltak for flergangsstrykere for å øke gjennomstrømmingen ved 3. avd. jus ved Universitetet i Bergen.* [*The Resource Group – an action-oriented programme to increase the throughput of third year students who repeatedly fail the exam at the law study, at the University of Bergen*]. Rapportserie 4. Program for læringsforskning, Universitetet i Bergen.

Russell, D. R. (1993). Vygotsky, dewey, and externalism: Beyond the student/discipline dichotomy. *Journal of Advanced Composition, 13*(1), 173–197.

Salomon, G. (1995). What does the design of effective CSCL require and how do we study its effects? In J. L. Schnase & E. L. Cunnius (Eds.), *CSCL 95. Computer support for collaborative learning* (pp. 147–156). Mahwah, NJ: Lawrence Erlbaum.

Strømsø, H. (2003). Hvordan arbeider jusstudenter med juridiske fagtekster? [How do law students work with legal texts?]. *Nordisk tidsskrift for ret og samfund, 26*(4), 3–13.

Säljö, R. (2003). Representational tools and the transformation of learning. In B. Wasson, S. R. Ludvigsen, & U. Hoppe (Eds.), *Designing for change in networked learning. Proceedings on computer support for collaborative learning 2003* (pp. 1–2). Dordrecht: Kluwer Academic Publishers.

Twining, W. (1994). *Blackstone's tower: The english law school.* London: Sweet and Maxwell.

Vines, A. (forthcoming). Multivoiced e-feedback in the study of law: Enhancing learning opportunities? In R. Krumsvik (Ed.), *Learning in the network society and the digitized school.* LEA.

Vygotsky, L. (1978). *Mind in society.* Cambridge, MA: Harvard University Press.

Vygotsky, L. (1962). *Thought and language.* Cambridge, MA: MIT Press.

Wenger, E. (1998). *Communities of practice. Learning, meaning, and identity.* Cambridge: Cambridge University Press.

Wertsch, J. V. (1998). *Mind as action.* Oxford: Oxford University Press.

Wertsch, J. V. (1991). *Voices of mind.* Cambridge, MA: Harvard University Press.

White, J. B. (1999). *From expectation to experience: Essays on law and legal education.* Ann Arbor: University of Michigan Press.

Wilhelmsen, L. S., & Lilleholt, K. (2003). *Fra pugg til problemløsning med IKT som mediator: Evaluering av et forsøksopplegg for 3. avdeling ved det juridiske studium, 2001-2002* [*"From cramming to problem solving with ICT as a mediator": Evaluation of a pilot project for 3rd year students at the law study, at the University of Bergen, 2001–2002*]. Det juridiske fakultet. Universitetet i Bergen.

Östergren, K. (2006). A case of organizational learning in higher education. In R. Lines, I. Stensaker, & A. Langley (Eds.), *New perspectives on organizational change and learning* (pp. 93–113). Bergen: Fagbokforlaget.

Åkvåg, I. M. (2000). *Jusstudentene fra A til Å*. [*Law students from A to Å*]. Særavhandling [master thesis]. Det juridiske fakultet, Universitetet i Oslo.

Arne Vines
Department of Education
University of Bergen, Norway

Olga Dysthe
Department of Education
University of Bergen, Norway

THOMAS RYBERG

UNDERSTANDING PRODUCTIVE LEARNING THROUGH THE METAPHORICAL LENS OF PATCHWORKING

Something old, something new
Something borrowed, something blue
And a silver sixpence in her shoe

The age old saying cited above – traditionally a list of good luck tokens for a new bride – captures the essence of how we can use metaphor of patchworking to help us understand learning processes. The metaphor of patchworking is used throughout this case study to highlight how learning processes, and processes of knowledge creation, consist of the stitching and weaving together of various patches into something new. The patches can be old, new, borrowed and of a widely different fabric; yet in combination they form a new patchwork. Empirically, the case study draws on a close examination of a short-term, open-ended, technology enhanced and problem oriented learning process, in which eight young people worked on the challenge of how ICT can be used to reduce poverty in the world. From this study, which formed the basis of the author's PhD thesis (Ryberg, 2007), the concept of understanding learning as a process of patchworking has emerged. The metaphor of patchworking is a perspective that emphasises the constructive, creative and productive aspects of learning. In this chapter the main aspects of this metaphorical perspective will be presented and discussed in relation to networked learning, indirect design and the notion of 'productive learning'.

INTRODUCTION

During 8–10 August 2005 six teams of young people worked intensively with a range of open-ended learning challenges. This took place within a larger event and symposium, which was itself part of the Power Users of Technology Project – a research project formed around the hypothesis that young people might be learning, working and solving problems in new and innovative ways due to their intensified use of technology (hence the term power users of technology). Moreover, it suggests that we can gain valuable insights about the future design of education by studying young people and their use of technology in relation to learning and problem solving processes.

L. Dirckinck-Holmfeld, C. Jones and B. Lindström (eds.), Analysing Networked Learning Practices in Higher Education and Continuing Professional Development, 201–221.

Each of the teams had chosen a specific problem to work with beforehand, and during the symposium. On the last day of the symposium they were to present their solutions and recommendations to the approximately 100 adults attending the event. Throughout this event the author in, collaboration with other researchers, closely followed the Nordic team of power users, who worked with the challenge of how to use technology to reduce poverty in the world. The eight young people that formed the Nordic team were: Angie, Diana, Jack, Jasper, Laura, Neil, Samuel, and Sophia (these are not their real names). Even though their work spanned almost three months, the majority of the time they spent on actually addressing the learning challenge and creating their presentation was much shorter; basically it covered just three days, during which time they managed to create quite an impressive final presentation.

In this chapter I argue for the metaphor of patchworking as a way of under-standing, analysing and approaching technology mediated learning processes. The notion of patchworking has emerged after a close observation and analysis of the work carried out by the team of power users, relying on video analysis, participant observation, interviews and document analysis (Ryberg, 2007). In the following pages I draw out and discuss some of the main methods and theoretical lessons in relation to the notions of networked learning, indirect design and the concept of productive learning. This is accomplished through initially presenting the case, and by discussing how we indirectly designed for productive learning. In relation to this I present an outline of the learning process, before applying the analytical concepts derived from the study and analysing examples of patchworking processes.

CASE DESCRIPTION

The empirical data in this chapter was the outcome of an event organised by the Power Users of Technology research project[1]. The event was called Power Users of Information and Communication Technology International Symposium[2], and took place between 8-10 August 2005 in San Jose, Costa Rica. The core assumption of the research project is that a new generation of young people is emerging due to societal and especially technological changes (Malyn-Smith, 2004; Malyn-Smith & Guilfoy, 2003; Ryberg, 2004). These tentative ideas and hypotheses crystallised into the Power Users of Technology Project, and the Costa Rica Symposium was the test-bed for these ideas and hypotheses (Dirckinck-Holmfeld & Ryberg, 2005; Ryberg & Dirckinck-Holmfeld, 2005).

The planning and staging of the Costa Rica symposium was a major task for many different people, although it was primarily headed and coordinated by the international, non-profit organisation EDC (Education Development Center Inc.). Although EDC was the main coordinator and project leader, each research team had a large degree of freedom in designing their own research and in the pedagogical design of the learning situation for their own power users team. Apart from sharing interview guides, adhering to logistic considerations and agreeing on the learning challenges as having a reference to the UN Millennium Goals, the individual research groups were free to pursue their own agenda. Therefore, this chapter only reports on the research design, the pedagogical design and findings related to the Nordic team of power users.

Our group's overall approach and research design employed mainly qualitative methods. We carried out an ethnographically inspired, open-ended investigation with close observations and documentation of their work during the symposium[3]. The data collected during and after the symposium were:

– Field notes from the participatory observation
– The proceedings of eight individual interviews and two group interviews with the young power users
– Hand-written notes and documents, as well as digitally produced notes and documents from their tablet PCs
– Approximately 20 hours of video footage, showing the team at work.

Thus, the work process of the young people during the symposium was quite extensively documented. In the following I shall describe how we framed and indirectly designed the work process and relate this to some of the central concepts presented in this book.

INDIRECT DESIGN AND PROBLEM ORIENTED PROJECT PEDAGOGY

Our pedagogical design was based on a very open ended problem based learning approach. Rather than designing specific sequenced events or deciding and controlling in detail what, and how, they should learn, we were more concerned with creating a setting or frame for the young people to act in. This is what we understand as an indirect approach to designing for learning (Goodyear et al., 2001; Jones et al., 2006). To understand the notion of indirect design we can turn to Peter Goodyear's visualisation of how to indirectly design for networked learning environments (Goodyear et al., 2001):

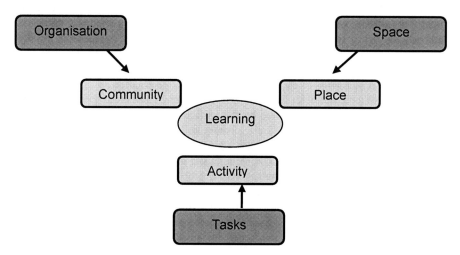

Figure 1. Indirect design - model adapted from (Goodyear et al., 2001, p. 98)

The basic claim of this model is that one should refrain from designing or interfering in detail with the components that are most closely related to learning. Instead one should focus on designing *organisational forms*, *learning spaces* and *tasks* which learners will respond to, appropriate and enact in an emergent, non-predictable way.

We aimed to realise this by drawing on a specific kind of problem based learning which is known as the Aalborg PBL model (Kolmos et al., 2004) or Problem Oriented and Project Pedagogy (POPP) (Dirckinck-Holmfeld, 2002). I refer to these terms to emphasise that notions of problem based learning cover many different ways of organising problem based learning processes. In some orchestrations of PBL the teacher has a more central role in governing the work and defining the problem than is the case with the Aalborg model, for instance.

To better illustrate the dynamics between different ways of organising for PBL, we can use the model below (Ryberg et al., 2006):

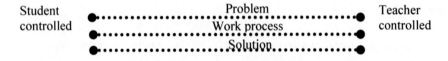

Student controlled ●··Problem··● Teacher controlled
●··Work process··●
●····························Solution····························●

Figure 1. Different orchestrations of PBL-processes

The model identifies three central dimensions of PBL/POPP-processes: the problem, the work process and the solution (Ryberg et al., 2006). These dimensions can be more or less controlled by either the students or the teachers. The axis of 'the problem' opens questions about who controls or owns the definition and framing of the problem: the teacher, the participants or others? Likewise 'the work process' is concerned with how the work processes are organized and who controls them. For instance, who chooses to investigate the problem and in what way (theories, methods, empirical investigations etc.), and who is in control of the project? Finally, one can ask questions about who owns 'the solution', meaning whether the solution is open-ended or fixed. Are the participants expected to come up with a predefined solution or is process one of exploration and knowledge creation?

In relation to the Costa Rica symposium we envisioned that these three dimensions should be predominantly controlled by the participants, and we conceived our role as one of supervisors who would help, discuss and facilitate their work. Therefore, we asked the young people to choose one topic from fifteen options, all very different but all connected to the UN Millennium goals (poverty, education, gender etc.), and we asked them to come up with a problem formulation by themselves. Furthermore, we wanted them to be in general control of the flow of the process and the distribution of work (apart from some things that we had to decide upon due to logistics or time pressure). Even though the pedagogical design was relatively open it was still situated within the larger design of the setting – something I shall return to in more depth when discussing the conditions for learning.

In relation to this case study and the setup of the Costa Rica event, we can use the categories of macro, meso and micro to identify three different levels of design and planning. These we can also relate to the concepts from Goodyear's model:

- A macro level being represented by the overall planning group of the event (which we as researchers were also part of)
- A meso level being the management of the Nordic team (a process also involving the power users to some degree)
- A micro level being the actual work of the power users (including us as researchers and facilitators).

As part of the overall design of the organisational forms the notion of team-work was established and the tasks were widely formulated as 'the UN millennium goals'. The space was designed in accordance with the practical necessities of having the event in the Marriot Hotel in San Jose.

This was the wider frame in which each of the research groups would have to navigate and choose a way of designing the environment for their specific team. Our group translated the notion of organisation and tasks into a PBL/POPP model of group work, which was organised around a common problem owned by the young people. Furthermore, we arranged some different spaces for them to engage with (the spaces, in Goodyear's terminology, are the physical learning environments, including all the artefacts embodying 'content' (Goodyear, 2001, p. 97). This can be understood as a kind of indirect design for learning and represents a meso level approach to pedagogical design.

We aimed at facilitating and indirectly designing the event by:

- Providing and nurturing a learning environment
- Providing and nurturing a social ecology
- Providing and nurturing a technological infrastructure.

I shall return to discuss these dimensions when reflecting on how this indirect design unfolded. In short we aimed at providing and nurturing a learning environment by creating connections to various resources for the power users to draw on. This was undertaken most visibly in the arranging on their behalf of interviews with resource people, and a lecture for the power users. We could call this 'arranging for learning opportunities', as there were no fixed learning goals for the different interactions. Secondly, we were conscious about establishing and supporting a sociable atmosphere. Before the actual symposium we spent some days together in Costa Rica, and we asked the young people to conduct short interviews with each other, so as to get to know each other better. Finally, we arranged for them to have access to various technologies, such as tablet PCs, video cameras, wireless access, a mini disc player, an Apple Mac and software packages for video editing, word processing, presentation and so forth.

DESCRIPTION OF THE LEARNING PROCESS

As mentioned earlier, the bulk of their work and learning process took place within the three days of the symposium. Even though three of them had already met on 27 July and discussed some aspects of their work (searching for information, conceptualising poverty and creating a provisional problem formulation), they had to re-negotiate and re-frame these ideas when engaging with the five other power users. In fact, they didn't have much to work with from the outset, as it was mainly vague ideas and concepts. Thus, their actual work began on 7 August in the evening, where they started to create interview guides for their expert interviews, and it culminated on 10 August when they presented their work to the symposium attendees[4]. Most of the time they all worked in a room, kindly provided by Universidad Nacional, but also they went out to interview various resource persons and experts. They interviewed two researchers: Ricardo Monge[5] and Manuel Bersone[6]. Furthermore they interviewed a manager of the Intel Clubhouse[7] in San Jose (Laura Aijalla) and a young user of the Clubhouse (Cynthia). Moreover, they had a small lecture on poverty, which was given by two local researchers (Mauricio Dierckxsens and Keynor Ruiz). The Nordic Team's final presentation was called 'how to improve a poor society' and the pictures below are from the presentation.

Figure 2. Pictures of their final presentation

The presentation was heavily multi-modal and combined many media and resources. On one projector screen a continuous slideshow with pictures of 'poor people' was displayed, and on another their main PowerPoint presentation was shown. The various types of media included music, pictures, a self-made cartoon show, small video clips from the interviews (some of them subtitled) and graphs carrying statistical information about poverty. In this way the presentation was a 'patchwork' of many different resources, means and media that were assembled to convey their conceptualisation of poverty and how to address this issue.

The multiple resources were foraged from various sources and by different means. Some graphs came from the PowerPoint slides used by the local researchers for the lecture; facts and information came from various web pages and books. Ideas came from the interviews, an informal conversation on a bus, and other sources. The four interviews they conducted were all recorded on video, edited and made part of the presentation. Pictures of poor people were found on the web, while the graphics in the animation were hand-drawn and animated in PowerPoint. The music used was carried on their computers from home.

Thus, the presentation was a complex patchwork of different media and resources, but also a conceptual patchwork representing complex arguments and lines of reasoning about poverty. The presentation outlined an overall argument that revolved to a large extent around taxes and education, although many other things were drawn in as causes of or solutions to poverty. These included corruption, lack of secondary education, Intel Clubhouses as an opportunity for young people to gain a new perspective on life, and more broadly, education as a means for civic engagement.

While it is difficult to convey in full the complexity of their arguments, the presentation and the whole process, I will try to illustrate it in the next section by analysing a single section.

ANALYSIS OF PATCHWORKING PROCESSES

Their final presentation was a very complex and impressive assemblage of different media, arguments and lines of reasoning. However, it should be noted that this claim rests on a very thorough analysis of the entire process. A central argument of the analysis and investigation in (Ryberg, 2007) was that it is not the final patchwork that should be made the object of study, nor its multimodality or the final assemblage of various patches, rather it is the patchworking process itself that we critically need to engage with. A guiding question of the analysis in (Ryberg, 2007) was whether the process was a mindless exercise of copy-and-paste or a creative, innovative and challenging process. In short, was it a process of knowledge construction rather than re-production?

Such questions are quite pressing in relation to youth, digital media and literacy. For instance, (Jenkins et al., 2006) building on a study of Guinee and Eagleton (2006) point out that young people's use and re-use of digital material in relation to learning processes might be less of a creative enterprise and knowledge creating process than anticipated:

"Guinee and Eagleton (2006) have been researching how students take notes in the digital environment, discovering, to their dismay, that young people tend to copy large blocks of text [...]. In the process, they often lose track of the distinction between their own words and material borrowed from other sources. They also skip over the need to assess any contradictions that might exist in the information they have copied. In short, they show only a minimal ability to create a meaningful synthesis from the resources they have gathered." (Jenkins et al., 2006, p. 51)

In this particular case the young people foraged quite a number of different resources from the web, but also, for example, from the PowerPoint slides of the researchers who gave them the lecture on poverty in Central America. From the pictures below one can see a particular slide which was presented by the researcher Mauricio Dierckxsens during his lecture. The very same slide was incorporated and used as part of the power user team's presentation (as were two other slides).

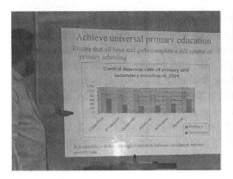

Figure 3. Example of slide re-used in their presentation

It would be justifiable to ask if this was an example of copy-and-paste plagiarism, or whether it was in fact a creative re-appropriation of this particular resource. In the subsequent analysis I shall take up this example and follow the 'itinerary' of the slides and how they were woven into their patchwork. Initially, I will just present some of the concepts that can be employed to analyse processes of patchworking.

Analytic concepts

The three main analytic concepts of studying learning processes through the metaphorical lens of patchworking are: Cycles, Processes and Threads.

Cycles are an analytical entrance path towards identifying some of the overarching structures of an event or series of events. They represent an overall rhythm or composition of such events. In relation to this case, two overarching cycles in the work flow were identified (Ryberg, 2007). These were called *cycles of remixing and patchworking* and *cycles of stabilisation work and production.* In the cycles of remixing and patchworking the team would work as one unit, discussing some of the more overarching questions facing them, such as 'what should be our focus', 'how should we do the presentation', 'what is actually the problem and the solution'. During the cycles of stabilisation work and production, which occurred within smaller and more fleeting groups, they would further develop the products of the overarching discussions. These developments and pieces of work would then again feed into the cycles of patchworking and remixing.

Processes are also open, flexible analytical categories. They are ways of looking analytically at how an entire process of patchworking is accomplished. Some of the processes that were identified in (Ryberg, 2007) were, for instance, how they foraged and gathered different patches, how they managed and engaged in planning work, how they created a sociable atmosphere, engaged in production of artefacts and how they were continuously stitching a conceptual blueprint.

Threads are employed in the analysis to point to some organising principles or common links in their work. Prominent threads were, for example, formulation of the problem and the ongoing construction of their presentation. The concept of threads also refers to some of the ideas that were prevalent throughout their work;

for instance, a notion of education as an important factor in decreasing poverty. This was a prominent line of enquiry throughout the process, but it developed from a more general 'education is good' to 'education can be statistically shown to have a major impact on poverty and is a key condition for civic engagement and democratic participation in a society'. Throughout their work, patches (ideas, interpretations, arguments, information, and digital files) started to cluster and form provisional patchwork that were woven together into the larger overarching patchwork.

The Itinerary of Slides – the Origin, Development and Reweaving of Patchworks

On 9 August in the morning the young power users were given a lecture by Mauricio Dierckxsens (and Keynor Ruiz) entitled 'Balance of Millennium Goals in Central American Countries'. As soon as the lecture was over the power users asked if they could have the PowerPoint presentation, and they transferred it onto a USB stick. This is a good example of the processes of 'foraging and gathering', which were ongoing, ever-present modes of operation, in which they collected, piled and shared different patches. The slides were quickly distributed to their respective tablet PCs and Nigel volunteered to look through the slideshow to make sense of it and choose slides that might be particularly interesting for their presentation. Although Nigel started this task he was often joined by Sophie (and others).

They saved a copy of the slideshow and together they began to re-order the slides, putting the most interesting first and deleting others. In selecting and re-ordering the slides they continuously discussed them in relation to some of the primary threads and their provisional 'conceptual blueprint'. Some of the prominent threads represented causes of, or solutions to poverty, and revolved around taxes, education and jobs. To understand the emergence of these threads we need to take a small step back in time. The threads emerged initially as part of their small-group discussions on the first night of work, where a group consisting only of Angie, Samuel, Diana and Nigel created questions for the expert interviews (as did the others in groups of two). In the document that Angie created as their shared representation, these three topics or threads structured their different questions. The next day (8 August), during a longer discussion and brainstorming sequence (or rather a cycle of remixing and patchworking), three topics (taxes, education and jobs) were reified on a whiteboard as a shared representation for the whole group.

These then became threads which acted as orientation devices, in structuring and framing their work with their new problem formulation ('How to improve a poor society'). This problem formulation was itself under intense negotiation on the afternoon of the 8th, and resolved some tensions in their previous framing of the problem. Basically, they were not sure if they wanted to approach Costa Rica as a success story, or whether they should point out that there are still problems with poverty (despite great improvements). Whereas, their previous framing of the problem explicitly positioned Costa Rica either as a success story or as still having unresolved issues, this new framing of the problem did not force them into positioning Costa Rica as one or the other.

In relation to this problem formulation the three threads were their main lines of enquiry, as hypotheses for the causes of, or solutions to poverty. An ongoing part of their work was the construction of a 'conceptual blueprint'; an ephemeral and continuously negotiated blueprint of the relations between their problem, the causes and solutions, and what their final argument and presentation should focus on. This conceptual blueprint became increasingly more elaborate and advanced. As their work and enquiries progressed, the threads developed and became thicker, and the relationships between the overarching problem and the different threads got more complex.

The threads and a provisional conceptual blueprint was what were discussed on 8 August; and this is what Nigel and Sophie were orienting towards (and developing) through their work with these slides. Whether a particular slide was relevant or not was negotiated and aligned with the emerging and continuously developing conceptual blueprint.

The work that Nigel and Sophie were doing in the above example was typical of the cycles of stabilisation work and production. During these cycles different patches were foraged, discussed, altered and negotiated in relation to the threads and the conceptual blueprint. From this type of work the young people would encounter patches that questioned their hypotheses and assumptions, and could challenge their current conceptual blueprint. Such disruptive items would be discussed, but deeper problems and contradictions would be taken up more intensively during the large group discussions (cycles of remixing and patchworking). The work done during cycles of stabilisation work and production was foraging and gathering for different patches, and thereby creating small, provisional patchworks of resources, ideas and arguments. In this particular example this is represented by the order, prioritisation, sorting, negotiations of and re-organisation of the different slides. Such little patchworks would then enter the cycles of remixing and patchworking where they would be discussed in relation to the work, ideas and resources (patch-works) created by the others. This is what we shall see an example in the following extract presented in Table 1, which is but a small part of a cycle of remixing and patchworking that lasted approximately two hours.

During the two hours they are discussing and brainstorming on the structure and content of their presentation. However, this is actually much more complex than 'merely' planning or outlining their presentation. In fact, what they are engaging in is the overall construction of the conceptual blueprint and their overarching arguments.

In Figure 4 we see an overview of the whiteboard as it looked shortly after the end of the extract presented in Table 1. On the left side of the board we see a number of topics, which represent individual slides from the researchers' slideshow which are then placed into the structure of the presentation outline by means of the arrows. In this sense the whiteboard acts as an unstable boundary object through which they reify the concepts, ideas and content suggestions that have emerged during their discussion of the presentation. The whiteboard, however, is used in a much more active way. It is not only used to reify, but to dynamically negotiate the content, form, structure and their overarching line of argumentation. The presentation itself is coming into being, with the whiteboard functioning as a dynamic space for the construction of their conceptual blueprint. This will be illustrated through analysis of the extract in Table 1, where Neil is introducing one of the slides foraged from the researchers' presentation.

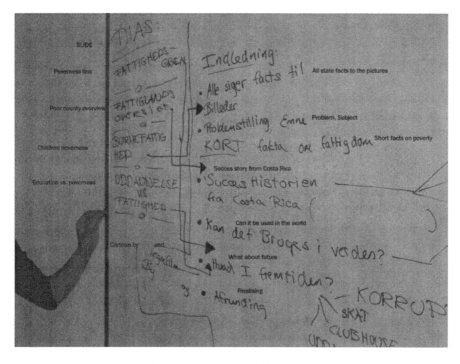

Figure 4. Overview of Whiteboard

Table 1. Extract of interaction: transcript with accompanying pictures

Neil: yeah then we the one that says that it is more the young and children that become poor (1.5)

Jasper: what?

Neil: ehm it is the children that become...

Samuel: it is, but it's...

Sophia: child-poorness

Neil: children below fifteen years are the most poor

Jasper: do we want to use that?

Samuel: it is those who live at home and can't really make any money

Jasper: should we use that?

Neil: yes, precisely

Samuel: and it is the poor families who have the most children

Laura: yes

Sophia: yes

Angie: that is because we must teach them something about protection (*TR: contraceptives*)

Jasper: should we use that or what?

Sophia: no we want to have children as ehm savings or whatever we want

Laura: as pension

Researcher: heh heh

Jasper: shall we use that

Jack: yeah why not

Samuel: why not

Laura: why?

Angie: it is good

Sophia: yeah, I think it is good, but I just don't know what it should appear under

Laura: what should we use it for?

Neil: (to Jack) I just think

Jack: (to Neil) ai okay okay okay it doesn't matter

Sophia: HELLO, hello how about we can put under that thing 'facts to pictures'

Jack: shh

Sophia: with ehm to you know that thing that it is actually kids under fifteen who are the most poor

??: yeah so we…

Jasper: that's actually something we could do put it under 'facts to pictures'

Neil: better there

Laura: yeah, but it should not be part of our work, you know, and make it to the conclusion

Neil: but it shouldn't really...

Angie: no

Jack: no it shouldn't be something for the conclusion - it should just be...

Laura: I mean we haven't made anything which especially...

Jack: some facts about...

Jasper: it should be a pretty good plan for what will come, else we will just forget it

The slide Neil introduces is entitled 'poverty by age group', showing that children are the most poor in Central America:

Immediately after the introduction Samuel starts to explain why this is so (which is partly because children do not really make much money, but also because the poor families have the most children). Here Samuel draws on earlier conversations about the topic, and also the explanations and interpretations of the slides, which were presented by the researchers.

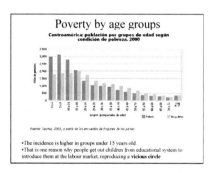

Figure 5. Slide: Poverty by age group

Sophia initially contests the use of the slide and says they "want to have children as savings"; or as Laura adds, "as a pension". This sounds rather odd, but originates in their wish to position the young population as resources, rather than a burden or problem. In their narrative they want the young population to appear as a hope for the future, rather than being a problematic group. Both Laura and Sophia point out that they do not know "what it should appear under" or "what they should use it for", which is a way of expressing that they do not see it as relevant to the overarching arguments of their presentation, and that it does not directly feed into the threads on either education or taxes.

Sophia is still in doubt about the use of the slide, but suggests they can put it under 'facts to pictures', which is a way of positioning it as a fact (but one that might need to be changed or dealt with to reduce poverty). Laura contests the use of the slide for other reasons, but agrees with the placement under 'facts', as she thinks they have not done a lot of work related to this particular perspective. Jack later suggests that it is moved from 'facts to pictures' to 'short facts about poverness (sic)[8]' (two categories that later merged). In both cases the positioning can be read as a 'demotion' of the importance of the slide. Each slide's argumentative weight is very much affected by its position in the presentation order, and whether it is placed within 'facts to pictures' or 'the success story of Costa Rica'. At this point the categories 'facts to pictures' and 'short facts about poverness' are envisioned as some rhetorical, oratory statements to highlight the importance of dealing with poverty. In contrast, 'the success story of Costa Rica' is seen as a point in the presentation where they will unfold the causes of and solutions to poverty, through more elaborated arguments. In this way it makes a big difference if a slide is positioned as a fact, or whether they position it as a part of a more elaborate argument.

From the extract in Table 1 we can see a glimpse of how these small patches are negotiated, discussed, contrasted and aligned with the threads and the conceptual blueprint. This also tells us that such resources, or 'knowledge artefacts', are not just uncritically stitched into the larger patchwork of their presentation. Rather, the larger patchwork is negotiated, unravelled, inspected and rewoven, as these different patches enter the discussions. This is because the slides are not treated as mere statistical facts (though in a sense they are); rather in the discussions they are transformed into particular argumentative resources.

Other examples are some of the facts about education (Figure 6), which they also foraged from the researchers' slides. While the statistical information on the slide was probably quite correct, its meaning was less straightforward. In this case the same slide was used in their final presentation to tell two different stories. For one thing it positioned Costa Rica as a success (compared to some of the other Central American countries). At the same time the slide it was used to argue that the relatively low secondary enrolment was a challenge that Costa Rica needed to address. This fed into a

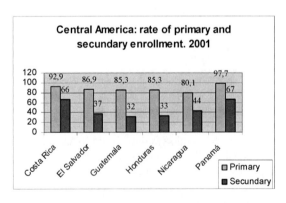

Figure 6. Slide: Primary and secondary enrolment in Central America

larger argument around the importance of taxes and how to encourage the Costa Rican people to pay higher taxes (which they coupled with the need to address corruption to regain the people's trust in the political system; and to invest even more in education to increase civic engagement and economic growth).

In both the examples we see how different digital patches that have been foraged enter into cycles of remixing and patchworking. Here they are negotiated, altered and enter into processes where the conceptual blueprint of their larger patchwork is rewoven and restructured. While I have only taken up small examples in this chapter this was quite a typical pattern of their work. Different patches were foraged, created, aligned and negotiated, before being crystallised into smaller patchworks (such as interview guides, facts about poverty, a self-made animation, foraged slides, video clips, a certain argument or way of arguing). This would typically happen during the cycles of stabilisation work and production, where they worked in smaller groups. Hereafter, all the smaller patches, or provisional patch-works, would enter into cycles of remixing and patchworking. During these cycles the conceptual blueprint of the entire problem space and presentation could be negotiated and rewoven.

THE METAPHOR OF PATCHWORKING

Having presented the notion of looking at learning as a process of patchworking, I shall relate this idea more intimately to some of the main ideas of this book; namely the notion of networked learning and productive learning. Research within the field of networked learning seems to have focused, in particular, on online courses, as embedded in various Learning Management Systems and supported by asynchronous or synchronous tools. This perspective is also prevalent from the other cases presented in this book. However, the chapter of introduction establishes a more varied interpretation of the interplay between online and offline contexts, as it focuses on movements and flows between these contexts. In line with this, the case presented here represents a slightly different constellation of people, resources and technologies.

My argument would be that the notion of networked learning actually has much wider currency, which can be illustrated when returning to the definition:

"Networked learning is learning in which information and communications (ICT) is used to promote connections: between one learner and other learners, between learners and tutors; between a learning community and its learning resources" (Goodyear et al., 2004)

While the interaction and communication between the young people was not mediated by ICT in the form of asynchronous or synchronous tools, for instance, many of the different digital patches were part of the fabric of their learning process. These were mediating their interactions through being shared representations or patches to manipulate, negotiate and alter. Thus, the digital patches were important parts of the processes of reweaving their conceptual blueprint and constructing the smaller and larger patchworks. Likewise, the access to many of the resources that became part of their presentation (facts, information, pictures) was only possible through the Internet.

A very important aspect of networked learning is the notion of promoting connections, both between learners and between learners and teachers; but also connecting people with resources. The resources, in my opinion, should be understood in a quite broad sense, as the young people were not only given access to a wide range of resources understood as material. Equally, we promoted connections between them, the researchers and other resource people (such as the Intel Clubhouse manager and the young girl using the club house). This gave them the opportunity to interact with professional networks or 'communities of practice'. In this sense we can understand their learning process as continuously traversing, connecting to or drawing on the resources, the content and knowledge from various networks; regardless of whether the patches that they worked into their developing patchwork were digital or analogue (e.g. whether it was a particular slide or a line of reasoning presented by the experts).

In fact, I believe this case shows us that the boundaries between digital and analogue are fleeting and mutable. Ideas may have come from an informal conversation, but would then be reified in a document with a certain structure, which would shape the team's enquiry. The ideas would then evolve and sharpen through the oral discourse from an expert interview, which would be digitised. These digitised resources would again enter discussions of what extracts should be used, where to place them in a presentation and what the argument or meaning of such a piece would be. They would then be further edited, negotiated and transformed into small video clips, which were embedded as part of the presentation and appear as part of a line of reasoning.

In this sense the young people engaged in many networked performances, where they traversed or connected to multiple networks and resources; but these resources were then entered into streams of remixing and patchworking, where they were discussed and transformed, becoming part of the processes of reweaving their smaller and larger patchworks.

These processes of remixing, patchworking or transforming are also important in order to understand the notion of productive learning. From the analysis and the discussion of digital and analogue we can understand the notion of productive learning as processes where 'material' and 'ideal' resources are seamlessly woven together into a product. Furthermore, I would argue that such productive learning processes can be seen as happening on different levels. For one thing, we can see how small, digital patches are transformed, shaped and repurposed into little patchworks, which then become parts in the processes of reweaving the larger patchwork and conceptual blueprint. This happens through unravelling and pulling apart the existing larger patchwork by critiquing or raising new ideas. Finally, follows a phase of reweaving the patchwork into a new provisional patchwork, which is done through rearranging and reorganising the different patches. This new patchwork can then again be unravelled.

Such processes of tangible knowledge construction, where various patches are foraged, created, negotiated and transformed into an increasingly larger patchwork and a progressively more coherent conceptual blueprint, are good examples of productive learning processes.

CONDITIONS FOR PRODUCTIVE LEARNING

So far in this chapter I have presented the case, the pedagogical design, the metaphor of patchworking and the related analytic concepts. Also I have discussed the metaphor in relation to the notions of networked learning and productive learning. Now I shall turn to discuss some of the conditions that are needed for such creative and productive learning processes to unfold.

The ways of organising the work process was largely controlled by the participants and there was no fixed solution for the problem. In fact, what actually constituted the problem was under continuous negotiation and reformulation. The case, therefore, is a good example of self-organised, horizontal peer-learning. They were a mixed group of young people, coming together for a short period of time to engage with an open-ended learning challenge. The problem and the solution were not given, and neither were the ways of working. All of these elements had to be identified, orchestrated on the spot and continuously negotiated. Secondly, the ongoing coordination of the work process, the distribution of the tasks and the decisions on groupings entailed a pulsating, organic and dynamic negotiation of roles and responsibilities that were horizontally distributed among the young people. In this sense an important part of the patchworking and learning process was also mastering and orchestrating the whole process.

However, this free and self-organised learning process was embedded in a wider design and planning process which made this possible. In this sense we can say that the pedagogical design and planning consisted in creating a learning infrastructure (Guribye, 2005; Jones et al., 2006) that supported well the kind of PBL learning process we had imagined and designed for. Our design and scaffolding operated more on a meso level where we indirectly designed for learning through providing and nurturing learning opportunities, a social ecology and a technological infrastructure. This meso level, however, was also dependent on the macro design of the event (and the micro level as I shall return to).

On a macro level the entire process was heavily reliant on a smooth and well run infrastructure of logistics and support, which was professionally orchestrated by people from EDC. In addition the whole setup, with speeches, guests and applauses, as well as the positioning and construction of the young people as being 'special', gave the entire learning environment an extra touch and layer of motivation. There was a whole setting, or macro level infrastructure, which had been designed for them to operate within. In this sense the meso level was dependent on and interacting with this macro level design, but this was equally true for the micro level. The meso level also had to be realised or enacted on a micro level during the actual interactions.

For the meso level we aimed at providing learning opportunities, such as through connecting the young people with the different resource people. I call these 'opportunities' as there were no fixed learning goals for the different interactions.

How to exploit these resources was something they would have to decide upon themselves. In this way it seems more appropriate to speak of providing resources and opportunities, rather than content. However, in engaging with these opportunities we, as researchers, also acted as mediators in helping them to interpret and make sense of the encounters with the resource people and the material they collected by, for instance, helping with the graphs on the slides.

We also aimed at nurturing a social ecology, which they themselves accomplished through continuously sustaining a sociable and humorous atmosphere. This was enacted, for instance, through their verbal interactions where they joked and teased each other, or through listening to music, singing and being noisy. Even though the creation of a social ecology was very much their own accomplishment, it was equally an ongoing process for us, which was enacted through allowing them to be noisy and humorous. Likewise, the notion of providing a technological infrastructure was dependent both on a meso level design, as well as an actual enactment on a micro level. We provided them with many different tools (tablet PCs, a mini disc recorder, video cameras etc.). But equally important was that the computers and equipment were not mere work tools that would be locked up in the evening, or that they were only allowed to use for special purposes. They were completely free to use the computers as personal tools for writing diary notes, store their personal pictures, play games, listen to music and draw funny drawings. Neither did we specify a certain way of using the computers as part of their work processes.

From these examples, I would argue that there is a transactional relationship between the different levels of design (Ryberg et al., 2006). We should not understand design as a vertical descend from macro to meso to micro, in the sense that, for instance, the macro level uniformly shapes the meso level and the meso level directs the micro level. Neither should we understand the micro level of interaction as a free floating entity, unaffected by the other levels (e.g. as the *only* place where structure is constructed or emerges[9]). Rather, we should understand the relationships between the levels as transactional.

While the whole learning environment was built on the central assumption that we cannot design learning in itself, but that we can design *for* learning to unfold (Guribye, 2005; Jones et al., 2006; Wenger, 1998), this ideal or assumption also has to be put into practice at the micro level. During the actual work we accepted and supported the fact that the young people were in control and that we were, therefore, horizontalised voices, rather than authoritative voices of control and management. The indirect design and the conditions we had provided them with were important vehicles in enabling the patchworking processes to flourish. The learning process was embedded in a setting that was designed and planned for, but simultaneously enabled through the interactional processes.

CONCLUDING REMARKS

In this chapter I have presented the notion of looking at learning through the metaphorical lens of patchworking. This concept has arisen from an empirical study in which eight young people managed, within a relatively short and intense period of time, to forage, pull together, create, negotiate and transform a number of different resources or patches into a final patchwork. The different patches encompassed both different digital media, such as pictures, music and animation, but also an assortment of ideas, perspectives and arguments that represented different knowledge abilities. Some of these were foraged from searching the web, while others emerged through dialogues and interviews with people that represented different networks, practices and forms of knowing. These patches were stitched together into a heavily multimodal presentation or 'final' patchwork that addressed the problem they had worked with.

I have argued that we can see this as an instance of networked learning. Even though the interaction and communication between the learners was not mediated by ICT (e.g. in the form asynchronous or synchronous tools) the different digital patches were important parts of the fabric of their learning process. The digital patches were mediating their interactions in their role as shared representations, and by being something which could be manipulated, produced, negotiated and altered. Thus, the digital patches were important parts of the processes of reweaving their conceptual blueprint and constructing the smaller and larger patchworks. Furthermore, an important part of their learning process came from the connections that were established to various people or networks of knowledge, as represented by the resource people.

The case also illustrates the mutable roles and fleeting boundaries between digital and analogue resources, where digital resources are re-worked into the overarching patchwork or line of argumentation. Likewise, discussions are reified on whiteboards, mediated by slides or transformed into, for instance, an animated narrative forming part of a larger argument. Here lie also the roots to better understanding the notion of productive learning as a fluid interplay between different modes, such as digital/analogue or ideal/material, and the movements and flows of these versatile resources through streams of remixing and patchworking.

The metaphor of patchworking is a perspective that suggests we analyse such flows, movements and transformations. The metaphor gives us a way of analytically looking at how different resources, or patches, of a widely different fabric are assembled into patchworks of different scale. It enable us to analyse the processes of how various smaller patchworks form around different threads and are aligned, contrasted and negotiated in relation to an emerging and developing conceptual blueprint, which is continuously re-woven and negotiated. In this sense the final product is not the primary object of analysis.

Finally, the case reported in this chapter is an example of an indirect design approach to learning, in which it is assumed that we cannot design learning, but only design for learning to unfold. The case shows how an open-ended PBL approach was afforded through creating and designing for a learning infrastructure and creating conditions for learning, rather than planning in detail how and what should be learned. The pedagogical design in the case was intended to create a learning infrastructure by means of focusing on the provision and nurturing of learning opportunities, creating and sustaining a social ecology and providing a technological infrastructure, rather than designing in detail the actual learning and work processes. In this sense the pedagogical design acted more on the macro and meso levels, where we provided the young people with a setting in which the patchworking processes could flourish. However, the case also highlights the need for realising and enacting the macro and meso level design on the micro plane, and how the interactional processes on the micro plane should reflect and support the pedagogical intentions of the design. We actively supported the fact that the young people were in control and that we became more horizontalised voices, rather than voices of control and management. As such the open-ended, problem-oriented learning process was embedded in a larger setting, and through the indirect design we provided a loosely structured frame to act within; but also this design was enacted and supported through the interactional processes on the micro plane.

NOTES

[1] For more information please refer to: http://powerusers.edc.org

[2] For more information please refer to: http://powerusers.edc.org/symposium/

[3] It should be noted that some work and activities also occurred prior to the symposium itself, but for the purpose of this chapter only data and descriptions from the work done during the symposium will be incorporated. For a more elaborated discussion I refer to Ryberg (2007).

[4] For a more thorough description of the presentation I refer to: http://www.ell.aau.dk/PhD-Thesis-on-Power-Users.429.0.html where one can find an appendix from the author's PhD thesis, which describes the presentation in more detail.

[5] Ricardo Monge is Executive Director of the Costa Rican High Technology Advisory Committee (CAATEC) and professor of International Trade at Universidad Latina de Costa Rica)

[6] Manuel Bersone is professor of economy and social politics and works as a consultant for UNICEF

[7] Intel Clubhouses are places where young (poor) people can get access to technology and training in how to use various multimedia and web technologies.

[8] On the whiteboard they initially used a wrong/non-existing form of the word poverty (fattigdom) in Danish. They initially used 'fattighed' (poverness) instead of the correct form 'fattigdom' (poverty) – something they later realised and joked about.

[9] Please note that I do not claim that structure, rules, directions etc. are not negotiated and emergent properties of interactional processes. I merely wish to point out the transactional relationship between the different levels, rather than claiming only one particular level to be the locus for studying structure.

REFERENCES

Dirckinck-Holmfeld, L. (2002). Designing virtual learning environments based on problem oriented project pedagogy. In L. Dirckinck-Holmfeld & B. Fibiger (Eds.), *Learning in virtual environments* (pp. 31–54). Frederiksberg C: Samfundslitteratur Press.

Dirckinck-Holmfeld, L., & Ryberg, T. (2005). An emergent agenda for the research on power users of technology. *Power users of information and communication technology international symposium.* San Jose, Costa Rica: EDC.

Goodyear, P., Banks, S., Hodgson, V., & McConnell, D. (Eds.). (2004). *Advances in research on networked learning.* Dordrecht, The Netherlands: Klüwer Academic Publishers.

Goodyear, P., Jones, C., Asensio, M., Hodgson, V., & Steeples, C. (2001). *Effective networked learning in higher education: Notes and guidelines.* Lancaster, UK: Centre for Studies in Advanced Learning Technology (CSALT). Retrieved January 10, 2008, from http://csalt.lancs.ac.uk/JISC/guidelines_final.doc

Guribye, F. (2005). *Infrastructures for learning: Ethnographic inquiries into the social and technical conditions of education and training*. Bergen: Department of Information Science and Media Studies—University of Bergen.

Jenkins, H., Purushotma, R., Clinton, K., Weigel, M., & Robison, A. J. (2006). *Confronting the challenges of participatory culture: Media education for the 21st century* (White Paper). Chicago: MacArtur Foundation. Retrieved August 15, 2007, from http://www.projectnml.org/files/working/NMLWhitePaper.pdf

Jones, C., Dirckinck-Holmfeld, L., & Lindström, B. (2006). A relational, indirect, meso-level approach to cscl design in the next decade. *International Journal of Computer-Supported Collaborative Learning, 1*(1), 35–56.

Kolmos, A., Fink, F. K., & Krogh, L. (Eds.). (2004). *The aalborg pbl model—progress diversity and challenges*. Aalborg: Aalborg University Press.

Malyn-Smith, J. (2004, June-August). Power users of technology—who are they? Where are they going? Why does it matter? *UN Chronicle*, (2), 58–61.

Malyn-Smith, J., & Guilfoy, V. (2003). *Power users of technology research initiative 2001–2020 - how power users of technology are shaping our world*. Education Development Center, Inc. Retrieved August 25, 2007, from http://eec.edc.org/pdf/PowerUsersGenevaReport.pdf

Ryberg, T. (2004). Initial queries into the notion of power users of technology—investigating ideas of production, competence and identity. *Power users of information and communication technology summit, New York 2004*. New York: Education Development Center.

Ryberg, T. (2007). Patchworking as a metaphor for learning—understanding youth, learning and technology. In *PhD thesis published in: e—Learning Lab Publication Series* (Vol. 1, pp. 1–477). Aalborg: Department of Communication and Psychology Aalborg University.

Ryberg, T., & Dirckinck-Holmfeld, L. (2005). Challenges to work and education in the knowledge society—studying power users of technology. *Power users of information and communication technology international symposium*. San Jose, Costa Rica: Education Development Center.

Ryberg, T., Koottatep, S., Pengchai, P., & Dirckinck-Holmfeld, L. (2006). Conditions for productive learning in networked learning environments: A case study from the vo@ net project. *Studies in Continuing Education, 28*(2), 151–170.

Wenger, E. (1998). *Communities of practice—learning, meaning, and identity*. New York: Cambridge University Press.

Thomas Ryberg
Department of Communication and Psychology
University of Aalborg, Denmark

VICTOR KAPTELININ AND ULF HEDESTIG

BREAKDOWNS, AFFORDANCES AND INDIRECT DESIGN

A Study of a Videoconference Learning Environment in Undergraduate Education

Undoubtedly, to designers contemplating the unpredictability of the uses and settings of what they design, grappling with context can appear about as attractive as wrestling with a whale: The task looks overwhelming, and the opponent offers few obvious handholds.

Brown and Duguid, 1994, p. 6.

INTRODUCTION

In this chapter we present a study of a videoconference learning environment, in which teachers located at videoconference studios interacted with students located at one or more student sites. The study focused on actual and potential breakdowns in the environment; the aim being to reveal the underlying causes of the break-downs, as well as the factors that helped prevent potential breakdowns from actually occurring. The case study presented here provides empirical evidence for discussing a number of issues that are common to the book as a whole, especially the notions of affordances and indirect design.

BACKGROUND

It is widely accepted that learning is a social process and should be supported as such. However, in network learning environments (NLEs) support for the social context of learning is often limited to providing text based communication tools for person-to-person communication and group discussions (e.g., online discussion forums). This support is important and is often used successfully. But the needs of participants in educational settings and the emerging technological affordances indicate that new and more advanced types of communication and collaboration tools and systems can and should be provided.

For the teachers, text based online communication imposes constraints on their ability to dynamically manage educational activities. The teachers miss out on rich, non-verbal indicators of group and individual response, such as emotional reaction,

L. Dirckinck-Holmfeld, C. Jones and B. Lindström (eds.), Analysing Networked Learning Practices in Higher Education and Continuing Professional Development, 223–239.

confusion, disagreement, readiness to ask a question or to contribute with a comment, and so forth. Limiting communication to text based mode can also present problems for students.

There are reasons to believe that network learning environments can benefit from more advanced, video based communication tools. The need to go beyond text based communication is indicated by the growing use of desktop video conferencing in online education (Kies et al., 1997). Until recently, the resolution and transmission speeds for this tended to be limited, so its educational possibilities used to be restricted. However, owing to the rapid development of information and communication technologies (ICT), it is likely that powerful and affordable desktop video based communication tools will soon be available for a wide range of educational uses.

Therefore, an understanding of the conditions for productive learning in a network learning environment requires an analysis of rich video based communication between remote participants. To explore the issues involved with this, we selected the case of an educational videoconference setting on a university campus, paying special attention to cases of coordination breakdowns and their underlying causes, as well as the role of the technician/ facilitator in the setting (see also Hedestig and Kaptelinin, 2002, 2005). The reasons for selecting the case are as follows:

– Special purpose videoconferencing settings are still typically more advanced than desktop video tools. We can expect personalised, mobile solutions, such as desktop video, to reach (and perhaps eventually exceed) that level in the near future. Therefore, videoconferencing settings provide a sneak preview of activities that we can expect to be possible with future NLEs

– Videoconferencing settings have developed over an extended period, allowing a substantial amount of experience to be accumulated on the likely problems and solutions when using them for distributed communication and collaboration. This experience, in our view, is important to take into account when creating more advanced NLEs

– The informant in our study was a competent technician/ facilitator, who greatly contributed to successful teaching and learning in the setting. Understanding the activities, strategies, and roles of that person was considered as a way to inform the design of video based environments, in which teachers will not be able to receive an immediate help from a technician/ facilitator.

The aim of examining this case was to identify the key issues in the transformation of educational activities that take place in a regular classroom into activities that occur in the media space of video sessions[1]. The study had two foci: breakdowns and success factors. It dealt with the breakdowns that occurred when expectations, competence, and skills developed in one educational context were applied by teachers and students in a different context. This was complemented by a focus on the success factors – those that helped prevent some of the potential breakdowns from happening, and so ensured that the learning environment functioned despite numerous threats.

In our view, the case study we selected for analysis provides empirical evidence that sheds light on several issues common to this book as a whole. Firstly, it supplies an empirical grounding for discussing the notion of *affordances*. In the paper we posit that the types and incidence of breakdowns in the videoconference environment under study are indicative of false and hidden affordances in the environments (cf. Gaver, 1991).

Secondly, the case raises a variety of issues related to design, or more specifically, to *indirect* design of NLEs. The notion of indirect design is related to the notion of affordances. Affordances, as we argue in this chapter, are not built-in properties of artefacts and environments. Rather, they are emerging qualities that can only exist in the interaction between human beings and the world. Therefore, the design of learning environments is not deterministic. The outcome depends on the actual interplay of various factors, including those that are not under control of the designer. Therefore, the decisions made by designers can only create prerequisites for a successfully functioning environment; they cannot directly determine how the environment is going to be used. Moreover, they cannot even determine the structure of a functioning environment, since this structure undergoes both short term and long term transformations.

The rest of this chapter is organized as follows. In the next section we describe the object of our study: a videoconference based learning environment employed in undergraduate education at a university in Northern Sweden. After that we summarise our findings and discuss them in the context of the current debates on affordances. Then we discuss another issue transpiring from empirical data collected in the study; namely, the indirect design of learning environments. We conclude with a general discussion of our findings.

VIDEOCONFERENCE LEARNING ENVIRONMENT: AN OVERVIEW

The videoconference learning environment analysed in the study was developed to support the distance and decentralized education programs of a university in Northern Sweden. The university has a strong history in developing such programs, and at the time of the study they accounted for over 5,000 students, all living at distances of 100 km to 700 km from the campus. The university is also a major educational and research centre in Northern Sweden, and to meet current demand for undergraduate education in the region, its involvement in decentralized education is increasing, so much so that it is gradually transforming itself into a "virtual" university. The gradual character of the transition is important, because it allows the university to try various forms of decentralization without radical changes to the whole system of education, and to capitalize upon the existing expertise of the teachers. The assumption, that the existing pedagogical skills and competencies of the teachers could be directly re-employed in videoconference sessions, was one of the main reasons why videoconference learning environments have been so widely used by the university.

At the time of the study the university had several videoconference studios on campus, each equipped differently, according to its specific intended purpose. They also varied in size, from a small room large enough only for a teacher and technician, to a classroom able to accommodate a teacher, technician and a group of students.

Videoconference-based learning settings at the university had two main types of components: (a) the *teacher site*, or videoconference studio, located on campus, and (b) the *student site* (or sites), a videoconference classroom at an off campus study centre[2]. The typical arrangement of these sites is shown in Figure 1.

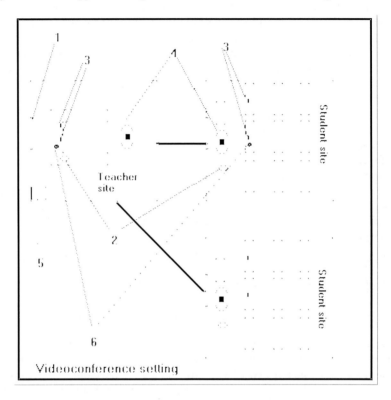

Figure 1. Typical structure of a videoconference setting. The teacher site has either a traditional or electronic whiteboard (1) and a computer connected to the videoconference system (5). At the student and teacher sites there are document cameras for slides (2), two or more stationary microphones (3), TV monitor(s), a video recorder and camera (4), and remote controls (6).

The teachers' site. Most on campus videoconference studios used by the teachers are relatively small, they include seating arrangements for groups of up to 10–15 persons. The equipment typically consists of a document camera, electronic whiteboard, computer, projector, TV monitors, and hands-free microphones. The most common type of activity in the videoconference studios is lectures delivered by teachers to one or more student sites.

The students' site. The videoconference equipment at the student site is usually installed in a traditional classroom with rows of tables and chairs. Such an arrangement directs students' attention towards the monitors, i.e., the teacher. The number of devices such as cameras and microphones can vary depending on how much equipment the study centre can afford. Most provide one camera, one document camera, one TV monitor for the incoming and outgoing image, and 1–2 microphones (see Figure 1). Usually, one student is given the responsibility for handling the equipment's remote control unit. At students' sites there are usually no technicians or facilitators to provide support during sessions.

Typically, during the videoconference sessions that were analysed, a teacher and a technician were stationed in a small on-campus studio linked to one or more study centres. The format of the videoconference based education included traditional lectures, seminars, and small group discussions, typically related to group projects.

The study was conducted during one year and employed ethnography as its main data collection method. The data was collected from several sources:

- Field observations conducted during one year and covering over 100 hours of learning and teaching at three different video studio settings. The technician was the same during all sessions, while the teachers were different, coming from different departments. In total there were over 20 teachers from the faculties of social sciences, natural sciences, and humanities. The field notes taken during and after the observations dealt mostly with the interaction between teachers, students, and the technician
- Interviews with the technician both at work and home. At work the interviews were conducted before and after video sessions. The numerous interviews and observations conducted at his home helped to eliminate a communication barrier between the informant and the researcher and reach a better understanding of the technician, his opinions, reflections, and personality
- Guided tours given by the technicians whenever an observation took place in a new setting. During the tours the technician explained and showed how he worked in each setting
- Interviews with other participants in the setting, including teachers, students and managers.

The conducting of field observations would often turn into a researcher's dilemma, where he is drawn into becoming both a participant and an observer. Such situations would occur quite unexpectedly; for instance, the technician would receive a phone call in the middle of a videoconference session and while distracted with the conversation would leave the remote controls with the researcher. Researcher's involvement in the setting also had a positive side: the researcher was able to gain direct experience of being a technician, and so achieve a better understanding of the interactions taking place in the setting.

BREAKDOWNS AND AFFORDANCES[3]

The findings of the study reported in this chapter suggest that the transition from traditional on-campus education to decentralized videoconference-based education is not as straightforward as it may seem. Teachers' attempts to directly apply the knowledge and skills they have developed in regular classroom settings, into videoconference learning environments, often cause coordination breakdowns. Videoconference settings may appear similar to regular classrooms and enable the same range of students' and teachers' actions. The teacher and students can see each other, talk to each other, show texts and sketches, and so forth. However, even though these possibilities for action are objectively present in the environment, the participants in the setting may overlook them. Or, conversely, they may perceive possibilities for action where none exist. Such cases lend themselves to interpretation in terms of *affordances*. Before proceeding to a detailed analysis of the findings from our study based on the concept of affordances, let us discuss the meaning of the concept and the current debate related to affordances in the area of human-computer interaction (HCI).

The concept of affordance originates from Gibson's ecological psychology (Gibson, 1979) and refers to the possibilities for action offered by the environment to an animal. A key notion of Gibson's approach, distinguishing it from more traditional perspectives in cognitive psychology, was that the possibilities for action can be *directly* perceived by the animal. The notion of affordances was introduced to the field of human-computer interaction by Don Norman (1989), where it became one of the most popular – and most controversial – concepts of all time.

The first wave of controversy surrounding the concept of affordances took place when it turned out that many user interface designers had interpreted Norman as stating that affordances are properties of an artefact and can be built into the user interface. In a more recent paper Norman (1999) criticized such an understanding as a grave oversimplification. The current wave of debates related to the notion of affordances mostly revolves around the relationship between affordances and perception, and between affordances and social actions.

Some researchers, most notably McGrenere and Ho (2000), emphasized the need to re-introduce and further develop the original Gibsonian concept of affordance. McGrenere and Ho (2000) indicated that Norman's (1989) definition of affordances did not include the actor, at least explicitly. They also highlighted what they believe to be a major contradiction between Gibson's and Norman's views: the relationship between affordances and perception. While Gibson differentiated between affordances per se and their perception by the actor, Norman defined affordances as both "perceived and actual properties of the thing" (Norman, 1989). Returning to Gibson's original notion, according to McGrenere and Ho, would mean to clearly acknowledge that affordances are "independent of the actor's experience, knowledge, culture, and ability to perceive" (McGrenere and Ho, 2000). This claim was recently echoed by Torenvliet, who observed that "Gibson labored to make affordances a characteristic of the environment that exists relative to an object but independent of perception." (Torenvliet, 2003).

There is no doubt that the attempts to bring the concept of affordances back in line with its original theoretical context have stimulated helpful reflections on the meaning of the concept. Unfortunately, however, the call to consider affordances as independent from a person's culture and their ability to perceive hardly achieves its goal of resolving conceptual contradictions surrounding affordances. Arguably, completely separating affordances from perception and culture is incompatible with the gist of Gibson's ecological psychology. Gibson specifically emphasized that the key issue for a theory of affordances is not whether or not affordances exist or are real, but whether or not optical information makes it possible to perceive them (Gibson, 1979).

Gibson's examples of affordances include those taking place in complex types of activities, such as business and politics. The possibilities for action in these contexts are not limited to physical actions; they are determined by culture. The canonical example of affordances of the mailbox also implies that affordances cannot be considered independently of their social, cultural context and learning. A wide variety of different types of mailboxes are used in different countries and settings, and they have different affordances. Even as simple an action as using a mailbox is a cultural action, and the possibilities for the action, provided by different mailboxes, depend on a particular culture. Therefore, separating affordances, experiences, and culture is in conflict with the underlying ideas of the Gibsonian approach.

There have been several attempts to address the issue of affordances from an activity theory perspective. (Kaptelinin, 1996; Albrechtsen et al., 2001; Baerentsen, Trettvik, 2002). These analyses articulated a few ideas that seem to help avoid a narrow understanding of 'action' and 'action capabilities' when developing a conceptually consistent view on affordances. The meaning of action in activity theory includes much more than purely motor responses, dissociated from perception. Perception is an integral part of human interaction with the world, so it plays a key role in both carrying out actions and determining what the action capabilities of a particular individual are.

The very existence of an affordance for an animal in a certain environment depends on the perceptual abilities of the animal. An experienced mountaineer might perceive a rock as affording climbing, even if most other people would wisely decide that climbing it is beyond the scope of their action capabilities. It is likely, however, that the same mountaineer will refuse climbing the rock blindfolded. Blindfolding in that case would not only affect the ability of the person to perceive an affordance but rather the very action capabilities of the person. In addition, the notion of affordance cannot be limited to possibilities for physical actions in the environment but should include the possibilities for social actions and learning, as well.

The above conclusions are fully applicable to the empirical findings of our case, the case of a videoconference learning environment in undergraduate education. Our data indicate that most of the breakdowns observed in the study can be explained as resulting from a mismatch between perceived and actual affordances in the environment. Following the terminology proposed by Gaver (1991), they can be interpreted as *hidden affordances* (there are possibilities for action but they are not perceived by the participants) and *false affordances* (the participants perceive nonexistent possibilities for action). In other words, to explain our findings we bring in the much criticized Norman's (1999) distinction between perceived and actual affordances. Does that mean that we are moving away from Gibsonian ecological approach and adopting a perspective that separates perception from action? As we argue below, we believe it is not the case. In our view, an ecological perspective on perception entails that perception is neither separated from action nor completely determined by action. The relationship between perception and action is a dialectical relationship rather than a dichotomy separating them from each other.

Before proceeding to a more detailed discussion of breakdowns we should also mention that the discussion has a limited scope. In our field observations we have identified different types of breakdowns, some of which have been beyond the scope of our study (for instance, technical breakdowns that are analysed in detail elsewhere, see, e.g., Dallat et al., 1992, Abbot et al., 1993, Rosengren, 1993). Here we focus only on coordination breakdowns, caused by the transition from traditional classroom settings to videoconference-based decentralized education.

It was found that, for reasons discussed below, students and teachers experienced different types of problems; and different types of breakdowns took place at student and teacher sites. Because of that, we are going to discuss these types of breakdowns separately. Let's begin with a rather typical statement made by one of the students we interviewed:

> Since it is necessary for us to push the mute-button at our site, it takes too long to ask a question of the teacher. Instead, many of us lie back, so to speak, and watch the 'program'. We see it more as a TV broadcast program - and a TV program you never interrupt! If there is something unclear we prefer to ask questions afterwards, if at all.

In this example, a combination of factors resulted in an interactive video session being experienced as a TV broadcast. A large screen or TV set, a presenter in a remote location, the lack of eye contact, loss of the use of subtle clues that show intent to ask a question – all these aspects combined were perceived as an affordance to resort to the role of a passive watcher of a TV broadcast (cf. Gaver, 1992).

Most of the student sites had the traditional classroom arrangement with few cameras and microphones. At sites where each student had an opportunity to control the cameras and microphones, spontaneous questions were more frequent than at those sites where they had to share a microphone and a remote control. Students from the sites with only one camera and microphone often had comments of the following kind:

> It's impossible to ask spontaneous or short questions during a video session. <...> First I have to ask someone to give me the microphone. Then I have to ask the student who has the remote control to push the mute button, so the teacher can hear me. At the same time the student also has to direct the camera towards me. This process takes too much time, so many of us do not bother to even think of asking a question.

Here, the perceived affordance of the videoconference environment, in terms of actions to be directed at the teacher (see previous example), was reinforced by the perceived affordances of actions directed at other students at the students' site. Student-student interactions were further complicated by the fact that the students were all facing in the same direction and not at each other. Therefore, they could not use non-verbal cues in their conversations; instead they had to raise their voice to make themselves heard by the students holding the microphone and the remote control. Asking a question required a substantial effort, and even a minimal degree of active involvement in the session caused social disruption.

Unlike their students, the teachers in the videoconference environment could not assume the role of a passive observer. Their objectives, competencies, and the structure of their immediate work environment were very different. Accordingly, so were the coordination breakdowns they experienced.

In face-to-face classroom teaching, teachers develop the skills of coordinating a 'physical' lecture with familiar technical artefacts. In a videoconference studio these skills were often not appropriate. Teachers had to change their practices to fit a different context that comprised various kinds of monitors and other technical artefacts. Let us consider two types of coordination activity that teachers had to carry out during a video session: coordination related to presentation (handling the outgoing image), and to student activity (handling the incoming image).

Coordination of the teacher's presentation. In regular classes the overall structure of the environment provides a number of affordances for gaining or retaining students' attention. The teacher can direct students' attention by pointing to the whiteboard or an area of a slide presented on the screen, or initiating a discussion by talking to an individual student or group. In our case some of the teachers' site features could be perceived as affordances of a regular classroom. But acting on these could result in breakdowns. For instance, if the teacher moved from the desk to the whiteboard the students would not see the teacher unless the camera view was changed accordingly. Placing a document under a document camera did not automatically result in the document being displayed to the students – for this to happen the image broadcast had to be switched to the document camera view. The specific problems and coordination breakdowns experienced by the teachers were dependent on whether they were using a whiteboard, document camera, or multiple technologies.

Teachers using regular whiteboards in a videoconference studio had to coordinate their movements in the studio with changing camera angles (camera movements) and zoom lengths. During the sessions we observed that all camera movements were controlled by the technician. The technician usually had 2–4 camera angles pre-installed, which could then be selected at the touch of a button on the remote control. In addition, the technician often were zooming the camera to adjust the image being transmitted to the students.

Table 1. Example of video sessions (T1–T5) where a teacher used a traditional whiteboard

Description	T1	T2	T3	T4	T5
Duration (minutes)	56	83	84	69	91
Change video source	0	0	0	0	0
Zooming	5	10	8	5	10
Camera movements	10	34	55	51	67
Audio adjustments	2	0	0	2	2

Table 1 shows examples of several sessions with such an arrangement. It is apparent that most actions meant for altering the way that information was sent to the students were those of adjustment of camera angles and/or zoom, these taking place every 1–4 minutes. These actions were carried out by the technician, since it was practically impossible for the teacher to handle the remote control at the same time as he or she was writing on the whiteboard. The teachers rarely looked at the incoming image. Most of the time they looked away from the audience and it was typically only when they finished a sentence, or had to look at their notes that they remembered to check the incoming image.

Those teachers, who used a document camera to present lecture slides, had no difficulties with camera movements. In addition, they were usually sitting in front of the monitors and so were able to coordinate both incoming and outgoing images. For them the main coordination problem was constant switching between the teacher view (the image of the teacher himself or herself) and the document camera view (the image of lecture slides or other documents).

Table 2. Example of video sessions (T6–T11) where teachers used slides on the document camera.

Description	T6	T7	T8	T9	T10	T11
Duration (minutes)	73	45	44	47	47	103
Change video source	43	29	26	23	13	80
Zooming	2	0	0	0	4	11
Camera movements	0	0	0	0	0	1
Audio adjustments	0	1	1	1	2	9

Table 2 shows that, in these instances, most of the interactions with technology were in changing the video source; that is, switching from the teacher view to the document camera view and back. The average frequency of these changes was one switching every 1–3 minutes. The more skilled teachers could do the switching themselves, but most of them relied upon the technician's help, as they found it difficult to concentrate on the lesson content while simultaneously operating the equipment.

The third method adopted by the teachers was in making use of the widest possible range of technologies available in the studio; that is, electronic whiteboards, computer applications and videotapes, document camera, and so forth. Examples of such sessions are shown in Table 3.

Table 3. Examples of video sessions (T12–T14) where teachers used multiple technologies.

Description	T12	T13	T14
Duration (minutes)	76	94	170
Change video source	19	26	20
Zooming	13	12	13
Camera movements	5	33	1
Audio adjustments	1	1	11

Teachers using this style were heavily dependent on the technician and a smooth functioning of each respective technology. It also required the technician to operate several remote controls and to follow the teacher's actions closely. However, it was not uncommon for the technician to have difficulty communicating with the teacher, who was totally concentrated on both the content of the lecture and controlling the technologies for he or she had taken responsibility.

Coordination of students' activities. Video sessions become especially difficult to coordinate when the teacher also had to manage the reactions and responses of the students. Regular classrooms offer a variety of affordances, including the possibilities for verbal and non-verbal communication with the students. But in a videoconference environment the teacher has to read these cues by watching the incoming image on the monitor, which in our study often resulted in communication breakdowns.

At many student sites the videoconference equipment was installed in traditional classroom settings. The student groups (typically, 15–25 in number) tended to spread out over the whole classroom, so the cameras would be zoomed out to their maximum to give the teacher a view of the whole class. Unfortunately, this resulted in a poor quality image, from which it was difficult for the teacher to discern the reactions of individual students.

The videoconference environment we studied also had other significant limitations over that of a regular classroom. For instance, it greatly reduced the possibility of direct eye contact and the use of spatial pointers, such as gestures. Therefore, it was problematic for the teacher to use intuitive pointing strategies to indicate which students the teacher was addressing. As a consequence, the coordination of each session became enormously complicated, especially in multipoint sessions, where more than two study centres were involved at the same time. As a result, some teachers decided to ignore student reactions altogether, focus exclusively on the lesson content and leave any remaining coordination activities to other actors, such as the technician.

Therefore, the central problem in creating successful videoconference environments for decentralized education is that of coordination. Traditional coordination mechanisms and structures often fail in new learning environments. A potential solution to this is 're-coordination', meaning the development and implementation of new, more appropriate structures. For this we need to understand both individual and collective activities within the setting. Furthermore, we need analysis of how different players set and accomplish their goals, resolve conflicts and maintain collaboration, and how their activities develop over time.

Traditional classroom education is a well-established genre with a history that goes back several centuries. The evolution of this genre resulted in the current forms of classroom education that may appear simple and straightforward but are in fact based on a sophisticated infrastructure that includes management of resources, expertise development, etc. The smooth functioning of traditional educational settings also depends on participants having adequate assumptions about the roles, norms, and values in the setting. Decentralized education implemented through videoconferencing is a relatively new genre. It may result, for instance, in conflicting expectations. Teachers, for instance, may well consider it as being very similar to a regular classroom setting, while students see it as a type of TV broadcast. In other words, the changing context of learning activities causes a mismatch between the actual affordances of the environment and what the actors might perceive as affordances. Students and teachers perceive affordances that are not actually present, while newly available affordances for physical and social actions are often not immediately obvious.

This conclusion is in agreement with a claim made by Gaver (1992), who observed: "With changes in the technologies come changes in their affordances; creating or emphasizing affordances is, in fact, a useful way to characterize the purpose of design" (p. 18). Arguably, the need to emphasize affordances, as noted by Gaver, suggests that it might be necessary for designers of new technologies to help users recognize whatever affordances their designs are offering.

Therefore, the findings of our study indicate that the distinction between perceived and actual affordances (Norman, 1999), as discussed above, can provide some useful insights. In our view, this distinction should be conceptually reframed rather than discarded altogether. Of course, affordances that are only perceived as such (or "false affordances", see Gaver, 1991) are formally not affordances at all, since they do not offer the implied possibilities for action. Rather, they are features of the environment that can be incorrectly perceived as affordances. However, if formally imperfect, the distinction between perceived and actual affordances is, in our view, consistent with Gibsonian understanding of the complex relationship between perception and action. It is true that Gibson makes a compelling case for the crucial role of action in the evolution and development of perception. But the coupling of perception and action, as essential as it is for survival, does not come automatically; if the environment changes, it is a continuous struggle for the actor to achieve and maintain such coupling.

It can be concluded, therefore, that affordances should be considered in the context of a dialectical relationship between perception and action. On the one hand, the very nature of perception is determined by the objective (and unforgiving) laws of survival and evolution. It is essential for survival to directly perceive the possibilities for action provided by the environment. On the other hand, in changing environments the tight coupling between perception and action cannot be taken for granted. New affordances can be hidden from an actor, while what is perceived as an affordance may turn out to be a false perception. It is important for the actor to restore the balance between perception and action, and it is precisely where design can and should make a difference.

LEARNING ENVIRONMENTS AND INDIRECT DESIGN

The discussion in the previous section indicated that affordances cannot be simply built in by the system designers. Affordances, including perceived affordances, are emerging properties that can only exist in the dynamic and developing interaction between individuals and their environments. This conclusion has a direct implication for the meaning of design in the context of learning environments. By making decisions regarding the shape (in a broad sense) of artefacts and their configurations, the designers of learning environments create prerequisites for interaction, but they cannot determine how their designs are actually going to be used.

The term 'interaction design' has been gaining popularity in recent years. While there is an uncertainty concerning its specific meaning (Bannon, 2005; Kaptelinin and Nardi, 2006), it is being used increasingly to denote the next phase of development of the field of human-computer interaction (HCI). Interaction design, according to Preece et al. (2002) is concerned not just with the interaction between people and computers, but between people and any kinds of interactive products, or artefacts, that have information-processing capabilities.

The discussion in the previous section (see also Dirckinck-Holmfeld & Jones, this volume) also indicated that interaction design is a somewhat misleading term. It is not *interaction* that is being designed, but rather properties of the product, which may or may not result in the types of interaction intended by the product's designer. In other words, designers of products can influence interaction only indirectly. Such influence can be strong and suggestive, but never deterministic. It is not accidental that widely accepted definitions of interaction design do not refer to interaction as the object of design. For instance, Löwgren and Solterman (2004) define interaction design as "the process that is arranged within existing resource constraints to create, shape, and decide all use-oriented qualities (structural, functional, ethical, and aesthetic) of a digital artifact".

We generally agree with Löwgren and Stolterman's definition when it refers to "use-oriented qualities of a digital artifact", rather than interaction, as being the object of design. However, in one respect this and other similar definitions are substantially limited. They tend to assume it is the designer alone who determines the qualities of the final product. However, this is not always the case, as there are many products whose properties can be defined by the users themselves. For instance, mobile phone covers can be easily changed, software customized by adding or deleting icons in the toolbar, or by installing additional plug-in modules. In the case of our videoconference setting end users could programme the buttons on the video equipment control panel to define camera angles corresponding to these buttons, depending on local needs and constraints. Therefore, in many cases, users are designers of artefacts in a very real sense. Using the terminology of the instrumental genesis approach (Rabardel and Bourmaud, 2003), to become instruments of meaningful activities artefacts provided for people's use have to undergo transformations within the process of instrumentation, in which they acquire new properties that make them suitable tools in real life contexts.

Of course, the importance of the contribution made by the designer – meaning the person with the formal design responsibility – should not be underestimated. However, his or her control over the use, and even the form and functionality of the product, is rather limited. This is the case even if the product is an individual artefact; for instance, a device or a software application. It is even more the case when the product in question is an environment; for instance a learning environment.

Environments can be characterized as 'ecologies of artefacts' (Krippendorf, 2006); they typically include configurations of artefacts, organized in a certain way. Decisions regarding the choice of particular artefacts to be included in an environment and how they should be organized within the environment are not always made by dedicated designers. In the case of the videoconference setting analysed in this paper the environment was composed of a number of nodes; that is, teacher's and students' sites. The configuration of material resources – space, equipment, furniture, and so forth – in each of these nodes was a cumulative result of numerous influences. The material resources could be dynamically rearranged just before or even during video sessions. The list of individuals and groups who influenced the design of the sites includes: the educational technology division of the university, university management, local authorities at the towns where the study centres were situated, study centre ICT experts, technicians, teachers, and students.

The problem of clarifying the meaning of 'design' and 'designers' in the context of videoconference learning environments is further complicated by the fact that such environments include not only material but also human resources. For instance, in our case the facilitator was probably the most valuable component of the environment. The facilitator performed a number of roles and made sure, for instance, that technical problems, such as problems with the communication line, were promptly recognized and taken care of before they could cause a major disruption of educational activities. The presence of the facilitator substantially influenced the functioning of the environment as a whole. In a similar vein, the presence or absence of students that could operate equipment at students' sites had a significant impact on the structure and use of resources in the videoconference setting during actual sessions.

This chapter does not set out to clarify the meaning of the words 'design' and 'designer' in the context of learning environments; such a thing would require the resolution of a whole set of conceptual issues. Our intention is to call for a systematic analysis of these issues, in order to develop a theoretical framework and practical methodology for design of learning environments that recognizes the limited control of the professional designer over the real life outcome of design, and strives to understand and coordinate contributions of a wide range of stakeholders.

FINAL REMARKS: CONTINUITY AND PEOPLE

While the main focus of this chapter is on breakdowns, affordances and indirect design – common issues for the book as a whole – we would like in this final section to bring in a more general perspective that emerges from the discussion above and from the empirical findings of our study.

Our study highlights the importance of ensuring continuity in the development of educational activities within a distributed learning setting. In the case analysed in this chapter the accumulation and transmission of experiences within a setting was achieved by the facilitator, who was the only link between otherwise fragmented episodes of teaching and learning. In addition, the case illustrates the importance of providing conditions for supra-situational activities, where participants assume roles and responsibilities that transcend immediate situational requirements.

Novel learning environments are characterized by numerous potentialities for breakdowns. We can conclude that an effective short term coping strategy can be stimulating supra-situational activities. It should be added that in the long run supra-situational activities should be crystallized in technological and institutional developments.

Concerning the role of the teacher, our study indicates that in geographically distributed learning environments a variety of roles should be assumed by the people who deliver the courses. In more traditional environments teachers are not always aware of certain coordination and resource management tasks – those carried out by other people or which are supported by the very structure of the learning setting. In new types of environments, teachers face the need to take on new roles. Our study indicated that the help provided by the technician/facilitator to the teachers was often a key factor in preventing the teachers from resorting to a sub-optimal teaching strategy – namely, simple lecturing while paying no attention to the students – so effectively inhibiting productive learning. In most NLEs, teachers are not provided with the type of support we found in our case, which means that the chances of breakdowns and the use of inefficient teaching strategies are increased.

Analysis of the support provided by the facilitator to the teachers in our case makes it possible to formulate tentative conclusions about how to ensure that similar support is available to any teacher operating in an NLE using desktop video-conferencing tools.

Firstly, teachers need to develop their awareness of the problems most commonly encountered within NLEs, along with the skills necessary to cope with them. The findings of our study give some guidance on what these should be. Secondly, the design of videoconferencing tools for NLEs should aim at making it possible for other people to support the teachers before, during, and after the video sessions. Such help, similar to the types of support found in our case, can be provided in the form of virtual coaching, when the teachers are new to videoconferencing and need the assistance the most. Thirdly, routine tasks should be automated as much as possible. Relatively simple solutions can be used for automatic attention management: for instance, the outgoing image can be set up to automatically switch to present-ation slides, either when the teacher changes a slide or deliberately points to an area of a slide. The proposed directions for research and development are tentative and need to be further explored in future research.

ACKNOWLEDGEMENTS

The authors would like to thank Nina Bonderup Dohn, Lone Dirckinck-Holmfeld, Frode Guriby, Chris Jones, Berner Lindström, and three anonymous reviewers for valuable comments on earlier drafts of this chapter.

NOTES

[1] The chapter does not intend to present a comprehensive analysis of similarities and differences between videoconference environments and regular classrooms. We compare these two types of environments because such a comparison was relevant to the participants of our study: the study

revealed that a common attitude toward videoconference settings was to view them as essentially similar to regular classrooms.

² In Sweden there is a national network of study centres, supported by local authorities, which provide resources, such as premises and technology, enabling people in the area to take part in various distance education programs.

³ The discussion of affordances in this section is partly based on a previous analysis of the issue by one of the authors (Kaptelinin and Nardi, 2006).

REFERENCES

Abbot, L., Dallat, J., Livingston, R., & Robinson, A. (1993). *Videoconferencing and distance learning.* Faculty of Education and Department of Adult and Continuing Education, University of Ulster.

Albrechtsen, H., Andersen, H., Bødker, S., & Pejtersen, A. (2001). *Affordances in activity theory and cognitive systems engineering.* Risø-R-1287 (EN). Roskilde: Risø National Laboratory. Retrieved from www.risoe.dk/rispubl/SYS/syspdf/ris-r-1287.pdf.

***Baerentsen, K., & Trettvik, J. (2002). An activity theory approach to affordance. *Proceedings of the Second Nordic Conference on Human-Computer Interaction* (Aarhus, October 2002) ACM Press, 51–60.

Bannon, L. (2005). A human-centred perspective on interaction design. In A. Pirhonen, H. Isomaki, C. Roast, & P. Saariluoma (Eds.), *Future interaction design* (pp. 31–51). London: Springer-Verlag.

Brown, J. S., & Duguid, P. (1994). Borderline issues: Social and material aspects of design. *Human-Computer Interaction, 9,* 3–36.

Dallat, J., Fraser, G., Livingston, R., & Robinson, A. (1992). *Videoconferencing and the adult learner.* Faculty of Education and Department of Adult and Continuing Education, University of Ulster.

***Gaver, W. (1991). Technology affordances. *CHI'91 Conference Proceedings* (New Orleans, Louisiana, April-May 1991), ACM Press, 79–84

***Gaver, W. (1992). The affordances of media spaces for collaboration. *Proceedings of CSCW'92.* ACM Press, 17–24.

Gibson, J. J. (1979). *The ecological approach to visual perception.* Boston: Houghton Mifflin.

Hedestig, U., & Kaptelinin, V. (2002, January 7–11). Re-contextualization of teaching and learning in videoconference-based environments. In *Proceedings of the 2002 conference on computer support for collaborative learning. Foundations for a CSCL community* (pp. 179–188). Boulder, Colorado.

Hedestig, U., & Kaptelinin, V. (2005). Facilitator's roles in a videoconference learning environment. *Information Systems Frontiers, 7*(1), 71–83.

Kaptelinin, V. (1996). Computer-mediated activity: Functional organs in social and developmental contexts. In B. Nardi (Ed.), *Context and consciousness: Activity theory and human-computer interaction* (pp. 45–68). Cambridge: MIT Press.

Kaptelinin, V., & Nardi, B. (2006). *Acting with technology: Activity theory and interaction design.* Cambridge, Mass.: MIT Press.

Kies, J. K., Williges, R. C., & Rosson, M. B. (1997). Evaluating desktop video conferencing for distance learning. *Computers and Education, 28*(2), 79–91.

Krippendorf, K. (2006). *The semantic turn: A new foundation for design.* Boca Raton, FL: Taylor and Francis.

Löwgren, J., & Stolterman, E. (2004). *Thoughtful interaction design.* Cambridge, Mass: MIT Press.

***McGrenere, J., & Ho, W. (2000). Affordances: Clarifying and evolving a concept. *Proceedings of graphics interface 2000* (Montreal, May 2000), A K Peters, 179–186.

Norman, D. (1989). *The design of everyday things.* New York: Basic Books.

Norman, D. (1999). Affordance, conventions and design. *Interactions, 6*(3), 38–43.

Preece, J., Rogers, Y., & Sharp, H. (2002). *Interaction design: Beyond human-computer interaction.* New York: John Wiley and Sons.

Rabardel, P., & Bourmaud, G. (2003). From computer to instrument system: A developmental perspective. *Interacting with Computers*, *15*, 665–691.

Rosengren, B. (1993). *När- och distansutbildning med dubbelriktad bild- och ljudkommunkation - en fallbeskrivning*. Department of Computer and System Sciences, report No 93-012-DSC, Royal Institute of Technology, Stockholm.

Torenvliet, G. (2003). We can't afford it! The devaluation of a usability term. *Interactions*, *10*, 12–17.

Victor Kaptelinin
Department of Informatics
Umeå University, Sweden

Ulf Hedestig
Department of Informatics
Umeå University, Sweden

HÅKON TOLSBY

VIRTUAL ENVIRONMENT FOR PROJECT BASED COLLABORATIVE LEARNING

A Case Study

Learning cannot be designed; it can only be designed-for; that is - facilitated or frustrated.

Wenger, 1998, p. 229

INTRODUCTION

A virtual environment for project based collaborative learning consists of more than software and computers. A virtual environment is situated in practice (Salomon, 1992; Pea, 1993). It encompasses a group of people working together with the aim of solving a problem. It also includes a curriculum to be studied and the pedagogical practice in which project work is founded as an activity of learning. All these aspects contribute to an understanding of the virtual environment and shape the practice that take place.

This chapter presents the study of a project group at Aalborg University who customized a groupware system and created a virtual project room, which they shaped and furnished to support their own practice. The decision for using a virtual environment was made by the students alone. They did that without any imposition from either teacher or institution, and they shaped the virtual environment according to their own needs and ideas. The virtual project room was not only a generic space for sharing material, but a joint place inhabited and constructed by the students.

Ryberg and Ponti (2004, 2005) argue that 'place making' is an important aspect of supporting social interaction on the Internet. They define place as the setting in which our intentions and behaviours become comprehensible and meaningful. It is a construction, consisting of reifications and shared experiences, that reflects a social practice. Furthermore, they argue that "fostering a social context cannot be disconnected from developing a sense of place in networked environments." The challenge is however to design and organise environments that can support place-making.

The aim of this study is to reveal how the students in the Aalborg case used a groupware system to construct a shared place on the internet where they collaborated to solve a project. The aim is to understand how they used the virtual environment

L. Dirckinck-Holmfeld, C. Jones and B. Lindström (eds.), Analysing Networked Learning Practices in Higher Education and Continuing Professional Development, 241–258.

to successfully coordinate their work on a joint project, how they shared knowledge, and how they engaged in each other's contributions.

Hopefully, the findings discussed below will contribute more knowledge to the field of virtual environment design, while improving our understanding of how virtual environments can be organised to support project based learning.

THE CASE

I learned about this case during a workshop with students and teachers at Aalborg University. The aim of the workshop was to discuss different approaches towards the use of ICT for supporting project-based learning. During the workshop a group of students presented their experiences with a groupware system called iGroups. Their presentation was particularly interesting, because it demonstrated how a virtual environment could be constructed in collaboration, and how the environment could be used to share knowledge and to coordinate the process of creating a joint project.

According to the students, comprising four males, iGroups was being used by several student groups at the University of Aalborg in similar ways. This was not something promoted by the institution, but chosen by the students themselves as a useful means to support their work with collaborative projects.

The students who were demonstrating their experience with iGroups had just finished their sixth semester project at Aalborg University's Institute of Humanistic Informatics, on which they all collaborated. The objective of their project was to design a prototype of a virtual learning environment that could be used in project based learning. This had involved some empirical research among their fellow students with the aid of questionnaires, workshops and observation of other students already using the iGroups groupware system.

Although they did not directly study their own experience as part of their project, it is natural to assume that the very nature of the project had impact on their creation and utilisation of the virtual learning environment, and vice versa.

In this case I consider the close relationship between the students' own project and their working methods as a strengthening of the case. It entails that they had strong interests and motives in reflecting on the processes involved in project-based learning and in the implementation of a best practice within a virtual environment.

The students gave me access to their virtual environment where I was allowed to study their constructions and activities. In addition, they gave me a copy of their project report that contained their own considerations and discussions of the topic.

The iGroups groupware system used by the students in this case is a free product, hosted by a Danish software developer. It is a flexible system, allowing the group of users a certain degree of shaping and building the environment according to their own needs. This customization is achieved over and above the basic structure of the system with the aid of a built-in set of tools. The main feature of iGroups is that it provides a file-sharing environment where the students can organize and structure their shared documents. Another important feature is that new workspaces can be added on demand. These are simple editable spaces where all group members can add and edit text and hyperlinks. Furthermore, the system provides tools like:

internal message system, forum for asynchronous discussions, news forum, link collections, chat, photo album and mailing lists. The architecture of iGroups is open and easy to navigate. It has a flat structure, and all links to available tools and workspaces are present in a menu bar to the left of the screen.

However, the purpose of this text is not to evaluate iGroups, which is by no means a perfect system, although it certainly has is advantages. The purpose is to reveal and discuss how project based learning can be supported by a virtual environment, what activities and processes are central, and what demands it places on technological solutions.

PROJECT BASED LEARNING AND POPP

Aalborg University is a project-organized university. The students learn to work in project groups from the day they arrive as freshmen, and 50 percent of each semester is devoted to project work (Kjersdam & Enemark, 1994). Project based learning, as practised at Aalborg University, has its own pedagogical foundation called Problem Oriented Project Pedagogy (POPP). In order to understand the practices in which the students of this case study are involved, it is necessary to know the basic aims and principles of POPP.

A central aspect of POPP is the focus on problem orientation. The students are defining and formulating their own problems. They do not work on predefined tasks with known solutions, but engage themselves in real problems that they find meaningful to work with. In addition, they are responsible for deciding which perspectives, theories and methods they want to use in the inquiry. The fact that the students have ownership of the problem and the inquiry is implicitly encouraging their involvement and motivation

POPP is also a collaborative pedagogy and the students are mutually responsible for creating and conducting a joint project (Dirckinck-Holmfeld, 2002). They are, therefore, not supposed to divide the project into discrete tasks for individuals to complete. While they are each responsible for their own leaning, the principle of mutual responsibility means they must engage in each others contributions and perspectives. The project work is a means of integrating individual constructions of knowledge, as well as constructing a shared understanding through negotiations and confrontations. It is a dialectic process based on a social constructivist understanding of leaning (Dewey, 1966; Piaget, 1969; Vygotsky, 1978; Illeris, 1981).

THE RESEARCH STUDY

The study of the project group and their virtual environment was conducted as a qualitative case study (Stake, 1995). The aim was to understand the meaning of the constructions and processes that took place in the virtual environment and how it afforded collaboration and learning among the students.

The research questions were focused on how the students shaped the environment and used the technology to support project-based learning. Stake (1995) describes such a case study, driven by specific research questions, as an instrumental case study. The aim is to provide insight into an issue by studying a particular case.

The case was not selected in order to be representative of project groups at Aalborg University. It was chosen because the group demonstrated a best practice, and it was assumed that it would provide valuable knowledge for understanding how a virtual environment can support learning and knowledge construction in a collaborative project.

Since the students had finished their project at the time I started to study them, the study of the virtual environment had the character of a retrospective observation, where I tried to recapitulate the processes and activities that had taken place some months earlier. Although I did not directly observe the project as it evolved, the virtual environment gave access to lots of useful information: documents, discussions, task lists, structures, constructions of work spaces etc. This made it possible to recapitulate at least parts of the activities and processes that had taken place.

Based on findings from the retrospective observation, I conducted an interview with one of the student participants, taking the approach of a semi structured qualitative research interview (Kvale, 1996). This means it was an explorative interview, where interpretations were present in all phases of the process, from the construction of the interview questions to the actual interview and in the resulting analysis.

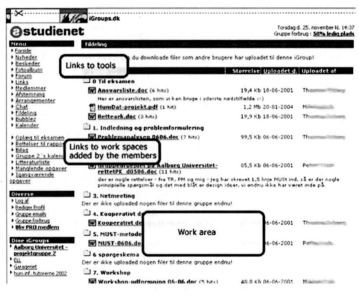

Figure 1. The virtual environment that the students furnished in iGroups

A computer showing the students' project environment was used during the interview to prompt the interviewee in his recapitulations and reflections on the activities and processes that had taken place.

After the interview a preliminary analysis was sent to all participants in the project group, including the interviewee, for verification and further comments (Merriam, 1988). Three out of four students responded to the request for verification, and their comments were incorporated in the final analysis.

In addition, I have used results from the research presented in the student's own project report as an additional resource in the analysis and discussions.

The analysis of the case study is organised into themes or concepts in order to understand the activities and processes in which the students were engaged. In the following text these themes are discussed and illustrated with examples from the virtual environment and statements from the interviewee. As the interview was conducted in Danish, these statements have therefore been translated into English.

A NEED FOR TOOLS THAT SUPPORT COLLABORATION

The interviewee gives two reasons why the project group chose to use a virtual environment as the working arena for their project. Firstly, they wanted to experience project-based learning with the aid of Internet based tools. This was the aim of their project. And although they did not investigate their own practice it gave them a useful insight into the problem area.

Secondly, they had found that working on a joint project can be simultaneously constructive and troublesome. In the introduction to their report, the students write the following about this:

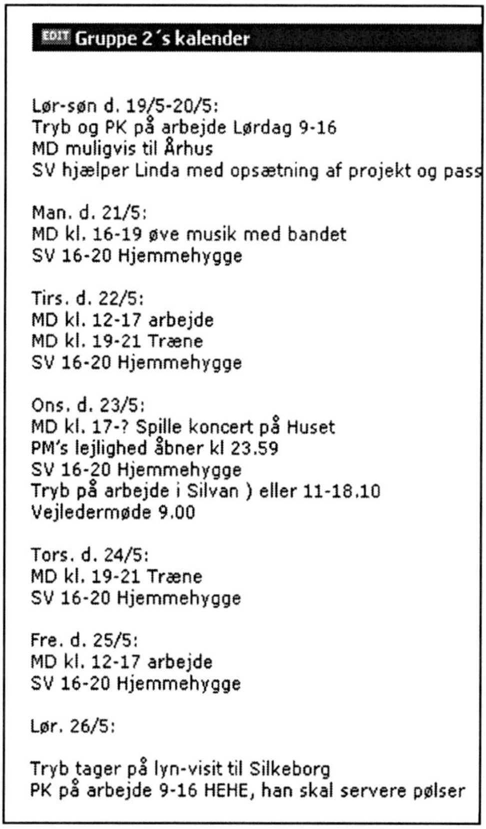

EDIT Gruppe 2´s kalender

Lør-søn d. 19/5-20/5:
Tryb og PK på arbejde Lørdag 9-16
MD muligvis til Århus
SV hjælper Linda med opsætning af projekt og pass

Man. d. 21/5:
MD kl. 16-19 øve musik med bandet
SV 16-20 Hjemmehygge

Tirs. d. 22/5:
MD kl. 12-17 arbejde
MD kl. 19-21 Træne
SV 16-20 Hjemmehygge

Ons. d. 23/5:
MD kl. 17-? Spille koncert på Huset
PM's lejlighed åbner kl 23.59
SV 16-20 Hjemmehygge
Tryb på arbejde i Silvan) eller 11-18.10
Vejledermøde 9.00

Tors. d. 24/5:
MD kl. 19-21 Træne
SV 16-20 Hjemmehygge

Fre. d. 25/5:
MD kl. 12-17 arbejde
SV 16-20 Hjemmehygge

Lør. 26/5:

Tryb tager på lyn-visit til Silkeborg
PK på arbejde 9-16 HEHE, han skal servere pølser

Figure 2. The shared calendar where the students wrote what they were doing at different dates.

There are euphoric moments, where one as a student sees connections that were earlier concealed. But there are also moments where the group members glow with frustration because the project is about to collapse. Papers are not delivered in time, the members have divergent goals and expectations and deadlines are postponed.

They had experienced the benefits of working together in solving a problem, but also the difficulties in maintaining and coordinating a joint project. Although they were on-campus students and could meet face to face, they were looking for tools to coordinate the process of writing and sharing material. They chose to use a virtual environment in order to strengthen the collaborative processes, to support coordination of work and to represent and make visible the project as a joint construction and enterprise.

COORDINATION

The required level of coordination between group members was a major reason for using a virtual project environment. Not unnaturally, the students had other activities besides their studies. Some were active in sports, while others also had jobs to go to, making it difficult to find time for meetings on campus. The interviewee explained:

We needed a virtual environment to coordinate our work. We could in fact not meet very often. So we thought that if we could place all our documents in a virtual group space, and make everyone read them and comment on them then we could work at home and meet in person once in a while

A project group is not a symbiotic union but it consists of individuals with individual lives, thoughts, beliefs and aims. From a constructivist perspective this is a prerequisite for project-based learning. Students bring their experiences into the project and a common understanding is reached through confrontations and negotiations of perspectives and beliefs (Dirckinck-Holmfeld, 2002).

However, this is a fragile process that can easily be destroyed if participants have diverging interests and priorities. Coordination between participants is therefore an important factor in project based learning to stimulate and maintain the mutual engagement and interdependency that is necessary for a successful project.

It is not only tasks and meetings that must be coordinated. The need for coordination extends across the entire mutual process of planning, structuring and creating a common understanding.

The case study revealed that, in practice, coordination falls into two categories, covering project activities and knowledge construction. Coordination of project activities is more of an administrative task while coordination of knowledge construction relates to the interactive negotiation process of reaching a common understanding in the project.

Coordination of Project Activities

In the first instance activity coordination is necessary for managing the presence of the students and arranging meetings.

All activities that the students were engaged in were registered. Since iGroups did not provide a proper calendar tool, they created a shared workspace for this purpose, which every one had access to edit. The interviewee explained:

> We tried to write down what we were doing at different dates, because then we knew when to drop a meeting, should a peer student be on vacation or working.

The main features of the calendar were that it was shared and accessible for everyone, and that it showed the activities of all the students simultaneously. When the students wanted to arrange a meeting, they used the calendar to find periods when everyone was available. Then they used the message tool in iGroups to negotiate the actual time for the meeting. The message tool is particularly appropriate for this purpose, because it is asynchronous. The messages are saved on a message board and do not have to bee answered immediately if one is not logged on to iGroups.

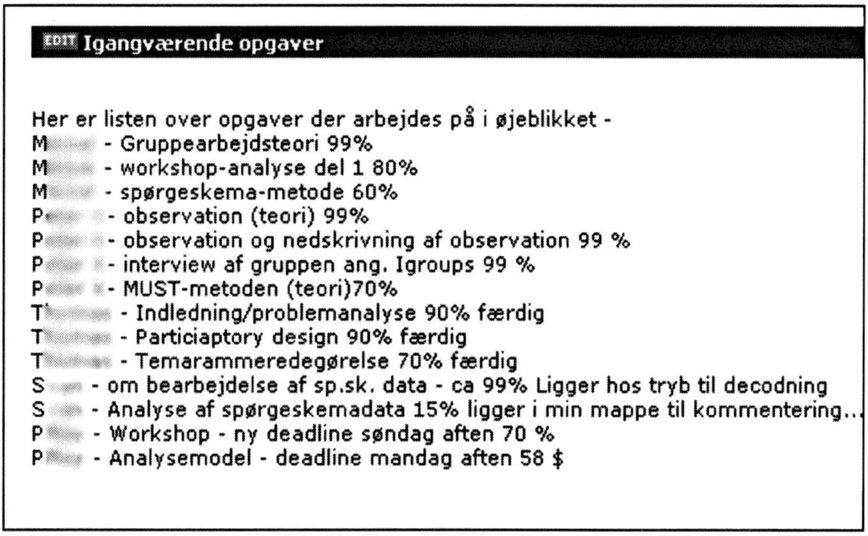

```
EDIT Igangværende opgaver

Her er listen over opgaver der arbejdes på i øjeblikket -
M       - Gruppearbejdsteori 99%
M       - workshop-analyse del 1 80%
M       - spørgeskema-metode 60%
P       - observation (teori) 99%
P       - observation og nedskrivning af observation 99 %
P       - interview af gruppen ang. Igroups 99 %
P       - MUST-metoden (teori)70%
T       - Indledning/problemanalyse 90% færdig
T       - Particiaptory design 90% færdig
T       - Temarammeredegørelse 70% færdig
S       - om bearbejdelse af sp.sk. data - ca 99% Ligger hos tryb til decodning
S       - Analyse af spørgeskemadata 15% ligger i min mappe til kommentering...
P       - Workshop - ny deadline søndag aften 70 %
P       - Analysemodel - deadline mandag aften 58 $
```

Figure 3. The shared workspace which the students created in order to register ongoing tasks and how far they had reached.

Activity coordination is also necessary for the identification, sharing and division of tasks. That is, which tasks will be solved through the project, by whom and when, and the status of ongoing tasks. In a joint project it is essential to be acquainted with the progress of the project and the responsibilities.

The students created two shared workspaces where the project tasks were coordinated. One of these was for ongoing tasks and the other for tasks yet to be started. The students wrote and altered in the shared workspaces and tried to describe what the new tasks were, which tasks people were working on and the problems they were dealing with. Using shared workspaces for these purposes gave a dynamic overview of the process, and it became a forum for idea generation and negotiation of the tasks involved. The interviewee said:

> We used the shared workspaces to write down what we didn't yet understand and what tasks and chapters we had started. It is very important to know which tasks other people have begun, so I can put any questions I may have to the right person. Who has had time to read this chapter, and who is actually responsible for the task now?

But as the interviewee further commented, it demands a certain discipline among the group members to maintain such information, and it was a task they didn't always fulfil. Hence the information became irrelevant and they could not trust it. The interviewee thought that the lack of a proper tool for task administration was a decisive shortcoming in the virtual environment, because the division of tasks, knowing what the others are working on and how far they have come, are all very important for project coordination.

Coordination of Knowledge Construction

The essence of project-based learning is that the students will reach a common understanding and construct a shared knowledge. This does not exclude individual contributions and perspectives. But neither does it mean they can divide the project into discrete tasks that are worked on by individuals and then brought together only at the end of the project. On the contrary, they are supposed to engage in each others contributions and perspectives, to negotiate meaning and understanding, and to construct a joint project.

If a project is divided into discrete tasks, coordination is only required when the partial results are assembled. On the other hand, constructing a joint project through genuine collaboration involves a coordinated effort to complete the project together (Roschelle & Teasely, 1995). It is an interactive process where all group members have to participate, share and negotiate.

iGroups provides a space for sharing uploaded files. This was the main arena for coordinating the construction of shared knowledge. The group members used the file sharing space to upload documents, to comment on each other's documents and to rearrange the structure of the project. Although important decisions concerning project progress were dealt with in physical group meetings, the file sharing space was the arena for the continuous co-writing and the negotiation of meaning throughout the project. Here they shared and discussed content simultaneously as they were writing.

iGroups identifies who has uploaded a document. It also provides information on how many times a document has been downloaded, but not by whom and it does not record the purpose of the download. In order to coordinate this process they used the facility offered by iGroups for writing meta-information into each document link. By this means they were able to inform each other what they had done to a document. The interviewee described the process:

> We had to use the meta-texts in order to relate what we had done with the document, and who had done it and why, because it could be that two people in separate locations had downloaded the same document simultaneously, corrected it and then uploaded it. Then it became a mess. So it was a matter of coordinating the order in which people should be performing their corrections on any given document. This was a bit hard (...) and wasn't always done consistently.

A major advantage provided by the file sharing environment is that one can edit directly in the document of a peer student. In order to keep the corrections separated from the original text they used the track changes utility in Word. Documents that were downloaded for commenting and rewriting by other group members were uploaded as new versions, and by this method a document history was created. Finally, the original owner of the document was given the task of reconstructing the document based on the contributions from his peer students. The interviewee explained:

> I download a document and start to change it. I do that using the track changes utility in Word, and thereby the changes are placed directly in the document, and they can be accepted or rejected. (...) The owner of the document can download it, look at it and say these corrections are good and these are bad.

The file sharing space was also the arena for more intensive negotiations about the content of documents. Simultaneously, the access to each others' documents provided both a source of inspiration and a guide for ensuring that the content and direction of one's own writings matched those of the project in general. The interviewee said:

> We could be two or three persons playing ping pong with a document; write corrections, refuse or accept them and quickly respond saying 'thank you for the corrections, they were damn good'. And if one got stuck while writing, or wondered where the project was heading, one always had access to what the others were writing, reasonably updated and simultaneously. Thereby it was also easier to adjust one's own writings according to the others.

In addition to iGroups they used Windows Messenger to send each other informal messages. It is faster than communicating in iGroups and they reported that it felt better for more spontaneous dialogue. Through a combination of asynchronous and synchronous forms of interaction they could confront each others' ideas and perspectives and establish a dialectic practice which has proven difficult to achieve in environments such as text based conference systems (Fjuk & Dirckinck-Holmfeld, 1999; Dirckinck-Holmfeld, 2002).

By using these various techniques, they coordinated the construction of a joint project through sharing and negotiation, and the interviewee described the process as far more manageable than the traditional way of using paper and pen. In an ordinary project it is normal to gather the whole project group and circulate the documents for comments and rewritings.

> Sometimes it is very disciplinary, the interviewee said. One sits together for a whole day and makes corrections to the documents, using five different pens with five different colours, and at the end you get a document with thousands of completely non transparent corrections. But it is a bit easier when you can do it directly in the document on a computer.

According to Gutwin and Greenberg (2004, p. 189) "coordinating actions in a collaborative activity means making them happen in the right order and at the right time to complete the task without conflicting with others in the group". But coordination in genuine collaboration, as described in this case, also includes the coordination of people who are negotiating their positions and their engagement in each other's contributions.

INTERDEPENDENCY AND COMMITMENT

The interviewee argued that coordinating the project in a virtual environment also created more interdependency and mutual commitment to fellow students:

> I felt more affiliated, he said. I got more interested in what the others were writing when I could go directly to a document in iGroups, correct it and get immediate feedback on my comments from the owner. I believe it means a lot that I could say 'Hi Fred, I have just added a correction, look at it and say what you think'.

He argued further that an environment that supports a continuously sharing and negotiation of content commits to participation and thereby strengthens the group process:

> It creates more commitment and one is more likely to focus one's attention. By keeping an eye on the system one is continuously participating. If a document pops up, one looks at it swiftly to see if there are any corrections, and sends it back right away with new comments. In this way I believe one gets to read more of the others' writings. People expect to get something back. And because it is fast, they expect to get a fast response. Commitments are created when one knows that others are checking what one has written.

The interaction between the students was improved by using Windows Messenger in combination with iGroups. They were synchronously writing their documents and maintaining a dialogue with the rest of the group. The interviewee considered the fast tempo of interaction and the fact that they all were online, constantly monitoring and checking for new uploads and messages, as essential for the collaborative process. "It became a sort of virtual group room", he said. In this room, belonging was demonstrated through continuously and concurrently participation, and psychodynamic factors such as interdependency and mutual engagement were nourished, in the sense that the students felt committed to share information, to complement each others contributions, and to focus on a joint project that they were all engaged in. "It worked well", he said, but then he added: "it is difficult to tell whether it is because of the system or the people you are working with."

Psychodynamic factors such as interdependency and mutual engagement are claimed to be crucial for genuine collaboration (Wenger, 1998; Salomon, 1992 and Dirckinck-Holmfeld, 2002). If the group doesn't pull together, if they do not engage in the same problems and tasks, and if they do not feel mutually responsible for the process, the collaboration will not work.

However, as the interviewee commented, the fact that they were collaborating so well could be due to factors other than the technology they were using. In fact it is not likely that technology alone can produce genuine collaboration, and according to Salomon (1992), factors such as interdependency and mutual engagement concern the orchestration of the whole learning environment, including curriculum, teachers' behaviour, collaborative tasks, learning goals and the like. This, in addition to the fact that some of the students knew each other, and had been collaborating earlier, laid the ground for a successful collaboration.

This doesn't make the virtual environment less important. This case demonstrates, to a certain extent that psychodynamic factors can develop in a virtual environment and even be strengthened if the necessary functionality is available, and the design supports the processes necessary for the students to engage in a joint project. These processes will probably vary form case to case, depending on curriculum, learning goals and the tasks in which the students engage. But in project based learning the interactive negotiation process, where material is shared and discussed, will be essential, and in this case it was supported by fast interaction and feedback between the students, by visualisation of participation, reifications of ideas and concepts, and the growth of a joint project.

TRANSPARENCY

Transparency is an important factor in project based learning and probably in all kinds of collaboration. It is a matter of being able to overview the process, to know what the others are working on, and to be able to place oneself into that context. Transparency is important with respect to coordination and sharing of knowledge, but also in order to stimulate psychodynamic aspects such as interdependency and mutual engagement, and to avoid possible problems and conflicts.

Transparency is closely related to what Gutwin and Greenberg (2004) describe as workspace awareness in distributed collaborative environments. They define workspace awareness as: "the up to the moment understanding of another person's interaction with the shared workspace". It is to know who is present and what they are doing where. Such information is taking for granted in the physical world, but in a virtual environment the system designer must explicitly program in such features that can gather awareness information.

In the file-sharing space the current project structure was visible for all members of the group. They could view what the others had done, how far they had come, and what they lacked. Furthermore, they could easily notice if someone in the group had problems with fulfilling their part of the project. The interviewee explained:

> It is invaluable to be able to watch what the others are doing. In normal group work people might say they are doing fine with a task, but then arrive two days before the deadline with half a page of analysis, and cry and say they that they can't come up with more. But here we had some control, because one could at any time see what the others were up to and be included in their process. And even though we were not sitting in the same room we could see whether someone was having problems or not by reading his documents, and we could say 'OK, Fred I think you are on the wrong track regarding the aim of the project.' ...It was essential that we could see each others documents and pay attention to them.

The virtual environment provided a visual image of the member's participation by showing a spatial representation of their file sharing space. Furthermore, iGroups gives information about who is online, or how long it has been since a group member was last logged in. The group used this information to assure themselves that no-one had dropped out or become passive, and if someone had not been active in the virtual environment for several days, he was contacted and asked to explain why he was not participating.

The students also discussed transparency in their own project report as a central factor in net-based project work. They concluded that transparency is important at different levels in relation to different actors. They concluded that transparency is necessary in order to maintain a mutual understanding of a project. It is a form of positive control that secures responsibility. In addition, they discussed the importance of opening the group process towards a tutor by giving him/her access to the virtual project room. This kind of transparency will provide the tutor with more insight into the project and probably improve the conditions for adequate guidance. A third aspect of transparency is that of other student projects; i.e. that former projects are available in a digital form, for easy access and inspiration.

A FLEXIBLE AND EXTENDABLE INFRASTRUCURE

Student projects are never homogenous. The problems they are investigating and the tasks they engage in will vary from project to project. Choosing an appropriate virtual environment for project-based learning is therefore problematic. The students in this case considered using a dedicated project management tool, but these tools were found not to provide the necessary flexibility. The interviewee explained that:

> (in a dedicated project management tool) one had to start defining a lot of tasks and create a lot of documents before one could even start on the project

(...) but when one starts on a project one does not have many ideas about where one is going.

Flexibility was the main reason for choosing iGroups as the virtual project environment. It didn't direct the students to work in accordance with a certain model, but instead let the students develop their own structures for the project. In the file sharing space they could add new folders, change the sequence and delete. "I believe one should be allowed to create the structure because it may change. Tasks may change", the interviewee said, and described how they were continuously restructuring the folders in the file sharing space and defining new folders with new headers where documents could be placed.

> This possibility that you can continuously enter (the environment) and change the structure gives an incredible flexibility. (...) You can see the structure develop, that the introduction and the problem formulation are almost ready and what will follow next.

The environment was also extended by creating several new workspaces as they were needed. In iGroups you can create simple editable spaces where all group members can add and edit text and hyperlinks. These were used for several purposes, for example link collections, literature list, exam preparations, idea generation etc. The interviewee said:

> The extendible work spaces were fantastic, because one can never foresee what people need. (...) We used them for example to maintain a literature list, which we could update during the project, and in the end we just copied it to project document.

Thanks to the simple facility that iGroups provides, the students were able to create their own environment, which they structured and extended according to their own needs. There was little pre-programmed structure that they were forced to follow. The system did not think for them, but afforded an environment that the students could change and restructure so that it supported the activities in which they were engaged.

AN IMAGE OF SHARED EXPERIENCES

The file sharing space, where the students were sharing documents, functioned as more than a space for sharing knowledge. As it developed over time, the project structure that gradually emerged in the file sharing space also became a dynamic representation of the progression of the project. The structures that emerged in the file sharing space provided an image of the experiences they were sharing, and it was reflecting the accumulated results of working together on the project. The interviewee said:

> The file sharing space is where the project is placed and at any time you could enter and see how far we had come and how many pages we had completed.

The structure in the file sharing space consisted of folders, documents and meta-texts, and the students were continuously changing it. It was structured to reflect the project and the group members' understanding of the project at any time.

The file sharing space was mirroring the structure in the project, the interviewee said. We did not have a structure to start with. At some point we had folders with our names on, where everyone could put their documents. But slowly and surely we realized that we had an introduction chapter and a problem formulation. And then we started to get more structure. But it was not until just before the end that the final sequence was lined up, because as the chapters changed so did their sequence.

The ability to see the project grow over time, and to get an overall picture of it, had a major influence on the coordination of the writing and the continuous reconstruction of the project structure. The file sharing space worked as a coordination element, around which they could negotiate their contributions and their positions. The result of this negotiation was a dynamically developing project that had undergone several changes and transformations before reaching its final status.

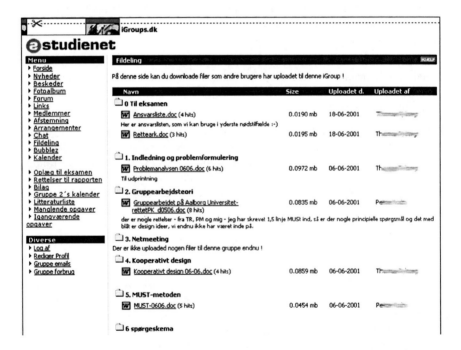

Figure 4. The file sharing space where the students shared files and jointly shaped the structure of the project.

There is an emerging understanding of cognition as distributed between mind and environment (Vygotsky, 1978; Säljö, 1995; Pea, 1993). Thinking is not exclusively an internal process, but is an integral part of human practice (Säljö,1995), which includes the use of psychological and technical tools. We use tools to interact with the world, to communicate, discuss and create understanding and knowledge. According to sociocultural theories, language is considered the most important tool for thinking. Language is used to create meaningful concepts that we can share and discuss with other people.

However, technical artefacts, including interactive computer tools, have a parallel function as mediators of knowledge, and as such they can extend our ability to think, act and collaborate.

The understanding of cognition as being distributed between mind and environment has consequences for the design of virtual environments and computer tools. It implies that in order to support cognitive demanding tasks such as problem solving, reflection, and negotiation of meaning, the virtual environment should provide tools and structures that can help the users to think, either alone, and/or in collaboration with others.

In response to this, Minken and Stenseth (1995) argue for the need to have elements in the user interface that can accumulate the user's experiences while interacting with the computer system. They call such elements images of experiences. These are objects, artefacts or structures that can help the user to see how far he/she has come in solving a problem and support him/her to find the further direction.

The image of experiences that emerged in the file sharing space was only partly a result of what was afforded by the system. It was just as much a result of the social practices in which the students engaged. In fact, the environment was quite simple and did not provide much interactivity, and in order to restructure and change the sequence of the folders the students had to number each folder, and have iGroups sort them into order. It is true that the environment afforded the students the possibility of structuring their project, but the invention of the structure and the process of negotiating and restructuring the representation belonged to the students.

It is obvious that the image of experiences did not reflect every aspect of the students' collaboration. However, it did capture essential elements. It captured the emerging project as they were adding and correcting documents and restructuring their sequence. The focus was on the representation of the project structure, and as they were changing it, so it was changing their own understanding and so laid the ground for new experiences.

CONCLUSION

A single study like this has its limitations as an explanation of collaboration and knowledge construction in a virtual environment. However, the case was chosen for study because it appeared to be a best practice and because the students had chosen to use a virtual environment of their own free will. It was not forced upon them, and they didn't know until later that their virtual practice would be a subject of investigation. Although it is a single case, the fact that they constructed a learning environment based on their own needs and desires and without any imposition from teachers and supervisors makes this case particular interesting.

The students in this case showed a desire to collaborate. Although the virtual environment supported this desire, it was grounded in the Problem Oriented Project Pedagogy as practiced at Aalborg University. The students were trained in collaborative learning and had several years of experience in it. Dirckinck-Holmfeld (2002) argues that POPP is a well qualified method for Computer Supported Collaborative Learning (CSCL) because it enables genuine collaboration. This study emphasizes that using a virtual environment can contribute to strengthening group awareness and the construction of a joint project.

The aim of the study was to reveal how the student group used the virtual environment to successfully coordinate the working on a joint project, and how they together created a shared space which they inhabited and structured according to their own practice.

Coordination was one argument put forward by the students for using a virtual environment. Two types of coordination were identified; coordination of activities, such as tasks and schedules; and coordination of knowledge construction, which is understood as the coordination of people who are negotiating their positions and their engagement in each other's contributions.

The extremely visible and interactive process of uploading, sharing and commenting on documents encouraged the students to be active within the virtual environment. They felt committed to work and to engage in each other's contributions. The group process was transparent, and the students could watch each other's participation within the virtual environment and adjust themselves to the others.

A flexible infrastructure made it possible for the students to shape and extend the environment after their own needs. The students were place makers who constructed their own collaborative environment.

Furthermore, the case demonstrated the signification of elements in the environment that function as images of experiences. These are objects and structures that can accumulate and reflect the shared experiences of the participants, and aid them in problem solving.

Finally, the case has shown that a virtual environment is constructed through the participation of its members; that it is a product of both ordinary participation and more explicit design decisions. The case points out that, given adequate tools, members of a project group can construct a productive and meaningful place for learning.

Tools supporting virtual environments are not neutral. They afford a certain practice (Norman, 1988; Pea, 1993; Dirckinck-Holmfeld and Jones, this volume), and one has to choose them according to the practice one wants to support. It is in the nature of POPP that the virtual learning environment must be open and flexible. POPP is a flexible pedagogy (Dirckinck-Holmfeld, 2002) with a flexible curriculum where the students define problems, theories and research methods themselves. Therefore the technology should not force the students to work according to a predefined structure. Instead, it should enable them to create their own knowledge constructions, around which they can negotiate their contributions and positions.

REFERENCES

Creswell, W. J. (1998). *Quality inquiry and research design. Choosing among five traditions.* Thousand Oaks, CA: SAGE Publications.

Dewey, J. (1966). *Democracy and education. An introduction to the philosophy of education.* New York and London: Free Press & Collier-Macmillan.

Dirckinck-Holmfeld, L. (2002). Designing virtual learning environments based on problem oriented project pedagogy. In L. Dirckinck-Holmfeld & B. Fibiger (Eds.), *Learning in virtual environments* (pp. 31–54). Fredriksberg, Denmark: Samfundslitteratur.

Dirckinck-Holmfeld, L., & Jones, C. (2009). Issues and concepts in networked learning. In L. Dirckinck-Holmfeld, C. Jones, & B. Lindström (Eds.), *Analysing networked learning practices in higher education and continuing professional development.* Rotterdam, The Netherlands: Sense Publishers.

Fjuk, A., & Dirckinck-Holmfeld, L. (1999). Articulation of actions in distributed collaborative learning. *Scandinavian Journal of Information Systems, 9*(2), 3–24.

Gutwin, C., & Greenberg, S. (2004). The importance of awareness for team cognition in distributed collaboration. In E. Salas & S. M. Fiore (Eds.), *Team cognition: Understanding the factors that drive process and performance* (pp. 177–201). Washington, DC: APA Press.

Illeris, K. (1981). *Modkvalificeringens pædagogik.* Denmark: Unge Pædagoger.

Kjersdam, F., & Enemark, S. (1997). *The Aalborg Experiment. Project innovation in university education.* Aalborg: Aalborg University Press.

Kvale, S. (1996). *Interviews. An introduction to qualitative research interviewing.* London: SAGE Publications.

Minken, I., & Stensth, B. (1995). *Brukerorientert programdesign.* Oslo: Nasjonalt læremiddelsenter.

Merriam, S. B. (1998). *Qualitative research and case study applications in education.* San Fransisco: Jossey-Bass Publishers.

Norman, D. (1988). *The psychology of everyday things.* New York: Basic books.

Pea, R. (1993). Practices of distributed intelligence and design for education. In G. Salomon (Ed.), *Distributed cognition: Psychological and educational considerations* (pp. 47–87). Cambridge, MA: Cambridge University Press.

Piaget, J. (1969). *Barnets psykiske udvikling.* Oversat (M. Uhrskov & J. P. Jensen, Trans.). København, Hans Reitzel. (Original work published 1964. Six etudes de psychologie, Paris, Société Nouvelle des Editions Gonthier.)

Ponti, M., & Ryberg, T. (2004). Rethinking virtual space as a place for sociability: Theory and design implications. In S. Banks, P. Goodyear, V. Hodgson, C. Jones, V. Lally, & D. McConell (Eds.), *Proceedings of the fourth international conference on networked learning 2004* (pp. 332–339). Lancaster, UK: Lancaster University.

Roschelle, J., & Teasley, S. D. (1995). Construction of shared knowledge in collaborative problemsolving. In C. O'Malley (Ed.), *Computer-supported collaborative learning.* New York: Springer-Verlag.

Ryberg, T., & Ponti, M. (2005). Constructing place: The relationship between place-making and sociability in networked environments—a condition for productive learning environments. In L. Dirckinck-Holmfeld, B. Lindström, B. M. Svendsen, & M. Ponti (Eds.), *Conditions for productive learning in networked learning environments.* Aalborg University/Kaleidoscope.

Salomon, GL. (1992, Spring). What does the design of effective cscl require and how do we study its effects? *Sigcue Outlook, 21*(3), ACM, 62–68.

Säljö, R. (1995). Mental and physical artifacys in cognitive practices. In P. Reimann & H. Spada (Eds.), *Learning in humans and machines: Towards an interdisciplinary learning science.* Oxford, UK: Elsevier Science.

Stake, E. R. (1995). *The art of case study research*. Thousand Oaks, CA: SAGE Publications.
Vygotsky, L. (1978). *Mind in society: The development of higher psychological processes*. Cambridge, MA: Harvard University Press.
Wenger, E. (1998). *Communities of practice*. Cambridge, MA: Cambridge University Press.

Håkon Tolsby
Department of Communication
Aalborg University, Denmark and
Department of informatics
Ostfold University College, Norway

LONE DIRCKINCK-HOLMFELD AND CHRIS JONES

ISSUES AND CONCEPTS IN NETWORKED LEARNING

Analysis and the Future of Networked Learning

This book began by positioning networked learning alongside of the rapid social and economic changes that began in the late 20th century and which have continued during the early years of the new millennium. The current rhetoric of technological change concerns the shift from what has been called Web 1.0 to Web 2.0 (O'Reilly, 2005). We begin this chapter by offering an historical perspective, one that suggests that these changes have been more incremental than many others have claimed and that the shift to Web 2.0 brings back into focus many issues that have been dealt with previously in relation to the Internet and Computer-Mediated Communication (i.e. pre-World Wide Web). Some of these issues date back even further to pedagogies and technologies for educational reform that pre-date both the modern Internet and Web (Cuban, 1986).

We go on to develop the theoretical and conceptual framework presented in the Introduction and to elaborate upon the core themes of this volume, namely an indirect approach to learning and design, institutional and infrastructural issues for networked learning, the affordances of networked learning environments, and the term productive learning. In making these elaborations we draw on the case study work presented throughout the volume.

HISTORICAL VIEW OF NETWORKED LEARNING

Some of the first experiments in networked learning took place as early as the late nineteen seventies based on the Internet and computer conferencing and several years prior to the development of the World Wide Web. In fact pioneering work using a computer conferencing system had begun in the 1970s at the Institute For The Future at Menlo Park in California (Vallee et al., 1974, 1974a and 1975). Soon after this Hiltz and Turoff, two educational pioneers in the use of Internet technologies, linked their work directly with the Institute For The Future reports (Hiltz and Turoff, 1978). A major problem with this early strand of educational research was its comparative approach. Hiltz, for example, clearly set out to compare traditional face-to-face teaching or traditional classrooms (TC) with the virtual classroom (VC) (Hiltz, 1990, p. 133). This comparative tradition was a spur to the development of the book and related web site, *The No-Significant Difference Phenomenon* (Russell, 2001), which suggested that comparisons alone did not provide any clear answers to the question of whether were any significant differences in outcomes

L. Dirckinck-Holmfeld, C. Jones and B. Lindström (eds.), Analysing Networked Learning Practices
in Higher Education and Continuing Professional Development, 259–285.
© *2009 Sense Publishers. All rights reserved.*

resulting from the deployment of technologies (Russell, 1999). Some of the conferencing systems developed in this period continue to be used today, for example the FirstClass computer conferencing system is still used on a large scale by institutions such as the Open University (UK) and Aalborg University (DK) (see Jones; and Dirckinck-Holmfeld et. al., this volume).

Research concerning educational use of computer conferencing had a different character to earlier research on the use of computers in education which had focused on human interaction with the computer itself and was often informed by behaviourist notions of stimulus and response (cf Jonassen, 1996, p. 4–5). Computer conferencing led to research that focused on interaction between people and on ideas of cooperation and collaboration (cf Harasim, 1990, p. 51; Mason, 1994, p. 25, Dirckinck-Holmfeld, 1990). It also had a focus on text and the forms of textual dialogue prevalent in computer conferencing (Vallee et al., 1974; Harasim, 1990; Sorensen, 1997). Synchronous and asynchronous interactions were analysed in terms of their comparative advantages for teaching and learning (cf Burge, 1993, p. 42). A general theme at this time was that take-up would be rapid and that the different forms of education, for example distance and place based education, would converge (Mason & Kaye, 1990).

It is worth pausing to reflect on this period because what happened next was in many ways a set back to the ideas that had emerged alongside the growth of the Internet and the computer conferencing and bulletin board systems it enabled. These narrow bandwidth applications had placed an emphasis on the largely written and text based interactions between people and between people and resources. This textual form of interaction was a generally familiar academic medium, even though there was a large amount of discussion about the newly emergent forms of online written text which seemed to have the flavour of informal speech rather than academic writing. The ideas that later become systematised into the characterization of networked learning became current at this time. Amongst the ideas that emerged were two contrasting models of online learning. An industrial model of online learning based on large scale courses with a systematic division of labour and marketing on a broad scale (Mason, 1989) and that of 'just in time open learning' (JITOL) which envisaged using the new technologies to enable small scale specialist courses with a very rapid turn around and small project teams that both produced and taught the courses (Goodyear, 1994; Steeples et al., 1994).

It was with the emergence of the World Wide Web in the mid 1990s that the interest in what became known as e-learning really took off. The popularity of e-leaning developed alongside the deployment of proprietary learning management systems (e.g. Blackboard, WebCT), and collaborative work tools which were also used for teaching and learning (e.g. Lotus Notes/Learning Space and Quick Place). These systems enabled the creation of large scale institutional learning environments and the integration of these into administrative and management systems. Many universities having made the investment in new technologies required their staff to use the new systems. This often led to a widespread but low quality take up of the new technologies for learning in the form of academic staff posting lecture notes and administrative details on course web sites but with little pedagogic thought going into the development of student activity online. Of course this movement was contradictory and whilst much of the use of e-learning systems was limited the pioneers of the previous wave of computer conferencing continued to make use of the enhanced provision that came along with some but not all of the new systems (see Pilkinton and Guldberg, this volume)

In some cases the move to a virtual learning environment (VLE) or learning management system (LMS) was seen by the pioneers of online learning as a retrograde step, with areas of functionality included in pioneer systems being absent from a largely 'one size fits all' e-learning strategy. In a recent book about VLEs Weller comments that "VLEs are perhaps not the most innovative of technology in recent years, but they are one of the most pervasive in higher education" (Weller, 2007, p. 2). A renewed interest in the delivery of learning via digital technologies was promoted by many national and regional (e.g. EU) programmes. It is against this backdrop that the interest in social networking and Web 2.0 has arisen.

The debate in e-learning has been characterised by Weller (2007) as one fought out between two competing approaches those of the broadcast and the discussion viewpoints. The broadcast view is the one we would associate most closely with the industrialized mode of e-learning as it is a viewpoint that emphasises the capacity of the Web to deliver content or resources globally and on demand to the user. A current issue of concern for those taking this approach is the potential of re-use and the deployment of learning objects (Wiley, 2003). The broadcast view can be found in higher education and national policies and it is also common in corporate training.

The discussion viewpoint can be identified as the inheritor of the first wave of Internet applications, and the view most closely associated with networked learning. The discussion approach emphasises communication, discussion and dialogue, all of which make use of the two-way or interactive nature of the Internet. However, as Weller points out, the Internet is both an excellent medium for the delivery of resources and for enabling dialogue. This duality fits well with the underpinning definition of networked learning which identifies connections between people and people and the resources they need. In this regard networked learning spans across the broadcast and discussion viewpoints because it recognises the importance of being able to supply resources, such as journal articles, e-books and multimedia artefacts within a discursive context. However it should be noted that networked learning stands distinct from the notion of content delivery that characterises the broadcast view. Networked learning emphasises the work that has to be done alongside resources both to make them available by de-contextualising them at source and in order to re-contextualise them at their destination. In this view knowledge cannot simply be delivered because it forms part of a social process of meaning making.

Many of the case studies presented in this volume report experiences from the end of what can be termed the Web 1.0 epoch. Whilst the authors of this volume worked together over a period of four years – a new social form of the Web has been developing, namely Web 2.0 or social software.

Table 1. From Web 1.0 to Web 2.0

Web 1.0	Web 2.0
The Web as platform	
Medium	Platform
Netscape	Google
Advertising and data collection from the user (DoubleClick)	Targeted advertising (Overture and AdSense)
Content delivery (Akamai)	Peer to peer (BitTorrent)
From communication to network environment	
Online Britannica	Wikipedia
Publishing	Participation
Personal web sites	Blogging

The origins of the term Web 2.0 are still debated but a primary source for, definitions of the term can be located in the article by Tim O'Reilly (2005): *What is Web 2.0?*. The figure above tries to illustrate some of the dimensions of change in the move from earlier forms of the Web, but Web 2.0 remains an elusive term that is as difficult to define as it is popular. The term Web 2.0 might be transient and simply fade into the background, however currently it helps to focus attention on the nature of a qualitative shift in the Web and to identify some of the emergent properties of the new form. It is worth reminding readers at this point of the previous qualitative leap that took place around 1994 with the emergence of the Web as a new form of the Internet. Howard Rheingold was just publishing his book The Virtual Community (1994/2000) as the change took place. In an Afterword he commented on a trip to Japan when he first saw a Mosaic web page:

> I knew I was looking at a new world. I literally jumped, the first time Joi pointed at the picture of a pop group and music came out of the speakers. (Rheingold, 1994/2000, p. 401)

Rheingold had written about virtual community in relation to a bulletin board system, The Well, which was largely text based. He was looking at our now familiar world of hypertext and multimedia. Arguably Web 2.0, though not so graphically shocking, is an equally powerful step change. For our purposes we have selected two features of the change that might be the most important for education. Firstly the idea of 'harnessing collective intelligence' and secondly the disruptive effects of the technological infrastructure in terms of institutional forms.

HARNESSING COLLECTIVE INTELLIGENCE

In Table 1 we pointed to the distinction between Akamai and BitTorrent. O'Reilly commented in relation to BitTorrent that:

> There's an implicit "architecture of participation", a built-in ethic of cooperation, in which the service acts primarily as an intelligent broker, connecting the edges to each other and harnessing the power of the users themselves. (O'Reilly, 2005)

It is this architecture of participation that we are pointing to when we speak about harnessing collective intelligence. A key feature of this is that the process naturally benefits from scale; the more a service is used the more value it has for the user. A second key feature is brokerage. The idea is that the service adds value by brokering between users such that each user brings something to the service themselves.

In education the idea of brokerage raises questions about the status of the students. It is possible that this concern increases as students progress through the levels of education such that professional learners in tertiary education often bring experience to a course that is beyond the level or scope of the course team. In these circumstances the role of the course creator moves away from a traditional didactic teaching role in a way that might remind the reader of the old adage from earlier Internet based learning that tutors had to move from being the 'sage on the stage to the guide on the side'. The new brokerage relationship may be viewed as a further development of this notion and suggests a different kind of support to that offered by a guide. Guides need to know where they are going whereas brokers need to know who to talk to, where to access information and how to negotiate between different views (Kanstrup, 2005). Some have suggested that the notion of the facilitator or guide 'democratised' education in some way (Hodgson, 2002). By contrast the notion of brokerage may suggest more market like relationships that whilst apparently equal hide serious inequalities in terms of access to information and divergences in levels of power.

Plagiarism is another hot issue in the context of collaboration and the use of the Internet. There is currently a great fear about plagiarism and the ease with which students can cut and paste materials or simply buy assignments online. One way to deal with this issue is not to develop anti-plagiarism search engines that seek out examples of copied work but to alter the product that is assessed. The problem and project oriented approach advocated by Dirckinck-Holmfeld et al. (this volume) relies on students developing their own unique problems and researching solutions. Solving the questions posed by the problems often involves re-using and re-appropriating information found in the Internet and from other sources. Such an approach undermines the usefulness of simply copying materials whilst at the same time emphasising the new skills involved in what Ryberg (this volume) has called 'patchworking'. Patchworking emphasises the positive and necessary aspects of accumulating and reworking materials that come in a variety of forms and from a variety of sources. This is itself a form of brokering that is the hallmarks of a successful professional learner in direct contrast with the stereotypical and negative view of all re-use as plagiarism.

Discussing Web 2.0 O'Reilly notes that "users must be treated as co-developers" in relation to the rapid development of software and the idea of software remaining in permanent beta versions and being in a process of continuous development. In education the question as to whether students can become co-creators of courses is one aspect of this suggestion. In problem based learning learners have some control over the learning they are involved with. This varies on a number of dimensions including the extent to which the process is teacher controlled and the degree to which it fits into a formal certification and accreditation procedure. In traditional forms of PBL the students acquire their knowledge and skills through staged sequences of problems presented in their context, in addition to learning resources and support from someone in a teaching or tutor role (Merrill, 2007) Amongst adult and professional learners and in the 'Aalborg model' a different approach has developed which is based on learners already having experience, working in small distributed groups using networked technologies and negotiating amongst themselves to define the problem on which they wish to work (Dirckinck-Holmfeld, 2002; McConnell, 2002; Kolmos, Fink, & Krogh, 2004). We would argue that the further development of problem oriented project based learning is highly suited to a Web 2.0 environment

PERSONALISATION AND MONITORING

In the introduction to this volume and in an earlier article (Jones, Dirckinck-Holmfeld, and Lindström, 2006) we raised the question of how to respond to the trend towards networked individualism when we are organising networked learning environments. Should designers respond to this by further individualising networked learning, in Personal Learning Environments (PLE) for example, or should they take the opposite approach and strengthen the interdependencies and genuine collaborative efforts of students working in networked learning environments. Weller suggests that there are two flavours of personalisation (Weller, 2007, p. 111). The first is personalisation of information and the second is personalisation of tools and services. It is the latter more Web 2.0 flavour that Weller suggests will lead to the realisation of a PLE.

> The idea behind a PLE is that users amass or create a collection of tools for themselves, which constitute their own learning environment... The PLE provides a way of linking these together for the user and then integrating them with institutional systems. (Weller, 2007, p. 114)

The more radical arguments for PLEs suggest an extremely individualised and learner-centric view of learning. In some ways this radical view ignores the political and institutional requirements built into educational systems for social cohesion, often derived from ideas of nationalism and the nation state. It is difficult to see an emerging economy such as China or India, or a developed country such as the USA or France abandoning education as a tool for the shaping of new populations, in both work related skills and civic and political ideals. Seen from a social cognitive or a social pedagogical perspective such a radical version of PLEs may be counter-productive if it hinders students' ability to engage in mutual inquiry processes. Weller notes four downsides to the concept of a PLE and these are worth repeating here:

– Commonality of experience. PLEs may threaten or loosen the shared experience of studying a course.
– Exposure to different approaches. The educational gain of broadening a local and personal experience may be lost. PLEs may encourage a narrow private view that is resistant to change and encourage a 'customer' focus that relies on

consumer choice of a educational goods that are often not appreciated until after the educational experience has taken place.
– Privacy. Personalisation requires the collection of user data and raises serious concerns in terms of privacy and surveillance. It may also have unintended consequences as once it is known that a system is monitored, user behaviour will adapt to the perceived requirements of the monitoring.
– Content focus. The drive behind PLEs is one that emphasises delivery of personalised content at the expense of communication with others
We can thus think of PLEs as one extreme in the choices offered by networked individualism.

Networked learning offers an alternative vision of a learning environment that emphasises connections rather than the privatisation involved in PLEs. Networked learning doesn't necessarily privilege the strong ties involved in collaboration or community but it does involve a connectedness of some kind, even if it only relies on weak links.

NETWORKED LEARNERS

The rapid pace of change in technology and society has generated an interest in understanding the kinds of young people who are becoming the new networked learners. The young people who are entering universities are likely to have had a lifelong engagement with computer technologies, especially games, and Internet based communication tools. Some extensive and longitudinal research on this group has been undertaken in the US context (Oblinger and Oblinger, 2005). However an interest in new learners is not exclusively focused on the developed world and there have been initiatives involving developing countries such as the Power Users of Information Technology Initiative (Malyn-Smith, 2004)) and the Virtual Mobius Project in South Africa (Brown and Czerniewicz, 2007). The research in the USA has developed alongside and in some cases informed a range of documents that provide advice to educators about the new generation and how the new generation of students might relate to learning and the institutions implicated in learning. At the time of publication an Australia a research project is underway (Kennedy et al., 2006; 2008). A project with similar aims led by one of the authors of this chapter has also begun in the UK funded by the Economic and Social Science Research Council (ESRC). A descriptive report has been issued by the Joint Information Systems Committee (JISC, 2008) and earlier research conducted with ESRC support investigated children in pre-university age groups and this UK research is now being extended into a pan-European context (Livingstone and Bober, 2005). The findings of the UK Children Go Online project suggest that policy should focus on how to improve levels of internet literacy and the development of critical evaluation skills. More recently a Demos report (Green and Hannon, 2007) has pointed to a number of different user types:
– Digital pioneers who were blogging before the phrase had been coined
– Creative producers who are building websites, posting movies, photos and music to share with friends, family and beyond

265

- Everyday communicators who are making their lives easier through texting and MSN
- Information gatherers who are Google and Wikipedia addicts, cutting and pasting as a way of life. (Green and Hannon, 2007, p. 11)

Overall the suggestion has been that new technologies may incline learners , if not force them, to adopt a new relationship with their teachers, one in which learners cease to be solely consumers of knowledge and begin to engage in the co-production of knowledge.

For clarity the claims about the net generation can be separated into a set of claims about:

- New technologies – primarily games and the Web (more recently Web 2.0)
- Digital natives – the general effects upon a generational cohort
- Net generation learners – the particular effects on learning.

New Technologies

The general assertion made about the current wave of new technologies is that previous media were primarily one-way broadcast media and that new media are principally interactive allowing two-way communication. However this kind of claim is not new, it has been made in one form or another since the earliest days of Internet based research, but it has been given a new impetus by the maturing and developing technologies of Web 2.0. A second claim made about the new technologies is that the way knowledge is represented is significantly changed in Web based multi-media, from written textual forms towards a range of audio and visual formats that involve new "intelligences" on the part of the person receiving and decoding the representations and enabling different ways of knowing and learning. Such general assertions can give rise to two separable claims:

- A claim about effects- the ubiquitous nature of certain technologies, specifically gaming (Oblinger, 2004; Prensky, 2001, 2001a) and the Web, have affected the outlook of an entire age cohort in advanced economies, the Digital Natives, who are now entering universities
- A claim about what the technologies enable - the new technologies generally labeled Web 2.0 have particular characteristics that afford certain types of social engagement and learning for a new generation of learners.

Digital Natives

Digital natives are part of a generation that have:

> .. not just changed incrementally from those of the past, nor simply changed their slang, clothes, body adornments, or styles, as has happened between generations previously. A really big discontinuity has taken place. One might even call it a 'singularity' – an event which changes things so fundamentally that there is absolutely no going back. (Prensky, 2001, p. 1)

Prensky's comments were made directly in relation to students but they were also about the entire generation currently in schools and colleges and not just those pursuing higher education. The discontinuity he describes is predominantly in their different ways of thinking and processing. He even makes the strong claim that the brains of the new generation are different (Prensky, 2001a). The biggest problem in education he claimed to identify was a disconnection between 'digital native' students who had a natural affinity with digital technologies and 'digital immigrant' staff who retained the 'accent' of a different era even when they were fully socialized into a digital environment.

Diana Oblinger of EduCause has called the generation born after 1982 the Millenials and claims that this group gravitates toward group activity, spends more time doing homework and housework and less time watching TV, believes "it is cool to be smart", and is fascinated by new technologies. This description of the Millenials is empirically based but like Prensky, Oblinger claims to have found a trend towards an Internet age mindset. She also agrees with Prensky that there is a disconnection between the new Millenial students and the institutions that they are enrolled with.

Net Generation Learners

The net generation is a term that has been in wide circulation for as long as or even longer than the idea of Digital Natives (Tapscott, 1998). John Seely Brown has identified several dimensions in the shift towards the net generation (Brown, 2000, 2005, 2006).
– New literacies: a move from text to multi-media and an ability to navigate large amounts of information.
– The move from learning from authority to discovery learning
– The move from linear learning and deduction towards judgement and 'bricolage'
– A bias towards action: characterised as 'link, lurk and try' (Brown, 2000, pp. 13–14)

The comments made by Tapscott and Brown reinforce the argument stated earlier that the development of new media technologies may involve learners adopting a new relationship with their teachers, one that involves learners in the co-production of knowledge.

The higher education sector taken as a whole has been relatively slow to adopt new networked and digital technologies. However the general pace of change within the sector has contrasted with an energetic, innovative, and fast moving consti-tuency that has developed in individual institutions around 'lone ranger' innovators and informal social networks. Across the tertiary sector there has been a gradual accumulation of expertise and capacity encapsulated by academic and practitioner organizations and depicted in their associated journals and conferences. These informal developments have been accompanied by a series of government sponsored policy initiatives which helped to embed and institutionalize this change.

Whilst we think that there are interesting developments amongst young users of digital and networked technologies we think that caution must be advised in relation to the uncritical use of the ideas summarized up by the terms digital natives,

Net generation and Millenials. We agree with a recent suggestion that naive use of the term Net generation as well as related terms and uncritical adoption of the ideas they promote has the hallmarks of a classic moral panic (Bennett *et al.* 2008). We would argue that the current need is for detailed research into the processes of learning that are taking shape amongst the new generations of learners. Ryberg (this volume) presents a detailed case study of the new generation of learners which contributes the concept of learning as patchworking. The metaphor of patchworking is focused on the dynamic process of knowledge creation and in particular on the constructive, creative and transformative aspects of learning. By focussing on the modest and small scale aspects of knowledge creation the analysis does not seek to find long-term regularities but rather to identify short term and provisional stabilizations in a dynamic process of production and learning (Ryberg, this volume).

RE-SKILLING AND UP-SKILLING – THE PROFESSIONAL LEARNER

For most national and international agencies the re-skilling and up-skilling of professional workers forms a key part of the discourse about what is described as a knowledge or learning society (e.g. the European Union, World Bank, United Nations). E-learning is seen as playing a major role in the development of more cost effective methods. However, networked learning as a particular approach to e-learning has many more potentials. It is possible that the new generation of learners, as they become professionals, will challenge traditional ways of organising higher education and training. They will have used new technologies and social software and be used to worldwide, just-in-time access to information and in their need for up-skilling and re-skilling they are likely to have participated in multiple communities and networks. Mobilising this trend as an approach to learning leads to what has been termed e-learning 2.0 by Stephen Downes (2005).

> This approach to learning [i.e. e-learning 2.0 Eds] means that learning content is created and distributed in a very different manner. Rather than being composed, organized and packaged, e-learning content is syndicated, much like a blog post or podcast. It is aggregated by students, using their own personal RSS reader or some similar application. From there, it is remixed and repurposed with the student's own individual application in mind, the finished product being fed forward to become fodder for some other student's reading and use. (Downes, 2005 not paginated.)

There remains the danger in the writings of Downes and others of conflating the use of new media with learning itself. The case studies in this volume show that we can find many examples of students collaborating, creating, remixing and repurposing learning content prior to Web 2.0. However, Web 2.0 tools and the increasing accessibility and organisation of information via the Internet certainly provide new potentials for making networked learning a reality.

Networked learning can be organised and designed to accommodate the needs of up-skilling and re-skilling the professional learner. In this volume we have focused on the following levels:

- Institution based networked learning environments for emergent professionals (undergraduate programme)
- Institution based networked learning environments for professionals organised by universities (masters programme)
- Informal networked learning environments created in collaboration between companies and universities (uncertified) and between universities and a community bringing together professionals, practitioners and carers (university certified).

The first levels are formalised within the institutional framework of higher and continuing education, while the third builds on informal learning practices. However, the dividing lines between formal and informal learning are blurring (Pilkington and Guldberg; Guribye and Lindström, both this volume). Universities are utilising informal learning elements as part of their accredited programmes, while informal business networks are taking up more formalised networked learning strategies.

A general characteristic of the learning environments analysed in this volume is that they go beyond thinking about learning as occurring as a consequence of the design of learning content and they illustrate the way that learning depends on how the content having been designed is used, renegotiated and repurposed. In the learning environments presented here the focus has moved from controlling content to facilitating and brokering activities, which allow the students to interact, to relate, and to produce.

CONCEPTUALISING ISSUES WITHIN NETWORKED LEARNING

We have presented a framework for understanding and designing networked learning that builds on socio-cultural foundations. An essential part of this framework is the interrelation of a set of conceptual tools including infrastructure, technology, institution and pedagogy with an indirect notion of design in relation to networked learning. We see these conceptual tools as interlocking building blocks for the development of a theoretically sound and coherent understanding of networked learning environments and their design. The conceptual tools have been explored in the case studies through the lived practice and engagement of educators, designers, students and professionals as they encourage productive learning activities in different networked learning environments. In the following section we revisit some of the conceptual tools building on the insights from the case studies concerning the conceptualization of networked learning.

Infrastructure

The concept of infrastructure outlined in the introduction to this volume was located at the macro and meso levels in which infrastructures took the form of largely given elements for those concerned with the day-to-day design process. This implies a relationship between design and learning in which infrastructures for learning are rarely designed directly by the academic staff who are usually involved in the detailed pedagogic design of courses and programs.

In the introduction to this volume we distinguished our view of infrastructure from others to be found in recent literature. We argued for an account of infrastructure located at the macro and meso levels, a level at which it involves largely given elements, set apart from the day-to-day design process and outside the control of academic teaching staff. The account we gave did not separate infrastructure from the local and temporally specific context. Indeed the emphasis in our account was on infrastructure as enacted and on infrastructure occurring in time at a point in which local and global factors combine. These two aspects of infrastructure, their location in factors that come into micro settings from outside and secondly being understood as relational, so that the elements become an infrastructure as they come into use in forms of practice, emphasize the interaction between levels. The key to understanding the apparent tension in this position is that whilst enacted at a micro level infrastructural elements cannot be changed at this level alone. The use of a VLE is an example of this tension because the infrastructure comes into being as the VLE is deployed locally but the choice of VLE and control over its technological and organizational support are largely beyond the local and micro level context.

An example of how critical infrastructure can be to educational change was provided by Vines and Dysthe (this volume)

> These recommendations sketched a complete transformation of the study of law. The immediate follow-up, however, was piecemeal. The infrastructure and pedagogical tools to manage such a deep restructuring of the teaching and learning environment were still lacking. The availability of a virtual learning environment was therefore a major factor in making the restructuring possible.

As illustrated by many of the case studies in this volume (see Pilkington & Guldberg; Dirckinck-Holmfeld et al.; Bygholm & Nyvang; Guribye & Lindström) infrastructure is not only a technical matter, it is a pedagogical and an organisational issue, which needs to be taken into account during theoretical conceptualization and practical implementation. Many of the case studies follow Star & Ruhledger (1996) in focusing on infrastructure in use and as a part of local practice. As noted previously in some accounts of infrastructure it fades into the background and only becomes visible upon breakdown. This notion when applied to a learning infrastructure fading into the background is questioned by Dirckinck-Holmfeld et al. (this volume). They suggest a dynamic relationship between the infrastructure and the activities that take place using it. In their view a learning infrastructure should actively stimulate and integrate with the learning activities taking place.

Infrastructures for learning

This sense of infrastructure has also been applied to learning in the preceding case studies. Guribye and Lindström provided the following definition of an infrastructure for learning:

An infrastructure for learning is a set of resources and arrangements – social, institutional, technical – that are designed to and/or assigned to support a learning practice (Guribye and Lindström, this volume).

In placing the focus on infrastructures that are "designed to and/or assigned to" learning this definition is related to the idea of work oriented infrastructures. Elsewhere Guribye has distinguished between work oriented infrastructure and infrastructures for learning by pointing out that infrastructures for learning do not necessarily have to be designed by the users and might commonly be designed by a variety of actors (Guribye, 2005, pp. 63 and 64). To this we might add the distinction that Hanseth and Lundberg make between work oriented infrastructures and what they term 'universal service infrastructures' that are intended for the use of all citizens (Hanseth and Lundberg, 2001, p. 365). Educational infrastructures are becoming intertwined with infrastructural elements that stand outside of educational institutions and which are neither designed for nor assigned to an educational purpose. We are thinking of services such as Google, YouTube and Facebook, all of which impact on the routine practices of students and teachers but stand alongside the infrastructures of learning as defined by Guribye and Lindström.

We would suggest that research concerning itself with infrastructures for learning should extend to these universal service infrastructures as it might be a serious mistake for designers of new networked learning environments to attempt to provide learning infrastructures that set up a 'walled garden' within which learning activity is intended to take place.

Affordances

We proposed an understanding of affordance as a *relational* property and proposed a return to a Gibsonian and ecological stance. The concept of affordance, as introduced by Gibson (1977; 1979), provides a way to describe the world that cuts across traditional subject-object dualities. Affordances go beyond a value-free physical description of the environment by expressing environmental attributes relative to a living creature and they go beyond subjective interpretations by describing meaning relative to an objective physical world (Gaver, 1996, p. 113–114) which has as a consequence that the affordance is there even it's not perceived as such.. We also noted that Gibson's understanding of perception still left the possibility that the second order nature of meaning was understated in his approach. Gibson's approach was based on the idea of direct perception and this could be taken to imply that the active agent had little or no role in interpreting the stimuli received from an external world. Our contention, in line with a socio-cultural approach, would be that culture and history will affect the appreciation of affordance even if it does not affect the existence of an affordance, as has been illustrated in the case studies in this volume.

The case study by Kaptelinin and Hedestig (this volume) makes use of the concept of affordance to analyse social action and social learning in a distributed video-based university setting. Kaptelinin and Hedestig focus on the breakdowns that occur when expectations, competence, and skills developed in one educational

271

context are applied by teachers and students in a different context. They study the coordination difficulties in a videoconference mediated classroom. Using the concept of affordance they point out the difficulties that occur when teacher activity, which is grounded in previous and different practices, is carried over into a new learning environment based on the decentralised use of videoconferencing.

The findings of the study suggest that the transition from traditional forms of education to that which is mediated through a new technology is not as straight-forward as it may seem. Teachers' attempts to directly apply the knowledge and skills developed in previous classroom settings to the videoconference learning environments often caused breakdowns. Videoconference settings may appear similar to regular classrooms, and from a formal logical perspective they provide the same functionality. However, even though these possibilities for action are objectively present in the environment, the participants in the setting may overlook them or conversely, the participants may perceive possibilities for action where such possibilities are not actually present. Kaptelinin and Hedestig argue "that completely separating affordances from perception and culture is incompatible with the gist of Gibson's ecological psychology" because as Kaptelinin and Hedestig show in their case study the possibilities for action in these contexts are culturally mediated.

From a socio-cultural point of view attempts to bring the concept of affordance back in line with its original theoretical context have stimulated helpful reflections on the meaning of the concept. A socio-cultural perspective implies that a human's ability to perceive and act cannot be separated from their experiential, social and cultural context and what is afforded in one context will not necessary be afforded in another. In the socio-cultural approach perception is integrated into human interaction with the world and can't be separated from meaning making. Not all human perception is a motor response because it is mediated socially and culturally through learning. Human action in relation to an affordance is determined in part by a person's socially and culturally mediated experiences of the situation. We accept that there are affordances in the environment, which are relational to the living creature. However how human beings perceive and act on such affordances is largely dependant on their acquired ways of interpreting and acting on affordances based on prior cultural and social experiences.

These conclusions are applicable to the empirical findings of the Kaptelinin & Hedestig case study. The study indicates that most of the breakdowns observed can be explained as the result of what they call 'hidden' affordances (there are possibilities for action but they are not perceived by the participants) and 'false' affordances (the participants perceive nonexistent possibilities for action). In the introduction we suggested that the distinction between perceived and actual affordances was flawed. When affordances are perceived a close link between perception and action may ensue, but affordances can also exist even when they are not perceived or if the perceptual interpretation is misleading about possibilities for action. In general we agree with Gaver that "the perceptibility of an affordance should not be confused with the affordance itself" (1996, p. 115).

In this view a false affordance is a false perception or understanding of an affordance as the affordance is not in fact available in the relationship between the active agent and the environment. Equally a hidden affordance is only hidden from perception as an active agent may avail itself of the affordance accidentally. For example a lizard may not register a surface as affording heat but still locate itself in relation to a warm surface and benefit from the heat. We would claim that in Kaptelinin and Hedestig's case study the participants have perceived the availability of an affordance based on cues in the environment and it is their false perception or understanding of the availability of an affordance rather than the affordances itself being false. In this we move the stress away from the falseness of the affordance to the process of being aware of and understanding what is available as an affordance.

The use of the term hidden affordance to represent those occasions in which there are possibilities for action that are not perceived or understood by the participants is very attractive. In these cases the affordance may be very apparent to others but merely not apparent for the specific participants. The missing action may not be caused by an affordances not being available to perception, but because there is a misalignment between the design and the understanding of and actualization of the design by the participants. This point emphasizes the relational aspect of affordances, which is that they are relational to the particular active agents in a specific context. Whilst affordances are analyzable in an abstract sense so that designers can consider what can be made available for users in general, any actual affordance only arises in a relationship that is particular and context specific.

Kaptelinin and Hedestig have provided a detailed account of a particular case and demonstrated that the concept of affordances can add new dimensions to the analysis. A socio-cultural perspective implies that a human's ability to perceive and act cannot be separated from their experiential, social and cultural context and such that what is afforded in one context will not necessarily be afforded in another. In the socio-cultural approach perception is integrated into human interaction with the world and can't be separated from meaning making. Human (higher order) perception is not simply a form of direct perception rather it is mediated socially, culturally and through learning. Human action in relation to an affordance in the environment is determined by the situation and by prior socially and culturally mediated experiences. By this framing of the argument we don't wish to deny that there are affordances in the environment, which are relational to active agents (i.e. humans, animals and machines). However how human beings understand and act on an affordance is strongly related to their cultural and social experiences, and their acquired ways of interpreting and acting on these. In this way the case study has thrown light on the theoretical discussions related to affordances. From a socio-cultural perspective there is still work to do be done in clarifying the theory of affordance and which will need to be discussed both in relation to the original insight in Gibson's writings, and to some of the newer positions, which we have touched upon in our work.

Genres and affordances

From a socio-cultural perspective another way of discussing the relation between affordance and action is to employ the notion of genres. The idea of using genres to study communication is not new. It has a rich tradition within the field of literary and media analysis and it has emerged as a useful way to explain social action in cultural studies (Brown & Duguid, 2000). Enriquez (this volume) states that a genre as identified by its socially recognised purpose and common characteristics of form and quotes Erickson's definition (2000):

A genre is a patterning of communication created by a combination of the individual, social and technical forces implicit in a recurring communicative situation. A genre structures communication by creating shared expectations about the form and content of the interaction, thus easing the burden of production and interpretation (Erickson, 2000, p. 2).

In short, genres provide a sort of a template – a commonly agreed way of interacting between members of a community. The particular 'genre template' of a community is an important resource in facilitating efficient communication. Problems in networked learning communities often occur because there are no common genres yet (and because the affordances of the material environments are not always obvious, see above). To facilitate a communicative act individuals draw on different genre norms out of habits based on previous experiences and this procedure does not always work. An example is the quandary of how to react to a message when we don't have time to answer immediately. Should we reply quickly to say that we will answer later, or should we respond later when we have time to do so fully, thereby risking the uncertainty that might be experienced by the sender? This demonstrates how genres and affordances are closely linked, because, if the communication system clearly displays that a message has been received and opened, then the requirement for a genre would be different than if the interface did not provide any information about the status of the message.

Genres are context-dependent and they shape, but do not determine their use. They are relational to the cues provided in a setting and influenced by the task design, previous genre use and the social relationships of those involved. As Enriquez remarks people participate in genre usage rather than having control of it (Enriquez this volume). Even though genres are dynamic entities that adapt to changes of circumstances, they develop regularities of form and substance. These regularities can become established conventions that influence all aspects of communication. Genres are not determined by affordance, but as shown by Enriquez (2008) they develop through people participating in the networked learning environment as a response to their understanding of affordances and they develop a regularity of form and substance as conventions on how to act.

The Concept of Technology and Affordances

In the introduction we argued that networked learning is necessarily learning mediated by technologies and we noted that Orlikowski has suggested that it may be helpful to make an analytical distinction between the use of technology and technological artefacts the latter being understood as the machine, devices, appliances or gadgets. (Orlikowski, 2000, p. 408). Seen from the practice of design, technologies do indeed embody features and properties and they also carry meaning having been designed with certain purposes in mind, embedding certain understandings of communication, interaction and collaboration in the design process. There are many examples of this within education. The design of learning management systems reflects certain models and understandings of communication, interaction, collaborations, teaching and learning, and they provide particular functionalities (Tolsby et al., 2002).

Information and communication technology vary in flexibility and in adaptability. Despite this, however, the tools embody particular symbolic and material forms which can become affordances in use, and make some kind of practice more available than others. How the technology is enacted is therefore closely related to the properties – social as well as technical – which are reified in the design. In order to assess productive learning in networked learning environments it becomes an interesting research question to ask what kind of technological, pedagogical and organisational affordances are realised in the technology, but also to understand how these features are given a new purpose by users in varying situations and institutional contexts, including how users find creative ways to deal with inappropriate design.

The use of open source software and the development of Web 2.0 tools as well as the general rise in digital literacy may add a new dimension to this discussion of affordances because technologies are becoming much more flexible and capable of adjustment to new practices and genres of use. An example of this trend is shown in the chapter by Tolsby (this volume). Tolsby shows how a group of students make use of a collaborative tool, how they enact their practices around this artefact and adapt the artefact to their needs in order to support their coordination effort in collaborative project work.

Summing up on Affordances

The socio-cultural view of affordance is non-essentialist, non-dualist and it is critical of both an information processing (cognitivist) and a simple direct understanding of perception. Affordances in this view could be discerned as a potential in a relationship between different elements in a setting whether or not the prospective user of an affordance perceives or understands its meaning but the affordance only arises in interaction between the user and the latent affordance. Because a socio-cultural view of affordance suggests that it is possible to analytically discern features of the setting or technology apart from the actual understandings and perceptions of particular groups of users, it explains the potential for the use of the term hidden affordance. Any actual group of users would have varied understandings and draw out different meanings from the setting and we suggest this undermines the notion of false affordance as in those circumstances an expectation of an affordance is not related to action because the affordance that is expected is not present when action is taken. This suggests that designers can only have indirect influence over those abstract structures that may become affordances in the relationship between the environments or tasks and the participants. Designers can design for certain affordances but how they are understood, perceived and acted on will depend on the participants' social and cultural history and their activity.

AN INDIRECT APPROACH TO DESIGN AND LEARNING

Design as noted by Kaptelinin and Hedestig in their case study can be understood in a variety of ways. Drawing on work in interaction design and the HCI tradition they note that writers with this approach assume that the designer in this context is a design professional and that this assumption is often inaccurate because some of the properties of a product can be defined by users themselves rather than the professional designer of the product. Professional design is less common in education but the ability of teachers and students to adapt and customize designed products for their own purposes is still an important feature. Whilst professionalized design is still uncommon there are wide variations in current university practices as the case studies in this volume demonstrate. There is also a current debate in education about what might be called the limits of design. This debate has taken place around the term Learning Design (Koper and Tattersall, 2005) and the related terms learning design (without capitalization) and design for learning (Beetham and Sharpe, 2007; Jones, 2007).

Learning design has two distinct meanings, often distinguished (as above) by capitalising the term, Learning Design (LD), which refers to the more formal technical specification of design through IMS LD (Koper and Tattersall, 2005, pp. ix–x). The term in lower case refers to learning design in a more general sense, to the human activity of designing units of learning, learning activities or learning environments (see also Britain, 2004; Beetham and Sharpe, 2007). In this volume we are generally concerned with learning design in this latter sense and not Learning Design in terms of IMS LD. The stronger sense of Learning Design is advocated by Berge and Fjuk in the context of the re-use of learning objects. They argue that a narrow focus on learning objects leads to a focus on low level, and unsophisticated views of learning and that Learning Design can allow for the adoption of innovative and diverse pedagogical strategies. Learning Design used in this strong sense relies on some quite definite assumptions.

- Learning can be improved by making the conditions of optimal learning explicit (Koper, 2005, p. 3)
- The quality of a unit of learning depends largely on the quality of the learning design (Koper, 2005, p. 4)
- A learning designer's basic task is to design a course that meets a set of learning objectives (Koper, 2005, p. 4)
- Learning design knowledge consists of a series of rules following the '*if* situation, *then* method' (Koper, 2005, p. 19)

This approach to IMS LD arose out of the experience of the Open University in the Netherlands (OU NL) and its desire to reduce institutional complexity by developing a 'pedagogical meta-language' that did not limit existing practice by reducing the range of pedagogical options available to one or two preferred forms (Koper and Tattersall, 2005, p. vii).

Learning Design competes for attention with other alternative approaches to the problem of how to abstract general design principles from specific instances of design, such as pedagogical design patterns (McAndrew and Goodyear, 2006, McAndrew et al., 2006) and scripts (Tchounikine, 2008). All of these approaches point to an important tension in higher education that arises when existing practices are disrupted by the introduction of networked and digital technologies on a broad scale. The approach taken in this volume is to stress the indirect nature of design which remains a creative and messy process emergent from a range of interconnected factors. While the authors of this chapter have serious reservations about the general applicability of IMS LD we are convinced that the problem area identified by learning design and design patterns is of major concern for the development of networked learning.

We noted in the Introduction to this book that the understanding we have of affordance is related to the claim that we cannot design learning we can only design for learning. It is nevertheless the ways that we can design for learning that provide some of the most pressing questions when technologies are applied to learning environments. This applies to the design of pedagogical processes and the organisational and technical infrastructure as well as to technological artefacts, media and resources.

The case studies deal with what we have termed pedagogical design which we identified in the Introduction to this volume as referring to those aspects of a setting that educators can organise for future activities and developments. This aspect of design lies at the meso level and takes other aspects of a networked learning environment as being relatively fixed in that they provide given parameters for ordinary design purposes. An example of this was given by Pilkington and Guldberg (this volume) who report a tutor stating that there was no point in evaluating a specific VLE (Moodle) because the university would not make a decision about replacing the existing system in the near future and when they did so they felt that the tutor's opinion would not be taken into account. The institutional selection of a VLE is an example of the macro level features of an infrastructure that lie beyond pedagogical design. We also argue that the enactment of any learning event will rely on micro level dynamics and the contingent interactions at a particular point in time of groups of students and their teachers with the designed environment and its resources. In this regard the case study by Vines and Dysthe of a law course shows how a strong sense of learning design in the law faculty interacted with the students' experience of the course, an experience characterised by the authors as a largely unintended "continual conflict between the demand to absorb new information and the expectation to demonstrate their own intellectual development" (Vines and Dysthe, this volume).

Within the case studies we have identified a range of approaches to indirect design, from a structured, institutionalised and professionalised design-process within the Open University (UK) (Jones, this volume) to the situation at Humanistic Informatics at Aalborg University, where the students are active in design (Tolsby, this volume). A further variation in the cases comes from approaches taken to the conduct of the research. There are examples in which the researchers have intervened as action researchers (Bygholm & Nyvang; Fulantelli; Berge & Fjuk, this volume) and others in which the researchers have taken a more analytic and distanced approach (Vines & Dysthe, this volume). Finally, there are a number of case studies (Dirckinck-Holmfeld et al.; Pilkington & Guldberg, this volume) in which the authors have taken on multiple roles as coordinators, designers, teachers and researchers.

The design process itself has also been dealt with in a number of different ways. In some cases (for example Jones, this volume and Vines & Dysthe), the design is one part of a more or less systematic institutional strategy. In these cases the design process itself takes place in an organised, phased, iterative and systematic way in which the various roles are enacted by professionals supported by evaluation and research. In the MIL and Web Autism cases (Dirckinck-Holmfeld et al. and Pilkington & Guldberg, this volume) the design forms a part of a much more incremental process. In these cases the different roles of researcher, designer and teacher are integrated in the same person rather than separated through a formal division of labour. The learning environments are being continuously refined and developed in a way that is founded on the engagement of the participants (teachers and co-ordinators). The improvement of the design is based on day-to-day insights from the design and research processes, and from participating in the learning environment. In this second design approach the ownership of the design is still largely in the hands of the participants.

The case studies based on action research were either trying to make the organisation and institution more aware of issues involved in the design of learning environment or they were a more directly intervention with the researcher themselves designing the learning environment (Berge & Fjuk; Fulantelli, this volume). One of the defining characteristics of this type of research was that the cases were not really integrated in an institutional design strategy and they were more focused on the researchers' own interests. In these cases the researchers have a somewhat detached role from the teachers although the researchers provide analytical insights which they feed back into the learning environment. In some cases (Berge & Fjuk; Bygholm & Nyvang, this volume) the research takes place in close collaboration with the teachers and has a potential to inspire future design work, while in other cases, it is a more indirect collaboration either with the teachers or the institution.

The research approaches are in all cases based on the assumption that design should reflect lived practice, and a number of research tools are used to capture these practices. These range from the more well known such as interviews and field observations towards more participatory approaches such as future workshops and design workshops. The cases illustrate that within much of higher education design is still very closely linked with the role of the teacher. There is still a limited division of labour and the teachers are the main designers at a local level. The cases also provide insights into the practices that arise as responses to design, and highlight unintended and unexpected responses to design. Moreover, the cases have broadened our view of who are likely to be pedagogical designers, and it raises questions for future research. Should the main locus of design continue to be the teachers or should there be a greater professionalization of design involving a greater division of labour and the further development of distinct professional roles such as learning technologists and instructional or pedagogical designers?

PRODUCTIVE LEARNING IN NETWORKED LEARNING ENVIRONMENTS

One of the challenges for this book has been to come closer to a theoretically sound concept of productive learning that is informed by the empirical study of networked learning environments. The case studies have all been asked to reflect on the notion of productive learning, a term that can have a number of different meanings. Dirckinck-Holmfeld et al. (this volume) define the term productive in relation to production and the use of tools in the transformation of nature. Using their case study as a basis they developed this definition by focusing on the notion of changes which they interpreted in a broad sense as changes in practice, identity, membership and trajectories. Ryberg in his chapter understood the notion of productive learning as processes in which both 'material' and 'ideal' resources were seamlessly woven together into a 'product'. He went on to argue that productive learning processes happened at different levels which he illustrated through the notion of patchworking. Vines and Dysthe argued that productive learning included more than the individual mastering of subject matter and that it must be understood in relation to the wider aspects of the learning ecology, including the institution's learning design and technological infrastructure, as well as the students' learning experiences, interactional processes and identity transformation. Productive learning can then be viewed in a number of different ways such as the production of successful students or as a contrast to 'unproductive' and 'reproductive' learning (Dysthe & Lillejord, 2005).

In their case study Vines and Dysthe (this volume) understand productive learning to have two possible meanings, as learning through activity and as effective learning. One of the issues of concern for Vines and Dysthe was that the networked learning environment tended to be less productive, than expected. They identified a number of tensions and contradictions between the well-structured learning design, the tailoring of the VLE-system, and the intended and unintended response patterns to these factors in the law students' actions. One of the critical aspects they found was the tension between conformity and divergence of which they provided a number of examples and showed how the authoritative voice of the teaching staff unintentionally came to dominate. This had the consequence that the students did not challenge the discourses they were offered leading to a rather stereotyped way of solving legal problems.

Vines and Dysthe also document the way that the learning design and the use of the VLE made education in Law 'productive' in the sense that the pass grades and drop-out rates improved. However their detailed study also identified counterproductive aspects of the learning design and aspects which were related to the specific way the design was realised in the VLE, particular institutional arrangement, and the way the students responded to the design.

The case studies in this volume all focus on conditions for productive learning. One result of this focus is to show that there isn't one single pedagogical method, which supports productive learning. Indeed productive learning seems to have more to do with the kind of engagement the students have with their activities. It also seems to depend on how this engagement is facilitated, nurtured and negotiated by their teachers and peers. It looks as if there is a delicate and context dependent balance between the reification of learning activities in tasks, learning designs and technological infrastructure, and the participation patterns of the learners.

CONCLUDING REMARKS

Networked learning can take on a variety of meanings especially as it is taken up in different contexts. At times it has been interpreted broadly and used interchangeably with other terms such as e-learning, online learning and currently, technology enhanced learning (TEL). As it has evolved, networked learning has often emphasised the importance of the collaborative aspects of learning and the cooperative possibilities available in online learning (c.f. McConnell, 2000; Steeples and Jones, 2002). The most common definition and the one that is provided in the introduction to this volume, comes from the Centre for Studies in Advanced Learning Technology (CSALT) team at Lancaster University in the United Kingdom:

> Networked learning is learning in which information and communication technology… is used to promote connections: between one learner and other learners, between learners and tutors; between a learning community and its learning resources. (Goodyear et al., 2004)

This definition arose from a series of projects during the late 1990s and it has also been associated with the Networked Learning Conference series since 1998. It has proved remarkably robust over the last ten years which has been a time of rapid technological change associated with the arrival and demise of a number of competing terms and definitions. We continue to believe this definition of networked learning provides a sound basis for future work.

The term networked learning is not simply a synonym for online learning or e-learning because it focuses on connections and emphasises human aspects of learning, even when that learning takes place in contexts mediated through a digital network. This emphasis on connections allows networked learning to be less partisan about the nature of the connections than other theoretical approaches such as 'communities of practice' (CoP) and 'collaborative learning' especially within CSCL. Commentary from a networked learning perspective has pointed out the way that notions of harmony and homogeneity can be privileged by theories of community and collaboration (Hodgson & Reynolds, 2002; Jones, Dirckinck-Holmfeld, & Lindström, 2006). Some of the authors are also concerned that CSCL and the theory of communities of practice focus too strongly on networks composed of strong ties and as a consequence overlook the potential value of weak ties between learners and between learners and their resources (Jones, 2004; Jones,

Ferreday, & Hodgson, 2008; Ryberg & Larsen, 2006). In this sense one characteristic of networked learning is that it does not privilege a particular pedagogical model.

Even though learning is not understood as being collaborative per se, the notions of relationships and connections suggest that learning is not confined to the individual mind, but rather it is located in the relationships and interactions between different entities, whether these are peers, teachers or resources. The work in the case studies expands the concept of connections as the determining factor for networked learning by focussing on activities, tools and artefacts as the central mediating principle of productive learning. Following on from the concept of productive learning it is precisely through activities and the artefacts used in those activities that humans produce themselves and their environment. In networked learning these activities take place as networked activities by way of communication, collaboration, interaction, negotiation and reflection. Basing our opinion on the case studies we suggest that productive networked learning is a way of conceiving of learning as a process which stresses the interrelatedness and connectedness of learners, the negotiation of meaning through activities, and the social and cultural mediation of tools and materials.

Networked learning is a socio-technical way of organising learning enabling learners to interact, connect, engage, relate and collaborate on joint enterprises and activities, through both strong and weak ties, and to dynamically accumulate and rework concepts, artefacts and knowledge in a variety of forms and from a variety of sources. Networked learning is as a consequence ever changing, with new constellations and relationships evolving depending on the engagement, interaction and contributions of the participants. Networked learning is characterised by learning processes that are organised horizontally as well as vertically in institutional settings. In institution-based networked learning teachers engage as designers, facilitators, and brokers in dialogue and collaboration with students and their peers. While networked learning is not reserved for any particular pedagogy we argue that problem and project based learning, taking the problem as the point of departure for the enquiry process, is a prototypical example of productive networked learning.

REFERENCES

Bennett, S., Matton, K., & Kervin, L. (2008). The 'digital natives' debate: A critical review of the literature. *British Journal of Educational Technology, 35*(9), 775–786.

Berge, O., & Fjuk, A. (2009). Operating outside regular opening hours. In L. Dirckinck-Holmfeld, C. Jones, & B. Lindström (Eds.), *Analysing networked learning practices in higher education and continuing professional development.* Rotterdam, The Netherlands: Sense Publishers.

Britain, S. (2004). *A review of learning design: Concept, specifications and tools.* A report for the JISC E-learning Pedagogy Programme. Retrieved October 3, 2008, from http://www.jisc.ac.uk/uploaded_documents/ACF83C.doc

Brown, C., & Czerniewicz, L. (2008). *Trends in student use of ICTs in higher education in South Africa* 10th Annual Conference of WWW Applications. Cape Town. 3–6 September. Retrieved October 13, 2008, from http://www.cet.uct.ac.za/files/file/ResearchOutput/2008_wwwApps_UseTrends.pdf

Brown, J. S. (2006, September/October). New learning environments for the 21st century: EXPLORING THE EDGE. *Change, 38*(5), 18–24.

Brown, J. S. (2005). *Commencement speech the university of michigan 30/04/05*. Retrieved October 3, 2008, from http://www.johnseelybrown.com/UM05.pdf

Brown, J. S. (2000). Growing up digital: How the web changes work, education, and the ways people learn. *Change, 32*(2), 10–20.

Brown, J. S., & Duguid, P. (2001). Knowledge and organization: A social-practice perspective. *Organization Science, 12*(2), 198–213.

Brown, J. S., & Duguid, P. (2000). *The social life of information*. Boston: Harvard Business School.

Burge, E. J. (1993). *Students perceptions of learning in computer conferencing: A qualitative analysis*. PhD, Department of Education University of Toronto.

Cavanagh, A. (2007). *Sociology in the age of the internet*. Berkshire, England: Open University Press.

Cuban, L. (1986). *Teachers and machines*. New York: Teachers College Press.

Dirckinck-Holmfeld, L. (2002). Designing virtual learning environments based on problem oriented project pedagogy. In L. Dirckinck-Holmfeld & B. Fibiger (Eds.), *Learning in virtual environments* (pp. 31–54). Frederiksberg C: Samfundslitteratur Press.

Dirckinck-Holmfeld, L. (1990). *Kommunikation på trods og på tværs* (Project pedagogy and computer-mediated communication in distance education). Dissertation. Aalborg: Aalborg University.

Dirckinck-Holmfeld, L., Nielsen, J., Fibiger, B., Danielsen, O., Riis, M., Sorensen, E. K., et al. (2009). Problem and project based networked learning—The MIL case. In L. Dirckinck-Holmfeld, C. Jones, & B. Lindström (Eds.), *Analysing networked learning practices in higher education and continuing professional development*. Rotterdam, The Netherlands: Sense Publishers.

Downes, S. (2005). *E-Learning 2.0*. Retrieved July 14, 2008, from http://www.downes.ca/post/31741

Engeström, Y. (1987). *Learning by expanding—an activity theoretical approach to developmental research*. Retrieved September 17, 2007, from http://communication.ucsd.edu/MCA/Paper/Engestrom/expanding/toc.htm

Enriquez, J. (2009). Genre analysis of online postings: Communicative cues do exist online. In L. Dirckinck-Holmfeld, C. Jones, & B. Lindström (Eds.), *Analysing networked learning practices in higher education and continuing professional development*. Rotterdam, The Netherlands: Sense Publishers.

Erickson, T. (2000). Making sense of computer-mediated communication: Conversations as genres, CMC systems as Genre Ecologies. *Proceedings of the 33rd Annual Hawaii International Conference on System Sciences, 3*, 3011.

Fjuk, A., & Dirckinck-Holmfeld, L. (1997). Articulation of actions in distributed collaborative learning. *Scandinavian Journal of Information Systems*.

Fulantelli, G. (2009). Blended learning systems thinking and communities of practice. In L. Dirckinck-Holmfeld, C. Jones, & B. Lindström (Eds.), *Analysing networked learning practices in higher education and continuing professional development*. Rotterdam, The Netherlands: Sense Publishers.

Gaver, W. (1996). Situating action II: Affordances for action: The social is material for design. *Ecological Psychology, 8*(2), 111–129.

Gibson, J. J. (1979). *The ecological approach to visual perception*. Boston: Houghton Mifflin Company.

Gibson, J. J. (1977). The theory of affordances. In R. Shaw & J. Bransford (Eds.), *Perceiving, acting and knowing*. Hillsdale, NJ: Erlbaum.

Giddens, A. (1984). *The constitution of society: Outline of the theory of structure*. Berkeley, CA: University of California Press.

Goodyear, P., Banks, S., Hodgson, V., & McConnell, D. (Eds.). (2004). *Advances in research on networked learning*. Dordrecht, The Netherlands: Kluwer Academic Publishers.

Goodyear, P. (1994). Telematics, flexible and distance learning in postgraduate education: The MSc in information technology and learning at Lancaster University. *CTISS File, 17*, 14–19.

Green, H., & Hannon, C. (2007). *Their space: Education for a digital generation*. London: Demos. Retrieved January 10, 2007, from http://www.demos.co.uk/publications/theirspace

Guribye, F., & Lindström, B. (2009). Infrastructures for learning and networked tools—The introduction of a new tool in an inter-organisational network. In L. Dirckinck-Holmfeld, C. Jones, & B. Lindström (Eds.), *Analysing networked learning practices in higher education and continuing professional development*. Rotterdam, The Netherlands: Sense Publishers.

Harasim, L. (Ed.). (1990). *Online education; perspectives on a new environment*. New York: Praeger.

Hiltz, S. R., & Turoff, M. (1978). *The network nation—human communication via computer* (1st ed.). Reading, MA: Addison-Wesley.

Hiltz, S. R. (1990). Evaluating the virtual classroom. In L. Harasim (Eds.), *Online education; Perspectives on a new environment*. New York: Praeger.

Hodgson, V. (2002). Issues for democracy and social identity in computer mediated communication and networked learning. In C. Steeples & C. Jones (Eds.), *Networked learning: Perspectives and issues*. London: Springer.

Hodgson, V., & Reynolds, M. (2002). Consensus, difference and 'multiple communities' in network learning. *Studies in Higher Education, 30*(1), 9–22.

JISC. (2008). *Great expectations of ICT: How higher education institutions are measuring up.* Retrieved September 1, 2008, from http://www.jisc.ac.uk/media/documents/publications/jiscgreatexpectationsfinalreportjune08.pdf

Jonassen, D. H. (1996). *Computers in the classroom: Mindtools for critical thinking*. Englewood Cliffs, NJ: Merrill, Prentice Hall.

Jones, C. (2009). Networked learning and postgraduate professionals. In L. Dirckinck-Holmfeld, C. Jones, & B. Lindström (Eds.), *Analysing networked learning practices in higher education and continuing professional development*. Rotterdam, The Netherlands: Sense Publishers.

Jones, C. (2004). Networks and learning: Communities, practices and the metaphor of networks. *ALT-J, The Association for Learning Technology Journal, 12*(1), 82–93.

Jones, C., Ferreday, D., & Hodgson, V. (2008). Networked learning a relational approach – weak and strong ties. *Journal of Computer Assisted Learning special section, 24*(2), 90–102.

Jones, C., Dirckinck-Holmfeld, L., & Lindström, B. (2006). A relational, indirect, meso-level approach to CSCL design in the next decade. *International Journal of Computer-Supported Collaborative Learning, 1*(1).

Kanstrup, A. M. (2005). *Local design: Volume I—An inquiry into work practices of local IT-supporters.* Unpublished Ph.D thesis, Aalborg University, Aalborg.

Kennedy, G. E., Judd, T. S., Churchward, A., Gray, K., & Krause, K.-L. (2008). First year students' experiences with technology: Are they really digital natives? *Australasian Journal of educational Technology, 24*(1), 108–122. Retrieved September 1, 2008, from http://ascilite.org.au/ajet/ajet24/kennedy.html

Kennedy, G., Krause, K., Gray, K., Judd, T., Bennet, S., Matton, K., et al. (2006). Questioning the net generation: A collaborative project in Australian higher education. In L. Markauskaite, P. Goodyear, & P. Reimann (Eds.), *Proceedings of the 23rd annual conference of the australasian society for computers in learning in tertiary education: Who's Learning? Whose technology?* (pp. 413–417). Sydney, New S Wales: Sydney University Press.

Kirschner, P. A., Strijbos, J., & Martens, R. L. (2004). CSCL in Higher education. In J.-A. Strijbos, P. A. Kirschner, & R. L. Martens (Eds.), *What we know about cscl: And implementing it in higher education*. Boston: Kluwer Academic Publishers.

Kolmos, A., Fink, F. K., & Krogh, L. (Eds.). (2004). *The Aalborg PBL Model – Progress, diversity and challenges*. Aalborg: Aalborg University Press.

Koper, R., & Tattersall, C. (Eds.). (2005). *Learning design: A handbook on modeling and delivering networked education and training*. Berline: Springer.

Latour, B. (1987). *Science in action*. Cambridge, MA: Harvard University Press.

Latour, B. (1998). *On actor network theory: A few clarifications*. Retrieved July 14, 2008, from http://www.nettime.org/Lists-Archives/nettime-l-9801/msg00019.html

Law, J. (2002). *Networks, relations, cyborgs: On the social study of technology*. Lancaster, UK: Centre for Science Studies, Lancaster University. Retrieved July 14, 2008, from http://www.comp.lancs. ac.uk/sociology/papers/Law-Networks-Relations-Cyborgs.pdf

Livingstone, S., & Bober, M. (2005). *UK children go online: Final report of key project findings*. Retrieved from http://www.lse.ac.uk/collections/children-go-online/UKCGO_Final_report.pdf

McAndrew, P., & Goodyear, P. (2006). Representing practitioner experiences through learning design and patterns. In H. Beetham & R. Sharpe (Eds.). (2007), *Rethinking pedagogy for a digital age: Designing and delivering e-learning*. London: Routledge.

McAndrew, P., Goodyear, P., & Dalziel, J. (2006, August 9). Patterns, designs and activities: Unifying descriptions of learning structures. *International Journal of Learning Technology, 2*(2–3), 216–242(27).

McConnell, D. (2000). *Implementing computer supported cooperative learning* (2nd ed.). London: Kogan Page.

McConnell, D. (2002). Action research and distributed problem-based learning in continuing professional education. *Distance Education, 23*(1), 59–83.

Malyn Smith, J. (2004). Working together: Power users of technology. Who are they? Where are they going? Why does it matter? *UN Chronicle, 2*, 58–61. Retrieved October 13, 2008, from http://www. un.org/Pubs/chronicle/2004/issue2/0204p58.asp#

Mason, R. D. (1989). *A case study of the use of computer conferencing at the open university*. PhD, Open University.

Mason, R. (1994). *Using communications media in open and flexible learning*. London: Kogan Page.

Mason, R., & Kaye, A. (1990). Towards a new paradigm for distance education. In L. Harasim (Eds.), *Online education: Perspectives on a new environment*. New York: Praeger.

Merrill, M. D. (2007). A task-centred instructional strategy. *Journal of Research on Technology in Education, 40*(1), 33–50.

Oblinger, D. (2004). The next generation of educational engagement. *Journal of Interactive Media in Education, 8*. Retrieved October 3, 2008, from www-jime.open.ac.uk/2004/8

Oblinger, D., & Oblinger, J. (Eds.). (2005). *Educating the net generation*. Educause. Retrieved October 8, 2008, from http://www.educause.edu/ir/library/pdf/pub7101.pdf

O'Reilly, T. (2005). *What is Web 2.0 – Design patterns and business models for the next generation of software*. [Online] Retrieved November 2, 2007, from http://www.oreillynet.com/pub/a/oreilly/tim/ news/2005/09/30/what-is-web-20.html

Orlikowski, W. J. (2000). Using technology and constituting structures: A practice lens for studying technology in organizations. *Organizations Science, 11*(4), 404–428.

Pilkington, R., & Guldberg, K. (2009). Conditions for productive networked learning among professionals and carers—The webautism case study. In L. Dirckinck-Holmfeld, C. Jones, & B. Lindström (Eds.), *Analysing networked learning practices in higher education and continuing professional development*. Rotterdam, The Netherlands: Sense Publishers.

Pinch, T. J., & Bijker, W. E. (1984). The social construction of facts and artefacts: Or how the sociology of science and the sociology of technology might benefit each other. *Social Studies of Science, 14*(3), 399–441.

Prensky, M. (2001, October). Digital natives, digital immigrants. On the horizon. *NCB University Press, 9*(5).

Prensky, M. (2001a, December). Digital natives, digital immigrants Part II: Do they really think differently? On the Horizon. *NCB University Press, 9*(6).

Rheingold, H. (2000). *The virtual community: homesteading on the electronic frontier* (Rev. ed.). (Originally published 1993 and 1994) Cambridge MA: MIT Press.

Russell, T. L. (2001). *The no significant difference phenomenon*. Raleigh, N Carolina: North Carolina State University.

Related web site Retrieved from http://www.nosignificantdifference.org/

Ryberg, T. (2009). Understanding productive learning through the metaphorical lens of patchworking. In L. Dirckinck-Holmfeld, C. Jones,& B. Lindström. (Eds.), *Analysing networked learning practices in higher education and continuing professional development*. Rotterdam, The Netherlands: Sense Publishers.

Ryberg, T., & Larsen, M. C. (2008). Networked identities: understanding relationships between weak and strong ties in networked environments. *Journal of Computer Assisted Learning* special section, *24*(2), 103–115.

Sorensen, E. K. (1997). *Learning in virtual contexts. navigation, interaction, and collaboration*. Unpublished Ph.D., Aalborg University, Aalborg, Denmark.

Star, S. L., & Ruhleder, K. (1996). Steps toward an ecology of Infrastructure: Design and access for large information spaces information systems research. *Information Systems Research, 7*(1), 111–134.

Steeples, C., & Jones, C. (Eds.). (2002). *Networked learning; perspectives and issues*. London: Springer Verlag.

Steeples, C., Goodyear, P., & Mellar, H. (1994). Flexible learning in higher education: The use of computer-mediated communications. *Computers and Education, 22*(1), 83–90.

Tapscott, D. (1998). *Growing up digital: The rise of the net generation*. New York: McGraw-Hill.

Tchounikine, P. (2008). Operationalising macro-scripts in CSCL technological settings. *International Journal of Computer Supported Collaborative Learning, 3*(2), 193–233.

Tolsby, H. (2009). Virtual environment for project based collaborative learning. In L. Dirckinck-Holmfeld, C. Jones, & B. Lindström (Eds.), *Analysing networked learning practices in higher education and continuing professional development*. Rotterdam, The Netherlands: Sense Publishers.

Vallee, J., Lipinski, H., & Miller, R. H. (1974). *Group communication through computers; Design and Use of the FORUM System*. Menlo Park, CA: Institute for the Future.

Vallee, J., Johansen, R., Randolph, R. H., & Hastings, R. C. (1974a). *Group communication through computers: A study of social effects*. Menlo Park, CA: Institute for the Future.

Vallee, J., Johansen, R., Lipinski, H., Spangler, K., Wilson, T., & Hardy, A. (1975). *Group communication through computers: Pragmatics and dynamics*. Menlo Park, CA: Institute for the Future.

Vines, A., & Dysthe, O. (2009). Productive learning in the study of law: The role of networked technology in the learning ecology of a law faculty. In L. Dirckinck-Holmfeld, C. Jones, & B. Lindström (Eds.), *Analysing networked learning practices in higher education and continuing professional development*. Rotterdam, The Netherlands: Sense Publishers.

Weller, M. (2007). *Virtual learning environments: Using choosing and developing your VLE*. London: Routledge

Wiley, D. A. (2003). *Learning objects: Difficulties and opportunities*. Retrieved August 31, 2008, from http://wiley.ed.usu.edu/docs/lo_do.pdf

Lone Dirckinck-Holmfeld
e-Learning Lab. Center for Userdriven Innovation, Learning, and Design
Department of Communication and Psychology
Aalborg University, Denmark

Chris Jones
Institute of Educational Technology
The Open University, UK

Lightning Source UK Ltd.
Milton Keynes UK
UKOW03f2021051113

220515UK00007BA/399/P